D1555741

Choral Societies and Nationalism in Europe

National Cultivation of Culture

Edited by

Joep Leerssen

VOLUME 9

The titles published in this series are listed at *brill.com/ncc*

Choral Societies and Nationalism in Europe

Edited by

Krisztina Lajosi
Andreas Stynen

BRILL

LEIDEN | BOSTON

NISE NATIONAL MOVEMENTS & INTERMEDIARY STRUCTURES IN EUROPE

This book is part 3 of the NISE Proceedings.

Cover illustration: Postcard depicting the eighth edition of the German Choral Festival in Nuremberg, 1912. Four color printing of E. Nister, Nürnberg.

The postcard is from Editor Krisztina Lajosi's own collection.

Library of Congress Cataloging-in-Publication Data

Choral societies and nationalism in Europe / edited by Krisztina Lajosi, Andreas Stynen.
     pages cm. — (National cultivation of culture ; 9)
     Includes bibliographical references and index.
     ISBN 978-90-04-30084-2 (hardback : alk. paper) — ISBN 978-90-04-30085-9 (e-book) 1. Choral
societies—Europe—History. 2. Nationalism—Europe—History. I. Lajosi, Krisztina, editor. II. Stynen,
Andreas, editor.

ML1520.C46 2015
782.506'04—dc23

2015023723

This publication has been typeset in the multilingual "Brill" typeface. With over 5,100 characters covering Latin, IPA, Greek, and Cyrillic, this typeface is especially suitable for use in the humanities. For more information, please see www.brill.com/brill-typeface.

ISSN 1876-5645
ISBN 978-90-04-30084-2 (hardback)
ISBN 978-90-04-30085-9 (e-book)

This book is printed on acid-free paper.

Printed by Printforce, the Netherlands

Contents

Acknowledgements

This book is the result of a workshop on Choral Movements and Nationalist Mobilization (Antwerp, February 2011), jointly organised by NISE (National movements & Intermediary Structures in Europe) and SPIN (Study Platform on Interlocking Nationalisms). The editors wish to express their gratitude to everyone involved in both the workshop and this resulting publication. Special thanks to the members of the 2010–2011 advisory board: Koenraad De Meulder, Koen De Scheemaeker, Jan Dewilde, Vic Nees (†), Michaël Scheck, Hugo Sledsens, Maarten Van Ginderachter, Frans-Jos Verdoodt and Staf Vos. We are also grateful to John Neubauer and Philipp Ther for their helpful advice. Special thanks also to Gene Moore for his help with copy-editing.

Notes on Contributors

Carmen de las Cuevas Hevia
is Senior Lecturer in Music Teaching at the Department of Music, Arts and Physical Education, School of Education, University of the Basque Country (Spain). An expert in both voice training and music education, she has worked since 1984 in the graduate and postgraduate programs in Teacher Training at the University of the Basque Country, where in 1998 she received her Ph.D. in Education with a dissertation entitled "Orfeón Donostiarra 1897–1997: proyección social, cultural y educativa," a case study involving the choral societies movement in the Basque Country. Her fields of interest are choral music teaching, primary education teacher training, and formal and informal aspects of music teaching.

Jan Dewilde
studied musicology at the Katholieke Universiteit Leuven and wrote his thesis on the Flemish composer Jules Falck (1881–1959). He publishes on Flemish music, and musical heritage and libraries. Currently, he is working on a biography of the composer Peter Benoit (1834–1901). He is also an editor for a sheet music series, The Flemish Music Collection (Repertoire Explorer), at Musikproduktion Höflich in Munich. Since 1998 he has been the scientific coordinator for the Study Centre for Flemish Music, a post he combines since 2006 with his work as a head librarian at the Royal Conservatoire Antwerp (Artesis Plantijn University College).

Tomáš Kavka
earned his Ph.D. in 2013 at the Institute of Social and Economic History, Charles University, Prague, where he specialized in art societies of the *belle époque*, Czech and German national movements and popular culture. He co-authored (together with Ondřej Daniel and Jakub Machek) a collective monograph entitled *Popular Culture in Czech Space* (in Czech, 2013). His areas of interest include everyday life and youth aspects of post-socialist popular culture. He is a chairman of Prague's NGO *Centre for the Study of Popular Culture* (CSPK).

Anne Jorunn Kydland
holds a doctoral degree from the University of Oslo (1996), and a position as research librarian at the National Library of Norway. Her various books and articles are focused on cultural history, in particular Norwegian literature and

music, especially the song culture of the nineteenth century, but also music history in the twentieth century. She has for instance studied Eivind Groven's life and work from a variety of approaches, for example by organizing activities involving Groven's recently tuned organ, and by editing a volume with contributions from different countries: *"East of Noise": Eivind Groven. Composer, Ethnomusicologist, Researcher* (2013).

Krisztina Lajosi

is Assistant Professor in the Department of European Studies at the University of Amsterdam, where her Ph.D. in cultural history examined the role of operas in nation-building movements in East-Central Europe. She is the coordinator of a research project supported by the Royal Netherlands Academy of Arts and Sciences exploring the transnational ramifications of European national styles in music.

Joep Leerssen

is Royal Netherlands Academy Professor in European Studies at the University of Amsterdam. In 2008 he was awarded the Spinoza Prize. His publications in nationalism studies deal with Ireland (*Remembrance and Imagination*, 1996), the Low Countries (*De Bronnen van het Vaderland*, 2011), and the intellectual and cultural history of nationalism in Europe, particularly in the nineteenth century (*National Thought in Europe*, 2006).

Sophie-Anne Leterrier

has taught art history and contemporary cultural history at the Université d'Artois since 2003. From 1994–2003 she taught cultural history at the Université Lille 3. She currently works mostly on popular musical practices in nineteenth-century France. Along with numerous contributions and articles, she has published five books: *L'Institution des sciences morales (1795–1850)* (1995), *Jérôme Paturot: A la recherche d'une position sociale* (with Louis Reybaud, 1996), *Le XIXᵉ siècle historien: Anthologie raisonnée* (1997), *Le Mélomane et l'historien* (2006), and *Béranger: Des chansons pour un peuple citoyen* (2013).

Jane Mallinson's

doctoral thesis was on the choral works of Hamish MacCunn (1868–1916). Her main research interest is the growth of choral societies in Scotland and the impact of Tonic Sol-fa. Other research interests include Andrew MacCunn (the younger brother of Hamish), the baritone Andrew Black, and concert life in nineteenth-century Scotland. With Moira Ann Harris she co-authored articles on Scottish topics for the new edition of Baerenreiter's *Musik in Geschichte und Gegenwart*. She is an Honorary Research Associate of the School of Culture and Creative Arts at the University of Glasgow and a member of the Advisory Board of Musica Scotica.

Tatjana Marković

is an Associate Professor teaching at the University of Arts in Belgrade and the University of Music and Performing Arts in Vienna; she has also been a guest professor in Ljubljana and Graz. She completed a postdoctoral project on South-Eastern European opera at the Austrian Academy of Sciences (2010–2014). She is an editor for the open access research journal *TheMA* and for a book series in SEE Studies (Vienna). She has published on 18th–20th century music (SEE, Russian, and German opera; music historiography). Her books include *Transfigurations of Serbian Romanticism: Music in the Context of Cultural Studies* (in Serbian, 2005), *Historical and Analytical-Theoretical Coordinates of Style in Music* (in Serbian, 2009), and (with Andreas Holzer) *Galina Ivanovna Ustovl'skaja—Komponieren als Obsession* (2013).

Fiona M. Palmer

is Professor of Music at Maynooth University—National University of Ireland, Maynooth, where she served as Head of the Department of Music from 2007 to 2014. Her research interests focus on music and musicians in the marketplace, performance practice, culture, commerce, canonization of the repertoire, and socio-economic issues in Britain in the long nineteenth century. Her publications include critical biographies of the virtuoso double bassist Domenico Dragonetti (1997) and of the church musician, editor and publisher Vincent Novello (2006). She is currently writing a monograph exploring the development of the orchestral conducting profession in Britain from around 1870 to 1914.

Karel Šima

earned his Ph.D. in historical anthropology at Charles University in Prague. In his thesis he studied Czech national festivities in the nineteenth century as performative processes of national identity formation. He has published several articles on nationalist festive culture in Czech journals. In addition, his research interests include theory and methodology of history (narrativism, memory, nationalism) and modern popular culture. He is also engaged in higher education research and policy, co-authoring various journal articles along with three books on Czech higher education and particularly on the Humboldtian idea of the university.

Andreas Stynen

is a researcher at the Antwerp-based ADVN—the Archives and Documentation Center for Flemish Nationalism. He obtained a Ph.D. in history from Leuven University with a study of nineteenth-century visions of nature and cities. His publications include titles on the collective memory of national movements, trans-Atlantic migration, and popular music. He is also editorial secretary of *Studies on National Movements*, NISE's online journal.

Dominique Vidaud

is associated with the Université Lumière—Lyon 2 in France. For five years he taught modern and contemporary history at the French Institute in Athens. His specialty is choral singing and nationalism in Catalonia, for which he received his M.A. in History in Lyon in 2000 with a thesis on "Chant choral et identité nationale en Catalogne, 1891–1931." For four years he was a teacher at the French Institute in Barcelona and a choir singer in the Orfeó Català.

Ivanka Vlaeva

graduated from the National Academy of Music "Pancho Vladigerov" in Sofia. She completed a degree in Cultural Studies at Sofia University "St. Kliment Ohridski" and a Ph.D. at Moscow State Conservatory. She is currently an Associate Professor at South-West University "Neofit Rilski," an associated member at the Institute of Art Studies of the Bulgarian Academy of Sciences, and a lecturer at Sofia University. Her interests are in music in Bulgaria, world music, and the music of Asia. She has participated in many conferences in Bulgaria and abroad, and is the author of dozens of academic works, more than one hundred reviews and popular articles, and books about the Bulgarian composer Lyubomir Denev and the music of Asia.

Jozef Vos

is a historian associated with the Research Institute for History and Culture at Utrecht University. He is the author of various books and articles in the general area of the social and cultural history of the past two centuries.

Gareth Williams

is Emeritus Professor of History at the University of South Wales in Pontypridd, in the heart of the Welsh coalfield. He has written and broadcast extensively in English and Welsh on popular culture in nineteenth- and twentieth-century Wales, particularly sport and choral singing. His books include *Valleys of Song: Music and Society in Wales 1840–1914* (2003), and he has written and edited books on oral history, rugby, and boxing. He is currently writing a history of the Welsh male voice choir.

Hana Zimmerhaklová

works as a head of the Department of Grant Administration at the Faculty of Arts, Charles University, Prague. In her historical work, she deals with modern cultural history, especially the ongoing interaction between society and art institutions. Her Ph.D. thesis focused on the Estates Theatre in Prague during the "long" nineteenth century.

Introduction

Krisztina Lajosi and Andreas Stynen

The nineteenth century, as is widely known, was an era of far-reaching changes. It is hard, if not impossible, to argue which evolution was the most decisive one. Not so for the Belgian periodical *L'Echo Musical*: its 1882 volume explained that the nineteenth century was to be labelled not the century of industrial development or democratic regimes, but rather "le siècle de la musique."[1] It seemed that music had become a greater priority than food or drink. Exaggerated as it was, this statement carried some truth: the rise of both instrumental and vocal societies was unmistakable, and so was their position in social life. Though *L'Echo Musical*—one of several periodicals devoted to music—was referring to the Belgian situation, the observation was valid for many European countries and regions, from Spain to Wales, from Estonia to the Balkans. This was no coincidence, nor a mere consequence of similar developments; the musical, and especially choral movements of the nineteenth century were a transnational phenomenon, with foreign models and practices often deliberately adopted, imitated, and modified—or rejected.

Logical though it seems, current historiography bears no witness to the transnational dynamics of the choral movement. Studies of choral history are rare, and the few that do exist are mainly limited to a clearly defined area—usually a town or a country. Even less examined is the potential of choral singing in mobilizing people for nationalist projects. In order to better comprehend these issues, a comparative workshop was hosted in Antwerp in February 2011. This two-day event—which opened with a performance of nineteenth-century music by two male choirs—was organized jointly by NISE and SPIN. NISE (National movements and Intermediary Structures in Europe), founded in Belgium in 2008 and continuously expanding, is a research, heuristic, and archival platform designed to promote comparative and transnational studies of the structures mediating between the authorities and the individual. SPIN (the Study Platform on Interlocking Nationalisms), founded the same year in the Netherlands, is a research hub designed to chart the cultural and historical roots of European nationalisms, bringing into focus the intellectual networks

---

1 "Le Siècle de la musique," *L'Echo Musicale* 14 (1882), 37–38.

which carried and disseminated the emerging ideals of cultural nationalism between 1770 and 1914.[2]

The primary objective of the workshop was to collate case studies and bring together specialists from different countries to work towards an integrated, Europe-wide, and comparative transnational study of the phenomenon of (male) choirs as vehicles for the assertion of separate national identities. This happened at a time before mass media and transregional communication reached full development, and in a great variety of contexts: in large as well as small countries, established states as well as emergent nationalities. Choirs could operate on their own or unite in larger federative structures; their practices ranged from weekly rehearsals to small- or large-scale festivals and competitions. To enhance the workshop's comparative dimension in this multi-faceted topic, participants were asked to keep in mind a number of perspectives, including the choirs' physiognomies, repertoires, rehearsals, performances, and representations, with particular attention to the extent to which trends were influenced by 'foreign' or 'domestic' circumstances. The inspiring enthusiasm and lively debates among the participants of the Antwerp workshop are now embodied in this volume, which contains a selection of reworked and fine-tuned papers along with some altogether new studies, all offering an important contribution to the history of musical nationalism in Europe, with an outspoken emphasis on the interaction between the local and the transnational. Our special thanks are due to Gene Moore for his invaluable help with the copy-editing.

Choirs in National Context

The dynamic interplay of choirs and national movements was a typically nineteenth-century phenomenon involving new forms of cultural and social activity. Choral singing and vocal societies, however, were nothing new. Singers have been performing in groups at least since the Greek tragedies, and Christianity had its *schola cantorum* (and consequently its choral tradition) since the fourth century. Outside the church, community singing was probably less practised during the Middle Ages; secular music was foremost a matter of soloists, and remained so until the seventeenth century. From that time onwards, opera composers periodically relied on choral singing, whereas oratorios, with their dramatic stories put to music, took religious singing out of

---

2   More information is available online at: http://nise.eu and http://spinnet.humanities.uva.nl.

the liturgy (and the church).[3] The secularization of choral singing was greatly accelerated in many parts of Europe by the French Revolution: in its fight against the Catholic clergy, many religious singing schools and chapels were closed. And even though choral singing often remained connected to church practices, the secularization of leisure activities was unprecedented.

The defining impetus for the choral movement's success, both internationally and undeniably, originated in the German-speaking world. Hans-Georg Nägeli, a Swiss composer, wrote in 1809 about a dream he had: if people started singing together with hundreds of thousands, from any background whatsoever, they would feel more closely related to one another to such an extent that it would mean a decisive step towards a more complete humanity. To realize this democratic, Enlightenment ideal Nägeli opened a singing school in his hometown Zürich, resulting in two choirs: one for young men and another for their female peers.[4] The dissemination of his pedagogical principles, inspired by his compatriot Johann Henrich Pestalozzi, provoked some controversy, but was influential, and not only in his own country. An extremely workable model for community singing, albeit for men exclusively and without democratic underpinnings, was that of the so-called *Liedertafel*, founded in Berlin early in 1809. The members met not only for the *a cappella* singing of (original) compositions, but also for the sake of social conviviality. Mainly middle-class, the choir members presented themselves in their activities and repertoire as a cohesive group with shared ambitions; friendship, liberty, and a Romantic world view colored their choral life, but also a longing for political unity in the territorial patchwork that was to become Germany.[5]

Although the German *Liedertafeln* would become an inspiring model for several generations of singing enthusiasts all over Europe, there were also other models of community singing. One important alternative approach was developed in France, based on the teaching method of the Paris music teacher Guillaume-Louis Bocquillon, better known as "Wilhem." When he introduced his method to the working class in 1830, free of charge, the so-called *orphéon* was born: again male *a cappella* choirs, but from a broader social background. Contemporaries emphasized how the *orphéons* were a means to lift the entire French people to new cultural heights.[6] Both prototypes—the *orphéon* and the *Liedertafel* (or *Gesangverein*)—found supporters all over Europe, though

---

3   Smith and Young, "Chorus," in *Grove Music Online* (http://www.oxfordmusiconline.com; accessed 17 Sept. 2010).

4   See Asper (1994), 11–12 and 18–20.

5   Brinkman (1970), 16–20; Langewiesche (2000), 142–45.

6   Fulcher (1979), 47–56; Gumplowicz (1987), 20–33.

mediated by local circumstances that differed widely from those found in the German lands or in France.

Among the differences the choral models encountered during their dispersal over the continent were different stages of nation-building and divergent nationalistic agendas. Several explanatory models exist to understand the historical development of nations and national movements. The most popular theories in recent decades have been those of constructivism and modernism: out of a sociological approach, the hypothesis arose that nations can be constructed by élites; 'imagined communities' are created thanks to the 'invention of traditions.' The nation is thus conceived as a product of modernization and without roots in history.[7] Some scholars, however, have criticized this intrinsically Western perspective and asked why the state is deemed necessary for the creation of nations. Ethnosymbolists like Anthony D. Smith and John Hutchinson argue that national identity and nations should be considered rather as specialized developments of ethnicity and ethnic groups. Smith defines a nation as "a named and self-defined human community whose members cultivate shared myths, memories and symbols, have a distinctive public culture, are attached to a historic homeland and observe shared laws and customs."[8] Ethnosymbolists move beyond the idea that nations are mere inventions or constructions, and in most cases emphasize continuity with ethnicity: nationalism comes into being as a process of secularization, in which (transcendent) ethnic motifs (myths, traditions, symbols...) are selected and codified.[9] Both the modernist-constructivist and the ethnosymbolist schools are important for understanding the choral phenomenon.

To comprehend the development towards nationalism as a mass movement, the Czech historian Miroslav Hroch conceived a renowned three-phase model in 1968 that is still useful and relevant today. In Phase A, intellectuals lay a foundation for a national identity by studying cultural, linguistic, and other traits to increase the awareness of a common bond; Hroch calls this the period of scholarly interest. Phase B is labelled the era of patriotic agitation: activists try to persuade as many people of the same ethnic group as possible to strive for a fully-fledged nation. Phase C, finally, witnesses the rise of a mass movement: nationalism is now the binding element of a full social movement, with several branches, occupying a wide ideological spectrum.[10] Nowhere is this

---

7   See Anderson (1983); Hobsbawm and Ranger, eds. (1983).

8   Anthony D. Smith (2004), 17.

9   For the position of ethnosymbolism in the historical debate on nationalism, see Boeva (2010), 11–22.

10   Hroch (2000), 22–24.

development visible before the eighteenth century, but it proliferates remark-ably in the nineteenth, also because it was a model disseminated through intense international exchanges.[11] This was a trait shared with the choral move-ment. Hence, it can be no surprise that choirs showed themselves as a poten-tially valuable vehicle in each of Hroch's phases. The chapters in this book also show how the societies embodied the working of what has become known as Romantic Nationalism: "The celebration of the nation [...] as an inspiring ideal for artistic expression; and the instrumentalization of that expression in political consciousness-raising."[12] Choirs offer a prime view into nineteenth-century burgeoning national sentiments.

Musical Cultures

To grasp the ideas and practices of nineteenth-century choirs—both national and otherwise—it is important to study much more than just the music itself. Music receives its meaning in a wider context that goes beyond the repertoire, composers, and directors. In other words, this book deals with the history of musical culture, including performances and processes such as identity for-mation or the transfer of knowledge. This dynamic approach also challenges widespread and fixed musical categories, such as the dichotomy between classical and popular music. Clinging to a view of choral music as a serious, even élite genre, as opposed to the preferences of the common people, would put from the beginning a strain on discerning any mobilizing force in choral singing. The (implicitly) supposed links between certain musical genres and the practices of specific social groups are subject to change. For instance: late eighteenth-century composers, including Wolfgang Amadeus Mozart, were very mild in their judgment of uninitiated audiences, and used similar musical motifs for both 'easy' *divertimenti* and more demanding forms such as symphonies.[13] A few decades later, middle-class connoisseurs began to dis-tance themselves from music that was deemed too easily accessible: overtures, operatic pot-pourris, virtuoso bravura compositions, dance music, and several types of songs—a group for which, halfway through the nineteenth century, the previously unknown term 'popular music' was coined. The counterpart was 'classical music,' more complex and often instrumental compositions to be savored in respectful silence. In the late nineteenth century this opposition

---

11   Thiesse (1999), 11.
12   Leerssen (2014), 5.
13   See William Weber (2008), 1–12.

between popular and élite/classical music gained general acceptance—
the so-called Great Musical Schism that is still very alive after a double turn
of centuries.[14]

Some musical genres and performances, however, lingered in the borderlands between both categories, a (changing) grey zone of the élitist and the
popular. Without this nuance it would be impossible to understand both
the acclaim of Jacques Offenbach's operettas among European rulers or the
programming of Georg Friedrich Handel's *Messiah* at factory choir concerts.
Processes of appropriation need to be taken into account to understand the
nationalist fervor surrounding choral singing. This observation is especially
true when considering folk music, a factor apparently further complicating the
popular-classical divide. Its advocates used the term to glorify music from the
(presumably) authentic people, thus opposing tradition to modern musical
aberrations.[15] Obviously this musical taste was no less an example of processes
of appropriation, usually taking place in Hroch's Phase A: folklorists presented
'genuine' tunes to their fellow countrymen as unalienable elements of a collective national identity. Hence, this book deals with constant negotiations, with
putting music to specific uses. An awareness of the changing reputations of
genres and practices is thereby indispensable, scrutinizing a wide cultural field
rather than reasoning within predefined visions.

The negotiations were in part between classes. Two distinct types of social
compositions dominated the European choral world: societies with a markedly middle-class membership versus choirs composed of working men. The
second type ranged from initiatives by factory bosses to singing unions initiated by the workers themselves. Nonetheless, everywhere a large degree of
societal self-organization was noticeable as were, apparently, singing practices.

Another aspect of the composition of choirs involves the issue of gender.
Choral singing began as a preponderantly if not exclusively male activity. In
most cases women's choirs came into being only after several decades, and
long before mixed singing became a common practice. In a society offering little room for female participation in public life, the male nature of choral singing seemed inevitable. Masculinity was also at the core of national thought:
the discourse in national movements was heavily centered around the male
patriot and overwhelmingly dominated by masculine interests and ideology;
the women's part was a domestic, motherly role.[16] *Gendered Nations*, a publication following a ground-breaking symposium in 1998, widened the scope

---

14   Van der Merwe (1992), 15–19.
15   Bruyneel et al. (2012), 13–14.
16   See Nagel (1998).

to musical practices: an image of the massively attended third Latvian Song and Dance Festival (1888) captured young rural women in (recently invented) national costumes, embodying peasant women's folk songs that (male) intellectuals had collected as evidence of an authentic collective identity.[17] Such a close entaglement of masculinity, nationalism, and music was deconstructed in the essays of *Masculinity and Western Musical Practices* (2009), postulating the key role of collective male singing in the (German) nationalist movement, and also the persistence of such thinking: at least until the early twentieth century the conviction was strong that women could be inspiring muses, but that actual musical creation belonged solely to the male realm.[18] These and other beliefs made the the singing patriot a cultural icon capturing the imagination and setting the practice of male singing in a positive light.[19]

Such masculine values as sacrifice, struggle, and fraternity were omnipresent in the European choral repertoire. The variety among nations was nonetheless considerable. Sometimes this was due to clearly identifiable local conditions: Austrian censorship limited the possibilities for Czech choirs; rehearsing in churches left its mark on the Welsh repertoire. Other differences are less easily explained. Flemish choirs had an essentially contemporary repertoire, while their Scottish counterparts favored folk songs and often sang centuries-old polyphonic compositions. The French *orphéons* developed their own repertoire, while elsewhere in Europe foreign melodies were imported—sometimes provided with altogether new texts, sometimes in translation. Such transfers took place even between the leading German and French choral traditions; in 1856 the German publishing house Schott found a ready market for *L'Allemagne Chorale*, a series of compositions made popular by touring German choirs but with French lyrics.[20]

The international mobility not only of repertoires but of choral societies themselves was striking. In the Basque case, participation in French competitions forced the choirs to steer away from their folk tradition. In many parts of Europe there was ample opportunity to compete with other choirs; specialized magazines published large numbers of announcements in each issue. The Enlightenment notion of Progress was an important catalyst: the urge to improve fostered rivalry not only in the economic sector but in the scientific and cultural world as well. Inevitably the musical struggle often ended in bitter fights, prompting many to adhere to another, more peaceful model of choral

---

17 See Novikova (2000).
18 See Taylor-Jay (2009).
19 Hoegaerts (2014), 15.
20 Stynen (2012), 201.

meetings: festivals where societies could not only learn from one another but which embodied the ambition to enlighten and instruct the masses. The formulas were numerous, from small-scale events to nationwide manifestations. Again, the German lands set the tone, with *Musikfeste* from 1818 onwards, followed by *Sängerfeste*; in August 1845 more than 1,700 singers gathered in Würzburg, bringing songs from several regions, thus giving a boost to the longing for unification.[21]

Performing Songs

By studying choral societies with a focus on nationalist mobilization, researchers naturally reach a point often missed in music studies and musical history: each concert, festival, competition or open rehearsal is a performance in which not only the musicians (in this case singers) take part, but also the audience. From an anthropological perspective, singing a song is a ritual with collectively entailed symbols and meanings, and this has always been so, from the Greek tragedies to present-day performances.[22] Rather than a homogeneous, anonymous and passive multitude, the audience is a dynamic group, often invited to sing along, or joining in spontaneously. In this act the boundaries between performers and audience were blurred and the music was transmitted and appropriated, all the more so because, in the days before recording devices, sheet music and live performances were the only distribution channels available. The crowd was musicalized, and often politicized as well. A memorial service for the famous Czech Romantic poet Karel Hynek Mácha in Prague in spring 1859 suffered from such repression by the Austrian authorities that a poem dedicated to his memory could only be read silently; but those present could then sing national songs aloud, imbuing the meeting and the vocal act with an enormous political charge.

The contributions in this book reveal a striking difference between choirs operating in established nation-states and in nations without an autonomous state. Since music and choral societies were deemed non-political, they were in the latter case all the more prone to politicization, as channels through which emancipation, both social and national, could be experienced and encouraged. Whenever a state system or another national movement challenged a nation, the political role of choirs became more obvious.

---

21   Porter (1996), 171–74.
22   See McCormick (2006); Geisler and Johansson (2014), 3–4.

Often, and both in the context of a nation-state and of nation-building, the nationalism present in the choral movement was of a banal nature. The repeated positioning of a repertoire as part of the nation's musical tradition and its multiple lyrical references to the nation's history, landscape, and people—with words like 'here' or 'us'—are an important part of what Michael Billig has labelled "flaggings [which] provide daily, unmindful reminders of nationhood." These ubiquitous references root people in a homeland, "made to look homely, beyond question and, should the occasion arise, worth the price of sacrifice," especially since the flaggings draw a distinction between 'us' and 'them.'[23] Indeed, among the most powerful traits of the nineteenth-century choral movement is its capacity to generate a feeling of unity. Group singing generates an acoustic resonance that exceeds individual ability. Ideally, this experience addresses the participant's heart, uplifting her or him into a larger, meaningful whole. Out of an emotional experience stem feelings of fraternity of greater importance than any political message.

This bonding could operate on several levels. Beyond the solidarity and conviviality within the choir itself—dinners, excursions, balls and festivities of all kinds abounded—the members explicitly reached out to the wider community. In line with nineteenth-century civic society, choral singing served a wider social utility. Besides the sometimes pompously stated ideal of disseminating art, this public service frequently involved fund-raising. A respectable status paid off, and many choirs became spear-heads of communal pride. Singers returning home after victory in a contest often received a very warm welcome, complete with a parade, a reception at the city hall, and fireworks. The most exuberant enthusiasm was perhaps to be found in Wales, where choral societies enjoyed a staunch support comparable to that of present-day football teams—sometimes even including hooliganism. Such an identification and mobilization was not incompatible with a more national scope, as the essays in this book demonstrate. Double and even multiple layers of identity were very common, even on the level of nationality, as the Flemish case proves, with choirs freely and in an *ad hoc* manner moving between (or combining) a Belgian patriotic and a Flemish nationalist stance. The longing for unity on a national scale, by the way, did not always imply (structural) solidarity or even feelings of equality with all fellow citizens: whereas the Association of Serbian choral societies managed to gather choirs from cities, towns and villages, elsewhere the tensions between urban culture and the countryside were very vivid. Also within a national framework, negotiations were a lasting and dynamic process.

---

23   Billig (1995), 174–76.

A European Phenomenon

The essays in this book cover large parts of Europe and mainly follow a geographical order. In a study focused on the transnational dimensions of the choral movement, starting with the German case is an obvious choice. It was in the German-speaking world that the modern choral societies originated, but Joep Leerssen also shows how the movement soon obtained a dynamic political role: choral practices and performances not only reflected an ideological position, they engaged in an ongoing interaction with political attitudes. The German model was hugely successful and was unabashedly invoked as an inspiration and consequently invested with other ethnic guises.

The other important model for choral societies was the French *orphéon* which Sophie-Anne Leterrier meticulously analyzes as a phenomenon closely related to the French regime. Sharing the authorities' centralizing ambition, the *orphéon* movement opposed any regional particularism, including folk music or the use of dialects, and thus contributed to the republicanization of even small towns. By the end of the century, French choirs were an embodiment of the state rather than the nation.

In Norway the choral repertoire and the vision of the moral and esthetic importance of choral singing bore witness to German influences. Anne Jorunn Kydland analyzes how, despite the transnational reality, the choral movement was partly positioned against Scandinavianism and contributed to a self-conscious nation stretching as far as the Norwegian migrant communities in the United States.

Great Britain offers an interesting set of cases because of the influence of a shared pedagogical technique for teaching sight-singing: the Tonic Sol-fa. Among the advantages of this system was that it replaced the usual staff notation with letters and punctuation marks, familiar symbols that made music scores appear less an alien code. The English case, as Fiona Palmer argues, is remarkable for another reason as well: the oratorio tradition, with large choirs as a common feature of public ceremonies, dates from the 1730s onwards, thus pre-dating the German choral model. With the popularity of foreign composers like Felix Mendelssohn, the protagonist in the choral movement in continental Europe, the transnational exchange was assured, though the Handel tradition in Victorian England remained strong.

Lacking any higher music education until 1890, the Scots were much more inclined to look beyond their own cultural traditions. Jane Mallinson explains how the Scottish repertoire was directly inspired by what was common in England, though small choirs in particular showed a Scottish (folk) nature; classical and folk music were less at odds than in most other European countries.

Such a repertoire was an expression of cultural nationalism, but without challenging the political reality of the United Kingdom. Gareth Williams makes a similar observation for Wales: the highly popular (labor) choirs pursued no openly political agenda, but were undoubtedly vehicles of national pride. The strongest symbol of this self-confidence is the eisteddfod, a Welsh festival formula with literary and musical competitions. Devoid of precedents for choral singing, the (national) eisteddfod together with an unprecedented industrialization fuelled a wide-ranging choral movement with some peculiar characteristics.

Western Europe holds a fascinating position due to the proximity of the two main choral models. In the Netherlands the preference was quite univocal: in two generations starting around 1825, the *Liedertafel* was imported from Germany. Until the 1870s the German repertoire held a dominant position, notwithstanding several pleas to replace it with a distinctively Dutch repertoire. Jozef Vos nuances these debates and emphasizes that for the average choir member the singing itself mattered more than the songs' origins. Also, the local identification of choirs was stronger than their national loyalty. Jan Dewilde observes that this is much less true for the Flemish choral movement. After independence, Belgian authorities promoted a patriotic culture that was both anti-French and anti-Dutch, including a choral repertoire aimed at glorifying the past. Flemish cultural activists, observing the spread of the French language (and culture) in public life, turned towards the German example and in 1845 a transboundary Singing Union was founded. Though short-lived, the inspiration of this initiative had a lasting impact and perhaps even mitigated against the success of the French *orphéon* model in Flanders.

Though fundamentally French, *orphéons* were founded in Spanish regions longing for autonomy, though sometimes only the name remained. In Catalonia, discussed by Dominique Vidaud, the Orfeons were primarily oriented towards the middle classes and drew inspiration from folk music. Moreover, the model was challenged by at least two other choral types. As a strong vector of identity, these choirs had a crucial role in the region's national awakening and resistance against the Spanish state. The situation in the Basque country was not entirely different. Carmen de las Cuevas Hevia equally notices different choral traditions, some founded in labor circles, some officially patronized: the city of San Sebastián provided funds to host an international choral competition in 1885 and favored the Orfeon Donostiarra as a catalyst of Basque music and language.

Choral movements in Central and Eastern Europe are often illustrations of an outspoken nationalist mobilization. Building on existing religious and military traditions, Czech choral life germinated after the turmoil of 1848.

Keeping a close eye to the symbolic and performative dimensions, Karel Šima, Tomáš Kavka, and Hana Zimmerhaklová trace how in the 1860s choral societies held an explicitly patriotic position. They developed in competition with (but also parallel to) networks of Germanized choirs, and combined a series of musical genres and traditions in order to achieve a maximal mobilization of national sentiments. In the 1870s this task moved into the political and economic spheres and the Czech choral movement diversified. Similarly, in Hungary the German choirs provided both a model to emulate and an obstacle to overcome. Krisztina Lajosi shows how Hungarian choral societies reflected complex social tensions that were both ethnic and class-related, and provided a form of sociability and entertainment in a fractured and often fractious society. In the Serbian national movement, choral singing played a key role in communication. Tatjana Marković shows how for the Serbs, who lacked a unified territory, singing was a way to build bridges between a shattered people. In the multi-ethnic Habsburg Empire identity was a complex issue. Serbian advocates mirrored their ambitions to the German example, including the exchange of magazines. In an effort to maximize the impact, concerts were organized both in concert halls and in public places, with varied programmes adapted to the audience. For Bulgarian nationalists choral singing was not only a vehicle of mobilization but of modernization as well; industrialization lagged far behind the situation elsewhere in Europe. Ivanka Vlaeva demonstrates how music obtained a central place in the Bulgarian Revival. At first, folk traditions and Turkish and Greek models were completely discarded and, through the mediation of foreigners, polyphonic singing was introduced instead. The wider gap between practices and traditions than in other European regions strongly indicates the presence and functioning of transnational transfers.

The studies in this book demonstrate how a flourishing choir scene was for nineteenth-century national movements a proof of being developed. Ambiguous combinations of foreign models and local profiling seemed to secure the membership of a modern transnational movement. If the chapters in this book teach one thing, it is that musical ideas and practices can and do cross boundaries, though in varying degrees and at differing speeds. Scholars studying local situations, and not looking primarily for cultural transfer or processes of nation-building, will also find it rewarding to look beyond what is immediately apparent.

Illuminating as these studies are, not all the questions have been answered. One obvious point is the absence of some nations. The choral situations in Italy, Poland, and the Baltic countries certainly deserve closer attention. Another opportunity for scholars is historical research into the actual singing practices of choirs; the songs they sang were arguably the most important aspect of their performances, but also a very fleeting and intangible one. Historical reconstructions of the sounds and the techniques used to produce them, on the one hand, and of the sentiments (for example of self-liberation) produced by choral singing, on the other, offer promising fields of study. Some pioneering studies also show how compositions can be analyzed in function of their acoustic representation of the country, including close attention to the issue of who was to produce which sounds.[24] There are possibilities not only for more in-depth research; the topic can also be broadened. Juxtapositions or comparisons with other types of societies can only contribute to a better understanding of the massive importance of transnational exchanges in the history of nineteenth-century national movements. As Joep Leerssen reminds us, the proliferation of choirs was never a matter of "spontaneous generation":

> The spread of male choirs is not a matter of parallel responses to similar circumstances; it is to a large extent a matter of diffusion, of *communicative procreation*. For that reason, understanding the emergence of choirs purely in terms of context and circumstances is insufficient.[25]

The aim of this volume is to understand the institutional self-replication of choirs and their role in the formation of national identity.

---

24   Dolar (2006), 59–60; Hoegaerts in Geisler and Johansson, eds. (2014), 14–32.
25   Leerssen (2015), 11–12.

CHAPTER 1

German Influences
Choirs, Repertoires, Nationalities

Joep Leerssen

The Choir's Message, the Choir as Medium

The German League of Choral Societies held its seventh festival in Breslau in 1906–07. The official programme gazette opened with a poem by the celebrated figure-head of cultural nationalism, Felix Dahn, distinguished professor at the local university, authoritative legal historian, former volunteer in the Franco-Prussian War, author of many a patriotic poem, and famous for his best-selling series of historical novels set at various periods of German and Germanic history.

In English translation, the poem runs like this:

> To the German people God has given / Music of richest sonority
> In order that rest and struggle, death and life / may be glorified to us in song.
> So sing on, then, German youth / Of all things which can swell your heart!
> Of the persistence of true love / Of true friendship, gold and ore;
> Of the sacred shivers of pious awe / Of the sheen of spring and the joy of the forest
> Of Wanderlust, roving from land to land / And of that darling son of sunshine
> —Do not neglect that!—the golden wine. / Yes, sing of all things high and lovely,
> But above all cherish one specific song / Which should resound inspiring and roaring:
> The song of the German heroic spirit! / The song of manly duty and honour,
> Of faithfulness uncowed by fear / Which jubilantly hurls itself onto the foes' spears
> And in death wrests victory! / Only he who is willing to die as well as live

For this song, unlike any other—/ Only he is worthy to intone it:
The song of the hard-won Reich![1]

Dahn's verse was aimed at a readership of middle-class, middle-aged, subur-
ban or small-town German males who once a week indulged in their leisure
pursuit of choral singing with a glass or two of beer afterwards. But the self-
image which it articulates and celebrates was far less anodyne: it addresses
its audience as a convivial *Bildungsbürger* with a slumbering readiness to go
berserk for the noble cause of the Fatherland. Dahn himself, chosen herald and
figure-head of the Festival, was the perfect embodiment of this type of 'manly
German,'[2] uniting scholarship, literature and military prowess in his career.
The verse also breathes Dahn's characteristic, fey heroism, which fetishizes
death in battle (joyously thrusting oneself onto the enemy's spears), and
which was most epically expressed in the vastly popular Ostrogothic historical
novel *Ein Kampf um Rom* (1876), which inspired its youthful readers (many of
whom would come of age post-1919) not only with rugged Germanic primitiv-
ism but also with a penchant for tragic, death-seeking, total-destructive defeat,
Götterdämmerung-style.

Given this undertone in the closing lines of the poem, it is all the more
surprising to see it twinned with the watered-down, sentimental remnants of

---

1   In the original: "Dem deutschen Volk hat Gott gegeben / Ein Harfespiel vom reichsten Klang /
    Daß Ruh'n und Ringen, Tod und Leben / Uns weihend schmücke der Gesang. / So singe denn,
    du deutsche Jugend, / Von allem, was das Herz dir schwellt: / Von wahrer Liebe ew'ger Dauer /
    Von echter Freundschaft, Gold und Erz, / Von frommer Ahnung heil'ger Schauer / Von ew'gen
    Sehnens Glück und Schmerz: / Von Frühlingsglanz, von Waldeswonne, / Von Wanderlust
    landaus, landein, / Und von dem Lieblingssohn der Sonne / Vergeßt ihn nicht!—vom
    gold'nen Wein. / Ja, singt vom allen Hohen, Schönen!—Doch eines Sanges pflegt zumeist, /
    Begeisternd, brausend soll er tönen: / Der Sang vom deutschen Heldengeist! / Das Lied von
    Mannespflicht und Ehre, / Von Treue, die kein Schrecken zwingt, / Die jauchzend in der
    Feinde Speere, / Im Tod den Sieg erkämpfend, springt! / Nur wer da sterben will wie leben /
    Für dieses Lied, dem keines gleich,—/ Nur der ist wert, es anzuheben: / Das Lied vom schwer
    erkämpften Reich!"; in Klenke (1998), 170. All translations are by the author.
2   Dietmar Klenke's benchmark analysis (1998) traces the history of the German choral move-
    ment in terms of the self-image its repertoire proclaimed, that of the 'singing German male';
    I here render Klenke's key concept of the *deutscher Mann* as 'manly German.' Alongside
    Klenke, my main source for the development of the German choral movement is the excel-
    lently-documented Elben (1887), written from within the movement whose values it cele-
    brates as *volkstümlich*, 'in touch with the national spirit.' On Felix Dahn as *völkisch*, see Frech
    (1996) and, more generally, Wahl (2002).

high Romanticism: the themes of love, friendship, life outdoors, the twinning of Nature and informal religious piety, far-flung foot-journeys, and wine-fueled conviviality. All these elements, capped and trumped by the overriding theme of heroic, militant love of the fatherland: all this is listed by Dahn as the thematic inventory of the national heritage of German song and German convivial singing; indeed, it is celebrated by him as something which constitutes the German's God-given national character.

It would be unfair to judge this hackneyed piece of occasional verse by poetical standards; it is a public speech in verse form, and aims for the lowest common denominator of rhetorical effect, glibly using all the established high-minded tropes and turns of phrase that one would expect. Dahn's piece of verse, similar to dozens, hundreds of similar effusions from the period, is highly exemplary and representative. Banal as it is, it forms part of that 'banal nationalism' (Billig 1995) which all-pervasively dominated and flavored the public climate of these decades; literary background noise, unremarkable in its individual instances, but present everywhere.

At the same time, Dahn's verse gives us not only a character-type of the 'manly German,' but also an excellent listing of the repertoire of one of the most potent platforms of patriotic mobilization in nineteenth-century Germany: the choral society.[3] With its roots in the late-Romantic decades after 1810, the choral society became an informal, self-organizing, bottom-up form of sociability which across all the German lands (and, indeed, beyond) united many young-adult to middle-aged males from a middle-class background around a repertoire of shared values: romantic, convivial, and feistily national. The repertoire, as aptly typified by Dahn, was a spontaneously generated reservoir of self-indoctrination; the bonding atmosphere of leisure-time glee clubs with occasional trips and festival participations helped to disseminate the ethos of the 'singing German male' both socially and geographically, until it merged into the groundswell of mass-mobilized militaristic chauvinism in Wilhelminian and Weimar times (cf. also Leerssen [2015]).

The spread of the choral movement brings together the spheres of cultural diffusion (the spread and canonization of a corpus of texts and ideas) and of social mobilization (the ramifying diffusion and self-replication of a pattern of sociability). It thus brings together the social-historical and the culture-

---

3   I conflate, in my use of 'choir' or 'choral society,' the various German terms *Gesangverein*, *Liederkranz* and *Liedertafel*. For the history of the choral movement I rely principally on Klenke (1998) and Elben (1991), as well as the relevant chapters written in the context of more broadly social or musical histories, such as Brophy (2007) and Minor (2012).

historical study of the history of nationalism. The latter has been better studied than the former, and it may therefore be useful to emphasize at the outset the culture-historical importance of the choral movement as a repertoire-carrier, a 'medium' no less important than media like newspapers, radio, or television. The repertoire issue will be addressed in the first half of this chapter, which involves two components: the ability of the choral movement to effect a very wide and deep social penetration of its repertoire, and the rhetoric of that repertoire itself.

Song Performance, Embodied Communities

Since the classic work of Benedict Anderson on the nation as an 'imagined community' we have got used to a default understanding that large-scale, long-distance and high-impact communication in modern societies requires mediatized mass-circulation broadcasting. That, after all, is one of the implicit but characteristic features of the modernization process upon which the rise and spread of national thought is contingent: the fact that (to invoke Tönnies's old *Gemeinschaft/Gesellschaft* distinction) modern societies no longer rely on the face-to-face communication (word-of-mouth, gossip) characteristic of small-scale traditional communities and centered around places of congregation such as the inn or the village pump, but instead *mediatize*. Communication does not move directly from sender to immediate receiver but is broadcast from sender to a diffusely general and anonymous audience by means of printed texts or other intermediary carriers (the etymology of terms like im*me*diate or inter*media*ry stresses the point).

Nation-building, and indeed the dissemination of all large-scale post-Gutenberg ideologies ever since Lutheranism, is usually seen as involving, unavoidably, the use of modern media, which in turn define the very idea of modernity and also underpin the rise of a Habermassian public sphere (beyond its first origins in the theatre, the coffee house, and other places of congregation). This model is, in its general outline, undoubtedly valid. But the rise of the mediatized, virtual or 'imagined community' should not blind us to the fact that the large-scale congregation of 'embodied communities' (Rigney 2011) was also an important factor in nineteenth-century public life, and that it, too, played an important role in the dissemination of culture and ideologies. These events left little documentation in the archive except the derived, more or less ephemeral and dispersed records of convocations, printed programs, and local, (semi-)private or press reports, and must be reconstructed from such secondary accounts and incidental sources. Indeed, to reconstruct these Woodstocks of the nineteenth century often requires a good deal of painstaking inventory and is often conducted at the local or regional level (e.g., Blommen 1960).

For this reason, the social impact of performed songs still has the capacity to surprise us, as something counter-intuitive. Songs that have left no documentary traces except dog-eared sheet music, banal catchphrases, and occasional, dispersed references-in-passing, partake of that condition of 'banality,' non-salience, analysed by Billig: something that is a matter of informal, private leisure pursuits—such as singing "Auld Lang Syne" on New Year's Eve, or celebrating Burns Night. Hence, to see the full force of the mobilizing power of, for instance, the Burns cult in mid-nineteenth century Scotland (Rigney 2011) is something that catches us unawares.

"Auld Lang Syne" has become known universally in the English-speaking world through wholly informal, non-institutional, word-of-mouth means. And it was no different for the much more politically charged, national verse of everyday nineteenth-century culture, which can easily reach from the informal, spontaneous celebration of an ad hoc company into something large-scale, public. "Land of Hope and Glory" or the other English-nationalist evergreens of the Last Night of the Proms are a case in point: they are disseminated across audiences and generations *as a performance*, in their cantatory, physical enactment. People do not primarily familiarize themselves with these songs as texts or musical scores (which function, except among the small minority of trained musicians, merely as a memory prop of secondary importance); people acquire their familiarity with this repertoire in the first place as a witnessed and shared performance, like learning how to dance or doing the Mexican Wave in a football stadium. The transmission takes place in non-mediated, immediate proximity: one learns to sing along with these songs as one hears them being sung, as a result of being present in the company of those who perform the song, in (I repeat the term) an embodied community, together in real time and simultaneously involved in a collective act.

Before the invention of the sound recorder and of audiovisual media, performed song could not be mediatized. That condition affects practically all of the nineteenth century. Music could only spread either through the medium of printed scores or by performative contagion. Informal as these lines of communication were (like the thin ramifying threads of underground mycelium that link together mushrooms in different spots), they ensured that almost everyone could come to recognize and, should they so wish, hum along with the Marseillaise, "God Save the King," the Internationale, and the Slaves' Chorus of Verdi's *Nabucco*. And this applies with even more force to the standard evergreens of the German-nationalistic repertoire such as E.M. Arndt's *Was ist des Deutschen Vaterland?* or Hoffmann von Fallersleben's *Deutschland, Deutschland über alles*. On two occasions do we see a collective, political acknowledgement of this ubiquitous presence of performative singing; in both cases, it involves a German parliament.

In 1949, the German parliament convened to adopt a new constitution. The constitutive session of 23 May was concluded by the delegates singing a stand-in national anthem, which could do in lieu of the discredited *Deutschlandlied*. They opted for the song *Ich hab' mich ergeben*, by the obscure philologist and versifier Hans Ferdinand Massmann. From what epistemic limbo did this song emerge into official status? It was part of the repertoire of the standard Students' Songbooks or *Commersbücher* which since the mid-nineteenth century had been a prop of the convivial social life of all German university students. The delegates were familiar with *Ich hab' mich ergeben* as part of their informal cultural repertoire, much as they were familiar with the students' anthem *Gaudeamus igitur* or the Christmas carol *O Tannenbaum*.[4]

A century earlier, in the Frankfurt Parliament of 1848, the second day of the proceedings had been overshadowed by a spontaneous acclamation of one of the old national-cultural icons, then present as an old man: Ernst Moritz Arndt. He was recognized by the assembly, called to the rostrum, and loudly applauded. The minutes then record the following exchanges:

> *Drinkwelder (from Krems)*: I move that we vote the nation's thanks to Arndt for his song "What is the German's Fatherland?" It inspired us in the times of oppression and united us.
>
> *Soiron (Mannheim)*: Just a small amendment: We want to thank him, not only for his song, but for all his activities for the entire Germany.
>
> (*A threefold, thunderous "Long may he live!" resounds in the Assembly and on the public gallery.*)
>
> *Jahn (Freiburg an der Unstrut)*: "Honorable German men! Once we were edified by Arndt's songs. May we ask him to compose, as his swan song, another one. We have often sung his song "What is the German's Fatherland?" and asked ourselves: *where* is the German's Fatherland? Now that the existence of Germany is an established fact, let us ask him to compose an additional stanza addressing Germany's present needs.
>
> (*A tempestuous "Bravo!"*)[5]

---

4   On the 1949 episode, see Widmaier (2011); on Massmann, see Richter (1992). All patriotic songs in the 19th-century *Commersbuch*, including *Ich hab'mich ergeben*, are now online as part of the documentation for the Encyclopedia of Romantic Nationalism in Europe, www.romanticnationalism.net.

5   In the original: "*Drinkwelder von Krems*: Ich stelle den Antrag, dem ehrwürdigen Arndt für sein Lied: 'Was ist des Deutschen Vaterland?' den Dank der Nation zu votieren. Es hat uns begeistert in der Zeit der Unterdrückung, und es hat uns vereinigt. *Soiron von Mannheim*: Ich

This scene is remarkable not merely for the way romantic-cultural enthusiasm was infused into, and galvanized, the political deliberations of the
Frankfurt Parliament, but also for the total, un-argued and self-evident obvi-
ousness with which everyone was familiar with Arndt as, first and foremost,
the composer of a song that was universally recognized and acknowledged as
a potent force in public life; and this, let me insist, occurred not on the basis
of its enjoying a mediatized or institutionalized official public status, but
on the basis of its grassroots performative popularity: again, like "Auld Lang
Syne" or *O Tannenbaum*.[6] In fact, it is possible to trace the trajectory of this
grassroots popularity along the stepping stones of its reception history: from
the inclusion in a seminal early *Commersbuch* or students' songbook (Albert
Methfessel's 1818 *Allgemeines Commers- und Liederbuch*), by way of the addition of Gustav Reichardt's four-part harmony musical setting in 1825, to the
apotheosis of its performance at the massive Cologne Song Festival of 1846, by
the mid-1840s Arndt's song had become the 'underground national anthem' of
nationally-minded Germans.[7]

---

habe nur einen kleinen Verbesserungsvorschlag zu machen. Wir wollen ihm nicht für sein
Lied, wir wollen ihm überhaupt für seine Wirksamkeit für das ganze Deutschland danken.
(*Ein dreimaliges donnerndes 'Lebe hoch!' erschallt in der Versammlung und auf der Tribüne.*)
Jahn von Freiburg an der Unstrut: Geehrte deutsche Männer! Es war eine Zeit, in der wir uns
erbaut haben an Arndt's Liedern. Wir wollen ihn bitten, daß er zu seinem Schwanengesang
noch ein anderes Lied dichte. Wir haben oft sein Lied gesungen: 'Was ist des Deutschen
Vaterland?' ich habe es ihm einmal als Zuschrift gesendet, und wir haben uns oft gefragt: Wo
ist des Deutschen Vaterland? und wenn nun nicht mehr Deutschland in Frage steht, so wollen wir ihm bitten, einen Vers dazu zu dichten, wie ihn die jetzigen Zustände Deutschlands
erfordern. (*Stürmisches Bravo!*)"; in Wigard (1848–50), vol. 1, 27.

6   Even the notorious culminating phrase in Goebbels's "Sportpalast" speech proclaiming total
    war ("Now, people arise, now, storm, unleash!") was quoting a songline: Theodor Körner's
    Männer und Buben, yet another favorite in the choral repertoire. The intertext was no doubt
    more familiar to 1943 audiences than to 2013 historians. Indeed, many propagandistic ges-
    tures of Goebbels invoked the spirit of the period 1813–1817: the book burnings harked back to
    the Wartburg Feast, the historical film drama *Kolberg* made allegorical use of 1813 historical
    events (including the singing of Körner songs).

7   Klenke (1998, 67) speaks of the *heimliche Nationalhymne*, since it was still suspect to the
    Metternich-style regimes of the period. For literary historians, the intriguing point (prob-
    lematizing Michel Foucault's analysis of the "author-function"), is that the poet was identi-
    fied by the poem, not the other way around. The canonicity of the text shed lustre on the
    author rather than vice versa; the text's autonomous popularity had in a manner de-autho-
    rized, collectivized it. In the field of memory study, the concept of the "collective text" (Erll
    2011, 164–66; Rigney 2012, 63) has gained currency to describe this trans-canonical "house-
    hold familiarity"; the fact that texts can be stripped of their authorial anchor indicates a yet

Nothing Succeeds Like Banality

Not the state nor any of its top-down institutions, but choral societies and their festivals were the platform that ensured the status of such a song in the public rather than the private sphere. From small semi-domestic beginnings in the 1810s, these choral societies multiplied across the map of the German lands, and clustered into trans-local, regional or national associations and federations. An established practice of guest performances and reciprocal visits crystallized into increasingly numerous and large-scale festivals; the formative stepping-stones appearing to be Stuttgart 1827, Esslingen/Magdeburg 1828, Stuttgart 1839 (in the context of a Schiller commemoration), Würzburg 1845, Cologne 1846, Coburg 1851, and Nürnberg 1861—the first to be organized by a new German-wide federative organization which also held the one at Breslau 1906–07 (mentioned at the beginning of this chapter). Active participants numbered 1600 in Würzburg 1845, 2200 in Cologne 1846, and 5500 in Nürnberg 1861 (also reflecting the rapidly increasing mobility ensured by the railway). Not only through their own attendance and increasing girth did these festivals and performances carry social clout: they also served to render the repertoire singable, and recognizable as part of a widely shared cultural reservoir. And what that consisted of, we have seen: students' drinking songs, songs of hunting, wandering, love and friendship, love of the fatherland.

"Love of the fatherland" is of course a long-standing civic virtue.[8] To assert that Love of the Fatherland is a Good Thing is almost tautologically uncontentious; Walter Scott's "Breathes There the Man" is but one of hundreds of instances of versifiers stating the obvious. It is no surprise to find this universally acknowledged trope of moral conformism part of the repertoire of Biedermeier sociability, alongside equally anodyne topics like the joys of nature and the charms of the innkeeper's daughter. Indeed, the very banality of the sentiment was an enabling condition for its success: social life in the early nineteenth century was deeply imbued with the need to keep political or religious controversy at bay and to exclude its harmful presence from the membership's convivial cheer. 'Safe,' uncontentious topics were therefore more widely acceptable, and among these, Love of the Fatherland was an obvious

---

further stage of popular collectivization. A modern-day parallel would be the chanting of the song "You'll Never Walk Alone" by supporters of FC Liverpool, who, were they to recall its provenance, would probably remember the rendition of Gerry & The Pacemakers rather than the authorship of Oscar Hammerstein II.

8 On the ideological intensification from Enlightenment-Patriotic *amor patriae* to Romantic nationalism, see Leerssen (2006).

trump card. Inclusion in the repertoire of the choral societies could therefore render national loyalty as unproblematic and uncontentious a theme as walking in the woods, raising a cheerful glass with friends, or wooing in the moonlight. Indeed, any uplifting emotive trope could, thanks to its qualification as 'wholesome and German,' be overlaid with the gloss of being national.

The song *Der Jäger Abschied* (The Huntsmen's Farewell, also known as the *Waldhymne* or Forest Hymn) is a case in point. The words are by Eichendorff and follow that poet's characteristic lyricism, combining religious awe with love of nature—a bit like Wordsworth's "natural piety," with no overtly nationalist connotations. Set to music by Mendelssohn, it was one of the highlights of the 1846 Cologne Song Festival, and became a choral 'hit.' This Festival in turn was fervently national-minded, held in the aftermath of the Rhine Crisis (1840) and during the run-up to the First Schleswig-Holstein War,[9] and wholly dedicated to proclaiming the virtues of the manly German against the effeteness of aristocrats and foreigners. In this context the virile Huntsmen in the "Forest Hymn" (directed by Mendelssohn himself, who was engaged for the occasion) became figures of Germany. The song was included in a songbook published in the fateful year 1848 with the telling title *Germania: A Wreath of Liberty Songs for German Singers of All Estates*.[10]

Banality was, then, the very condition which rendered nationalism successful, and which could allow it to piggy-back onto all other moral virtues.[11]

---

9   The galvanizing presence of a Schleswig-Holstein delegation at the Würzburg 1845 feast (Klenke 1998, 55–63) followed a declaration of autonomy of the Holstein Estates (1844) which provoked a Danish centralist backlash and, on the rebound, strong anti-Danish feelings of Schleswig-Holstein solidarity throughout the German lands. The intensive cultural opinion-making that preceded the outbreak of war in 1848 is illustrated also by Emmanuel Geibel's *Zwölf Sonetten für Schleswig-Holstein* (Lübeck 1846) and by the fact that the prestigious, nationwide scholarly meeting of *Germanisten* organized by Jacob Grimm in 1846 in Frankfurt was wholly dominated by the issue (*Verhandlungen* 1846; see Netzer 2006). Grimm himself moved a declaration of unremitting war against Schleswig-Holstein as a delegate in the Frankfurt Parliament of 1848.

10   Klenke (1998), 66. Original title: *Germania: Ein Freiheitsliederkranz für deutsche Sänger aller Stände* (ed. Th. Täglichsbeck; Stuttgart, 1848).

11   This piggy-backing capacity to inflect other political doctrines appears to be a peculiar quality of nationalism. Michael Freeden (1998) concludes that this is because nationalism is "thin-centred," i.e. having little by way of a concrete, explicit agenda for the ordering of social or political relations beyond a vague, generalized notion of national self-determination. The point is valid but tends to be overstated by those who, like Freeden, pay insufficient attention to the agency of culture in setting political agendas and in mobilizing people for those agendas, and are therefore unduly dismissive of nationalism as a powerful and influential ideology—which it undoubtedly was. The 'banality' and unfocused

This was possible largely because cultural nationalism was itself the political projection of a more general, moral-national self-image: that of German
manliness (*virtus* in the ancient Roman sense of the word, involving stern
dedication to duty, self-abnegation, forthright honesty, and imperviousness
to flattery and vanity). This gender-national auto-image was of long standing
and was traditionally opposed to its implied counterpart or 'hetero-image,' the
frivolous French. Anti-Napoleonic intellectuals (including Jahn, the Grimms,
Fichte, but most prominently Arndt in his prose writings as well as his verse)
had instrumentalized this German auto-image into a political, anti-French
agenda. Indeed, much of the rhetoric of German nationalism can be understood as precisely that: a politically instrumentalized national auto-image. The
auto-image of the 'manly German' was everywhere, and was perhaps most effi-
ciently adopted and (in a century-long sustained praxis) proclaimed by the
choral movement, from Arndt to Felix Dahn.[12]

The centrality of this German self-image in the rhetoric of cultural nationalism makes it legitimate to define nationalism, in imagological terms, as the
political instrumentalization of a national self-image. Thanks to its adoption
by the choral movement, a nationalistic verse repertoire obtained a huge distribution and all-pervasive social penetration, and by 1900 was as universally
inculcated in Germans as the Lord's Prayer among practising Christians or the
pledge of allegiance to the flag among American school children.

From 'Love of the Fatherland' to Nationalist Mobilization

Although its pious banality ensured widespread acceptance, 'love of the
fatherland' was not just a woolly celebration of 'all things bright and beautiful.' From the outset it had sharp claws under its fluffy paws and fangs behind
its simpering smile; these claws and fangs had become fully evident in Felix
Dahn's 1906 poem and were to continue, across the anti-Versailles revanchism

---

idealism of nationalism can certainly be analysed in term of 'thinness,' but this should not
be mistaken for weakness; the fact that viruses lack muscles makes them 'thin,' but does
not make them weak or inconsequential.

12   This application of imagology (which has long recognized and analysed the rhetoric of
characterological opposition between 'upright Germans' and 'frivolous French' (in the
wake of the pioneering work of Hugo Dyserinck; cf. Florack 2000, Beller and Leerssen
2007) lends additional support to the analysis of Klenke cited in note 2 above. On the
ultimate roots of the ethnotype in the early-modern German appropriation of Tacitus's
Germania, see Leerssen (2006) and Krebs (2011).

of the Weimar Republic, into the 'steel romanticism' of the period 1933–1945.[13] Sharp political edges were never far away: Arndt's *Was ist des Deutschen Vaterland?* already predicated the German's love of his native land on his hatred of all things French; and Hoffmann von Fallersleben's *Deutschland über alles* was written in exile after the author had been banned from Prussia for political subversiveness.

Arndt's songs and the verse of Körner (set to music by Schubert, Weber and others) first became popular in the aftermath of the anti-Napoleonic wars of 1813 and its popular-Romantic enthusiasm, when, as Gneisenau convinced the Prussian king, the "security of the throne is founded on poetry," and all German lands were united in their common hatred of the French hegemon (see Leerssen [2008], 114–18; and more generally, Kohn). Thus, the beginning of national-romantic song issued from militaristic, radicalized beginnings, and indeed its early cultivation was strongest among those who had been most strenuously radicalized in the years 1810–1813: the young males who, after reading Jahn and Arndt, had joined volunteer militias, gymnastic clubs, and student fraternities. In these circles the songs remained an important convivial bonding agent, and the first *Commersbuch* anthologies were assembled; it was in and for these groups that Massmann composed his *Ich hab' mich ergeben.* Gymnasts and student clubs were, throughout the century, looked upon with mixed feelings by the authorities: they were appreciated for their national fervor but feared for their radical populism and 'demagoguery.' As a result, they were frequently banned or suppressed, and in requital they often denounced dynastic conservatism and the authoritarian state in their rhetoric and songs.[14] Meanwhile, a canonical repertoire crystallized; not the *oeuvre* of any one particular poet (though the names of Arndt, Schenkendorf, and Rückert occur saliently alongside the posthumously glorified Körner), but rather the collectivized, anthologized corpus of cherry-picked verse by many authors, prestigious (like Uhland) and second-rate (like Massmann). This verse did not survive as an autonomous *textual* corpus (any more than an opera libretto is remembered in literary history), but, set to melodies (and thanks to this melodic setting), as the semi-anonymized lyrics to a performative musical repertoire.

All this provided a latent subtext underneath the pious conformism of 'love of the fatherland' and the generalized moralism of songs like *Freiheit, die ich*

---

13   Klenke (1998) aptly traces the development of growing militarism into the *stählerne Romantik*, and also identifies the dual antagonism, typical of pre-1848 national liberalism, against *Adelsherrschaft und äußere Feinde* in the radicalization of the choral movement.

14   Cf. Lönnecker (2003) and Richter (1992). Also, for verse disseminated in periodicals, Vanchena.

meine or *Der deutsche Mann*. While the male choirs emanated from a much more stolid middle-class background (no radical students and gymnasts there), they and their repertoire could easily adopt the radical implications of the nationalistic repertoire. The international crises of 1840 (over the Rhineland and, at recurring moments, over Schleswig-Holstein) saw increasingly combative and militaristic sentiments displayed in the choral repertoire, which in turn became triumphalistically fixed into that mode after 1870–71—which explains Dahn's rhetoric of 1906.

At the same time, the choral tradition should not be seen as a mere passive reflector of political attitudes. It had its own inner consistency and autonomous dynamics. The song cycle *The Soldier's Life* (*Soldatenleben*, by the Dresden composer and organist Julius Otto) became a favourite from 1849 onwards, and in turn rendered this repertoire more warlike. Arndt's lyrics remained a constant inflammatory factor in the decades after 1815—not only the enduring popularity of the 1813 corpus, which was recycled and adapted for changing circumstances, but the continuing productivity of Arndt himself, who remained a stalwart radical presence into advanced old age. It was his "Festive Song" written for the Würzburg Festival of 1845 that helped to give that event a more radical, militaristic tone; its rhetoric is a half-way house between the spirit of 1813 and Dahn's poem of 1906:

> Well befits you the straightforward word,
> Well the spear which stabs straight in,
> Well the sword wielded openly
> Which pierces the breast from the front.
> Leave furtive assassination to those French;
> You be reasonable, pious and free.
> Leave ostentatious servitude to those French;
> Simple honesty be your part![15]

The simple, honest, pious, non-French German is here kitted out with weaponry, as he was in 1813, and as he would be again from the 1860s onwards, to the tones of Otto's *Soldatenleben*. The rattling sabres and brandished spears had been references to the real business of actual warfare in 1813; by the 1840s they had become mere verbal posturings, eroded martial-heroic metaphors for

---

15 In the original: "Wohl steht dir das grade Wort / wohl der Speer, der grade bohrt, / wohl das Schwert, das offen ficht / und von vorn die Brust durchsticht. / Laß den Welschen Meuchelei, / du sei redlich, fromm und treu. / Laß den Welschen Sklavenzier / schlichte Treue sei mit Dir!" (cited in Klenke 1998, 56).

a run-of-the-mill consumer culture; but in the approach to 1870 they gained again a real-world resonance in the increasing militarism of German national unification. 'Banal' it was, and remained; but from banal-trivial it became banal-virulent.

The repertoire, with its repeated performances and mnemonic resonances, in fact functioned as a cultural echo chamber in which the passing crises of evenemential history were preserved and re-activated, amplifying political emotions in a self-stoking loop after the events had passed which had triggered those emotions in the first place. The idea of a Rhine coveted by French expansionism was a political reality in 1813; in 1840 Schneckenburger's *Die Wacht am Rhein* and Julius Becker's *Rheinlied* were already a hysterical over-reaction fed by the intense, Arndt-mediated memory of 1813 more than by the actual political reality of the day. And the combined memories of 1813 and 1840 were sufficient in 1861, without much in the way of a real political threat, to make German choirs froth at the mouth and declare *fortissimo*: "And if the foe approaches, then a united Germany will march to the Rhine, to do battle for the Fatherland!" This was sung by a huge massed choir at the National Song Festival of Nuremberg in the relatively peaceful year 1861, and the line "Hurrah! We Germans, we march to the Rhine!" was drowned in loud acclamations. The Franco-Prussian War was still ten years in the future; but together with its triumphalist aftermath it was foreshadowed in the field of culture and emotionally pre-programmed through this self-stoking, self-amplifying choral flag-waving.[16]

What we see, then, is a qualitative intensification and a quantitative amplification of informal cultural nationalism. Publicly performed culture in nineteenth-century Germany became inculcated with a nationalist rhetoric which, for all its pretended uncontentiousness and consensual nature, was increasingly strenuous and militaristic; and the forcefulness and socially penetrative power of the inculcation itself was increased quantitatively by the growing presence and impact of the choral movement.

---

16   On the massed-choir programme of the Nuremberg Festival, with its fervently anti-French
      militarism, see Klenke (1998), 110–15. The quotation is on p. 114. In the original: "Und naht
      der Feind, dann zieht ein einig Deutschland zum Rhein, zum Kampf für's Vaterland!" and
      "Hurrah! Wir Deutsche, wir ziehen zum Rhein." In the visual arts as well, the image of
      Germania vigilantly guarding the Rhine was a constant long-term iconographic trope,
      outlasting the evenemential crises of the day: thus Lorenz Clasen's *Germania auf der
      Wacht am Rhein* (1860), Hermann Wislicenus' *Germania auf der Wacht am Rhein* (1873),
      and the cover illustration of Hermann Müller-Bohn's patriotic geographical album *Des
      Deutschen Vaterland* (1913).

That growth of the choral movement brings us to the second part of this chapter: how institutions like these could ramify and proliferate within and beyond Germany.

Institutional Self-replication: Social Setting, Cultural Reach

The importance of sociability is by now well established in the study of eighteenth- and nineteenth-century Western modernity. The growth of musical societies is a Europe-wide phenomenon, starting either in or around existing associations (churches, masonic lodges) or as private convivial gatherings. From the outset, they were also seen as a suitable platform for social pedagogics, training body and mind and instilling the values of harmonious collaboration around an edifying pursuit. As a result, collective musicianship, especially singing, also thrived in educational settings: in schools and universities, and, later, in the context of workers' organizations. Musical societies often emerged alongside sports/athletic/gymnastic clubs, teetotalling societies, etc.

These social-infrastructural factors help to identify the choirs' social catchment and role, and explain the conditions that made their emergence possible; but there remains the more historical question of the temporal/geographical dynamics of their growth and activities. Various country-based studies have charted these dynamics, and by now we are in a position to collate the various findings and move to the stage of a transnational comparison.

At first sight, two basic types appear to have been operative: the French-style *Orphéon*, and the German-style *Gesangverein* or *Liedertafel*. In most individual instances, from Wales to Catalunya and from the Basque Country to the Balkans, we find, as might be expected, a combination of local infrastructural determinants (church structures and educational patterns; agricultural, civic or industrial aggregations) and a diffusionary exchange of models and examples adopted from elsewhere and inspiring local activities— not only in the availability and choice of repertoire, but also at the level of organizational structures.[17]

The emergence of social structures from social infrastructure is not, or almost never, a matter of spontaneous generation—as if all over the map fresh wheels were being invented all the time by different people. The spread of

---

17   Some non-German cases are covered in standard works like Philippe Gumplowitz (1987) on the *Orphéon* and Gareth Williams (2003) on Wales. For Catalonia, see Nagore (2001) and Narváez Ferri (2005). See also Milojković-Djurić (1985), Kuhn (1990), Corten (2009), and of course the other chapters in this volume.

male choirs is not a matter of similar responses to similar circumstances; it is to a large extent a matter of diffusion, of communicative procreation. For this reason, understanding the emergence of choirs purely in terms of context and circumstances is insufficient. It is, as Bruno Latour would put it, 'using the social to explain the social.' Having established the social-historical context in which the choral movement could emerge, the question remains of the diffusionary dynamics and filters through which choirs spread and ramified. They were spawned not just by the social conditions of the time, but also by each other, by following the examples of other choirs and setting an example for others in turn.

This institutional self-replication is relatively straightforward within a given sociopolitical setting. The establishment of *Liedertafeln* and *Männergesangvereine* within the ambit of the Lower Rhine, for example, took place within a homogeneous society unified by the condition of Prussian rule since 1815, and may be seen a single process affecting the entire area as a whole.[18] Germany as a whole was, however, a much less homogeneous space consisting of various autonomous states with different constitutional structures and different political regimes, different religious confessions, different degrees of urbanization and industrialization, different party-political landscapes. The picture painted by Otto Elben in his *Der volksthümliche deutsche Männergesang* of 1887 shows, accordingly, a diversified dissemination trajectory emanating from the twin foundational hives of Zürich and Berlin.

In the North, and in the Prussian Rhineland, the private *Liedertafel* established by Zelter in Berlin in 1809 became a prototype; in the South, the first initiative by Nägeli (1810) found widespread dissemination through the relay station of Stuttgart, which Nägeli had visited on a lecture tour in 1819–20 (which also included Karlsruhe, Darmstadt, Mainz, Frankfurt, and Tübingen), canvassing the male choir as the ideal interface between popular sociability (*Volksleben*) and artistic education.

The Stuttgart *Liederkranz* was founded in 1824 and in turn inspired copy-cat initiatives in Ulm (1825), Munich (1826), Esslingen (1827), Frankfurt/Main (1828), Schweinfurt (1833), and elsewhere. By the time the prototypical Stuttgart

---

18   Blommen (1960, 250–52) lists the foundations of some 120 choirs between 1840 and 1870 in the *Niederrhein* region. The process appears to be fairly evenly distributed over the chosen region and over the chosen period. The peak years showing significantly more than the annual average of four foundations (1846–48, 1850, 1853, 1859–60, 1862, 1868) are spread fairly evenly over the period, indicating a sustained process. On the social/cultural history of the (greater) Rhineland generally, see Brophy (2007).

choir was founded, Berlin spin-offs had already taken root further north: foundations in Frankfurt/Oder, Leipzig, Göttingen, Weida, Thüringen, Magdeburg, Dessau, Münster, Hamburg, Danzig, and Minden all date from between 1815 and 1824.

Between the Berlin and Stuttgart hives there was a zone where the spreading Zelter and Nägeli models met and overlapped: Franconia and the southern part of the Prussian Rhine Province. Some of the more notable foundations in the post-1824 decades include Koblenz 1824, Bremen 1827, Nuremberg 1829, Bielefeld 1831, Aachen 1832, Trier 1835, Paderborn 1838, Mannheim 1840, and Cologne 1842.

In this diffusion of choral foundations, we see that such institutions, locally anchored though they were, operated translocally and were involved in translocal, transregional communicative dynamics. The foundation of regional and, ultimately, national federations took place in tandem with the regular organization of mutual visits and regional festivals for a variety of choirs from different places. Thus, an association between the choirs of Hannover and Bremen formed the nucleus of the "League of United North-German Choirs" in 1831; it attracted other local choirs and organized a series of regional festivals.[19] Similar patterns were at work in Bavaria, Thuringia, and Franconia; and these federations in turn entered into a nationwide meta-federative league in 1860. Thus the organizational history of these choirs in a sense offered a template of Germany's political unification.

The institutional history of the choral movement, no less than the history of its repertoire, is to a large extent characterized by self-propelling, translocal communicative development. Choirs were rooted locally but active translocally, and this combination of local rootedness and nationwide outreach characterized both their organization and their outlook. The communicative translocal ramifications of the male choirs rendered them in themselves a manifestation of the middle-class pan-German unity that they celebrated in their repertoire and helped to prepare in their activities.

---

19   Affiliations came to include Nienburg, Osnabrück, Kinteln, Minden, Bückeburg and, ultimately, some twenty-five others. Annual festivals were held at Nienburg 1831–33, Porta Westfalia 1834, Rehburg 1835, Bremen 1836, Hameln 1839, Hildesheim 1840, Pyrmont 1841, Minden 1842, Osnabrück 1843, Hameln 1844, Bielefeld 1845, Detmold 1846, Pyrmont 1847, Hannover 1851, Bremen 1852, Detmold 1853, Braunschweig 1856 (celebrating the League's 25th anniversary), Pyrmont 1857, Osnabrück 1858, and Bielefeld 1860 and 1861.

Beyond 'Germany': Cultural Transfers

As the choral movement became pan-German, so did Germany itself. The coalescence of the German lands into a united whole was proposed idealistically by Romantic intellectuals and 1848 parliamentarians, then realized first by the various Prussian acquisitions and annexations and later in the 1871 *Reichsgründung*. Precisely where this process was going to stop was not obvious. Intellectuals like Arndt, Grimm, and Hoffmann von Fallersleben had always been vague in their gesture towards the German nation's geographic footprint, and were loth to err on the side of modesty. That Alsace and Schleswig-Holstein belonged to an aspirational Germany was self-evident. Grimm found philological reasons to claim all of Jutland, and there were widespread, more or less overt or euphemistically phrased notions to effect a reconnection with the Low Countries; while in the East, pockets of German communities dotted the map from Transylvania to the Baltic. There, too, the fashion for choral societies spread, as indeed it took hold among the German diaspora in the United States.

The spread of choral societies should not be seen finalistically, from a latter-day viewpoint, as affecting that 'Germany' which took political shape in 1871 or 1945. The pre-1871 process of scale enlargement and infederation was open-ended. German-style choirs were founded in the cities of the Low Countries (Ghent 1843, Rotterdam 1847, Arnhem 1845) and by the German urban communities of Central and Eastern Europe (Königsberg, Prague, Budapest, Pressburg, Siebenbürgen).

The choral movement affected Flanders from two directions. One Ghent choir, the *Mélomanes*, was founded in 1838 on the model of the French *Orphéon*; the other (the *Lion de Flandre*, founded in 1843) was inspired from the Rhineland (as was the Antwerp choir *De Scheldezonen* of 1844). Indeed, as in the early 1840s the Flemish Movement, inspired by go-betweens like Hoffmann von Fallersleben, became increasingly German-leaning in its opposition to French-speaking hegemony, Flemish cultural nationalism (which took shape principally among the urban bourgeoisie of Ghent and Antwerp) adopted the model of the patriotic-convivial choir as well. This honeymoon of Flemish and German choral natonalism culminated in reciprocal visits in the mid-1840s, and a massive Flemish presence in the Cologne Festival of 1846.[20] Something

---

20   On Hoffmann's role in Flanders, and on the Flemish-German interaction between 1837
      and 1848, see Von der Dunk (1996) and also Leerssen (2011b). On Cologne 1846 (and
      its run-up, as well as its sequel: Ghent 1847) as Flemish-German festivals, see Leerssen
      (2011a), 155–62, and Blommen (1960), 114–121.

similar went on in the borderlands between Germany and Holland, near the German town of Kleve. Here, cross-border choral festivals were held with a pronounced Dutch participation (from Amsterdam, Nijmegen and Arnhem, which on the Dutch side were seen as international fraternization and among German patriots as a reconnection between Dutch and *deutsch* [Blommen 1960, 113]). Such contacts dwindled after 1848 as the German movement, in the 1850s, grew increasingly militant in its national chauvinism.

While, in the West, some spillovers occurred across the border, the situation in the ethnically mixed territories of Central Europe, especially in the Baltic area, was different. Certain cities which are now de-Germanized (Königsberg, Breslau/Wrocław) were at the time unquestionably German, with a non-German native population present at best as a mere cultural substratum and a social underclass. In Prague, the establishment of a *Liedertafel der deutschen Studenten* (1844) at the university bespeaks, perhaps, a certain defensiveness in the face of increasing anti-German, Czech challenges to German hegemony there.[21] In these mixed towns and cities of Central-Eastern Europe, the male choir model seems to have functioned both as a social-cultural bulwark for local Germans and, in adopted form, as a mobilization platform for emerging non-German national movements.

This transnational aspect is best borne out by the extraordinary repercussions in the Baltic area. Although the Baltic Provinces had all come under Russian rule, city life in towns like Riga, Reval/Tallinn and Dorpat/Tartu was still dominated by the German townspeople and their culture. In 1851, German-style choirs (possibly following the example of the Königsberg choir) were founded in these three cities. Significantly, these foundations occurred at precisely the time when Latvian and Estonian cultural awakenings began to stir (stimulated, if anything, by the paternalist-sympathetic interest of local Baltic-German intellectuals). The vernacular culture of the Estonian and Latvian populations proved a highly congenial ambience for choral singing, uniting performativity and face-to-face conviviality in an 'embodied community.' In the later decades of the nineteenth century, the song festivals of Estonian and Latvian activists took flight. A first all-Estonian song festival was held in Tartu in 1869 to commemorate the fiftieth anniversary of peasant emancipation in

---

21   Besides the well-known episode of the Slavic Congress of 1848, a tell-tale example involves the philologist August Schleicher. This prominent scholar had been called to a Slavicist chair at the Charles University in 1850, but soon became deeply unpopular among Czech-speaking students owing to his German-centered pedantry; in 1857 he was driven to resign from the university, which in 1882 was split into German-speaking and Czech-speaking parts.

Livland, with 845 singers before an audience of from ten to fifteen thousand. The movement gathered in strength with further festivals held in 1879, 1880, 1891, 1894, and 1896; and from 1873 the cue was taken up in Latvia as well.[22] The Baltic Germans had delivered the inspiration, the organizational design, and the community-bonding and nation-mobilizing function; the native populations fitted these *made in Germany* vehicles with their own ethnic (Estonian, Latvian, Lithuanian) payload.[23]

The Baltic choral movement became a very broadly based cultural mass rally with an important role in the accelerating national movements of the post-1900 period, and an enduring social presence throughout the twentieth century. This emerged in 1989 as the most powerful survival of pre-Soviet public culture: it was above all in choral demonstrations (the so-called Singing Revolutions) that the power of the USSR was exposed to public, collective challenges, and the nationalist mobilizing power of mass singing found its most extraordinary manifestation (cf. Ginkel).

Rooted and active locally, but ramifying through processes of cultural communication and institutional contagion, the voice of the choral movement carried far and wide. It proved an ideal means to generate local mobilization for national ideals, and thus offers an almost ideal-typical example of the interaction between the social and the cultural, the local and the transnational, in the history of nationalism in Europe.

---

22   Raun (1991), 75–76; Tall (1985).
23   See Brüggemann and Kasekamp (2014).

CHAPTER 2

Choral Societies and Nationalist Mobilization in Nineteenth-Century France

Sophie-Anne Leterrier

In nineteenth-century Europe, national movements found expression and support in convivial sociability and shared cultural interests. Choirs could galvanize or mobilize a part of the population with national fervor, and choral festivals became tribunes for the assertion of a separate identity. Choral societies made an important contribution to nationalist mobilization, mostly in east European and Balkan countries, but also within empires (as in Wales). In France, the choral movement was not divisive; instead of challenging the national state, the male choral societies or *orphéons* were among its supporters. This came about for historical reasons that will be examined below.

The Legacy of the French Revolution

The history of France in the nineteenth century is defined by the French Revolution, with the government and the people either celebrating revolutionary principles and conquests, or seeking to discredit and eradicate them. Among the principles of the French Revolution, the most important was the idea of the nation. This idea made possible a rupture with absolutism, privileges, and feudal order. Reference to the nation legitimized post-revolutionary powers (through the Constitution, the parliamentary system, and the rule of law). But at the beginning of the century the nation was more a utopian concept than a reality. France already existed as a state, which meant that the choral societies did not have to build an 'imaginary' nation,[1] but to cope with a real one. In a sense, the orphéons' mission was precisely what the French Revolution had in view: to make a nation by creating unity among different people. The orphéons were a concrete way of learning democracy by incarnating and practicing it.

After the nation, education was perhaps the second most important principle of the Revolution. In Georges Danton's famous words, "After bread,

---

1   See Benedict Anderson's famous concept of nations as 'imagined communities' (1983).

education is the first need of the people." The revolutionary project was also a pedagogic project, not only involving the school system but leading to a real conversion from subject to citizen, from alienation to reason and freedom. Education is another word for Regeneration. The orphéonic movement was strongly committed to this progressive concept of education. The idea of the orphéons emerged from the Society for Elementary Instruction, a small circle of philanthropists.

The French Revolution had to deal with an absolute king and a state religion. In the beginning, deputies tried to favor religious freedom, but to preserve the Catholic church. They integrated it into the new state, with priests becoming civil servants if they agreed to sign the *Constitution civile du clergé*. But the king never accepted these dispositions, nor did many priests, whose resistance was one of the causes of the division of the nation, leading to civil war. In nineteenth-century France, religious questions were still very political. Restoration was also a religious reaction. Religion was always involved in decisions about schools, morality, or power. The claims of secularism were a result of the Revolution. Nineteenth-century republicans called themselves sons of Voltaire; they might be Catholics in private, but they refused a ruling Catholic church. Even in the field of leisure and art, in France religious structures did not offer an open and welcoming frame. On the contrary: where religion divided, singing would unite.

Before being real institutions, the orphéons were the utopia of the singing nation. The choral movement carried big hopes at the beginning; it appeared as a mean of bringing art to the people, making artists from everyone. The ideal of music as a noble, moralizing, 'social' art, was kept alive by the social movement of the mid-century.

In the first decades, Saint-Simonians were eager to make the arts more accessible to the masses, but rejected the utilitarian view that the arts should be an after-hours distraction for the workers, a placid after-dinner diversion. "Instead, they directed music to enter as active participant into the struggle for social reform. They demanded that music sing forth the ideals towards which society should be striving and that it draw people's attention to what one of them called society's 'hideous sores' (such as prostitution and social parasitism)."[2]

Saint-Simonians were numerous among the first orphéonists, and some, like Félicien David, wrote choral music. By the same token, some Polytechnicians were involved, which was not surprising given their contribution to the liberal movement in general. From 1836, former schoolmates created an association

---

2   Locke (1986), 230.

dedicated to the professional formation of workers, which included music, using the method of "Wilhem" (Guillaume-Louis Bocquillon). Six months later, four hundred Parisian workers performed before the musical élite of the capital city with great success. Baron Taylor, the founder of the Association of Musician Artists in 1848, belonged to the same circles.

The Orphéons

In France, the initiators of the orphéons were passionate music lovers and concerned democrats. Alexandre Choron, who was first invited to direct the movement, declined the proposal; a mathematician, musician, and specialist in ancient music, he was engaged in the creation of his own musical institution (the *Institution royale de musique classique et religieuse*). Guillaume-Louis Bocquillon, known as "Wilhem", was then chosen by the Society for Elementary Instruction to be in charge of musical education in the schools that had opted for mutual schooling.

Wilhem was born in 1781 into a family of soldiers. He studied music from 1800 to 1802 in Paris, at the Conservatory, under François-Joseph Gossec, Louis Joseph Daussoigne-Méhul, and Pierné. He loved the patriotic compositions of Gossec, which determined his musical orientations. As he could not make a living from music, he worked as an employee at the Ministry of the Interior. There he was under the direction of Edme-François Jomard, a member of the Society for Elementary Instruction, and came to meet Pierre-Jean de Béranger. Both of them earned their living as obscure employees, but lived for their art. Both were democrats, and wanted to bring art to the people. They collaborated in songs, with Béranger writing the lyrics and Wilhem the music. Both left the Ministry in 1819, Béranger to become the *chansonnier de l'opposition*, and Wilhem to take up the musical direction of the Ecole Saint-Jean-de-Beauvais. Two years later, Wilhem published his manual (*Tableaux pédagogiques de la méthode Wilhem*), which was sent to provincial schools. In 1826, ten Parisian schools adopted Wilhem's method. After the Revolution of July 1830, all the schools in Paris adopted it. At the same time, Wilhem created the first orphéon, a choir assembling pupils from all these schools, and published *L'Orphéon*, the first musical periodical dedicated to choral music. In 1842, when Wilhem died, more than 5,000 children and 1,500 adults (attending evening classes) belonged to the Parisian orphéon.

In its early years, the movement was firmly grounded in liberal principles and groups or institutions, such as the Society for Elementary Instruction. After the July Revolution brought liberals to government, the orphéon had powerful protectors. Major members of the musical institutions—Cherubini, Berton, and Berlioz—attended the first public performance in 1838. They were enthusiastic and gave much attention and help to the movement for some years. In 1845, the Queen herself, the Duchess of Nemours, the Duchess of Orléans, and the Duke and Duchess of Aumale listened to the annual performance. So did the new republican government in 1848. In the 1850s the orphéon was protected by Hippolyte Chelard (who was also chapel master of the Grand Duke of Saxony), Adolphe Adam, Ambroise Thomas, Napoléon-Henri Reber, and Louis Clapisson, all members of the Institute. Halévy, Gounod, Niedermeyer, Auber, and Meyerbeer were also members of the Commitee. Under the Third Republic, if they could no longer rely on the musical establishment, the orphéons were still encouraged and protected by the government. All through the century, everyone considered the orphéons as a democratic and progressive institution.

Numerous texts document the orphéonic movement: materials emanating from the societies themselves, from their patrons and sponsors, from the local press, or local erudition, but also political speeches, mostly from senators, deputies, or mayors, at the openings of meetings or exhibitions or at banquets. These texts generally contain praise for music as an agent of order, of civilization, of morality—that is to say: an agent of progress, in two ways. First, collective singing is supposed to keep choristers away from depravation, give them self-pride, and illustrate social cohesion and consensus. It offers a kind of leisure and pleasure absolutely commendable, "The good, the brave pleasure which does not disturb anyone."[3] Second, the discourse of Meunier, a republican deputy (Seine-et-Marne) at the opening of the Universal Exhibit in 1878, connected the orphéons with the movement of history itself: "Your work is democratic. Before, art was the property of a few. Music found shelter only in fashionable circles and theaters. Today it has taken wing; it mingles with everyone's life. It tells its secrets to young ones, its notes no longer resemble the scribbles of an alchemist, it is understood and loved by all. This evolution is part of the democratic evolution of our society. The organization of the orphéons is universal suffrage applied to music."[4]

---

3 F.-J. Vaudin, cited by Gumplowicz (1987), 121. Unless otherwise noted, all translations are by the author.
4 Cited by Marie-Claire Mussat in Tournès (1999), 197–98.

The Orphéons and Nationalism

In French terms, 'nation-building' and 'nationalism' are quite different notions. According to Raoul Girardet, since 1789 the French have produced two kinds of nationalism.[5] The first is rooted in jacobinism and was generated by the ideology of the French Revolution. It mixed two ingredients: chauvinism and humanitarian messianism, whose compatibility later came to seem problematic. The second, which appeared during the Boulangist crisis and matured with the Dreyfus Affair, was a reactionary nationalism, conservative and xenophobic, and mostly a meditation on decadence.

As the orphéonic movement spread during the whole century, it had to deal with both types of nationalism. As we will see below, most orphéons were patriotic rather than nationalistic. After 1870, like other French groups, the orphéonists were obsessed with revenge and expressed nationalistic feelings and hostility towards Germany and Germans in general.[6] In the '80s, it became more common for a society to be founded to meet political needs. One could easily underline the relation between a partisan group and a musical society, including the same members and wanting to use different means—either discursive or emotional—to propagate their opinions.[7] Sometimes the very creation of a musical society was a political gesture, for instance in Rennes for the Choral Rennais in 1880 (an overtly republican society) or in Valensole in 1884 (an orphéon for the reaction, as the city major suspected).[8]

By the end of the century, the names of some groups reflected their nationalist engagement: *La Jeunesse française, La Jeunesse gauloise, L'Alsacienne*. Some musicians gave attention to the choral movement for political reasons. Louis-Albert Bourgault-Ducoudray, a member of the *Action française*, one of the founders of the *Societe nationale* (1871), considered music a mean of propaganda.[9] In 1881, he dedicated to school pupils and French orphéonists a "Hymne à la patrie" composed for the national holiday of 14 July. In 1895, he

---

5 Girardet (1983), 8–9.

6 Gumplowicz (1987), 120.

7 For instance in Rugles in 1882, where the *Ligue des patriotes* and the City Musical Society were dissolved and reorganized as the *Union Musicale de Rugles* (Jean-Yves Rauline in Tournès [1999], 182–83).

8 Mussat in Tournès (1999), 198, 205.

9 "Selon moi l'Action française, comme la patrie française, devrait chercher dans l'art, et particulièrement dans l'art musical, moins un moyen de recette qu'un moyen de propagande par le sentiment"; cited by Francfort (2004), 51.

set to music a poem by Victor Hugo dedicated to the soldiers killed in action ("Those who died devoutly for their native land / Have the right that to their coffin the crowd should come and pray").[10] But his effort failed; the choral societies preferred other compositions, and rarely expressed an overtly nationalist hostility against foreign countries, even in the '90s.

Generally speaking, the orphéonic movement was conditioned by domestic circumstances; but in some places, mostly along the frontiers, choirs could result from foreign influences. For instance, in Alsace, the oldest choirs developed from vocal quatuors created in the 1820s in the Austrian manner.[11] In Flanders, the development of orphéons in Lille was clearly influenced by the model of the *Réunion lyrique* in Brussels, founded in 1820 by François de Marneffe, itself created on the German model, which was dominant on an international scale, either as a model or as a challenge to other patriotic vocal societies.[12] By the end of the century, the repertoire reveals no real foreign influence, but offers an imaginary trip to other countries through musical *clichés* ("false Spanish, excentric Viennese music, tropical music, Scottishes and other polkas"),[13] a "shoddy exotism" ("tyroleans, barcarolles, false Spanish or Neapolitan music").[14] Alsace after 1870 is a special case, where old French societies and new German choirs competed in many different ways concerning their ethnic and confessional compositions, their repertoires (German *Lieder* versus popular French songs and mostly French opéras-comiques), and the contexts of their execution (official ceremonies versus protests against annexation).[15]

The chronology of the orphéons is clearly structured, and begins during the Restoration, in June 1819, among the founders of the Society for Elementary Instruction. Wilhem, the first director of the orphéon, formed many disciples, who, using his method, taught music during the July Monarchy, either in Parisian schools or to workers. Expansion followed in the forties and fifties all over France, flourishing mostly in the provinces. In the north (including Normandy) the movement was very strong from the start, but weaker in the south and west (Britanny). By the mid-century, the orphéons were at their peak everywhere in small towns.

---

10   Francfort (2004), 55.

11   Geyer (1999), 154–55.

12   Gumplowicz (1987), 77. The *Réunion lyrique* was founded after a German recital in Brussels. The Czechs formed their own choirs in opposition to German choral societies.

13   Ibid., x.

14   Ibid., 194.

15   Geyer (1999), 170 ff.

Wilhem's disciples continued his work. Eugène Delaporte is one of the most important during the time of the expansion of orphéons into the provinces: by 1836 in Strasbourg and Toulouse, by 1838 to Lille; by 1845 to Burgundy. Delaporte was supported after 1848 by the Association of Musician Artists, founded by Baron Taylor. He brought artists and primary teachers to give music lessons, established competitions, and organized the major festivals of the second half of the century (including the first national choral festival at Troyes in 1859).[16] Unfortunately (and rather injustly), he was excluded from the movement after the failure of the London Concert in 1867,[17] and would not be remembered.

In the meantime, the nature of the movement evolved. The first orphéons were purely vocal, and mostly Parisian. Their aim was chiefly to bring music to workshops. Under the Second Empire, orphéons were created everywhere: they were increasingly instrumental, and appeared in public along with regimental music or theatrical artists. They were both an occasion for local pride and the vector of a new national culture, as agents of mass musical events. At the first national orphéonic festival in Troyes in 1859, some six thousand singers from 204 societies were acclaimed by 50,000 spectators. After 1860, the movement continued to expand until the First World War. By 1867, it represented 3,400 societies with 247,000 singers. The number of registered members grew continuously during the Third Republic, but mostly in favor of instrumentalists. Between 1860 and 1908, the number of wind ensembles and bands increased twentyfold (from 400 to 8,000); while the 800 choirs in 1860 grew to 1,500 in 1895 and 2,000 in 1908. This means that among amateurs, by 1908 three musicians out of four were instrumentalists. After 1918 came a decline for both bands and vocal societies.[18] The orphéons, which in the nineteenth century offered the principal (and often the only) popular leisure, were challenged by sport. The shift was very quick and devastating.[19]

Unlike the 'sociétés savantes,' the orphéons paid little attention to the exact registration and archiving of their members, which makes it difficult to study their social composition. In Rouen, one of the two societies studied by

---

16   Gumplowicz (1987), 58.

17   Ibid., 100.

18   The trend since 1945 seems again to be more favorable to choral societies, but the context is very different. Since World War II, music has become a commodity that anyone can buy, but its consumption is individual. Participation is no longer a necessity. Music lovers may be simple listeners. Choirs are legal, registered associations, including different social groups, but they mostly consist of classical music singers with no roots in popular tradition. Choral singing is most often a leisure activity, a way of personal development, not a militant engagement, but nonetheless a challenge for the Ministry of Culture.

19   Gumplowicz (1987), 212.

Loïc Vadelorge (the *Cercle musical de Rouen*) was mostly middle-class, including traders, shopkeepers, artisans (cabinet-makers, engravers, string-instrument makers), and rentiers. The other one (the *Musique municipale*) counted mostly shopkeepers and employees.[20] Members of the élite, mostly the economic élite of the city, were named honorary members.

Orphéons appeared before the industrialization of France. Vocal societies relied on and consisted initially of independant workers, except in the north, where industrial concentration arrived earlier. In 1828 the society *La Soie de Valenciennes* had three bands: two for the workers in crockery in Saint-Amand and Orchies, and one for glass workers in Sars-Poterie. But generally, relations between bands and corporate labor existed mostly at the end of the century. For instance, the *Anjou Lyra*, founded in 1897, was the musical society of Bessonneau (a textile factory). It gave two concerts each week after work, performed in public gardens, alternating with the military band, and participated in charity concerts. Most factory music belonged to large companies like coal mines or iron works. As in the army, the position of a musician in the industrial world was privileged and envied. But sometimes they had to be at the disposal of the directors, or play in religious ceremonies (masses for Sainte-Barbe, Sainte-Cecile, or the Fête-Dieu) and at big receptions.

The directors of the choirs were also middle-class men. During the 1840s and '50s, choirmasters were often instrumentalists or journalists like Eugène Delaporte, François-Jules Simon, or Henri-Abel Simon. Specialized composers conducted orphéons in the second half of the century, among them Laurent de Rillé, Mathieu de Monter, and Marcel de Ris. Choir directors were typically educated musicians who had followed classes at a conservatory in the provinces, were organists at the cathedral, or taught music in private schools. During the Third Republic, teachers played an important part in founding and conducting choral societies, while the conductors of bands were usually military musicians, mostly wind players. Some of them worked in factory bands (without pay,[21] or most often as accountants).

The composition of the orphéons is rather stable during the century. "The orphéon is a story of men."[22] Male choirs always predominated. Among workers, mixing was generally discredited. Both inside the choirs and outside, singers gathered to consort with their peers—same class, same sex. But mixed choirs also existed. In 1865, Eugène Delaporte created two societies in the factories of Godillot and Dusautoy in Paris, one for male workers (the *orphéon*

---

20   Vadelorge (1997), 73.

21   As *emplois de complaisance*.

22   Gumplowicz (1987), 153: "L'orphéon est une histoire d'hommes."

Saint-Auguste) and one for females (the *orphéon Sainte-Hortense*). Other societies did not hesitate to add female singers to the choir when the repertoire requiered it (for instance in Strasbourg).[23] But even around 1900, mixed choirs were exceptional.

Since they were the future of the nation, young people were the privileged public of the movement. The first disciples of Wilhem, for instance Foulon, mostly taught male children (at the *Lycée Louis le Grand*, the *Collège Chaptal*, the *Collège des jeunes Polonais*, and the *Collège des jeunes détenus*), but also taught girls (at the *Ecole supérieure des jeunes filles*), and young adults (in 1843, at the *Régiment de dragons*, and among associations). During the Third Republic, there was no segregation in the orphéons. Everyone was welcome, whether young or old.

The number of members varied widely in relation to the size of the village or town where the choir was located. Thirty to forty was average at the end of the century. But the number of singers in public performances could sometimes be very large: in 1836 the first Parisian orphéon counted 300 performers; in 1838, 450; in 1842, 700; in 1844, 760; and in 1846, 1,600.[24] The performances were transformed into mass spectacles. In 1855, 3,500 orphéonists (from sixty-seven French societies and twenty-nine Belgian societies) sang eight choruses in front of more than 20,000 spectators in the Palace of Industry. In March 1859, for the first general meeting of French orphéonists, 204 societies with 6,000 singers faced an audience of 50,000 people. In June 1860, 3,000 French singers (in formal dress) gave three concerts in Sydenham Palace, London, for an audience of 20,000. In 1878 Jules Pasdeloup conducted 15,000 singers from 700 societies performing *La Marseillaise* in front of 200,000 people. In this context, the power created a social ritual far beyond royal processions or religious ceremonies, and one specifically republican, with the choral singing of the national hymn, supposed to abolish the distance between citizens and reinforce national community.

As for the repertoire, the principles of the founders of the orphéon drove the choices. For them, popular music did not exist; there was only one kind of music for everybody, 'la grande musique'; this music, which had once been an aristocratic privilege, would become a national good. *L'Orphéon*, the first choral publication edited by Wilhem in 1833, was a compilation. The first song, "Du Ciel, éternelle harmonie," was composed by Wilhem himself, to a poem by M. d'Epagny. The rest of the volume collected choruses by classic composers like Palestrina, Philidor (*Tom Jones*), Gluck (*Alceste*), Handel ("Dieu de Bonté"),

---

23   Geyer (1999), 153.
24   Gumplowicz (1987), 44.

and Mozart (*Don Giovanni*); from musicians of the French Revolution (Gossec, Gretry, Méhul, Cherubini); and from living composers from theatre and opera: Monsigny, Sacchini, Rossini (*Tancrède*), Piccini, Dalayrac, and Spontini. Around 1840 Mozart, Auber, Rossini, and Wilhem contributed equally to the repertoire, which was not commissioned (at least regarding the music, with specific lyrics being written), and relied on German and Italian music, like many other repertoires at the time.

The same attitude could be observed in the public schools, and among republican pedagogues. The French case appears to contradict the assertion of Didier Francfort that the relation between a musical tradition and an efficient musical school system able to transmit it is a condition of musical nationalism.[25] The French public school system was never able to teach national music to pupils. Instead, French music was almost entirely represented by composers trained in a cosmopolitan musical tradition. Whenever schools were used to teach music to the people, it was 'universal' music.

Meanwhile, the orphéonic repertoire resulted from negative choices in many ways. Wilhem refused folklore, because the orphéon was modern by definition. A child of the French Revolution, it adopted its cosmopolitism. Its conception of the nation hated particularisms. Because he did not want to 'form' artists (in the sense of specialized, professional artists), Wilhem refused melody and music written for the salons.[26] For moral reasons, he kept away from actual popular songs (commercial songs), because too many of them were corrupted by broad joking.

In the second part of the century, the selected repertoire became the responsibility of the directors, who were also often in charge of the formation of the interpreters, of public relations. Numerous periodicals furnished musical materials to performers and interconnected societies: *L'Orphéon* (Eugène Delaporte, 1855) and *La France chorale* were among the most influential. The orphéons' directors approved the initial choices, and tried to compose a specific music, avoiding both the illusions of Art and the depravity of popular songs.

---

25   "Le nationalisme musical trouve systématiquement sa genèse dans l'existence d'écoles autant que dans la révélation d'une mission individuelle du génie créateur." "Une logique musicale de filiation esthetique est ainsi reliée au processus de formation nationale par l'école"; Francfort (2004), 24, 28.

26   "L'orphéon forme des chanteurs, non des artistes." "Mon orphéon ne va point en ville"; Gumplowicz (1987), 46, 48.

As a consequence, the repertoire was almost entirely secular. Bach, Handel, classical polyphony, cantatas, or oratorios were rarely sung.[27] Meanwhile, at Wilhem's funeral service, 500 orphéonists sang large pieces from the *Requiem* of Pierné; but they did so for special occasions only. The repertoire was mostly contemporary, and made especially for the choirs. Bands also used Sax instruments, which (as industrially produced instruments) signified modernity.

The choice of repertoire was thus determined by ideological principles; but it was also directly related to the composition of the choirs, whose members often had no special training in music. Since they lacked musical instruction, these singers were not able to read music. They learned by hearing and imitating more than reading. The musical work was done during rehearsals; people rarely worked by themselves at home. As a result, the level of difficulty remained low (in terms of the character of the melody, the rhythms, and the intervals used). Beside, choirs were not mixed, and real basses were rare, which handicapped most of the classical choirs and condemned composers to write under many constraints (and with poor results).

The orphéonic repertoire was divided into two kinds of compositions. The first consisted of transcriptions, reductions, or adaptations of theater music for male choirs. Here the original music was 'reduced' but the text remained the same. The second part was made up of *scènes chorales* written (both text and music) specifically for the choir. Henri Maréchal, one of the most prolific and popular composers for orphéons, was also inspired by Belgian musicians (Gevaert, Riga, Radoux) who wrote long pieces for male choirs.[28] The lyrics for these compositions were usually descriptive, and rarely inspired in a poetic sense.

For decades, opera and opéra-comique furnished the major contributions. Ambroise Thomas (director of the National Conservatory) and Charles Gounod (*Sapho* and *Faust*) were among the famous opera composers who wrote for the orphéons. In 1859, Thomas composed the opening chorus of the Orphéonist Meeting. Charles Gounod personally directed the Orphéon for eight years (1852–60) and wrote a number of songs for its members. Circa 1860, the usual repertory consisted of some religious pieces (like the Psalm of Marcello, "Veni Creator" by Bezozzi), mostly classical music from Mozart (the Priests' chorus from *The Magic Flute*), Kreutzer ("Hunters' Departure"), Adolphe Adam

---

27   In England, oratorios, being "sacred but not liturgical, unstaged and yet dramatic" (William Weber 1992, ch. 4), were considered appropriate for vocal societies, and dominated musical life rather than opera. In France, the preference for opera can also be related to its religious neutrality.

28   Gumplowicz (1987), 190.

("Les Enfants de Paris"), and some specialized repertory: a chorale by Hasler, "Ambres et Teutons" by Lacombe, or "La Retraite" by Laurent de Rillé.[29] But during the 1860s, except in national competitions, the usual repertoire changed radically in favor of 'choral scenes' by composers such as Laurent de Rillé, Armand Santis, or Henri Maréchal. In major cities like Rouen,[30] some societies maintained the old repertoire, singing masses by Bach and Mozart, French music from the nineteenth century (Thomas, Franck, Gounod, or Fauré), and even some living composers (Paray); but the orphéon programmes rarely included classical chorales from the seventeenth and eighteenth centuries or any kind of religious music. In 1867, in the context of the Exposition Universelle, the orphéonists sang "Hymne à la nuit" by Rameau and mostly pieces from popular contemporary theater composers.

Free public concerts and local festivals or competitions were the normal modes of performance for the orphéons. In the nineteenth century every small town had its musical festivals. Any occasion would serve: the inauguration of a monument, an agricultural meeting, a carnival, a local exhibition, or simply to give a summer concert. "The Orphéons follow both a local and a national agenda."[31] The *Harmonie d'Auxerre* performed in various contexts: for the feast of Saint-Amôtre, but also under civil patronage, at commercial exhibitions, and for the local sports alliance or the horticultural society.[32] In Rouen, the orphéons participated in local anniversaries (the *Fête de Jeanne d'Arc*, the anniversary of the *Théâtre des Arts*) along with national holidays (14 July, 11 November). By the end of the century, international exhibitions reveal the extent to which international networks determined orphéonic performances.

They performed in various places. The first concerts in Paris were held in the Sorbonne, the Cirque des Champs-Elysées, and the Salle Saint-Jean de l'Hotel de Ville. In the provinces, choir concerts took place in concert halls, but also in churches, schools, factories, or town halls; and for orchestras and brass bands, in the parks and streets. Marie-Claire Mussat rightly emphasizes the revolutionary connotations attached to open-air concerts. Songs proceeded from the people, and were easily transmitted. They could be political symbols. Singing was not only a technique but also a form of social behavior, creating

---

29   Ibid., 101. With the addition of the national anthem, "God save the Queen," this was the
      program of the London concert of 1860.
30   Vadelorge (1999), 98.
31   "The time of the orphéons was both the local time of the city and the national time of the
      Republic"; Vadelorge (1999), 90.
32   Gumplowicz (1987), 151.

interactions between singers and listeners, and it was therefore a matter of political concern. Not until 1848 could choirs and musical societies perform publicly, at the risk of police intervention in case of trouble.[33] But after 1850, and mostly between 1880 and 1890, bandstands were constructed specifically for music and dance.[34]

Encouraged by local powers as much as by government, the orphéonic movement also received financial support. Choir singing was reputed to unite, to discipline, and eventually to galvanize. It was not thought of as a revolutionary force but as an expression of leisure. Like other cultural associations in France, choral societies existed mostly by public subsidy and the voluntary involvement of their members. In 1854, the Prefect of *Seine-et-Marne* decided that in each town where an orphéon existed, the primary school teacher would have to lead and conduct the society, and give free lessons, and the commune (district) would have to pay for the method and for the scores. In 1862 the same process occurred in Seine-et-Oise, and a public grant of 500 francs was regularly voted to each society.

Despite a few cases under the Second Empire,[35] in the nineteenth century there was no real propagandistic use of orphéons, in the way that the Vichy government used singing for instance, through school, army, youth movements, and public celebrations, with a special repertoire (marches and hymns) and a special manner of singing (exhibiting masculinity and collective participation).[36] The democratic engagement of their founders implied no partisan orientation of the choirs themselves. A large majority of the orphéons expressed a political consensus, although in some places choral societies reflected local political divisions, with each party having its own group.

In different ways, orphéons played a major role in the republicanization of small towns, although the orphéonists kept away from political debate *stricto sensu*. After 1849, the orphéonists traveled frequently to competitions, usually by train, and mostly in France. The expansion of railroads facilitated trips, and sometimes the railroads gave special fares to orphéonists. Before 1936, among

---

33   Mussat (1999), 194.

34   Public bandstands were erected in Metz in 1852, Strasbourg in 1855, Colmar in 1858, Angers in 1862, Montluçon in 1863, le Puy and Nice in 1865, and Cambrai in 1867 (Mussat, 196).

35   Rauline (1999), 178. Rauline explains the kind of arrangements that existed between a Prefect and a musical society, with the Prefect furnishing the society with instruments and materials, and the society going along on electoral trips.

36   See Dompnier (1996).

miners, the musicians were the only ones who traveled to the coast (for festivals in Malo-les-bains or Ostende).[37]

Since the 1850s the orphéonists provided a civic model of community and acculturated republican ideals, ideas, and forms. At a time before political life was structured by parties, republican feasts were a major link between citizens and power.

> The main element of republican mysticism is not the equality of all citizens, but the link that unites them. Festivals actualize this link, not only because people gather, but because they gather on specific days ... Singing songs in unison strongly contributes to the actualization of this unity.[38]

The orphéons also figured as a moral, recreational, and unifying activity. They invited and inclined to charity, and later to mutuality or solidarity (or 'solidarism' according to Leon Bourgeois).

Since they tried to provide elementary musical education, which the public school system was almost never able to provide, they represented education and cultural diffusion. In small towns, they also offered free musical auditions to the citizens, and played an important role in the general musical education of audiences. No professional aspirations were ever mentioned, since the orphéons clearly refused to train professionals in the field of music. Orphéonists were judged with benevolence and obvious sympathy, which was not the case for professional singers. The praise of orphéons was usually an indirect praise of the national culture.[39] It was also an illustration of the local heritage, through works of native composers who were systematically preferred over others, especially when they had achieved national or international recognition.

The genesis of the orphéons, their composition, their unusual repertoire, and the values they embodied and diffused, cannot be understood outside the context of post-revolutionary France. This implies some specificities relevant to an integrated, Europe-wide and transnational study of the phenomenon of choral societies.

---

37   Gumplowicz (1987), 151. For instance, between 1897 and 1912 l'Harmonie d'Auxerre traveled to Troyes, Dijon, Pantin, Honfleur, Mantes, Chablis, Toulon, Versailles, and La Rochelle.

38   Tournès (1999), 36, 41.

39   "L'orphéon local n'est pas à la musique ce que le roman populiste est à la littérature"; Vadelorge (1997), 76.

French Orphéons in the European Context

Most choirs in nineteenth-century Europe emerged from, or were closely related to churches, and their repertoire was predominantly religious. In Wales, for instance, amateur choral singing was bound up with the Methodist religious revival. People found basic musical literacy among chapel congregations; churches were the (only) places of rehearsals, meetings and shows. In Serbia, choral societies were often established in Orthodox churches. In both cases, religious specificity gave the choral movement a national character.

In France it was different. If a large majority of people were faithful and Catholic, quite often the cause of liberty and progress was identified more with the Enlightenment than with religion. Free thinking was vivid, and sometimes aggressive. The question of public education and the question of national independence (from Rome) interfered with religious choices and make the way to religious peace difficult. The statute of Catholicism—legally the religion of the majority of the people in a state guaranteeing freedom of religion, but culturally the pillar of the Ancien Régime—had an impact on the orphéonic movement in two ways: it influenced the repertoire, which was usually secular, and expressed a new religiosity in the sacralization of the nation. After 1870, the shift between Church and State (resulting in Separation in 1905) incited some choral societies to adhere to a strict republican secularism.

The first societies agreed to participate in religious celebrations, even when they indulged in banqueting and had a rich social life as well. For instance, the *Crickmouils* of Lille, founded in 1838, sang masses every Sunday. In Dieppe, the choral society was conducted by a clergyman and active in charity. But there were often different societies in the same local context, with one particularly devoted to sacred music, as the names indicate. For instance, in Lille, *Sainte-Cecile* specialized in sacred music, while the workers' societies (*Les Lièvres, Les Mélomanes, Les Rasoirs, Les Bluets, Le Cercle du Nord*, all founded in 1848) preferred secular music. In Rennes, the religious society was the first, and a secular society appeared in 1862 (the *Orphéon rennais*) with the explicit support of the mayor who hoped to counterbalance the influence of the other societies directed by clergymen.[40] From 1870 onward, the shift was quick between republican and clerical societies; some choirs refused to sing at masses or religious feasts, while others refused to sing the national anthem.[41] Schisms

---

40   Gumplowicz (1987), 87.

41   Mussat (1999), 204. She cites the example of the *Société Musicale de Josselin*, which refused to participate in the national feast on 14 July 1880 and claimed that Brittany was in no way an exception.

and reorganizations were the result. The phenomenon became general in the 1880s. Usually the names of the societies reveal this process, along with their choice of honorary members or a meeting place. Instrumental societies were mostly republican, while vocal societies were more conservative.

While art music is a universal language spoken by individuals, the Romantics regarded folk music as specific to a linguistic community and region and, at the same time, as a shared, collective expression of the *génie du peuple*. In nineteenth-century Europe, folk music played a central role in the construction of various European national identities, for example in Romania, Serbia, and Hungary. The Welsh, the Irish and the Scots, together with the Slavic and Scandinavian countries, based their national music on folk songs. In Scotland, even if the nationalism felt or expressed in music was cultural rather than political, harmonized folk-songs with Scottish texts and compositions by Scottish composers formed an important part of the choral repertoire.

In other cases, native folk songs were not welcomed because they did not appear as a national patrimony, but rather as a feature of peasant culture. Thus, in Bulgaria, music was conceived in terms of 'non-national intonations from outside,' that is to say Serbian, Russian, Ukrainian, Czech, or Polish melodies.

In France, the status of folk songs was different. Early in the nineteenth century, a few folk songs were still current in French peasant culture. They fascinated some Romantic poets and gave way to erudite research, but from the beginning they were clearly expelled from the orphéonic repertoire, for ideological reasons. The democratic engagement of the orphéonic movement made references to regional heritage problematic. The orphéonic identity was founded on a refusal of both folkloric roots and formal, intellectual music.[42]

In a way, the Exposition Universelle in 1889 marked the climax of the orphéonic movement as well as a major republican event, and shows very clearly the way the orphéons remained on the side of official culture instead of incarnating the nation through popular culture (i.e., folklore or 'picturesque music'). Picturesque music was everywhere at the Exposition, whether authentic or fake. It was cheerful, and performed with costumes and instruments that were also picturesque.[43]

Unlike the picturesque music from afar, French folk music was not part of the wave of local color exhibited in taverns, restaurants, cafés-concerts, or

---

42   "Moins qu'un autre pays, la France, du fait de son brassage de populations et de ces frottements particuliers entre peuple et élites, laisse entendre des particularismes musicaux nationaux, à la manière par exemple des musiques bulgares, dont le temps de maturation interne serait à même de garantir une quelconque authenticité"; Gumplowicz (1987), 15.

43   Fauser (2005), 253.

exotic theater productions at the Exposition Universelle. While some French folk-music ensembles performed in the various bandstands, the music from the French provinces was mainly located in the concert hall, in exhibitions of instruments, and in museums.[44]

French folk music was at the center of two annual events: the official competition on 4 July related to Southern French regionalism, which at the time adopted a nationalist speech of 'enracinement,'[45] and the official *Congrès international des traditions populaires* concert on 1 August. Neither of these concerned the orphéons, who were clearly excluded from the competition by the rules regarding the repertoire,[46] and from the Congress by the jury's implicit criteria (wearing uniforms, or being able to read music, did not meet the expectations of the organizers).

The prejudices against both artistic music and popular music led the orphéons to a dead end. During World War II, they were condemned by André Coeuroy,[47] who argued that their disdain for traditional music had deprived them of a great resource. He deplored their rejection of their heritage (they had "no connection with the French popular base") and their 'purely democratic' ideology: "Instead of mining their own regional treasures, the orphéonists sing choruses composed by their directors."[48] The orphéonists celebrated "Democratism, Saint-Simonism, Humanitarianism. But nothing really popular or nationally musical." Coeuroy's point of view was very partisan, but his diagnosis was quite correct.

Given their aims and social composition, the French orphéons sang in French, but usually in a schoolish, artificial French, the national idiom imposed on school children since the French Revolution. In the nineteenth century the French language was a token of citizenship. Bilingualism was a reality, but each language had its proper sphere.

Eugen Weber has described some uses of dialects in singing (as an expression of political opposition, coming from anti-clericals), but he explained that the government intervened only when the conflict did not stay at the local

---

44   Ibid., 268.

45   "Through the celebration of regional roots, especially in Latin cultures of the Mediterranean, France was to strengthen national identity and patriotic pride"; Fauser (2005), 270.

46   "Programmes may include only popular melodies from the performer's region; all arrangements, fantaisies or selections from operas or chansons from the *café-concert* will be rigourously excluded"; Fauser (2005), 272.

47   Coeuroy, cited in Gumplowicz (1987), viii–ix.

48   "Au lieu de puiser dans leur propre trésor provincial, les orphéonistes chantent les choeurs composés par leurs chefs."

level.[49] Even if choirs sometimes sang in dialect, they would usually use French for public performances, which made them instruments of the official culture.[50] The first collections of songs by individuals in the middle of the nineteenth century tended to privilege the poems belonging to official culture over those coming from oral tradition. Alsace was an exception, even before 1870. There, popular songs formed the core of the repertoire.[51] But in the main part of France, it was only after the war of 1870 that vanishing traditions encouraged some people to collect and present popular traditions as a national heritage.

The preference for French over dialects found allies in teachers, for whom traditional singing, like other expressions of popular culture, had to give way to a superior form of art and culture.[52] Teachers certainly thought that being able to speak French was an asset, and that national unity required linguistic unity. But it was mostly because they considered the national language richer and better able to express ideas.[53] In schools, songs were clearly the vehicles of patriotic and moral values. Singing was also conceived as the ideal way to regulate particularist pulsions and civilize people. Before 1914, school songs were mostly patriotic, even military songs: "Le Drapeau de la France," "Le Départ du régiment," "Mourir pour la patrie," or the "Choeur des soldats" adapted from Gounod's *Faust*.[54] Explaining his choices in a book written for teachers, *Chants populaires pour les écoles*, Maurice Bouchor insisted on the internal limits of this kind of music, on the distance between a childish imagination of war and the reality; he invited teachers to contextualize the songs as much as possible. This perhaps explains why, if young singers learned patriotic songs at school, *La Marseillaise* was rarely among them.[55] The school repertoire was divided into different sections: some conveyed patriotic, civic, and moral values, while others were traditional work songs, or regional songs, evoking nature, friendship, or the pleasures of family. More and more, at the end of the century, school songs expressed love for the local heritage, but textbook authors and

---

49   Weber (1976), 437.

50   "Even in Nîmes, Marseille, and Montpellier, where workingmen had separate societies and sang works in local dialect of their own devising, they avoided public performances of 'songs in the vulgar tongue' " (Ibid., 442–43).

51   Geyer (1999), 166.

52   Weber (1976), 441 and Chanet (1996), chap. VI.

53   Chanet (1996), 209: "A ces esprits fatalement fermés ouvrons le monde en leur apprenant la langue de tout le monde" (quoting the School Inspector of the North, 1888). Cf. p. 212.

54   Ibid., 308.

55   Alten (1999), 236. She explains that in 1911 a circular from the ministry was obliged to underline the meaning and value of a song, probably because the school was conceived as a way of freeing pupils through the use of reason, not as a place of indoctrination.

teachers always tried to extend this love above the local level, to have it shared by all pupils all over France.

"In 1864 a school inspector in the department of Aude proudly reported that 'the lewd songs that wounded even the least modest ears have been replaced by the religious and patriotic choirs of numerous orphéons due to schools and the initiative of teachers.' "[56] Under the Third Republic, there were even more cross-links between the repertoire taught in public schools and that of the orphéons. In the regions where orphéons were well implanted, the teachers used in class what works in those societies.[57] Conversely, school songs were not intended to remain only in schools. As living and moving songs, they should be able to transcend this space.[58]

The repertoire of the orphéons was obviously national and patriotic. It was meant to transmit the values of revolutionary France (liberty, humanity, progress), expressed in French. References to France as a leading nation, 'the great nation,' the fatherland of liberty, were very frequent. Songs rarely expressed nationalist hostility against foreign countries, as they might have done in Germany, except when they referred to a threat of invasion, as in the Orphéonist Chorus. Most songs refer to the present, or to the future, in a very optimistic way. They rarely refer to the Ancien Régime, but sometimes to the French Revolution, as a time of giants, an epic, heroic time. Evocations of wine and of Gaul are also metaphors of nationality, mingling references to Gauls and Franks not as enemies, but as two elements of the nation. This is significant because of the long historiographic conflict between conservative historians who asserted that France was a conquest of the Franks (justifying the power of the nobility), and others who spoke up for the Gallic people (with more democratic views).

The orphéons appeared in the public space as incarnations of these values. Every orphéon had its emblems, uniforms (an expression of uniformity, as in schools), banners, medals, conviviality, and shared memories. The orphéons chose emblems that illustrate music (any harmonic instrument, mostly the lyre) and mottos that proclaimed their principles. The motto of the *Annecy Lyra*, founded in 1861, was "Harmony, Fraternity, Fatherland"; its banner

---

56   Weber (1976), 442.

57   Alten (1997), 53.

58   "Les chansons d'écoliers ne sont pas faites exclusivement pour l'école. Si elles ne pouvaient en sortir sans être offusquées par la lumière du dehors, si dans tout autre milieu elles paraissaient gênées ou prenaient l'air un peu maussade que, pour certains, évoque le mot 'scolaire,' je crois que même à l'école, elles ne seraient pas ce qu'elles doivent être pour émouvoir et pour agir: quelque chose de vivant"; Bouchor (1909), 27.

depicted the cross of Savoy, a lyre, and two crossed hands. The iconography of the orphéons insisted on the collective and the prestigious. In the context of international events, mostly artistic competitions, their iconography could also emphasize their regional character (costumes).

Eugen Weber relates how the orphéons propagated an official culture, as against oral singing, which faded continuously after 1870, as old pastimes and leisures disappeared and the identity of providers and performers of popular music changed.[59] By the end of the century, while vying with other nations through major exhibitions, France had led the orphéons to become a metaphor for the regime, and to embody the state more than the nation.

---

59   Weber (1976), ch. 26, "Fled Is That Music," esp. pp. 442–44.

CHAPTER 3

Song in the Service of Politics and the Building of Norway

Anne Jorunn Kydland

In 1811, when King Frederik VI of the double monarchy of Denmark-Norway conceded to the demand for a university in Norway, the board of directors of the Society for the Benefit of Norway encouraged their thirty branches and regional commissions to hold a celebration of thanks. This developed into a countrywide national holiday, Norway's first. The idea was to stimulate the king to keep his promise—through thanksgiving to oblige him to act, purely and simply. To document the festivities, regional groups were asked to send in descriptions of their local events, which were gathered in a book and sent to the king: *Reports on the National Celebration December 11, 1811, on the Occasion of His Majesty King Frederik the Sixth's Ordering of a University in Norway.*[1]

The reports included an appendix where the publisher, Ludvig Stoud Platou (1778–1833), collected all the speeches, songs and 'cantatas' performed across the nation during the celebration. Generally the king's resolution was celebrated with 'a song written for the occasion,' or a so-called cantata, sung by a choir or the participants. Speeches were usually held in the local church, and the songs commonly written to familiar melodies, though larger cities could often afford to perform a newly composed cantata. The publisher Platou saw several reasons why the reports should become known to the general public. National celebrations could be important for inspiring and preserving the national spirit, he said, and it was obvious how weak this had been in several European countries. In Platou's opinion the reports were strong proof of the fact that the desire for a university was the *people*'s will, and that the ceremonies were not "the invention of a few men" or "mere empty pompous parades."[2]

---

1 Parts of this essay are related to two earlier articles of mine (Lysdahl 2004 and 2005).
2 Platou (1812), xliv. Unless otherwise noted, all translations are by the author.

Political, Ideological and Musical Framework

The first Norwegian university and the Norwegian constitution date from the
same period: in 1811 the University of Christiania (the old name for Oslo) was
founded,[3] and the constitution of Norway dates from 1814. The ideas of self-
government and a national university went hand in hand. From the beginning, the university was not only a temple of wisdom but also a symbol of
freedom. When the union between Denmark and Norway was dissolved after
the Napoleonic Wars, Norway established its own constitution in the spring
of 1814 before a new union with its neighbour Sweden was established. The
constitution was signed on 17 May 1814, which was soon considered Norway's
national holiday.

The official celebration of 17 May had a difficult start. In the years after 1814,
young students fought for the right to celebrate the anniversary of the sign-
ing of the constitution. They often stood alone—against the Swedish king
and government, the university, and the police—and demonstrated a bold-
ness that could lead to disqualification for employment. Because the students
participated so strongly in marking the national holiday, they had a decisive
influence on the forming of celebration traditions. Singing acquired a central
function, which it still has.

Singing was not only social and festive, but also channeled political
attitudes—attitudes which, for example, King Karl Johan did not like. The
king's disapproval came to the fore in 1829. On 17 May that year, crowds of
people gathered in the streets of Christiania. Military power was used to dis-
perse the crowd, and the famous 'Battle of the Square' occurred. During the
dramatic celebration, it was considered a bold provocation to hold a small,
modest booklet of *Selected National Songs, to be used for the Celebration of
May 17*.[4] In the course of the following summer a number of people, especially students, were interrogated. It was imperative for the authorities to learn
whether the people were singing, and, if so, which songs they sang.

How did song prosper otherwise in the early 1800s? In 1815 Lars Roverud
(1776–1859), a tenant farmer's son and music teacher, expressed his dismay:
"the nation knows music almost only as a word."[5] Roverud himself contributed
markedly to the improvement of the conditions of song, both at the university
in the capital city and in classrooms around the countryside. He wanted to

---

3 Christiania (preferably written Kristiania after 1897) was the official name of the capital from
   1624–1925, when the previous name of Oslo was re-established.
4 Published in Christiania in 1827.
5 Roverud (1815), 1.

improve the common people's knowledge and skills in song and music, and started the first music printing office in Norway. There was a marked dearth of music teachers. There were only two musical professions: organist and city musician. Only instrumental instruction was offered, and only to wealthy people. Norway needed a basic education in music that would make song an obligatory subject at school.[6] Roverud felt that his work met with resistance, but when the movement for choral singing first emerged about 1850, it did not take long before it spread throughout the whole nation. The way was paved in city and town.

Roverud stressed that song stimulates the creation of a meaningful social community. Multi-part choral singing can, for example, lead to a deeper sense of harmony. The performers of song not only influenced people's musical tastes, but also their "religious and moral upbringing."[7] In his publication *A Look at the State of Music in Norway* (1815),[8] the Danish theologian Peder Hansen (1746–1810) is cited: "Gymnastics and music are the unmistakable means by which the people can be led out of slavery, brutality, and savageness."[9] As a bishop in Norway for some years (Kristiansand diocese, 1799–1803), Hansen was engaged in educational work and wished to reform schools for the peasantry and the poor.

When Roverud asserts the importance of song for the individual and for society as a whole, he takes the side of the German-Danish composer Hardenack Otto Conrad Zinck (1746–1832), who in 1810 emphasized the influence of music on "our aesthetic and moral education" and was of the opinion that music should not be "just for pleasure."[10] The composer and orchestra conductor Johan Abraham Peter Schulz (1747–1800), also of German-Danish descent, likewise emphasized the importance of song and music instruction and the publishing of songbooks. In the little pamphlet *Gedanken über den Einfluss der Musik auf die Bildung eines Volks* (1790), he wrote that music education beautifies and improves human existence, and heightens the people's sense of aesthetics and thus their ethical character. There is no doubt, he points out, that

---

6   Herresthal (1993), 20–21.

7   Roverud [1827?], 1–2.

8   The complete title is *A Look at the State of Music in Norway, with a Proposal for its general Dissemination throughout the Country, by an Institute's Founding in Christiania.*

9   Roverud (1815), 9.

10   Zinck [1810], 8. H.O.C. Zinck, a composer of German descent, lived in Copenhagen from 1782.

to the same degree their musical ear is developed and becomes susceptible to the higher powers of this beneficial art, feeling for beauty is aroused, which will undoubtedly influence customs, all domestic and social pleasures, courage and manner of thought, the enrichment of work, the lightening of burdens and suffering, as well as the enjoyment and bliss of life.[11]

Lars Roverud probably became familiar with Schulz's and Zinck's music-educational thoughts when he studied music in Copenhagen in the middle of the 1790s before Norway received its own university.[12] Schulz's thesis was translated into Danish in 1790, the year before the Blaagaard Seminarium, the first teachers' school in Denmark-Norway, opened. Here Zinck tried to launch Schulz's and his own reforms of the educational system in Denmark. Future teachers were to receive a broad education in music so they would be competent to teach song in the schools. Already by 1799, the kingdom required training in "proper harmonic song," especially chorales and good folk songs, in pauper- and free schools.[13] Zinck spoke out in favour of the mandatory teaching of music—especially song, "the truest music":

an instruction, whereupon the smallest child and the most neglected youth could obtain a suitable practice in musical perception and comprehension; whereupon each could learn to appreciate all of the benefits nature has put into music; whereupon our most magnificent talents are cultivated, our noblest feelings raised—whereupon all could raise their voices together in a common choir to sing: "All that has breath, praise our God."[14]

Schulz's and Zinck's thoughts were similar to the ideas of French philanthropists of the Enlightenment, and especially of the Swiss educators Heinrich

---

11   In German: "daß in eben dem Grade, worin sein Gehör sich bildet und für die höheren Kräfte dieser wohlthätigen Kunst empfänglich gemacht wird, auch Gefühle für Schönheit in ihm erweckt werden, deren Einfluss auf die Sitten, auf alle häusliche und gesellige Freuden, auf seinen Muth und seine Denkungsart, auf Versüßung der Arbeit und Erleichterung jeder Last und Leiden, auf den Genuß und die Glückseligkeit seines Lebens, unwidersprechlich ist"; Schulz (1790), 6.

12   Probably sent by Peder Anker (1749–1824), Norway's first prime minister and owner of Bogstad estate near Christiania; cf. Hopstock (1997), 112. Roverud's father was managing clerk for Anker for a while; cf. Herresthal (2004), 11.

13   Schiørring (1978), vol. 2, 123 (cited in Herresthal [1993], 18).

14   Zinck [1810], 9.

Pestalozzi (1746–1827) and Hans Georg Nägeli (1773–1836). Their enthusiasm for national independence stimulated by song festivals and folk festivals, and their ideas about the sovereignty of the people and the life of art were nurtured and brought to Norway. Through song one could express patriotism and stimulate fraternization. When a large group sings with the voices nature has given them, that, claims Pestalozzi, is "the image of the majesty of the people."[15]

Nägeli preferred men's singing because, among other things, he was of the opinion that a men's choir could articulate the text more clearly than a mixed choir. Just as people in France right after the revolution in 1789 made a point of leaving the musical salon and going outdoors, where the voices of the people could resound in large musical performances, Nägeli emphasized that large choirs, not small quartets, were necessary for the ideal development of men's song. The ideal was large amalgamations, such as those that finally manifested themselves in the mass choirs at song festivals.[16]

The European democratic choir movement influenced Norway. Ideas from France about national festivals in which all classes participated in song intertwined with Nägeli's and Pestalozzi's cultural politics as imparted by, among others, Lars Roverud's speeches, writings, and complaints at home in Norway.[17] Song and music were emphasized not only as an important means of education in the humanities, but also as a means of knowledge. Nineteenth-century enlightenment ideologists and music educators were rooted in antiquity's consciousness of the cosmos and harmony and the aesthetics of music, imparted through Romantic theories of knowledge and art. The poet and cultural ideologue Henrik Wergeland (1808–45) passed on this heritage from the ancients (Platon and Pythagoras), German Romanticism, and the French Enlightenment.

Singing is itself a bridge-builder that reconciles differences and binds together social classes, a medium which promotes harmony and reconnects the human soul with its divine origin. The agent of reconciliation, the unifying factor, was song. In all of the Nordic countries, one finds strong

---

15   Nägeli's "Die Pestalozzische Gesangsbildungslehre" from 1809; quotes from Huldt-Nyström, ed. (1958–59), vol. 1, 202.

16   Hanssen (1919), 3.

17   In his book about the minister and public educator Hans Peter Schnitler Krag (1794–1855), Olaus Arvesen (1830–1917) cites one of Krag's pupils, Fredrik Hougen from Sel (a small rural district in the valley of Gudbrandsdalen), saying that Krag held courses for teachers and liked to talk "a lot about Rousseau, Pestalozzi and other famous educators"; Arvesen (1916), 92. At the school Krag founded in Vågå (another district nearby) during the 1830s, he emphasized gymnastics (!) and song.

representations of song's harmony-producing, unifying, reconciling power. *Harmony* in Greek thought is a power that holds opposing elements in place within the universe. The multifarious and the contrasting are not absent where harmony reigns; quite the contrary. Harmony includes the heterogeneous. Its order provides meaning and beauty. The first person to call this universal wholeness the *cosmos* was Pythagoras. Likewise, music is a world governed by certain order-producing principles, namely fixed ratios, and these ratios allow the principle of harmony to express itself in sound. These inherent regularities, which the tonal world reveals, lie also at the foundation of human life, and of reality as well. This organic thinking returns in Romantic epistemological teaching.

The Greeks thought of man's inner self as a lyre. Like other instruments, the soul can become out of tune and distant from its cosmic model. Thankfully, music can retune a person's lyre in accordance with the macrocosm. The lyre appears as a symbol on the banners of several men's choirs in the Scandinavian countries.

The Physiognomy of the Choirs

Norway's oldest public choir, the Norwegian Student Choral Society, was founded on the initiative of Johan Diederich [Didrik] Behrens (1820–90) in the summer of 1845. A meeting of students that year in the Swedish and Danish cities of Lund and Copenhagen was the external occasion for its establishment. Musical interests were actually not central when the choir was formed. Rather, the choir came into being to promote through singing the essential ideas of the time: national awareness and dreams of community among Scandinavian countries. The conflict with Sweden, then Norway's union partner, was suppressed, and the feeling of kinship with Denmark, Norway's former union lord, was renewed. The Scandinavian movement for tighter cooperation ('Scandinavianism') flourished. That same autumn, Johan Gottfried Conradi (1820–96) founded the Christiania Craftsmen's Choral Society and the Commercial Community's Choral Society. Earlier there had been four-part singing in freemasons' clubs and small private choirs, but choral singing as a public movement started in the 1840s. Soon men's choirs were formed among workers as well. The radical movement that Marcus Thrane (1817–90) started in 1849 was not just political. It also had a cultural goal. Thrane wanted to engage in general education in an environment marked by uncleanliness, disease, drunkenness, malnutrition, poverty, and illiteracy. He managed to gather several hundred workers in Christiania in an association, and in 1850 a choral society was founded. The Thranites' choral society disappeared after a while, but in 1864 the Christiania Workers' Society was founded (by Eilert Sundt, 1817–75), and that same year this group established its own choral society, which was soon considered the capital's fourth largest choir.

Conradi understood early on that men's choral singing had a future. In 1843 he tried to form a choir of academics *and* artisans, and later stimulated song gatherings and the formation of choirs in several places in eastern Norway. He emphasized the democratic aspects of a choral movement: song for *everyone*, not limited to an élite. When the sixth large national song festival was arranged in Trondheim (1883), there were about two hundred men's choirs in Norway (with almost two million inhabitants). These were located not only in cities; several small places in the countryside could also pride themselves on having a men's choir. Early in the 1900s a series of choir tours within Norway and abroad increased interest in men's song. The public and the press were preoccupied with these tours in a remarkable way. People were eager to attend the concerts. In the little town of Hammerfest, when the student singers were on tour in the north of Norway in 1907, the windows of the local prison were opened so that prisoners could also listen.

For quite a while, men's choirs did not have to compete with other institutions in the life of music as they did in the neighbouring countries. Mixed choirs first appeared towards the end of the 1870s. These existed side by side with the men's choirs and attended to other tasks. By the turn of the century the mixed choirs took the lead. Among the founders of mixed choirs were teachers inspired by the Danish minister and author Nikolai Frederik Severin Grundtvig's (1783–1872) folk high school and leaders from religious milieus.

Women could participate actively when large compositions from oratorio literature were performed. In the Philharmonic Company (founded in 1846 in Christiania), songs for mixed choir had an important place in the programs. There was also a small group of women in Norway who composed songs for men's choirs in the 1800s, apparently a unique phenomenon in Scandinavia. Norway's oldest women's choir, the Christiania Workers' Community Women's Choral Society (known today as the Oslo Ladies' Choir), was founded as early as December 1870. When women students formed their own choir (the Women Students' Choral Society) in 1895, only twelve years after the first women were allowed to take A-levels, this aroused enthusiastic wonder in international university communities. This was women's history; the world's oldest academic women's choir was established. The capital city's men's and women's student choirs wanted to provide an active forum for contemporary music in addition to keeping up tradition. More than a hundred choral compositions were dedicated to and originally performed by these two choirs.

Repertoire

The men's choirs acted as essential fora for the composition and performance of new music in the nineteenth century. Norwegian composers experienced a rare luxury: they were in demand. There was room for diversity; famous composers mixed with what we call the 'underbrush' in Norwegian music. The texts often came from important poets. On the wings of song, Norwegian poetry—both secular and religious in nature—could reach the common people.

Johan D. Behrens and his first song quartet of students stood behind the first publication of songs for men's choir: two small booklets with Norwegian, Danish, and Swedish songs, as well as a booklet with German songs from well-known contributors of literature for men's choir, reproduced with Norwegian texts.[18] He also published the *Samling af flerstemmige Mandssange for større og mindre Sangforeninger*, booklets that appeared in the course of several decades in the 1800s. Many of the altogether 750 songs in these booklets dominated repertoire lists for men's choirs throughout the whole country and served as a source of songs not only for singers in the capital. Here we find most of the Norwegian men's choir songs from the 1800s, about 250 in all, most of which were given to Behrens by the composers themselves with printing in mind. Friedrich August Reissiger (1809–83), originally of German descent, composed most of the songs with Norwegian texts, some seventy-four items. Otherwise, songs from all of the Nordic countries are represented in the collection, a majority by Sweden's Carl Michael Bellman (1740–95; thirty-five items), and Otto Lindblad (1809–64; fifteen items). The largest numbers of German songs are by Franz Abt (1819–85; thirteen items) and Felix Mendelssohn Bartholdy (1809–47; eleven items). Over one hundred of the songs are folk melodies, mostly of Norwegian origin, many from the Nordic countries, and the rest from various European countries—from Italy in the South to Russia in the East and Scotland in the West.

While in smaller élite choirs or quartets the focus was often on a demanding foreign repertoire (although with Norwegian/Nordic texts), the large choirs mostly favoured their own Norwegian songs when giving concerts instead of looking to the repertoires of other Scandinavian countries. The 'Song Festival's Father' himself, Johan D. Behrens, wrote new lyrics to imported tunes, translated foreign texts, and arranged foreign melodies for choir and school children. He was well connected to many of the poets and musicians of the time. Nearly all the major composers supplied material to the men's choirs, often through Behrens' encouragement. Numerous songs were introduced into the

---

18   [Behrens, ed.] (1845–46) and (1846).

country for the first time through Behrens' school songbooks or men's choral publications. One example is the Norwegian national anthem, which was presented through Behrens' leadership on the occasion of the fiftieth anniversary of the Norwegian constitution in 1864 and immediately published in Behrens' large collection of men's choral songs.

Why did Norwegian composers write so many songs for men's choirs? Compared with other Nordic countries, musical institutions in Norway were less developed. In Sweden, for instance, the men's choir was less important as a forum for new music. Several of the compositions spread throughout the country and also became popular abroad. In Denmark and Sweden complaints were heard about having little new material when it came to a national song repertoire, while in Norway (and Finland) it was noted that the large song festivals stimulated creativity.

A look at repertoire policy for men's choirs in the four Nordic countries between 1840 and 1920 shows that the need to acquire song material from neighbouring countries—for use in concerts—was weakest among the Norwegians. At the same time, it is interesting to note that no compositions were as popular among the neighbours' students as the Norwegian ones.

The flow of Norwegian culture to Sweden, the union partner, on the whole increased constantly after the meeting of Nordic students in Christiania in 1869. This was a fact that August Strindberg (1849–1912) was not entirely happy to have to admit. He complained of a cultural invasion from Norway into Sweden in three fields (literature, painting and music), and cited an expression from Latin literature, abbreviated thus: *Graecia capta, Romam cepit.*[19]

> Rome took Greece, but Greece captured Rome. Sweden took Norway, but now Norway has captured Sweden.... Ibsen and Bjørnson broke into Sweden; Tidemand and Gude were victors at the art exhibition of '66; Kierulf and Nordraak mastered song and the piano.[20]

However, if song is to be the property of all people, then choral direction and vocal education in school must go along with it, according to Behrens. He saw early on the importance of developing vocal talent among children: "A fundamental school education in song is the most important means to awaken and

---

19   Horace, "Epistulae" 2, 156–57: *Graecia capta ferum victorem cepit et artes intulit agresti Latio* ("Greece, the captive, made her savage victor captive, and brought the arts into rustic Latium"; Horatius (1929), 408–09.

20   Strindberg (1913), 354; see Jonsson (1990), 223.

develop people's musical sensibility."[21] The need for vocal literature was great. Through his steady and systematic efforts, he laid the foundation for the cultural climate of song in Norway, for adults and children with regard to religious and secular song as well as choral and unison singing.

Right from the start, Behrens had a broad cultural aim. Just as Luther was eager to create church songs for congregations in their native tongue, Behrens felt that melodies and texts must have a national character if singing was to take root in *all* milieus. He would probably have understood Grundtvig's enthusiasm for the mother tongue, depicted, for example, as follows:

> The mother tongue speaks from our heart,
> all foreign speech is but skin-deep,
> it alone in mouth and book
> can awaken a people from their sleep.[22]

Grundtvig was highly regarded in Norwegian spiritual life, among other things for his concept of a singing people. During the student meeting in Christiania in 1869 (as during the national song festival in Bergen in 1863) the poet Bjørnstjerne Bjørnson spoke, influenced by Grundtvig's spirit and folk high-school idea. He emphasized how important it was that *everyone* should participate in culture and knowledge. Education needed to focus on building *people* (not masses of knowledge) and to be based on popular values. Thus students must attempt to leave 'the student framework' and enter 'the nation's framework.' The prerequisite for respecting other nations is familiarity with and love for one's own culture; then one will discover common traits between countries. One recognizes one's own in others, and such a process of identification creates understanding and removes differences.[23]

Representation

Although the establishment of Norway's first public men's choir was stimulated by the first student meetings in Scandinavia, the development of Norwegian men's choral singing must be viewed more widely, from aesthetic, social, political, and cultural-historical perspectives as well.

---

21   Behrens (1868), 3.
22   From "Moders navn er en himmelsk lyd," Christmas 1837 (*Folkehøjskolens sangbog* 1942, no. 300).
23   Wallem (1913), 572–73.

The fact that Pestalozzi's idea about choral singing as 'the image of the majesty of the people' was well received during the 1840s was due to the flowering Romanticism in Norway at that time, and the awakening feeling for the nation's cultural treasures. The voice of the people was about to speak out in various ways. The widespread collection of folksongs, fairy tales, and folk music had begun. The movement of men's choirs became "the thrush in the spring effervescence" that was experienced in cultural life.[24] It seemed that poets, composers and conductors were just waiting for tasks. For that reason, art could spread very quickly.

It had long been held that song could provide delight in good times and strength in bad. It could create a sense of community both within and between various milieus and across borders. Through words set to music, the practitioners of song could learn about their own country and themselves. One can express one's individuality, or that of a group or a people, and at the same time display the face of a nation. In connection with the idea of popular education, song helped to create an independent cultural identity after 400 years of subordination under Denmark. While students in Scandinavia often met each other during the nineteenth century and sang and made speeches about the old *common Nordic* identity, the national song festivals consolidated the *nation* and the *inner* community in Norway.

Scandinavianism worked like an infection. The historian Jens Arup Seip (1905–92) said it produced "antibodies,"[25] a new national self-esteem, often present at song festivals which consolidated the nation and inspired the establishment of new choirs. In Denmark and Sweden, Scandinavia was looked upon as a big native country; but in Norway (influenced by long union relationships) it was difficult for most Norwegians to understand nationalism and Scandinavianism as anything other than two opposing movements. After all, in Norway the Scandinavian movement became a superficial phenomenon (often conservative), whereas nationalism became a *radical reality*.

As early as the summer of 1846, the pharmacist Harald Conrad Thaulow (1815–81) wrote an enthusiastic article on "Christiania's Song Societies" for *Morgenbladet*, an important newspaper in the capital:

> Song and choral societies will spread to all social classes throughout the whole country, and a new period in our nation's inner history will date from the founding of choral societies.[26]

---

24   Hanssen (1919), 3.
25   Seip (1981), 43.
26   Thaulow (1846).

With great joy the author noted the positive effects of song on people's social gatherings. One evening he heard "sonorous song" through an open window of the town's school. He wondered who the singers could be, and was surprised by the answer:

> *Trade workers?*—No!—it couldn't possibly be trade workers!—Such singing could only be heard from the *students*, who would most certainly have a more thorough foundation and longer practice in refinement and taste!... The last tones seemed still to hover on their lips, which would certainly not be opened *this* evening to praise the brandy devil, nor be profaned by drunken reveling.[27]

According to Thaulow, it was unfortunate that the police felt the need to forbid the "harmonious performances" of choral societies outdoors. In Rotterdam he experienced a choir that wandered through the streets singing at night. Something similar would be possible in Norway if the prohibition of song in the streets was lifted. The night watchmen themselves could start a choir!

Bjørnstjerne Bjørnson remarked in a speech at the celebration of the Norwegian Student Choral Society's twentieth anniversary in 1865 that song was an "extraordinary help" in involving everyone in a cultural life that had previously been reserved for state officials only. Song did not seem frightening to those who earlier had stood outside "art and the like." Seemingly, song was only for entertainment; but by means of song, the office worker was taken from his counter, the student from his desk, the craftsman from his workshop, Bjørnson said, and all were lured into the realm of art.[28]

Reconciliation and Rehearsal

Gradually a nationwide movement of men's choirs developed, stimulated especially by the many central and local song festivals which provided important fora for contemporary thought, music, and literature. The first song festival was held in the middle of the 1800s, probably earlier in Norway than in any other Nordic country. While in Sweden, Denmark, and also Finland, only student singers were invited to such gatherings (and often turned down the invitations), it was the opposite in Norway. Here the members of the Norwegian

---

27   Ibid.
28   Anderssen (1895), 117.

Student Choral Society were not only obvious participants but also organizers and chief ideologists. One important reason why Norwegian students became leaders of a popular choir movement was the fact that Norway was the *last* Nordic country to found a university. For this reason, it took some time before the student milieu could become a more established, reserved, and dignified circle. Student singers represented not only an academic milieu, but also a free group of people representing a whole nation. The educational power of song was emphasized. Perhaps it was not enough to be "the chivalrous guard of the light," to quote a line from a Swedish song: one had to be transmitters of "the light" as well.[29]

What can be the reason for this? Two hundred years ago the people in power in most European countries were noblemen or tradesmen. In Norway it was different: the country had no nobility, and the tradesmen suffered great losses after the Napoleonic Wars. As opposed to other countries, the ruling class in Norway was recruited from the University. University graduates came to mark Norwegian public life throughout the 1800s both politically and artistically. At the same time, many university graduates saw themselves as teachers of the common people and builders of the nation through writing and speaking. Norway was influenced by the ideals of the Age of Enlightenment. Knowledge led to status, and the public school system saw to it that common children could read already two hundred years ago, according to Jan Eivind Myhre.[30] In his comprehensive comparative study of national movements in Europe, Czech professor Miroslav Hroch has investigated which social groups the patriots came from: nobility, merchants, clergy, farmers, or artisans. Hroch registers that in Norway in the 1800s *higher officials* lead the liberation movement. He sees this as a unique phenomenon in the European context.[31]

Because Norway was run by university graduates, a small educated élite consisting of jurists, clergymen and officers, Jens Arup Seip has called the political system between 1814 until 1884 (when parliamentarism was

---

29   In his travel descriptions *Rundt i Norge* (1892), the Danish poet Herman Bang tried to describe the difference between the students' position in the various Scandinavian countries. Copenhagen integrates the students. In Lund and Uppsala the students become the ruling class; in Christiania they become a group of foreigners, a caste. Concisely, one could say that in Sweden the student milieu was aristocratic, in Denmark of the middle class, in Norway popular (Jonsson 1990, 23).

30   Nickelsen (2011), 15–16. Myhre is a contributor to the latest work on the history of the University of Oslo (Collett et al., eds., 2011).

31   Hroch (2005), 114 says that the patriotic élite in Norway also was made up of rich tradesmen, but according to Myhre they lost their influence after the Napoleonic Wars.

introduced) "the state of educated officials." When the Norwegian "state of educated officials" began to dissolve and decline in the later 1800s, a kind of paradigm shift took place: "a dissolution of both a political system and a social order," according to Seip.[32] At the same time, an outburst of new forms for social gatherings or associations was experienced, which provided opportunities for both companionship and influence. Different determining factors were involved in the establishment of clubs and associations, such as:

> *economic* interests, common *occupations*, an interest in *missionary* work of a religious or other nature, *philanthropic* interests, *general cultural* interests (e.g., in art, historical memorials), *group activities* (e.g., sports, singing), and finally *political* interests.[33]

Groups representing various convictions and attitudes could, through common endeavours, show their colours outwards and intensify solidarity inwards. The establishment of choral societies and the organizing of song festivals were part of the group endeavours of a flourishing of societies that characterized the middle of the 1800s; various social groups experienced community and equality through a common pursuit: singing. The harmony of tones produced a deeper harmony between countries, especially within Scandinavia, and between social classes and regions in Norway itself.

Through the community created by song, it was possible to increase the awareness that Norway's inhabitants, despite differences in class and residence, were Norwegians, children of the same mother. Mutual respect would strengthen the country. "Norway was a *kingdom*, it shall become a *nation*," says the medieval King Haakon in Henrik Ibsen's *The Pretenders*.[34] Ibsen completed this play in the autumn of 1863, inspired partly by the song festival in Bergen the same year, which emphasized the idea of unification and the importance of song for the individual, the society, and the country. Song established a new kind of national unification! While some organizations created new differences partially across the old lines, the choral societies had a unifying effect.[35] Having roots in a common culture stimulates security and openness for the unknown, and contributes to the feeling of community and reconciliation, prerequisites for building and preserving a democracy. Several builders of the nation shared this opinion, for example poets and important cultural personalities such as Henrik Wergeland and Bjørnstjerne Bjørnson.

---

32   Seip (1981), 44–45.
33   Ibid., 54.
34   Ibsen (1963), 283.
35   Seip (1981), 65.

In the nineteenth century, men's choirs seldom gave concerts alone outside the festivals. Sometimes they assisted other musicians, or gave concerts for a charitable purpose. In the second part of the century, several mixed choirs were established, and they collaborated with orchestras in large performances, for instance in some new Norwegian music dramas.

The Scandinavian movement ('Scandinavianism') was an interlude in the middle of the century, but was weakened after the Danish-German war in 1864. Near the end of the century, however, the movement woke up again. Several Scandinavian festivals were arranged with contemporary Nordic music, more often big choral and orchestra works than short *a cappella* songs such as earlier. The music was important, but so were the political implications; by keeping musical company, less discord between Norway and Sweden would be generated during the years around 1905.

When Norway achieved its political emancipation from the union with Sweden in 1905, the Norwegian choir movement had managed to conquer all of Norway, inspired by the appeals which resounded in student circles in the early 1900s: 'Contact with the outside world' and 'Know your country.' Men's choir singers had sung in various parts of the country thanks to tours and singer gatherings. In 1905 it was time to expand the tours to make contact with Norwegians who had emigrated to the United States.

The status of men's choral singing in the nineteenth century is illustrated by the World Exhibition in Paris in 1889. Just as Norway and Norwegian contemporary music were to be presented, a choir made up of men stepped forth. Not only student singers had the honourable task of representing their country; singers were also selected from the choral societies of freemasons, workers, officers, businessmen, and craftsmen in Christiania. One claimed that the choir's composition appeared to be a visualization of the time's desire to amalgamate the various social classes artistically. Not only the performers, but also the compositions (by ten different Norwegian composers) impressed the French press.

As the number of musical institutions increased in Norway, the difference between professional and amateurish activity became more obvious. At the same time, choir singing from a public educational perspective received less attention after a while. Singing's ability to create community and identity was less appreciated. Earlier the *activity* itself was important: *to sing*; by the beginning of the next century, more attention was paid to the *performance*: *how to sing*. Several leaders wanted to create élite choirs with high *musical* ambitions, rather than to "sing the spirit of community, fraternity and patriotism into our warm-hearted, but disunited people," as one famous singer said, expressing the old Romantic, optimistic confidence in the ability of singing to create a nation.[36]

"Much that was Norway, started with a Song"[37]

Nevertheless, Norwegian choir history shows that song—first by men's choirs and later by women's choirs and mixed choirs—became, alongside folk music, the way for common people to experience the sonorous side of art without being able to read music. Choral song is an art form that suits both the musically ambitious and happy music-makers. The same songs that were heard on the capital's concert stages were also heard at song gatherings in the dusty squares of small towns and in rural districts. Several sources indicate that when workers' choirs performed, they did not necessarily sing specifically workers' songs, but rather the old repertoire of songs with national and religious content.[38] By way of household song collections and school songbooks, the song material reached even further afield and became part of the spiritual and national heritage of Norway.

From the national celebration of 1811 via the efforts to create an official celebration of May 17 through the flourishing and spreading of the choir movement to the strong experiences of 1889 (the World Exhibition in Paris) and 1905 (visits to Norwegian America), the development of choral singing emerges as a common cultural expression for Norwegians, and a symbol of solidarity and community.

In the story "Knut Veum" (1910), the writer Jacob Breda Bull (1853–1930) describes the development of choral singing in a Norwegian valley. The main character, Knut Veum, comes to the village as a new schoolteacher. Eagerly, he passes out a songbook by Behrens and gets the village people to part-sing together. When he speaks enthusiastically about singing, it is like hearing an echo of Pythagoras and Pestalozzi. Choral singing's high status may perhaps be ascribed to the century's great faith in the innate forces of a people and to art's ability to build nations and nurture life:

> Song—that was what was deepest inside us all, our dreams and yearnings and what we otherwise couldn't express. And it wasn't in unison; it

---

36   Fredrik August Bekkevold (1830–1911), brother-in-law of Henrik Wergeland, famous speaker and singer.

37   From Nordahl Grieg's (1902–43) poem *Bjørnson* (1932).

38   Hegtun (1984), 100.

was a hundred different things. It was actually as many voices as there were people who sang! But, nevertheless, it was a matter of getting it to resound together. Polyphonic song was actually like a free people. Not the old unison singing with a parish clerk first and all the others carefully following, but a thousand minds and a thousand thoughts and a thousand wills, which found each other in a great harmony, because they all bent themselves in under freedom's eternal law. No power on earth could stop such singing by such a people. It lifted the roof and lifted burdens and created a great, pure joy which was never forgotten and which always could be found in times of need. Singing was like freedom, the people's best friend![39]

---

39   Bull (1910), 33–34.

CHAPTER 4

Choral Societies and Nationalist Mobilization in the Nineteenth Century

A Scottish Perspective

Jane Mallinson

A meaningful examination of Scotland's choral societies in the nineteenth century and their role in society cannot be undertaken in isolation. Some knowledge of Scotland's historical, political and cultural background and institutions is required to put the study into context.

Along with England, Wales, and Northern Ireland, Scotland is one of the four constituent parts of the United Kingdom. Since 1999 Scotland has had its own devolved parliament in Edinburgh. Prior to 1603, Scotland was a nation state, often at odds with England, its larger southern neighbour. When Queen Elizabeth I of England died without an immediate heir, the English crown passed to the Scottish king, James VI, who was her distant cousin. For the next hundred and four years, the two countries were ruled by one monarch based in London, while continuing to have separate parliaments in Edinburgh and London. In 1707 the Act of Union brought both the parliaments together, with the seat of government fixed in London. Thereafter, despite the guarantee of continuing independence of the church, the educational and legal systems, and the mint, Scotland, subsumed into the Union as North Britain, experienced a loss of identity. Many Scots welcomed the Union and the economic advantages they saw it would bring, in the wake of several years of very poor harvest and the failure of the disastrous Darien venture (1698–1700).[1] However, many others vigorously opposed and resented the treaty, as it was alleged that English money had been used to buy votes. Discontent continued to be felt at the apparent loss of nationhood experienced at the time of the treaty, and was articulated for a later generation by the poet Robert Burns in his poem "Such a Parcel of Rogues in the Nation."

---

[1] This was an enterprise to establish a Scottish colony on the isthmus of Panama to trade with both the Atlantic and Pacific simultaneously. Half of Scotland's total available capital was lost, and the ensuing failure had wide-ranging economic and political repercussions. For full details, see Prebble (1968).

© KONINKLIJKE BRILL NV, LEIDEN, 2015 | DOI 10.1163/9789004300859_006

After the Act of Union, Edinburgh "awoke painfully to the fact that it had become, culturally and politically, a satellite of London."[2] London set the tone for all matters cultural, and Scottish culture and language were perceived by many Scots to be inferior. Thus the English language replaced Scots as the language of the law, the educated classes, writing and publishing.

Although Scotland was a small and poor country, the Scottish court had enjoyed a relatively rich cultural life prior to the Union of the Crowns. Several Scottish monarchs married into European royal families. There were trade links with France, the Low Countries, and the Baltic. Thus European ideas of music, literature and architecture were introduced and developed into a peculiarly Scottish renaissance. The Protestant Reformation (begun in 1560) and the ensuing religious turmoil that continued for more than a century effectively ended all cultural activity identified with the Roman Catholic church. Music in particular was badly affected. In the Presbyterian Calvinist church, music was limited to the plainest singing. Instrumental accompaniment was forbidden, and the debate as to whether it was appropriate to have an organ in a church was to continue well into the nineteenth century.[3] The use of elevated liturgical music continued solely in the Scottish Episcopal Church, whose musicians tended to be imported from England, among them Musgrave Heighington (1679–1764), who in his later years was organist at the Episcopal Church in Dundee and founded the Dundee Musical Society. A later example is the London-born Thomas Poulter (1837–1901), who trained as a church musician in Warwick. Around 1855, he moved to Greenock to take up the post of private organist to Sir Michael Shaw Stewart, 7th Baronet, who had built a private Episcopal chapel, St Michael and All Angels, on his Ardgowan Estate.[4] Poulter took an active part in the musical life of Greenock. At various times he was organist at the Mid Parish Church and at St Paul's Church, and he also held the post of town organist.[5] He was director of the Greenock Choral Society from 1864 to 1870[6] and also conducted his own Select Choir. Most significantly he was the first harmony and composition teacher of one of Scotland's best-known composers, Hamish MacCunn (1868–1916).

2 Johnson (2003), 133.

3 For a detailed account, see Farmer (1947), 365–79.

4 Baptie (1894), 150. Baptie incorrectly gives Poulter's year of birth as 1838. He also misspells Wasperton as "Warperton." The "Specification of Work Relative to Plans of Chapel at Ardgowan" (Mitchell Library, Glasgow T-ARD/1/6/623) required the work to be completed by 1855.

5 Idem.

6 Marr (1889), 22.

In the eighteenth century, although some Scots were composing in the classical tradition,[7] many musicians, following the trend set by the Romantic movement, tended to concentrate on the collection, arrangement, and publication of traditional songs[8] and traditional instrumental music.[9] In Scotland there was not the same degree of separation between classical and folk music as there was in most European countries where a classical tradition was firmly established. To quote David Johnson:

> Eighteenth-century Scotland possessed two distinct types of music: 'folk' and 'classical.' These coexisted within the same cultural framework and even, to some extent, interacted, while retaining their individualities and behaving, in a sociological sense, quite differently from each other.[10]

Organized classical music flourished only in the small number of cities and towns able to support professional musicians. As in England, most musical activity and knowledge was confined to the wealthy and professional classes. The capital city, with its Edinburgh Society of Musicians founded in 1728, was the centre of musical excellence, and there was also musical activity in Dundee and Aberdeen.[11] In Glasgow, organized music emerged only towards the end of the century with the establishment of societies such as Gentlemen's Private Concerts (1788) and the Sacred Music Institution (1796–1805).[12] In the early nineteenth century, musical activity in Scotland continued to be at a low ebb. To quote from Henry George Farmer's *History of Music in Scotland*, it was "almost as barren as the Outer Hebrides."[13] In Scotland, as in England, there were some choral societies, but they were few in number and in general remained the prerogative of the wealthier educated classes.

In the 1840s there was a major expansion in the number of choral societies in the United Kingdom with the growth of the sight-singing movement, first in England, then closely followed by Scotland. This movement, which originated

---

7   For example, Thomas Alexander Erskine, sixth Earl of Kelly (1732–81) and James Oswald (1711–69).

8   For example, Allan Ramsay's *The Tea-Table Miscellany* (4 vols., 1723–37), and *The Scots Musical Museum* (6 vols., 1787–1803), a collaboration between the Edinburgh publisher James Johnson and the poet Robert Burns.

9   For example, by William McGibbon (c. 1690–1756) and Charles McLean (1712–ca. 1770).

10   Johnson (2003), 3.

11   Aberdeen Musical Society (1748); Dundee Musical Society (1757); [Glasgow] Amateur Music Society (1831).

12   See Moohan (2005), 231–50.

13   Farmer (1947), 382. The Outer Hebrides are islands off the west coast of Scotland.

in France, had as its main aim the education and improvement of the adult working classes. In Britain this aim coincided with the Victorian desire for the betterment of the lower classes; time spent singing was time spent away from unsuitable activities such as drinking. "Popular song was thus seen to constitute an 'important means of forming an industrious, brave, loyal, and religious people.'"[14] Choral singing was now open to a much wider participation, and to some extent allowed for the breaking down of the rigid class barriers which operated in Victorian society. An 1849 account of a choral class in a market town on the borders of Norfolk and Suffolk gives ample evidence of this.

> Seated in groups, arranged with methodical irregularity, so that none should be 'below the salt,' in their best dresses and in their best behaviour too, everyone feeling as much at home as when at home, and yet brought into free and friendly intercourse with the classes that are separated from them in ordinary life by an impassable barrier of convention; a pleasanter sight than these working people cannot well be imagined.[15]

The advantage of teaching singing in preference to an orchestral instrument or piano is immediately obvious: the voice is the most portable of instruments, costs nothing, and everyone has one. The two rival sight-singing systems which were to have such an impact on singing in the United Kingdom, those of Wilhem[16] and Mainzer,[17] arrived in England at approximately the same time. These methods use staff notation in combination with a system of letters or names using a fixed 'doh'; each note of the scale is given a fixed name, using those of the Guidonian gamut, with the addition of 'si' for B.

Both Mainzer's and Wilhem's methods proved to be extremely popular. Enthusiasm for choral sight-singing swept through the whole of the United Kingdom. Many thousands of people attended classes in towns throughout the country and learned that competence in music was indeed possible. In the words of one student:

> Before attending the [Wilhem] class, I had concluded that music was a study beyond my capacity, but the first night I was there and saw the

---

14   Rainbow (1967), 120.

15   "Music, a Means of Popular Amusement and Education," *Musical Times* 3 (1849), 240, 245.

16   Guillaume–Louis Bocquillon, known as "Wilhem" (1771–1842), French music teacher.

17   Joseph Mainzer (1801–51), German educator who came to England ca. 1840.

adequateness of the method to the initiated, I got quite interested, and became, I rather think, a musical enthusiast.[18]

To assist students with their musical study, Mainzer published a manual entitled *Singing for the Million*,[19] and given the impact of his and other sight-singing methods, the notion of one million is no exaggeration. Although Mainzer's system is no longer used in the United Kingdom, his substantial and lasting legacy is the *Musical Times*, which began life in 1844 as *Mainzer's Musical Times*. A perceived weakness of both the Mainzer and Wilhem methods was that because they relied on the fixed 'doh' system, they were not able to take the majority of students beyond the very rudimentary stages of singing at sight.

A major change in direction was introduced in 1855 by John Curwen (1816–1880), a Nonconformist English minister, when he published his adaptation of the system developed by the Norwich schoolteacher Sarah Jane Glover.[20] This method, Tonic Sol-fa, uses a movable (as opposed to a fixed) doh and dispenses with the stave altogether. Letters are used to represent pitch, and punctuation marks indicate the duration of each note. Since its symbols are familiar, it was possibly less intimidating to people with no musical knowledge and little education.

IF HAPPINESS (A round for four voices)   KEY D   M. 60

:s | d¹ : d¹ | r¹ :r¹ | m¹ :m¹ | d¹ : d¹ | l :l | t: t | d¹ : – |–
If | hap- pi- ness has | not   her   seat, And |cen - tre in the | breast,

:s | f : f | f : f | m : s | d¹ : s | l : f | r: s |d ; –| –
We |may be wise or | rich or great, But| ne - ver can be |blest..
EXAMPLE 4.1   *Example of Tonic Sol-fa notation.*[21]

18   George Lewis, *Observations of the Present State of Congregational Singing in Scotland, with Remarks upon the Means of its Improvement* (Edinburgh, 1851); quoted in Marr (1889), xcvii.
19   Mainzer (1841).
20   See Curwen (1855).
21   Curwen (ca. 1857), 36.

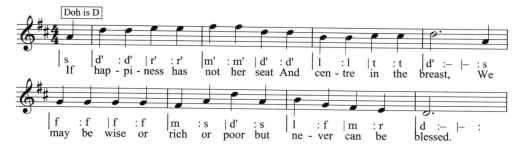

EXAMPLE 4.2   *Example 1 transcribed into staff notation.*

The sight-singing movement reached Scotland in 1842 when Joseph Mainzer moved from London to Edinburgh, where he set up his headquarters and taught for the next six years. In Glasgow and the west of Scotland the rival Wilhem system, favoured by John Hullah,[22] was the preferred teaching method. Both these methods attracted thousands of pupils, before being supplanted by the increasingly popular Curwen or Tonic Sol-fa system. It gained further ground when its founder John Curwen was appointed music lecturer at the Anderson's University[23] in Glasgow in the years 1866–67. Although some choral societies had been in existence prior to the rise of the sight-singing movement, the Curwen system was the catalyst for the creation of many more societies throughout Scotland. The method was attractive for its simplicity. Since music could be set using ordinary letterpress type and required less paper, scores published in Tonic Sol-fa notation were cheaper to produce and therefore more affordable for the target market.

In Scotland, although the term 'choral society' is frequently used, other titles are also found, of which 'Choral Union,' a direct translation of the German *Chorverein*, was apparently the most popular. Other titles used include: Harmonic Choir, Harmonic Society, Harmonic Union, Lyrical Society, Musical Association, Musical Society, and Philharmonic Society. Some of the earliest Scottish choral societies were the Glasgow Choral Union (1843), the Aberdeen Harmonic Choir and the Selkirk Choral Society (both 1847), the Perth Choral Society (1850), the Edinburgh Choral Union (1858), and the Montrose Harmonic Union and the Stirling Choral Society (both 1860).[24]

---

22   John Hullah (1812–84), composer and teacher, was an advocate of the Wilhem system.
23   Now the University of Strathclyde.
24   Marr (1889), xcvii–ciii.

Many societies were formed as the continuation of a singing class; a course of lessons on the Wilhem method led to the formation of the Selkirk Choral Society,[25] and in Pollokshields, a district of Glasgow, the Pollokshields Lyrical Society was formed from the senior pupils of the Popular Music Classes taught by Mr. Daniel McColl.[26] It gave its first concert in 1887 and the following year gave the final concert at the Glasgow International Exhibition.[27]

By the 1880s, the impact of the sight-singing movement was such that nearly every Scottish town, large or small, from Thurso in the north to Stranraer in the south, from Campbeltown in the west to St Andrews in the east, had its own choral society. In these smaller towns, the societies drew their membership from the community at large. The cities of Glasgow and Edinburgh each had their élite choral society—the Glasgow Choral Union and the Edinburgh Choral Union—while less prestigious local societies were to be found in most of the cities' districts. For example, in Glasgow, there were choral societies in the districts of Bridgeton, Crosshill, Dennistoun, Hillhead, Maryhill, Mount Vernon, Partick, Pollokshields, Queen's Park, and Springburn. While many churches of all denominations (Presbyterian, Episcopal, Roman Catholic) had choirs whose sole function was to lead church services, others had choirs which gave open concerts of both sacred and secular music, among them the Greenhead United Presbyterian Church, Queen's Park United Presbyterian (Dissenting) Church, St. Columba['s Church] Musical Association, and the St. Vincent Street United Presbyterian Church. Choral societies drew their membership from educational institutions (Glasgow Academy Choir, Glasgow Normal School, Glasgow University), from societies (Glasgow Foundry Boys' Religious Society, Glasgow Tonic Sol-fa Society, Kyrle Choir), from a military unit (the East Lanarkshire Rifles), or from the temperance movement (Glasgow Temperance Choral Society, Leith Total Abstinence Choral Union—with no post-rehearsal visits to the pub for members of these choirs!).

Despite their distance from the centres of cultural activity, island communities also had their societies—in the north on Orkney (Kirkwall) and Shetland (Lerwick), in the Firth of Clyde on Cumbrae (Cumbrae Musical Society), and in the Western Isles on Lewis (Stornoway). The discovery that there was a choral society in Stornoway performing English repertoire is somewhat surprising, as the Outer Hebrides were areas where Gaelic was the first language of most of

---

25   Ibid., xcvii.
26   Ibid., 26.
27   "Glasgow International Exhibition," *Glasgow Herald* (9 Nov. 1888), 9.

the inhabitants.[28] Gaelic, once widely spoken but now confined mainly to the north and west of the country, has a rich, orally transmitted musical and literary heritage, very different from that of English-speaking Scotland. One might have expected a society in Stornoway to have had a Gaelic repertoire. However, the Stornoway Choral Union, established by 1862, performed in English.[29] The first Gaelic choir on Lewis was not founded till much later.

Perhaps the best indicator of the extent of choral societies' engagement with nationalist mobilization is an examination of their repertoire. Again this cannot be done in isolation, given that in the nineteenth century most Scots did not have one, but three separate, inter-related identities: as citizens of Scotland, the United Kingdom, and the British Empire, a concept which may be illustrated by three concentric circles with ever-increasing radii. Scots, because of the high standards of Scottish education[30] and the lack of opportunities at home, contributed disproportionately to the development of the British Empire.

The repertoire of all the Scottish choral societies so far identified in this research does not vary greatly from that of their English counterparts. This is hardly surprising, given that London was the cultural capital of the United Kingdom and exerted a very strong influence over regional cultural affairs and activities. Another driving force in the selection of repertoire was the music performed at English music festivals. While some of the oldest festivals—for example the Three Choirs Festival (1737), Birmingham (1768), and Norwich (1770)—predate the start of what was disparagingly termed the 'oratorio industry' by Rosa Newmarch,[31] more festivals came into being when it was at its height in the second half of the nineteenth century, for example Leeds (1859), Bristol (1873), and Lincoln (1888). There were no equivalent festivals in Scotland.

In the early nineteenth century, Handel's oratorios, many of which were written for the English market, dominated the choral repertoire, with *Messiah* the work most often performed. However, the first performance of Mendelssohn's *Elijah* at the Birmingham Festival of 1846 and its reception broke the stranglehold of Handel's music in Britain. This, in Nigel Burton's opinion:

---

28   In 1800 nearly 20% of the Scottish population spoke only Gaelic. By 1901, 4.5% were bilingual and a mere 0.5% spoke only Gaelic.

29   A report of a concert by this society appears in the *Scotsman* (9 Nov. 1862), 9.

30   Prior to 1832, Scotland had four universities to England's two.

31   Newmarch (1904), 14.

... did more than anything else to drag British choral music belatedly into
the Romantic era. Mendelssohn was to exert a vital and beneficial influence on the course of Victorian music: his style, whatever its faults, flexed
sufficient musical muscle to effect several immediate and long overdue
improvements.[32]

Music festivals were responsible for commissioning many new works, both
from European and from British (mainly English) composers. The Birmingham
Festival of 1855 commissioned eight new works, of which five were choral: Gounod's *Mors et Vita*, Dvorak's *The Spectre's Bride* (*Svatebni košile*), *The
Sleeping Beauty* by F.H. Cowen, *The Three Holy Children* by Charles Villiers
Stanford, and *Yule-Tide* by Thomas Anderton. Festivals were well reported and
reviewed in the music press, particularly in the *Musical Times*, which had a
wide circulation. The advertisements it carried for scores of the new works
performed at festivals would certainly have influenced societies to explore
new repertoire and to keep up with other forward-looking societies.

In Scotland, as in England, the societies' programmes were dominated,
indeed almost monopolized, by Handel, especially *Messiah*, Haydn, and
Mendelssohn. However it is evident from press reports that there was a willingness and indeed a desire to perform and understand new works. Notices in the
Musical Times about repertoire for the forthcoming season very often talked
in terms of works 'being studied' rather than being rehearsed. This implies a
serious commitment. Contemporary works, in vogue because of their status as
a festival commission, feature frequently; for example, works by Cowen (1852–
1935), Gaul (1837–1913), Macfarren (1813–87), and Sterndale Bennett (1816–75)
feature in programmes, as do those of other, lesser native composers. English
part-songs and glees were performed in miscellaneous concerts. As noted previously, many musicians active in Scotland were English by birth and training; they programmed the repertoire with familiar works in which they had
been trained.

Although much of the repertoire in Scottish choir programmes follows the
English pattern, there is evidence of Scottish music being included in concerts.
This material falls into three categories: harmonized folk songs, compositions
by Scottish composers, and settings of Scottish texts by non-Scots. At the most
basic level, Scottish content was introduced into choral societies' programmes
by the inclusion of Scots songs harmonized in four parts, often by composers who were not Scottish. This repertoire tended to feature in miscellaneous
concerts and in concerts given by smaller choirs. These songs were either

---

32   Burton (1981), 218.

traditional folk songs or songs composed in a folk style. In Stornoway in 1879, the Choral Union, with twenty-one members, included the following Scottish songs in their programme: "John Anderson, my jo," "The Blue Bells of Scotland," and "Our ain bonnie Scotland."[33] The melody of "John Anderson" is traditional, with lyrics composed for it by Robert Burns.[34] "The Blue Bells of Scotland" has lyrics by Anne MacVicar Grant (1755–1838) set by an unknown composer.[35] The final song has not been identified to date. Scots part-songs would later become a feature of the repertoire of the Glasgow Select Choir (founded in 1878), a semi-professional choir which achieved national fame, performing in the Albert Hall in London to very large audiences, and of the later and world-renowned Glasgow Orpheus Choir (1901–51).

Although Scotland in the nineteenth century was not a centre of cultural excellence, it should not be assumed that there was a total absence of native musical talent. The problem for many musicians was that prior to the establishment of the Glasgow Athenaeum School of Music[36] in 1890 there was no provision for advanced music study in Scotland. In an article advocating the provision of a Scottish College of Music, Hamish MacCunn pointed out how the lack of a music training establishment in Scotland disadvantaged Scottish students.[37] Anyone wishing to pursue advanced music studies was forced to choose between London and Europe. He remarked that for the Scot, "London is in effect no nearer to the Waverley Station [Edinburgh's railway station] than Leipsic or Berlin are to the pier of Leith [Edinburgh's port]."[38] In the later part of the nineteenth century, some Scots who took advantage of a 'foreign' education rose to prominence, in particular Alexander Campbell Mackenzie, Hamish MacCunn, and Learmont Drysdale. All three, in keeping with the fashion of the time, composed many choral works.

The first Scottish composer of note in the nineteenth century was Alexander Campbell Mackenzie (1847–1935), whose musical education was obtained in Germany and London. All of his choral works, for example, *The Rose of Sharon* (1884), *The Story of Sayid* (1886), or *The Dream of Jubal* (1889), were performed by Scottish choirs; but only one, *The Cotter's Saturday Night* (1888), a setting

---

33   "Concert at Stornoway," *Inverness Advertiser* (7 Mar. 1879), 3.

34   First published in James Johnson (1790).

35   An arrangement of "The Blue Bells of Scotland" by the German composer August Neithardt was published in the *Musical Times* 7 (1856), 215–17. This was possibly the version sung at the concert.

36   Now the Royal Conservatoire of Scotland.

37   See MacCunn (1913), 153–58.

38   Ibid., 154–55.

of a lengthy poem by Robert Burns, used a Scottish text for libretto. One section of the poem mentions three Scottish psalm tunes—"Dundee," "Elgin,"
and "Martyrs"—which Mackenzie incorporated into his setting, thus adding
another layer of Scottishness.

Hamish MacCunn and Learmont Drysdale (1866–1909) were educated in
London at the Royal College of Music and the Royal Academy of Music, respectively. Both wrote cantatas and dramatic ballads based on Scottish texts, for
which they employed distinctive features borrowed from traditional Scottish
music: imitation of folk instruments (bagpipes, fiddle, harp), gapped scales,
double tonic, and the distinctive rhythm of the Scotch snap. MacCunn's choral works set texts by major Scottish poets—James Hogg, Walter Scott, and
Thomas Campbell—and texts drawn from the ballad tradition of the Scottish
Borders. These texts treat Scottish subjects and to a greater or lesser extent
use Scots vocabulary and expressions. A reviewer of the first performance of
MacCunn's *Lay of the Last Minstrel* wrote:

> Hamish Maccunn [*sic*]—whose new cantata "The Lay of the Last
> Minstrel" we refer to—is the first Scotch composer who has treated the
> legendary history of Scotland in music on a large scale, in the attempt to
> give adequate expression and illustration to wild grandeur, the pictur-
> esque beauty and warm feeling of Scottish character and poetry.[39]

MacCunn, who spent all of his adult life in London, never lost his sense of
identity and was vocal in proclaiming his Scottishness. This somewhat dis-
tanced him from English audiences, but earned him the respect and admiration of all Scottish music lovers. The positive reception accorded to MacCunn's
music in Scotland may have acted as a catalyst to encourage other Scots to
persist in composing. Many minor composers wrote for the choral market, and
some, following MacCunn's example, used Scottish texts. Three such composers were Archibald Davidson Arnott (1870–1910), William Augustus Barratt
(1873–1947?), and David Stephen (1869–1946), who set works by Scott, Ossian,
and Lady Carolina Nairne, respectively.

Large-scale cantatas composed by non-Scots using a Scottish libretto are
rare, possibly because it was feared that the language, Scots English, might
present problems to choirs in the larger English market. In the United Kingdom
it was the practice for all choral works to be performed in English translation.
In Scotland the first performance of Bach's *St. Matthew Passion* in German
did not take place till 1937. Alexander Campbell Mackenzie's remark about a

---

39   "Hamish MacCunn," *Quiz* 16 (1888), 145.

performance of his setting of Burns's "The Cotter's Saturday Night" in London's Albert Hall by an English choir "[who] courageously grappled with a foreign tongue" gives some indication of the difficulties experienced by choirs singing in any language other than Standard English. One Englishman who did attempt and succeed with a setting of Scottish literature was George Macfarren. His *Lady of the Lake*, based on Scott's epic poem, was commissioned for the opening of the Glasgow City Halls in 1877. It was well received, and reviews mention the "'local colouring'... achieved by writing in the style identified with our National melodies."[40] Subsequently it was performed throughout the United Kingdom, proof that its appeal was not limited to Scottish audiences.

Performance of any of the above-mentioned repertoire might have instilled a certain amount of fleeting national pride in the singers and their audience because of its familiarity and resonance. However, it is debatable whether it contributed in any way to an increased feeling of nationalism, either in the choir members, their audiences, or the population at large. In the nineteenth century most Scots were content to assert their Scottishness within the context of the Union (a concept described by Graeme Morton as 'Unionist Nationalism')[41] and of the wider British Empire. At this time, in seeking to assert its identity, Scotland looked back to four Scots—William Wallace, Robert Bruce, Robert Burns, and Sir Walter Scott—who, more than any others, had assumed iconic status. The specific events which brought them to public attention were the death of Scott in 1832, the centenary of Burns's birth in 1859, the construction of the national monument to Wallace completed in 1869, and plans for a Wallace/Bruce monument in Edinburgh. William Wallace and Robert Bruce were warriors who led the Scots in their fight against English domination in the Wars of Independence, culminating in Bruce's victory at the Battle of Bannockburn in 1314. Robert Burns and Sir Walter Scott were writers who in their literary works glorified Scotland's distant past—for example, in Burns's poem "Robert Bruce's March to Bannockburn" (1793) and Scott's epics *The Lay of the Last Minstrel* (1805), *Marmion: A Tale of Flodden Field* (1808), and *The Lady of the Lake* (1810). With the advantage of distance, they reinvented the more recent past by portraying a form of sentimental, romanticized Jacobitism to which many Scots would not have subscribed politically but to which they were emotionally attracted.

For the United Kingdom, with the exception of Ireland, the nineteenth century was a time of relative political stability, with Queen Victoria reigning from 1837–1901. Although there was an increasing awareness of Scottish sentiment

---

40   *Aberdeen Weekly Journal* (16 Nov. 1877), 3.

41   See Morton (1999).

and identity, this was not mirrored by any political movement, principally because Scots for the most part were content with the status quo. The National Association for the Vindication of Scottish Rights, founded in 1853, had as its aim the protection of Scottish interests and the pursuit of equal treatment for Scotland within the Union. Membership was drawn from a wide range of social classes.[42] Similarly, the membership of the Scottish Home Rule Association founded in 1886 came from a wide range of backgrounds and beliefs, including romantic conservatives, unionists, radicals, and Gladstonians.[43] It was founded to campaign not for Scottish independence, but for a Scottish Parliament in Edinburgh operating within the framework of the Union. This is in contrast to the situation in Europe, where there was a rise in national sentiment in many countries in response to political oppression. A growing desire for self-determination in countries such as Poland, Czechoslovakia, and Finland was expressed in literature written in the vernacular and in music which employed folk melodies and idioms.

In conclusion, the evidence shows that in Scotland in the nineteenth century, choral societies were chiefly the result of the sight-singing movement; the number of choral societies in Scotland substantially increased; they had an educational and social intent; and although the core repertoire was European, they gave performances of arrangements of traditional Scots songs, and large-scale works by Scottish composers. If inclusion of Scottish repertoire in programmes had any significance, it was as an expression of cultural nationalism within the context of the United Kingdom. For the members of a choral society in Scotland, in the nineteenth century, there was no underlying agenda. Two factors were important—the singing and the sense of belonging—both of which are aptly conveyed by the term 'choral society.'

---

42   Webb (1978), 55.
43   Harvie (1998), 17.

CHAPTER 5

Fighting Choirs

Choral Singing and the Emergence of a Welsh National Tradition, 1860–1914

Gareth Williams

In broad terms, the key determinants in the growth of amateur choral singing in Wales between 1860 and the First World War are: Protestant Nonconformity (different from the Anglican Church of England), whose places of worship functioned as concert halls; the eisteddfod (local and regional competitive musical and literary events, culminating in an annual week-long national festival); industrialization (notably the dramatic growth of the south Wales coalfield); and an accelerating demography which saw the population of Wales quadruple in the course of the nineteenth century. These were the critical factors that shaped the musical life of Wales down to the 1920s, when the onset of industrial depression derailed all these engines of growth.

Within this framework amateur choral societies were formed in nearly every industrial township. Parallel developments like the temperance choral unions in mid-century and the Tonic Sol-fa movement (doh, ray, mi) from the 1860s instilled discipline and a basic musical literacy among chapel congregations, so that the local choral societies which emerged in the 1860s were based on chapel choirs and adopted a predominantly religious repertoire. These new industrial communities, lacking the benefit of aristocratic patrons, centres of sophisticated taste, cities, princely courts, or (until the late nineteenth century) even universities, literally found their voice and their identity in collective musical articulation in the form of congregational singing festivals, choral concerts and competitions, and, for the talented, individual vocal and (to a lesser extent, for these were materially poor working-class communities) instrumental expression. This was a competitive society that was based on delivering and being rewarded for productivity, and on beating rivals. The performance culture nurtured by the chapel, Sunday School and eisteddfod esteemed and encouraged an uninhibited vocalism. From the 1870s Wales became known as 'the Land of Song,' as choirs from Aberdare in the south to Caernarfon in the north, composed almost entirely of working-class men and women, and conducted for the most part by formally uneducated amateurs from their own number, began to attract the attention of outsiders with their full-blooded, dynamically colourful performances, particularly of oratorio choruses. Choirs became as much the focus of community loyalty as football teams, and down

© KONINKLIJKE BRILL NV, LEIDEN, 2015 | DOI 10.1163/9789004300859_007

to the early twentieth century their rivalries excited passions that often spilled over into disorder.

Although attempts were made to invoke precedent ('the appeal to the past') to explain the Welsh fondness for singing, there were in fact *no* precedents for what happened to Wales in the nineteenth century. Its population doubled in fifty years, and doubled again during the next fifty. The engine of this growth was the sudden and unprecedented industrialization of Wales, as the expansion of the coalfield transformed the valleys of the south into one of the great fuel-producing regions of the world, and ports like Cardiff made the channel that lies between south Wales and the southwestern English counties of Somerset, Devon, and Cornwall (known as the Bristol Channel) as economically significant as the Persian Gulf is today.[1]

Into this region, to dig the coal and make the iron and steel, came office workers, railwaymen, shopkeepers and assistants, clerks, schoolteachers, policemen, doctors, surveyors, solicitors, publicans, drinkers, Christians (and others)—they arrived in their thousands. Most ordinary workers were in search of higher wages than they could command in the agricultural counties of the rest of Wales and the west of England. They were often single men seeking employment and lodgings, and were given a room near the front door, through which after work they went in search of company, recreation, and fellowship. And they found these in the public house, the workingmen's club, the lodge meeting, the sports club, the chapel, the band, and the choir.

The Methodist religious revival of the eighteenth century had in Wales been noted for its lusty harmonized singing. When rural migrants poured into the valleys in the nineteenth century, they brought with them their traditional culture, their Welsh language, their Nonconformist religion, and their fondness for robust congregational hymns. In their unfamiliar new surroundings, they found solace and sociability in song, for in a materially poor society the voice was the most democratic of instruments; it cost nothing. Men and women found comfort from the daily industrial grind in their chapels, which were places of song as well as prayer. This was where choirs took shape, rehearsed and performed, for where else was there? In the early industrial years, before welfare halls and workmen's institutes, let alone concert halls were built, chapel buildings were also the people's theatres, their venue for entertainment.

This had consequences, for even outside the hours of worship one couldn't sing music-hall ballads and popular songs in a sanctuary; the music had to be suitably respectable. But this didn't mean it couldn't be enjoyable, and the

---

1   Davies (2007), 456.

rousing choruses of Handel, Haydn and Mendelssohn, whose dramatic narratives of the Israelites fleeing captivity from Egypt and their wars with the Philistines were expressed with thrilling climaxes that fired the passions of their audiences. The Welsh responded enthusiastically to these accessible choruses with their familiar diatonic harmonies, comfortable progressions and lively fugues, and they delivered them with strong vocal projection, richness of tone, rhythmic drive, and emphatic articulation. Also, the phonetic consonants and open vowels of the Welsh language, like Italian and German, encourage an emphatic pronunciation of English as well as Welsh, and clearly articulated expression.

The south Wales coalfield is the longest continuous coalfield in Britain, and its choral tradition is just as unbroken. It began in 1855 when the first tram load of the best steam coal in the world trundled out of the Bute Colliery in Treherbert at the top of the Rhondda valley. This heralded the birth of a new society, as south Wales in the late nineteenth century pulled in migrants on a scale second only to the U.S.A. Culture, it has been said, is the steam that comes off the back of a galloping horse, and our galloping horse is the breakneck growth of the Welsh population, which in the course of the nineteenth century reached over two million by 1900. The combined population of the towns of Cardiff, Swansea, Merthyr, and Newport totalled barely 18,000 in 1800 but 530,000 by 1920.

Most dramatic of all was the rapid growth of the Rhondda valley, originally tree-lined and secluded, and populated by fewer than a thousand people according to the census of 1851, the valley floor so thickly wooded it was said that a squirrel could travel its ten-mile length without ever touching the ground. By 1920 there were few trees and fewer squirrels but many people: the population of the Rhondda was then over 165,000 and still growing. A horse galloping so fast was bound to draw attention to itself: to change the metaphor from the equine to the industrial, we recall the Welsh socialist Aneurin Bevan's observation that culture comes off the end of a pick, the miner's tool for hacking at the coal. There were many picks in south Wales by 1920, wielded by a quarter of a million coal miners; there were fifty-six working collieries in the Rhondda valley alone.[2]

We could equally well chart the seismic effects of this demographic earthquake by measuring the rise of religious Nonconformity in Wales, and its dominant cultural influence. Throughout the nineteenth century a Welsh Nonconformist chapel was opening somewhere every eight days, virtually one

---

2   E.D. Lewis, in Hopkins, ed. (1975), 22 –30, 110–15.

a week: there were five thousand in Wales by 1900, 188 of them in the Rhondda.[3] Everything about them was imposing, from their command of the skyline to their influential and often controlling social roles, and from their lusty congregational singing to their massive Sunday Schools, which were attended by adults as well as children. A century ago, according to the *Report of the Royal Commission on Religious Bodies in Wales* (1910), 730 attended Sunday School in Bethania chapel Dowlais near Merthyr Tydfil, and 835 at Mount Pleasant Swansea; the overall figure for Sunday School attendance in the Rhondda was 48,000, a third of the total population. It can be argued that Nonconformity hijacked Welsh culture, with baleful effects on an appreciation of the fine arts and the theatre; but who needed drama when you had some of the greatest actors of the age giving impassioned histrionic performances every Sunday in the pulpit?

It was singing, however, at which the Welsh had always excelled. In the twelfth century, as was gleefully pointed out in the nineteenth, the astute Gerald of Wales had observed that

> When they come together to make music, the Welsh sing their traditional songs not in unison, as is done elsewhere, but in parts. . . . When a choir gathers to sing, which happens often in this country, you hear as many different parts and voices as there are performers, all joining together in the end to produce a single harmony and melding in the soft sweetness of B-flat (*sub B mollis dulcedine blanda*).[4]

This description sounds for all the world as if anticipating the solid four-part harmony found in later congregational hymn books and which marked the sturdy church singing of the Victorian era. The more fastidious, who took Gerald's claim with a pinch of salt but were still keen to track the spoor of the historic Welsh proclivity for song, found exciting aromas in the eighteenth century. Hadn't the great Handel, while staying in Hafod, Thomas Johnes' mansion in Cwmystwyth (i.e., the vale of the river Ystwyth) in rural mid-Wales been inspired by the joyful cries of the local Methodists at their open air revivalist meetings to compose the "Hallelujah Chorus," the cornerstone of his great work the *Messiah*? Unfortunately, Handel wrote his great work in 1741; Thomas Johnes wasn't born until 1748, and didn't acquire Hafod until 1783. So if Handel ever did stay in Wales en route to the famous first performance in Dublin,

---

3   Anthony Jones (1996), 46.
4   *Gerald of Wales*, 242.

there is no record of it, and even if he did, it certainly wasn't anywhere near Aberystwyth.[5]

In actual fact, when the English music critic John Graham spoke in the 1920s of 'the sudden rise of Welsh choralism' he was exactly right.[6] A formative influence in Wales—possibly a feature of capitalist society's desire for results, productivity, and beating rivals in the manufacture of both—was the competitive urge; and this was embodied in the growth of the National Eisteddfod, an ancient institution modernized in the nineteenth century. The 'sudden rise' can be quantified: when the National Eisteddfod was held in Carmarthen in 1867 only seven competing choirs appeared; but when the event next was held there in 1911, there were sixty-nine. Giving this fondness for singing an individual inflection, at the Aberdare Eisteddfod in 1861 four sopranos and four tenors competed, whereas at the same event in Swansea thirty years later the participants numbered thirty-three sopranos, twenty-four contraltos, fifty-three tenors, seventy-two baritones, and seventy-one basses.

Historians were once fond of distinguishing between 'rough' and 'respectable' cultures, and the popular enthusiasm in Wales for rough sport on the one hand and the more respectable pursuit of musical excellence on the other would seem to offer support for this distinction. The Welsh evidence also indicates its limitations, however, for the argument of this paper is that these two cultures were essentially one: each demonstrated the same need in what were essentially new industrial communities seeking what Dominique Vidaud in his chapter in this volume usefully calls a 'vector of identity.'

Of course we might wish to stress the desirability, indeed the necessity on the part of employers and industrialists, to provide some of the facilities for the creation of a literally harmonious society. What is not in doubt is that the people expressed their identity by responding with equal enthusiasm to victorious heroes—whether winning sportsmen or choristers—who would be welcomed home by a battery of civic dignitaries at the railway station, a brass band, fireworks illuminating the midnight sky and detonators exploding on the track, and the conductor and the football captain alike borne aloft through the milling crowds. Talented sportsmen and singers, winning teams and successful choirs were locally celebrated as representatives—identity vectors—who embodied the values of their communities even before they moved on to receive national recognition.

Clearly there were legitimate grounds for mutual suspicion between the rough and the respectable. Welsh choralism owed its origins to the temperance

---

5   See M.I. Williams (1959).

6   Graham (1923), 4.

choral unions of the mid-nineteenth century, which were often large in number. The public house had been an important enabler in the transition from the bibulous popular entertainment of rural Wales to the new industrial settlements of the coalfield, but the location and nature of this culture was anathema to abstinent temperance reformers. Regional temperance choirs of the 1840s and 1850s, like the Temperance Choral Union of North Glamorgan and Monmouthshire and, further west, the Swansea Valley Temperance Choral Union, enjoyed competition, but their size as well as their resolute sobriety ruled out the public house as a suitable venue for their meetings.

Where then could they be accommodated? While the Merthyr and Aberdare Temperance Halls date from the 1850s, they were the exception rather than the rule. Until more spacious workmen's institutes and welfare halls were built in the early twentieth century, there was only one possible auditorium: the chapel. There was no shortage of these places of Nonconformist worship, but the music sung in them had to respect its surroundings; one couldn't sing street ballads, pub songs, ditties and doggerel in a sanctuary. Happily, the beefy cheerfulness of the oratorio choruses of Handel, Haydn and Mendelssohn with their familiar narratives were now accessible, especially after the advent of the Tonic Sol-fa notation and the removal of the paper tax in 1862 made music publishing cheaper, and they fitted nicely with the tradition of vigorous congregational singing that had been a feature of eighteenth-century Methodism. Choirs emerged from chapel congregations, and their own native composers wrote for them too in the familiar Handelian idiom with their anthems often constructed in a tripartite structure with a rollicking fugue in the final section.[7]

The industrial areas were the choral crucibles of 'the Land of Song'. These were not necessarily all in south Wales: in north Wales there was and still is a robust choral tradition in the former quarrying and coal-mining areas of Gwynedd and Clwyd. But undoubtedly the great nursery of choristers was the thickly-populated south Wales coalfield. This is where the famed South Wales Choral Union came from: 450 voices drawn from the heads of the valleys from Brynmawr, Ebbw Vale, and Tredegar in the east, through Rhymney, Dowlais, Merthyr, and Aberdare, and across to the Swansea Valley and Llanelli. This choral juggernaut was driven by a formally uneducated but harmonious blacksmith called Griffith Rhys Jones (1834–97), better known by his *nom-de-plume* 'Caradog,' whose statue stands in the centre of Aberdare.[8] It was Caradog who described Wales as 'the Land of Song' in 1877, four years after his second triumph at the Crystal Palace with the South Wales Choral Union: unopposed in

7   Gareth Williams (2003), 17–18, 25–6, 32–3.

8   Ibid., 35–46; Cf. Herbert in Bashford and Langley (2000), 255–74.

1872, but deemed worthy of the thousand-pound prize and challenge cup, they returned the following year to defend it against Joseph Proudman's middle-class London Tonic Sol-fa choir. Even *The Times*, so often supercilious when it deigned to mention Welsh matters at all, was moved to observe that

> When it is remembered that this chorus is almost entirely drawn from the labouring classes of the Principality, miners, colliers etc., their wives, daughters and relatives, we cannot but wonder at the excellence they have attained, an excellence unattainable except through assiduous and continued study.[9]

The point was not lost on a prickly press in Wales itself:

> The vast majority of the English have been accustomed to speak disparagingly, and generally have a low opinion, of the Welsh. When it comes to achievement, knowledge and imagination Wales is assumed to be as lifeless as a graveyard.... [The South Wales choir] demonstrated there is life here, and ability and achievement, and the Welsh in Wales are no longer to be despised ... we are in a new era and the impact of this Welsh choral victory will contribute significantly to raising the standing of the Welsh both here and abroad.[10]

This choral culture became self-sustaining, producing after Caradog other charismatic conductors like Tom Stephens, who led the Rhondda Gleemen to victory in the World's Fair Eisteddfod in Chicago in 1893; William Thomas, who, like Stephens, had sung under Caradog's baton at the Crystal Palace, and whose Treorchy (Rhondda) male choristers were the first Welsh choir to be invited to sing before Queen Victoria at Windsor Castle in 1895; Harry Evans of Dowlais, who was described by no less a figure than Edward Elgar as "a great conductor";[11] and Glyndwr Richards, whose Mountain Ash male voice choir was invited to sing to President and Mrs. Theodore Roosevelt at the White House in 1908. These were all competitive choirs for whom competition and winning prizes were their *raison d'être*. Of no one was this more true than of fiery Dan Davies (1859–1930), 'Terrible Dan,' the conductor of the Dowlais 'Invincibles,' who used to threaten Eisteddfod adjudicators never to set foot in Wales again

---

9   *The Times*, quoted in the *Aberdare Times*, 13 June 1872.
10 *Y Cerddor Cymreig* [*The Welsh Musician*], 1872, p. 59. Unless otherwise noted, all translations are by the author.
11 *Y Cerddor* (1909), 311.

when their decisions went against him. It requires a leap of the imagination to conceive of choral competitions attracting bigger crowds than major sporting events, but this was the case: when, for instance, in the Triple Crown year 1893 the Welsh international rugby xv beat England at the Cardiff Arms Park, they were cheered on by 15,000 spectators; but at the National Eisteddfod held later that year in Pontypridd, a partisan audience of 20,000 packed the Pavilion to hear the chief choral competition.

If we were to ask what choristers got out of this, the enjoyment to be derived from collective and individual expression would have to figure high on the list. Nor should we underestimate the spiritual uplift of engaging with the oratorio's religious repertoire; it is likely that through choir membership some singers acquired familiarity not only with scriptural texts but with reading itself, and literacy learned through the letters of the Tonic Sol-fa method of musical notation. The collectivity of choral singing also provided consolation, all too often in demand in south Wales, the most accident-intensive coalfield in the UK, which in the decades 1880–1900 employed 18% of the British mining work force but suffered nearly 50% of its fatalities. What has been dubbed the 'cruel inheritance' of the Rhondda valleys, from the 114 killed by an explosion at the Cymmer colliery in Porth in 1856, to the 119 mostly young men and boys under twenty blown to bits at Wattstown in 1905 (thirty-one miners had been killed in an explosion at nearby Clydach Vale only three months earlier), guaranteed that a chorus from the *Messiah* like "Surely he hath borne our griefs" was sung with particular intensity of feeling in the Welsh coalfield.[12] On a happier note, choirs—like the hymn-singing festival and the so-called monkey parade of young people promenading after the Sunday evening service—provided opportunities for sociability, flirtation, and courtship.

It also worth reflecting that although their historic roots in Nonconformity might give them the appearance of being exclusive institutions, in fact choirs could play an integrative role in their communities. We must remember that these were new settlements with a need for such 'vectors of identity.' Soon choirs sprang up in almost every town and village of over five thousand inhabitants. To adopt Ivanka Vlaeva's phrase about Bulgarian choirs, they were 'polyfunctional'—that is, they appeared on all kinds of public occasions from celebratory and civic events to trade-union marches; and as in Bulgaria and other parts of Europe, they gathered strength from the 1880s parallel with the growth of the nation (though, as Dietmar Klenke notes, this development, happened in Germany much earlier, after 1806).[13]

---

12   See Williams and Jones (1990).

13   See Vlaeva's chapter in this volume, and Klenke (1998).

One of their functions was to overcome religious and social barriers, which were temporarily transcended when not only local Nonconformist ministers but the Roman Catholic Father Bruno and a clutch of Anglican clergymen would attend the Merthyr Philharmonic's final rehearsal, as well as local dignitaries and civic worthies; ordinary mortals from whatever class were charged admission, and 'spies' from rival choirs, as soon as they were identified, summarily ejected.[14]

Choral singing was also one of the few acceptable recreational outlets allowed working-class women in this predominantly masculine world. To those mothers, wives, and daughters alluded to by the *Times* reporter, confined to the house by the unremitting demands of an unpaid seventeen-hour shift of domestic chores, choir practice, concerts, and bank-holiday travel to a competition offered a respite beyond washing-day gossip and attending chapel. At the Newport National Eisteddfod in 1897, we are told, "the Merthyr choir seemed to have come to a wedding feast. All the girls [*sic*] wore white blouses and Jubilee bonnets... [and] to heighten the effect the sopranos had blue sashes around their waists and the contraltos red ones." Another choir's female members "wore white dresses and pink sashes from shoulder to waist, and the altos wore the same with blue sashes and all were under sailor hats." The adjudicator was forgiven for ostentatiously turning his back on them as they formed up, for "no one could pay attention to the music with eyes on that dream of dressed bliss on the platform."[15] The sexist male gaze offends our modern sensibilities, but we dismiss at our peril the self-esteem provided by such sartorial displays. 'Ladies' choirs' in their own right were a regular feature at competitive meetings from the turn of the century; eighteen of them from the strike-bound coalfield competed at the National Eisteddfod in 1926. Similarly, for the vocally gifted individual a solo role was a further opportunity for self-respect and wider esteem.

However, women's active participation in this ostensibly civilising and popular cultural practice had its rumbustious aspect too. At an eisteddfod in Treharris, near Merthyr, in 1891, the barracking by choristers in the audience of the choir performing on stage was led by Dowlais, with the female members especially prominent "in a way which even abashed their male companions." One reporter compared them to "quite an army of Amazons" whose "bad language led them to be expelled from the eisteddfod, and even at the train station they continued to behave in an unseemly manner."[16] Here is a salutary

---

14   Croll (2000), 115.
15   *Western Mail*, 5 Aug. 1897.
16   *Merthyr Express*, 16 May 1891.

reminder that the line between rough and respectable leisure activities was porous indeed. At the 1885 Aberdare National Eisteddfod, where Dowlais mounted a strong challenge to the favourites, Llanelli ('six to one on Llanelli' were the odds being shouted around the field), the vast and impatient crowd amused themselves by hurling clods of earth at each other. The police were called when Merthyr and Dowlais' sulphurous rivalry spilled over into a riot at the annual Porth (Rhondda) eisteddfod in 1896, and it did not help that when the result was announced, the placings of the first two choirs were inadvertently transposed. Since the choirs concerned were Merthyr and Dowlais, bedlam ensued.[17]

The Welsh-language music monthly *Y Cerddor* (*The Musician*, 1889–1913, modelled on the London *Musical Times*), published articles on music history, biographies of composers and musicians, lessons in harmony, reviews of competition and concert reviews, but also condemnations of what it called 'mob law' (*mobyddiaeth*) of the kind that required the police to be called to restore order even in a chapel schoolroom, as choristers and their supporters would square up to each other and to the adjudicators on and off the stage. At an eisteddfod in Llandybie on the edge of the western, anthracite coalfield in 1897, two nationally known musicians who had unwisely withheld the prize in the male voice choir competition were chased and hooted all the way to the train station by disappointed choristers and their frustrated supporters.[18] The adjudicators had been similarly 'menaced, hustled and pushed' at Abergavenny the previous year, while at an August bank holiday eisteddfod in Swansea in 1904 chagrined choristers invaded the platform and barred the eminent Signor Randegger, who was adjudicating, from leaving it. So serious was the demonstration that the police had to be called to protect him from physical assault, "and the veteran musician's trouble did not end there... he was mobbed in the street and must have deemed himself fortunate at getting out of the town whole in body."[19] Little wonder that the English adjudicator, librettist, and *Daily Telegraph* critic Joseph Bennett, a frequent visitor to the Principality, thought that "there were in Wales fighting choirs, and fighting choirs were an abomination." The *Cerddor* agreed that "too many choirs scented battle from afar," and were over-eager participants in what it termed "musical prizefights."[20]

---

17   *Merthyr Express*, 5 Sept. 1885, 30 May 1896.

18   *Y Cerddor* (1897), 103.

19   *Y Cerddor* (1896), 54; Nat. Lib. Wales, "Music in Wales 1899–1912." D. Emlyn Evans papers, vol. 2 (10 Sept. 1904).

20   *Y Cerddor* (1893), 33; (1897), 103.

Although such behaviour has been censoriously viewed as "irrational antics,"[21] it was legitimized in the eyes of its perpetrators by a belief in a musical moral economy which needed defending against, for instance, choirs perceived to be deriving unfair advantage from tactics such as not meeting or exceeding the prescribed number of singers (to maintain discipline or to produce greater volume, respectively); hiring singers from another organization to bolster the ailing section of a competing choir (such mercenaries would be paid); the decidedly mature look of some female members of ostensibly juvenile choirs; or lengthy delays due to poor organization that led to audiences becoming restive. All these were seen as legitimate objects of audience heckling and protest. As Sophie-Anne Leterrier puts it, "singing was not only a technique but a social behaviour, creating interactions between singers and listeners."[22]

In Wales this 'interaction' expressed itself as restlessness and disruption, and was the inevitable accompaniment to large-scale working-class participation. With the chief choral competition always the main event, "Thousands crowded into the pavilion and excitement ran high," recorded the *Musical Times* reporter at Newport in 1897, "for next after a football match Welshmen enjoy a choral fight";[23] and they attracted intense media coverage. There were sixty-six pressmen at Newport, sixty at Merthyr in 1901, and they were shrewd observers of the contemporary scene. "The eisteddfod will soon vie with football and the prize ring for disorderly scenes and rowdyism," noted the *Manchester Guardian*, for "eisteddfod audiences displayed all the partisanship of the race-meeting class as a whole."[24] So many of the 12,000 in the audience were familiar with the choruses from Mendelssohn's oratorio *St Paul*—the test pieces at Llanelli in 1903—that they sang along with the competing choirs in a kind of collective karaoke.[25]

Was choral singing therefore as morally improving as it was meant to be in so many other parts of Europe? Were Welsh choristers, like the French and Belgian *orphéonistes*, agents of social reform, a civilising influence? We have to wonder whether in Wales there was any meaningful distinction between rough and respectable behaviour, between choristers and football supporters. They appear to be not really so different when a distinguished musician like Sir Alexander Mackenzie, principal of the Royal Academy of Music and chief adjudicator at the Newport National Eisteddfod in 1897, having awarded

21   Croll (1992), 24.
22   See her essay in this volume.
23   *Musical Times*, quoted in *Y Cerddor* (1897), 115.
24   *Manchester Guardian* quoted in the *Musical Herald* (Aug. 1898), 250.
25   *Y Cerddor* (1903), 96.

the palm of victory to the more refined choristers of Builth from rural mid Wales over the strenuous choral phalanx that was the Merthyr Philharmonic, was advised to leave the pavilion by a rear exit since a posse of threatening-looking men was loitering outside the main entrance.[26] A few years earlier, when the writer and educationalist Owen M. Edwards visited the Eisteddfod at Swansea in 1891, he was amazed by the smoking, swearing, spitting, cudgelling and fighting on the back-benches of the pavilion—though he adds that once the competition began, the audience settled down and listened intently.[27] This contradictory behaviour manifested itself in the 'wild shout' that went up from sections of what was clearly a boisterous but knowledgeable audience when one of the competing choir's sopranos came in early, and fatefully, on the last page of the main test piece at Aberdare in 1885.[28]

While some critics found this behaviour repellent, others were fascinated and curiously attracted to it. The composer Samuel Coleridge Taylor was among the latter. When he informed Dr. Turpin, principal of the London Trinity College of Music, that he had been invited to judge at the National Eisteddfod, Turpin told him, "You have no idea what adjudicating in that place is like. Why, I had my hat knocked in and only got safely away with great difficulty." Coleridge Taylor ignored the advice, as may be gauged from his assurances to an American agent organising a tour on his behalf:

> Please don't make any arrangements to wrap me in cotton wool . . . I do a great deal of adjudicating in Wales, among a very rough class of people where most adjudicators have eggs and boots thrown at them. I mention this so that you may know my life is not spent entirely in drawing rooms and concert halls but among some of the roughest people who tell you what they think very plainly. Yet I have four more engagements there for next January.[29]

Coleridge Taylor was the composer of the popular cantata *Hiawatha's Wedding Feast*, whose attractive and accessible choral writing and lyrical tenor aria "Onaway, awake, beloved" guaranteed its warm reception by amateur singers in Wales, a popularity which also reflected the contemporary fixation with the American West. The West had recently been 'won' and the frontier closed, the native peoples herded onto reservations and their leaders dead, killed, or

26   Bennett (1908), 400.
27   Edwards (1907), 89–91.
28   *Merthyr Express*, 29 Aug. 1885.
29   Sayers (1915), 119, 154–55. See also Jones (1999).

imprisoned: Custer had been revenged, and the last great battle of the Indian Wars had been fought at Wounded Knee in 1891, so the West was now safe to sing about. Interest was further stimulated by Buffalo Bill's Wild West Show, which visited several venues in Wales between 1890 and 1910, and by the flickering, grainy images of the early cinema's cowboys and Indians. This fixation with the West was musically reflected at exactly this time (1899–1900) by Coleridge Taylor's *Hiawatha*, Puccini's *Girl of the Golden West* (*La Fanciulla del West*), and a rollicking chorus by the Welshman T. Maldwyn Price called "Crossing the Plain," little if ever heard outside Wales, but much enjoyed within it, where it remained for the better part of a century a favourite among men's choirs.

These male choristers were the pride of Wales, and of the southern industrial belt in particular, as the first year's issue of the *Cerddor* (1889) makes plain with its references to men's choirs in the coalfield from Gilfach Goch, Kenfig Hill, Tongwynlais, Brynaman, Dowlais, Pontycymmer, Ferndale, Tylorstown, Treorchy, and Treherbert, the last four from the Rhondda alone. For this was a man's world, a male domain where, in the 1880s, among migrants into the Rhondda aged between fifteen and thirty, there were a thousand men for every six hundred women, a gender imbalance which accounts for much of the masculine culture that is still a feature of the Welsh valleys today: their fondness for physical sports like boxing, rugby, and football, the workingmen's club—and the male voice choir.[30] Miners constituted the bulk of the workforce—nearly a third of the entire working population of Wales—and had as neighbours in their terraced houses men they saw underground as well. This was an industry that bred intense pride among its workers in their manual skills, their villages and townships, and their loyalty to the collective institutions that represented them on a wider stage and received their unwavering support: the Miners' Federation, lodge and institute, the rugby team, the band, and the choir— especially the choir, an assertion of working-class male bonding, of harmonious fellowship expressed through the most inexpensive instrument they possessed: the human voice. Underground the work was unremitting, the dust and heat suffocating, and the daily casualty rate from roof falls and runaway trams exceeded only by the horrific explosions of gas and fire damp that made the south Wales coalfield the most dangerous in Britain. Its people sang with a corresponding passion that could lacerate the emotions, in circumstances that bred faith and fellowship, concerted endeavour, and a profound awareness that truly they lived, in the words of the Psalmist, in "the valley of the shadow of death."

---

30   *Census* 1891; Lewis (1959), 239.

It was not unknown for choristers physically to attack rivals, and given a repertoire that headlined battle, collective struggle, and sacrifice, is not difficult to appreciate how the inhabitants of what were raw, unrefined industrial communities became aroused by these pieces of vocal artillery, so that all became infected by the general atmosphere of excitement, menace, and belligerence that emotionally committed performances were able to whip up. And in these communities the constant awareness and fear of death, by industrial accident in particular, might go some way toward explaining the appeal of the entreating or dramatic chorus and the intensity with which it was rendered. There was no shortage of poverty, hardship, and crime in what was for many a grim environment; it was this very grimness that engendered such a vigorous and expressive community existence.

All this was reflected in the repertoire of the Welsh male voice choir (and still is, for it has changed little even by today). Because they articulated many of the principles that featured in their working lives, they relished choruses proclaiming conflict, sacrifice, struggle, and hardship. Hence the appeal of operatic choruses that combined militarism with patriotism, and at the same time brought ordinary people into contact with high art, as happened elsewhere in Europe. Equally compelling and popular were the compositions written for the French *orphéonistes* by for example Adolphe Adam ("Les Enfants de Paris," sung in English as "Comrades in Arms"), Laurent de Rillé, (especially his "Les Martyrs" or "Martyrs of the Arena," hugely popular in Wales), Dard Janin, Boulanger, de Saintis, and Ambroise Thomas, whose yodeling number "The Tyrol" has been condemned as "shoddy exoticism"![31]

Unlike the *orphéonistes* who, it appears, confined themselves to secular songs only, Welsh male voice choirs sang religious numbers quite happily. Their concerts would take place in chapels and typically consisted of arrangements of hymn tunes, traditional Welsh melodies, minstrel songs (i.e., plantation songs popularized by black-faced touring groups like the Christy Minstrels), English glees and part-songs, and after 1900 the challenging unaccompanied part songs of Elgar and Granville Bantock, and the derivative pseudo-motets of Peter Cornelius, as well as more militant numbers like "Les Martyrs," the "Soldiers' Chorus" from Gounod's *Faust*, or Verdi's "Slaves' Chorus" (*Nabucco*), "Bandits' Chorus" (*Ernani*) or the "Anvil Chorus of the Gypsies" (*Il Trovatore*). Not to be outdone, there were also pieces by Welsh composers writing in the *orphéoniste* idiom, like Joseph Parry and Daniel Protheroe—both Doctors of Music (of Cambridge and Toronto, respectively) who were born into humble

---

31   See the chapter in this volume by Sophie-Anne Leterrier.

Welsh surroundings, migrated to the U.S.A., and wrote compositions aimed as much at choirs of Welsh migrants in America as for native choirs back home. This confirms the point made in this volume by Anne Jorunn Kydland about Norwegian choirs serving as 'agents of reconciliation.' *Liederkranz* choirs in Pennsylvania and Norwegian groups in Wisconsin (two states where there was also significant Welsh migration) sing pieces written for them by German and Norwegian composers and are visited by choirs from home. The Welsh experience was similar. Welsh male choirs—for obvious reasons it was less easy for house-bound *women*—are to be found touring in the U.S. from the late 1880s. Having visited there in 1906, the Treorchy choir went further and in 1908 embarked on a round-the-world tour of 30,000 miles, giving over 300 concerts, while another Rhondda choir's earlier triumph at Chicago's Columbian Exhibition in 1893 is best understood in terms of the competitive milieu in which Welsh choirs thrived. The invitation to the touring Mountain Ash male voice choir to sing at the White House in 1908 also reminds us how its choirs were putting Wales on the map.

There is, however, no political project at work here as was apparently the case in Germany, Bulgaria, or Serbia, except in the sense that it is by its choirs, and male choirs especially, that the Welsh asserted their identity and a popular nationalism. As Jane Mallinson observes of Scotland in this volume, music was cultural rather than political; and the same was true of Wales, which was not a national state either. If in Wales choirs did not play a part in nationalist mobilization, they were certainly agents of cultural nationhood and vehicles of national pride; and while the economic circumstances that gave birth to them no longer exist, their legacy remains as a continuing badge of Welsh identity.

If by the civilizing process we mean the declining role of violence in leisure and recreation, then this process had some way to go in the Welsh coalfield of the late nineteenth century. The ordinary people who sang with and followed these choirs as choristers and supporters were stubbornly resistant to attempts by their superiors to 'civilize' them. They had their own ideas of what constituted performance style, and of what was expected of them as representatives of the aspirations and values of their communities, on the performance stage as much as on the field of play. Different classes appropriate a cultural practice and do it their own way. In late Victorian Wales this happened on the football field, when the English public-school game of rugby became the consuming passion of a working class who brought to it their own values and sense of the significant; and it happened in the field of collective music-making too: a readiness to reward materially an exceptional talent among their number; a stubborn refusal on the part of predominantly working-class crowds to obey middle-class admonitions to accept unquestioningly the decision of the referee or the adjudicator; and a reluctance to be fair to the opposition (to refrain from booing opposition kicks at a goal or a rival choir's efforts).

In this way Welsh choral performances were the authentic expression of a distinct musical culture honed by economic circumstances, the competitive eisteddfod and the Nonconformist singing festival, which in British terms distinguishes the Welsh choral tradition from the industrial areas of England (the Potteries, Lancashire and Yorkshire) where choral singing and Nonconformity enjoyed comparable popularity but without the boisterous allegiances and disorder that the intensely competitive Welsh environment peculiarly nourished.[32]

As for mixed choirs, while a work like Handel's *Messiah* was the preserve of high culture throughout the second half of the eighteenth century and reached lower down in society only in the course of the next, it was sung by the amateur working-class choirs of industrial Wales until well into the twentieth century, in a manner, as visiting musicians were quick to notice, that was emotionally different from the treatment it was accorded by, say, the Birmingham Festival Chorus or the Bradford Choral Union, let alone the Royal Choral Society. We can analyse this style in terms of a wide range of vocal colouring, solidity of attack, and exaggerated dynamics; but essentially these full-blooded performances were the authentic expression of a distinctive culture. Undeniably this culture and this wilful defiance of 'civilizing' middle-class norms of acceptable behaviour owed something to the unsophisticated manners of a rough, industrial society; but until the emergence of professionally-trained musicians at the turn of the century, these were the stylistic characteristics of enthusiastic but musically unrefined singers and their amateur conductors. Tatjana Marković's remarks in this volume about Serbia are equally applicable to Wales: choral singing was "the most accessible form of cultural and musical life for numerous amateurs ... and membership did not require a professional musical education." Like Anne Jorunn Kydland's Norwegians, Welsh choristers sang for entertainment and self-fulfillment, not for the furtherance of any political agenda. Unlike many of the countries discussed in this volume, however, they were rarely conducted by trained musicians. Indeed, we wonder how these amateur conductors, situated at some distance from major musical centres in a pre-gramophone era, perceived style and sound, and what models they imitated. We salute their achievements, for while we must always be critical in our engagement with the past, we need to be humble too.

---

32   See Nettel (1944) and Russell (1992, 1997).

CHAPTER 6

The Large-Scale Oratorio Chorus in Nineteenth-Century England

Choral Power and the Role of Handel's Messiah

Fiona M. Palmer

We, as an imperial race, should appreciate the master's imperial effects. Handel is the Napoleon of his order, without a Moscow. The French Caesar used to win victories by launching masses at his enemy's centre. Handel too fights in masses and overwhelms by straightforward blows. You cannot give him too large a force. Expand the Sydenham transept till twice four thousand executants find room on its orchestra, and his power is doubled without encumbrance. Such a musician deserves to be the musician of an empire. Rome would have decreed him divine honours, and sent her legions to battle with his music at their head.[1]

The lives of many Englishmen and women, regardless of class, were touched by large-scale choral singing in the nineteenth century. As both audience members and practitioners (amateur and professional), vast numbers of people experienced the striking effect of grand oratorio performances via regular concert life and festival culture nationwide. This article examines the contexts and origins of this choral culture and considers its role in shaping a sense of national belonging and identity. Handel's *Messiah* plays an important role in this process because of its canonical status, its longevity and widespread familiarity. As Charles Dibdin observed while touring northern England in 1788, "Children lisp 'For unto us a child is born' and cloth makers, as they sweat under their loads in the cloth-hall, roar out 'For his yoke is easy and his burden is light,'" which confirms both the place of Handel and the role of choral activity in the lives of working people.[2]

A comprehensive and detailed study of the multiple kinds of choral activity in nineteenth-century England remains to be undertaken. Available scholarship currently includes focal studies of important institutions (such as the Bach Choir and the Huddersfield Choral Society), of sacred choral activity

---

1 Joseph Bennett, *The Musical Times* (1877), cited in Smither (1985), 346.
2 Charles Dibdin, *The Musical Tour of Mr. Dibdin* (Sheffield, 1788); cited in Ehrlich (1985), 22.

(the work of Nicholas Temperley is crucial here), and of educational movements including the transformational Tonic Sol-Fa method. In the meantime, the main survey available is found in Dave Russell's thought-provoking chapter in his monograph, *Popular Music in England 1840–1914*.[3] Russell exposes the absence of systematic comparative studies of the social origins of choir members among these many thousands of organizations. In short, no large-scale study currently exists which attempts to explore fully the data relating to the choral activities of various kinds across the nation in this period. Such extensive work would require a dedicated grant-funded project.

From the separate studies that have been undertaken, and from evidence available in the newspaper columns of the period, it is possible to trace the standing and role of grandiose performances of oratorio in England during the nineteenth century. The trajectory of large-scale choral activity from the watershed performances of Handel's *Messiah* in 1784 makes it clear that the appetite for momentous performances of oratorio with highly-populated choruses continued throughout the Victorian era. The reasons for this undiminished appetite, and the nature of the structures supporting its continuity, reveal a great deal about the socio-economic tapestry of the period.

The status of the Handelian tradition, the overwhelming importance of grandiosity, and the impact of the visual and aural power of the masses is encapsulated within the epigraph to this article. The quote is apposite because it captures the force of the Handel oratorio tradition in England, invested as it was with intensity, enterprise, widening education, communal effort, and the dissemination of culture. The choruses of Handel's *Messiah* were popularly considered to be 'sublime.'

The author of the epigraph adopted for this article, Joseph Bennett (1831–1911), occupied an influential role from the 1870s until his retirement. He depicted and commented upon England's musical life via the pages of *The Daily Telegraph* and *The Musical Times*, among other widely-read publications. His rousing comment quoted here dates from thirty years after the death of Mendelssohn. Portraying Handel as omnipotent Emperor, Bennett leaves us in no doubt that the composer's music enjoyed primary popularity. This emblematic metaphor, bolstered by the military terms employed, resonates ideally with the empowering sense of a masterful, far-reaching and still expanding British Empire. After all, Queen Victoria had become Empress of India as recently as May 1876.

In his 1985 article, Howard Smither examined the fortunes of Handel's *Messiah* in Victorian England and traced its provincial and metropolitan progress employing the contemporary periodical literature as his source. His

---

3   Russell (1997), ch. 10: "Choral Societies," 248–71.

findings revealed that Handel was regarded as "the imperial composer *par excellence*" and that *Messiah* was the most-performed oratorio of the era.[4] The conclusions that Smither drew relate to the role of this work in uniting the lives of otherwise disconnected people. He summarized the power of this oratorio as a popular, familiar, acceptable manifestation of positive endeavour and shared knowledge, as follows:

> From a social aspect, *Messiah* participated in the progress of choral music away from being the exclusive preserve of the élite to the humble classes, a progress which resulted from Victorian efforts toward mass education and the amelioration of the conditions of workers. Sacred choral music, epitomized by *Messiah*, played an immensely important role in these efforts. The vast numbers that made up both the audience and the performers at the Crystal Palace were drawn from a variety of social strata. Those performances symbolized metropolitan, national and imperial progress and achievement. And underlying all this progress, from early to late Victorian times, was the strong religious and moral significance of oratorio, as embodied by *Messiah*.[5]

The accession of the young Queen Victoria to the throne in 1837 brought with it a new impetus for social change and improvement. The need to create a national education that included music was topical.[6] By the time of the six-month Great Exhibition in 1851—an international showcase of Victorian industry and culture in the largest industrial city in the world—the census shows that half the country's population was settled in urban areas.[7] Nineteenth-century England was at the heart of a vast and far-reaching conglomeration: the British Empire.

English society was adapting to urbanization and industrialization. In his discussion of models of civic nationalism across Europe in the early nineteenth century, Jim Samson argues that to the view of industrialization and its community-creating agency should be added the understanding that it enhanced a greater sense of cosmopolitanism.[8] The impact of industrialization and of laws that reduced the working week and increased the size of wage packets allowed the working classes increased access to free time and leisure pursuits. These changes engendered an ever-increasing emphasis on education and culture.

---

4   Smither (1985), 346.
5   Ibid., 347.
6   Mackerness (1966), 153.
7   Evans (1999), 306.
8   Samson (2002), 569.

The emerging middle class, with its encouraged desire for self-improvement via rational recreation (and its philanthropic attitude to education) found an aspect of its leisure time satisfactorily served through diverse musical activities. As the century progressed, music was performed domestically, in church, in schools, at the seaside, in parks and in the streets.

We need only look at the statistics relating to domestic piano activity in order to appreciate the daily role of music in the lives of many. By the 1850s it was *de rigueur* for middle-class homes to contain a piano. Cyril Ehrlich's groundbreaking study *The Piano: A History* shows that by 1850 approximately half of the world's pianos were manufactured in England; he estimates that 50,000 pianos were made worldwide per annum.[9] Entirely possible without investment in equipment, singing featured within mechanics institutions, which established their own choruses, and also in junior, infant, day, and Sunday schools. In the mechanics institutes the working classes were provided with a curriculum encompassing intellectual, moral, and religious aspects.

Musical institutions including choral societies, orchestras, brass bands and travelling opera companies—all aided by the railway network—were commonplace. In his comprehensive essay on choral music in the nineteenth century, John Butt situates the role of oratorio and choral society performances in England within the wider European festival context and traces the secularization of choral activity and its establishment as a leisure pursuit via amateur choral institutions.[10] Dave Russell has outlined the presence of a choral society in all English towns with a population of 20,000 or more by mid-century. Russell defines three common ensemble units: the medium-sized mixed-voice choir; the large mixed oratorio choir (often ca. 300 voices or more); and the male-voice choir (relatively unknown in England until the 1880s).[11]

The infrastructures that produced such large numbers of musically educated and flexible people able to contribute usefully to a chorus were gradually embedded in the routines and expectations of work, faith, education, and purposeful leisure and self-improvement. Various influences were at play in helping to improve musical literacy. The rise of Methodism and evangelical faiths led to an increased involvement in hymn singing within these denominations. The publication of hymn-books and associated music theory and Sol-Fa materials was incorporated into the extensive activities of Sunday schools and mechanics institutes.[12] Educationalists and social reformers led

---

9   Ehrlich (1990), 9, 10.
10   In Samson, ed. (2002), 213–36.
11   Russell (1997), 248.
12   Smith and Young, "Chorus (i)"; accessed 5 Jan. 2011.

what was described as a 'mania' for choral sight-singing. This widening of access to printed music originated in London in 1841 with the pioneering work of Joseph Mainzer (1801–51; *Singing for the Million*) and John Hullah (1812–84; *Wilhem's Method of Teaching Singing*).[13] Hullah was inspired by Mainzer's work, having observed him in Paris. Through his collaboration with James Kay, the Secretary to the Committee of Council on Education, Hullah was commissioned to translate *Wilhem's Method* and was appointed as music instructor at a college in Battersea (later named St John's) in 1840. St John's was the training ground for four hundred schoolmasters and mistresses per week.[14] A sense of the vitality and reach of Hullah's work in these early years can be detected in the following review, taken from *The Era*, and dating from 1860:

> Mr. Hullah gave a sublime performance of this grand oratorio [*Messiah*] on Tuesday evening at St. Martin's Hall, which was very fully attended. There was, as usual, a fine and complete orchestra and the numerous choral phalanx from the members of the first upper singing school.... There is nothing to say about this *Chef d'Oeuvre*, which has been so frequently executed of late years, but as it contains some of the grandest choruses of Handel, it offered many opportunities for displaying the strength and efficiency of the members of Mr. Hullah's upper singing school, whose training does great credit to the talent and perseverance of their director. Most of the choruses were admirably rendered, but the greatest effects were produced in "And the glory of the Lord," "For unto us a Child is born," "Glory to God," "Lift up your heads," "The Hallelujah," and the final "Amen." All through the *piano* passages were sung with the utmost truth of intonation, and the balance of power was admirably preserved in the different parts.[15]

However, the limitations of the Hullah-Wilhem system—*solfège*—which employed a fixed 'doh' were criticized; as D. Leinster-MacKay puts it, "Kay had backed the wrong horse";[16] and gradually John Curwen's method (with its

---

13   Hullah was appointed as Government Inspector for musical subjects in 1872.

14   See Rainbow, "Hullah, John," in *Grove Music Online. Oxford Music Online*, accessed 28 Jan. 2012.

15   "Handel's 'Messiah' as performed under the direction of Mr. John Hullah," *The Era*, no. 1124 (Sunday 8 April 1860), p. 12, col. 1.

16   Leinster–MacKay (1981), 165.

movable 'doh') supplanted Hullah's system.[17] The congregational minister John
Curwen (1816–1880) promoted his more flexible Tonic Sol-Fa Method (*Singing
for Schools and Congregations*, 1842) which drew on the work of Sarah Glover.
In 1867 he founded his Tonic Sol-Fa College, and networks of singing teachers continued to spread around Britain.[18] Mackerness asserts that the outcome
of the singing-class movement was felt by the second half of the century via
its generation of "a great enthusiasm for singing among the lower and middle
classes."[19] It was considered that singing instilled moral virtue and was thus a
force for good. According to statistics in a report relating to Curwen's Sol-Fa
College dating from 1897, the reach of the system by then extended to millions
of people across the colonies.[20] The data provided shows that nearly four million children in the English and Scottish education system were taught according to the Curwen method, and that more than 25,000 examination certificates
were issued, mainly to the adult evening class students. These extraordinarily
high numbers underline the continued strength of choral singing as recreational activity at the end of the nineteenth century. They also make explicit
the role of the Sol-Fa movement as an agent. The movement allowed access
to underprivileged and privileged alike. The value and effect of music within
the education system was continually promoted and developed in this period.
In 1882 Hullah was succeeded by John Stainer (1840–1901) as Music Inspector.
Thus, Tonic Sol-Fa played a vital role in demystifying music among the masses.

Dave Russell shows that there was considerable diversity in relation to the
make-up of choirs which could be exclusive or inclusive. There were socially
élite groups (e.g. the Bradford *Liedertafel*) together with those drawn from a
cross-section of class in the Yorkshire textile community in the 1890s.[21] Russell
believes that there was no defined 'choral movement' in England. He paints
a picture of the choirs derived from northern industrial clubs, and those
from local festivals which became more continuous in their activity (e.g. the
Birmingham Festival Choral Society and the Bradford Festival Choral Society).
Choral competitions began to feature only late in the century—this was very
different from the infrastructure of competition that underpinned the brass
band movement. Later in the century, choirs came from every conceivable

---

17   For fuller background on these developments see, for example, Cox and Stevens (2010).
      The work of the Norwich-based Sarah Glover as a springboard for Curwen is touched
      upon here and the broader context of music education and its systems is explored.
18   Smither (1985), 343.
19   Mackerness (1966), 164.
20   "The Tonic Sol-Fa College," *The Daily News*, no. 15956 (18 May 1897), p. 8, col. 5.
21   Data is provided for Huddersfield and Leeds.

organizational background, due in no small measure to the exponential increase in the numbers of voluntary organizations. As Russell states, such organizations as "Temperance societies, chapels, Pleasant Sunday Afternoon organizations, banks, mills, political parties, and numerous other bodies spawned choirs."[22]

In London the division was clearly drawn between professional choristers—used exclusively at such occasions as the 1834 Westminster Abbey Commemoration—and the amateur choristers who founded the Sacred Harmonic Society (1832) and based themselves in Exeter Hall until 1880.[23] In his history of the London Bach Choir (established 1875), Basil Keen notes that the initial rules of the Sacred Harmonic Society dictated that members should be admitted only if they were of 'high moral character' and that the repertoire should be restricted exclusively to sacred music.[24]

From the 1730s onwards, the inclusion of large choirs in state and civic occasions became established as a regular feature in English culture. Towards the end of the eighteenth century these choruses increased in size still more. Indeed, large numbers of voices came to be regarded as a prerequisite for a satisfactory and worthwhile oratorio performance. Central to these events in England was a work by a German-born composer. Handel's oratorios and in particular his *Messiah* formed the bedrock of the repertoire.[25] The British composer Dr. Samuel Arnold issued a collected edition of folio scores of Handel's music between 1787 and 1797.[26] From its beginning *Messiah* was strongly associated with charitable events. Donald Burrows has traced its journey through the English provinces in the eighteenth century.[27] As he notes, *Messiah* was designed to be performable by professional singers after a very limited number of rehearsals, and was therefore generally within the compass of amateur singers within a matter of months. Appropriate rehearsal provision, with its logistical complexities in harnessing the effort and energy of hundreds of singers, was a crucial component in the oratorio-performing process. As we shall see in relation to the Westminster Abbey and Crystal Palace Handel Festivals, when

22   Russell (1997), 249.
23   Smither (1985), 342.
24   Keen (2008), 2–3.
25   Smith and Young (accessed 10 Dec. 2010) provide details of the emergence of *Messiah* performances in venues other than churches; they state that the oratorio was first performed in a cathedral in 1759 at the Three-Choirs Festival. The link between the performances and charitable causes (e.g. hospitals) reinforced the sense of purpose and the association with the collective good.
26   Landon (1992), 232.
27   Burrows (1991), 57.

gathering up individuals from the provinces in combined scratch choirs, the allocation of adequate rehearsal time was a priority and a problem.

Rather than the opera, which featured large in Europe, it was oratorio that dominated musical life in Britain in the nineteenth century. Nigel Burton provides a convincing explanation for this: "oratorio, a form that was sacred but not liturgical, unstaged and yet dramatic, was an ideal compromise for a nation whose Established Church sought to combine and resolve both Catholic and Calvinist traditions in its worship and theology."[28] Nineteenth-century music festivals around the English provinces provided local opportunities for large-scale, visually and aurally striking performances of choral music. These were obvious manifestations of civic activity and business prowess, a by-product of the industrial revolution. Handel's status as an adopted Englishman was unquestioned. Coronations and commemorations featured his music (e.g. Westminster Abbey in 1784, involving 300 singers)[29] and this was also the case in Germany.[30] The Three-Choirs Festival (established in 1754) featured his music performed by the members of the three cathedral choirs (Gloucester, Hereford, and Worcester) and amateur members of music clubs in the towns. In 1834 Sir George Smart, himself a veteran of the festival circuit and propagator of Handel, directed a festival in Westminster Abbey at the command of William IV. Like its predecessors, the event incorporated performers from throughout the country. The large forces—644 performers—comprised singers from cathedral choirs and other professional choristers.[31] However, religious non-conformists were excluded, leading to the formation of the Sacred Harmonic Society, whose membership was drawn from the middle classes.[32]

Starting from the 1820s and 1830s festivals were held in Birmingham, Derby, Hull, Manchester, Norwich, and York which nearly always included performances of *Messiah*. The Lenten Oratorio tradition—in which performances of oratorios, in full and in part, were delivered in combination with secular instrumental and vocal music in concert halls for profit—offered another arena for choral activity. The case of the Liverpool Philharmonic Society (founded 1840) provides a useful example of an organization whose origins lay in oratorio performance via the town's festivals. Musical festivals were held in Liverpool

---

28   Burton (1981), 214.
29   This involved 300 singers (drawn from around England) and 250 instrumentalists. Smith and Young detail the growth in forces associated with commemorations later in the eighteenth century. Such events were held in 1785–87, 1790, and 1791.
30   Ferdinand Hiller's Berlin *Messiah* in 1786. See Butt, in Samson, ed. (2002), 213–36.
31   Smither (1985), 341.
32   Keen (2008), 2–3.

in early October in 1794, 1799, and 1805; the French wars intervened and the Festival was revived again in 1817, 1823, 1827 and held triennially thereafter until 1836.[33] This final Festival included the English premiere of Mendelssohn's *St. Paul* conducted by Sir George Smart. The Society's remit stemmed from the long-standing, large-scale choral festival activities so popular in the town. The new institution, comprising an orchestra and a choir, was built on amateur involvement; professional musicians had no obvious means to develop an economically viable career in the town. Indeed, the process of professionalization was a very slow one for the Society.[34] The Liverpool Festival Choral Society, which included amateur and professional musicians, was already in existence and continued its work. It became known as the Auxiliary Society and exercised powerful brokerage rights in the running of the Liverpool Philharmonic Society for many decades. This power was derived from the central core of repertoire programmed by the Society's orchestra and choir—choral repertoire.

A telling example of the demanding, indeed limiting, attitude of the chorus dates from 1850 when the Society mounted a catastrophic performance of Mendelssohn's *Elijah*. So badly did the performance go astray that it provoked published rebukes from the critics, denial of any responsibility on the part of the organist, letters of complaint from the Auxiliary Society to the Society's Directors, and a strong rebuttal from the conductor of the ill-fated event, J. Zeugheer Herrmann. This very public unravelling of reputations came about because of the historic power of the Society's chorus. In their combined strength and shared negativity towards the conductor, they managed to derail the performance. The subsequent restructuring of power in the Society was to take time, but by 1851 the Auxiliary Society had been disbanded.

Back in the capital city, a significant trial event took place in 1857. On this occasion the Sacred Harmonic Society (whose secretary was Sir George Grove) marshalled 1,200 singers from London and 800 more from towns around the country. A three-day festival was mounted garnering audiences of 48,474 and performing *Messiah, Judas Maccabeus*, and *Israel in Egypt*. From this large audience a profit of £9,000 was realized.[35] Two years later, the Handel centenary of 1859 spawned the Great Handel Festival Chorus with its linked

---

33   Pritchard (1969), p. 1.

34   The Liverpool orchestra remained entirely local and did not perform its first London concert until 1944. In the mid-1940s signings with *His Master's Voice* and *Columbia Recordings* increased its notoriety. All of this came more than a century after the Society was instituted on 10 January 1840.

35   Keen (2008), 3.

amateur divisions around England.[36] This 1859 Crystal Palace performance in Sydenham marshalled a gigantic chorus of 2,765 singers and an orchestra of 460 players under the baton of Sir Michael Costa.[37] The chorus thus outnumbered the orchestra five times over, giving us pause to consider quite what the aural effect was of the gathered ensemble. There were over 81,000 people in the audience across the four days, and they listened to Handel's *Messiah* and *Israel in Egypt*. This event illustrates not only the dominant role of the chorus in oratorio but also the outreach of Handel's music to vast numbers of the listening public. The Crystal Palace Festival was held on a triennial basis until 1926. The bicentennial anniversary of Handel's birth in 1885 was an exception to this triennial pattern, and events under the direction of August Manns began on Monday 20 June with *Messiah*.[38] Wednesday's fare comprised a 'selection' and Friday brought a performance of *Israel in Egypt*. Manns had undertaken extra rehearsals with the chorus, and it was reported in the press that of the 2,782 singers, 2,008 were drawn from London while the remaining 774 emanated "from Yorkshire, from Wales, from Cornwall and Devon, from Norwich, from Ireland and Scotland."[39] The status of Handel remained undiminished, continually drawing on the commitment and enterprise of singers from across the nation.

As we have noted, festivals and choral societies were found in nearly every town in England. The association of many of these oratorio and festival activities with charitable causes added to their moral status. These events brought an upsurge in local trade at performance time and must have boosted a feeling of collective engagement and even a sense of 'national morale,' as E.D. Mackerness puts it.[40] The promotion of oratorios by Handel (always dominant), Beethoven, Haydn, Mendelssohn, Mozart, and composers such as Spohr and Neumann was widespread.

Improvements in the economies of music publishing helped to allow cheap printed copies to be widely disseminated and individually owned. Composers who wished to raise their profiles and to succeed had to write oratorios. Festivals commissioned choral works—one obvious example being

---

36   Smith and Young (accessed 10 Dec. 2010).

37   Smither (1985), 345.

38   August Manns (1825–1907) had become conductor of the Crystal Palace concerts in 1855; his Saturday Concerts (1855–1901) operated with Sir George Grove were a vital source of popular classical music. Costa died in 1884 and Manns was asked to conduct the Handel Bicentenary. Manns was given a knighthood in 1903.

39   "Handel Festival," *The Era*, no. 2440 (27 June 1885), p. 9, cols. 1–3.

40   Mackerness (1966), 209.

the Birmingham Festival's premiere of Mendelssohn's *Elijah* in 1846. After Handel it was Mendelssohn who had the greatest influence on musical society in England during the nineteenth century. His friendship with Victoria and Albert, his popularity as performer, composer, and conductor, and his ties with the house of Novello all contributed to the security of his position in English consciousness.

Founded in 1811, via the entrepreneurial work of the Roman Catholic organist and choirmaster Vincent Novello (1781–1861), the Novello publishing house capitalized throughout the nineteenth century on the appetite for choral music making. It also nurtured the sense of piety associated with the owning, learning and performance of sacred works at home, in church, and in concert venues. Vincent Novello ardently believed in opening up general access to the great works of the masters. By supplying cheap octavo vocal scores in large numbers, Vincent's son, Alfred Novello (who was a sought-after bass soloist on the oratorio circuit), equipped a burgeoning market with material suited to amateurs.[41] From 1846 the Novello firm's bound *Messiah* vocal score (priced six shillings and sixpence) or the unbound six-shilling vocal score became affordable. This was followed by the Novello pocket-sized score in 1856 at the bargain price of one shilling and sixpence. Obtaining the English copyright to Mendelssohn's *St. Paul* in 1836 fuelled Novello's market share and reflected and supported the taste for oratorio fare. The company harnessed the power of the press in promulgating taste by establishing the periodical *The Musical World* as a mouthpiece for the promotion of *St. Paul*. By the time of its premiere in Liverpool the publisher had made *St. Paul* available in full- and piano-score formats. The Novello company also sponsored oratorio concerts, thus creating practical opportunities for the application of its products. The firm of Novello was responsible for providing its customers with accessible copies of seminal works in a format designed to be not only affordable but clear and practical. At the same time it built on the popularity of the familiar and the trust that this created among its customers, and used this as a springboard for investment in new works in the genre.

Doubtless the massive choral phenomenon brought with it a sense of collective unity and mutual agreement. Handel's *Messiah* sung in English represented a link with the past and an endless tradition of performance and familiarity, and therefore provided a solid foundation. Activities originating in the eighteenth century provided a training ground by establishing madrigal and glee clubs which fostered musical knowledge, creativity, and participation

---

41   See Palmer (2006).

among middle-class males.[42] The concert and town hall, designed to accommodate large forces, effectively became a place of religious communion. The work of the Sol-Fa movement, combined with affordable printed music, allowed formerly musically illiterate people access to repertoires, memberships, rehearsals and performances.

Much more remains to be discovered about the separation and interrelation of people of varying classes and backgrounds within these and other abundant choral activities across England. Statistics relating to the supply of women and children within these choruses are currently unavailable. Handel's *Messiah*, a work accepted as the epitome of canonized music in the repertoires of choirs nationwide, provided a vital and accessible continuity, connecting disparate choirs in combined performances and making possible participation from diverse locations and social backgrounds. *Messiah* can thus be seen as a force for positive leisure-time activity with its built-in personal and collective development and enjoyment. As such, and perhaps particularly in its large-scale performances, *Messiah* was a vehicle for national pride and unity.

---

42   The Madrigal Society (1741); Anacreontic Society (1766); Noblemen and Gentlemen's Catch Club (1761); Glee Club (1783). See Smith and Young (accessed 10 Dec. 2010).

CHAPTER 7

National Art and Local Sociability
Dutch Male Choral Societies in the Nineteenth Century

Jozef Vos

Here croons the *Amstel choir*, there three *Euterpes* cheer,
Eutonia, at rest, is tuning throat and ear,
While all *Cecilia*'s powers are at work...[1]

Liedertafels are among the most widely discussed musical phenomena of the nineteenth century. These male choral societies made a significant contribution to the revival of Dutch musical life.[2] In addition, the many groups with names like Apollo, Amphion, or Orpheus performed regularly in a distinctly national setting. In the sixty years from 1853 to 1913, some twenty-five Dutch National Songfests were organized, each lasting for several days. The significance of such large public gatherings has been the subject of a number of studies, among them Mona Ozouf's well-known volume on the festiveness of the French Revolution, and, closer to home, Frans Grijzenhout's dissertation about Patriotic and Batavian festivities. Both scholars were inspired by anthropology, which possesses a vast expertise concerning the social and cultural significance of celebrations. Anthropology teaches us, here in the words of the American social scientist John MacAloon, that "cultural performances... are occasions in which as a culture or society we reflect upon and define ourselves, dramatize our collective myths and history, present ourselves with alternatives, and eventually change in some ways while remaining the same in others."[3] German research on the culture of public celebration also acknowledges the importance of studying the ways in which collective myths and histories are enacted.[4] In France and the Netherlands as well as Germany,

---

* The author wishes to thank Henk te Velde for his comments and suggestions for this essay.

1 Heydenrijck (1861), 3. Unless otherwise noted, all translations are by the author.
2 Reeser (1986), 21. The original name *Liedertafel* came in the course of the century to be increasingly associated with social functions. To place greater emphasis on their artistic pretentions, many *Liedertafels* changed their names to "male choral societies."
3 MacAloon (1984), 1.
4 See for example Düding, ed. (1988) and Schneider (1995).

such festive public gatherings have also been studied in relation to the process of modern state formation.

In this essay I wish to consider the national orientation of Dutch choral societies in greater detail. First I shall offer a general sketch of the rise of male choral societies in the Netherlands, and then trace their specifically national aspects by examining the nature of their disagreements about the kinds of songs to be sung at the annual Dutch National Songfests. I conclude by considering various aspects of male choral societies from the perspective of studies of nineteenth-century sociability.

The Rise of Dutch Choral Societies in the Nineteenth Century: Two Generations

Insofar as literature has concerned itself with the origins of nineteenth-century choral societies in the Netherlands, all the sources agree that the *Liedertafels* were imported from Germany. Invented in Prussia soon after 1800 in the form of distinguished societies of composers, musicians, and poets, the *Liedertafels* soon became popular among the middle classes. In South Germany and in Switzerland, where they became part of the pedagogical program of Nägeli, the *Liedertafels* were more middlebrow in character from the beginning. That the *Liedertafels* and male choral societies were imported from Germany we also know from the articles of Florentius Cornelis Kist (1796–1863) in the musical journal *Caecilia*. According to Kist, at that time one of the foremost authorities on Dutch musical life, the organization of the *Liedertafels* and the holding of songfests could only be seen as "mimicry of what our artistic neighbors the Germans are doing." In the Netherlands people kept up with these developments "either by reading German newspapers or by going to their festivals."[5]

The earliest known Dutch *Liedertafel* was set up in Dordrecht in 1827 by Anthonie Kist Ewz., a brother of F.C. Kist. Known as 'Aurora,' this group remained active until around 1840. Between 1827 and 1915, nearly five hundred male choral societies were established in the Netherlands. Some existed only briefly, but a larger number remained active for decades. Some sixty male choral societies established before 1915 were still active in the 1990s.[6] The phenomenon of the *Liedertafel* arrived first in the major cities, in the west of

---

5   Kist (1852), 211.

6   These remarks are based on evidence gathered from sources such as the membership lists of the Royal Dutch Singers Association, memorial books, programs of song competitions, musical almanacs, and studies of local and regional musical life. See also Vos, *Rapport betreffende*

the country and in North Brabant, and then spread quickly into the smallest villages in the countryside.

The rate at which choral societies were being founded in the nineteeth century makes it possible to distinguish two generations, the first of which lasted from 1825 to 1865 and reached its peak in the years 1846 to 1850. Certainly connections can be made with other expressions of a cautiously burgeoning cultural self-consciousness in this period, for example the launching of *De Gids* in 1827 or the Society for the Furtherance of Music in 1829. The liberalizing climate of 1848 and the sense of new possibilities to assemble and form associations doubtless also played a role. In 1830 F.C. Kist founded the *Liedertafel* 'Caecelia' in The Hague.[7] The governing board of Caecelia bore a striking resemblance to the local branch of the Society for the Furtherance of Music established the year before. At first the Society for the Furtherance of Music was very interested and involved in the formation of *Liedertafels*, although its members saw male choral societies chiefly as an intermediate stage towards a higher musical art. Caught between the unbridgeable barriers of class difference and the cutting edges of musical trends that struck more refined ears as harsh, the Music Society showed little enthusiasm for male choirs after 1850.[8]

'Song and Friendship' was established in Haarlem in 1830 by men who described themselves as "tradesmen and suchlike and those belonging to the respectable middle class."[9] Its director and co-founder was J.E. Schmitz (1800–72), a blacksmith and musical autodidact. He was an organist who also gave music lessons at the training college.[10] It is worth noting that many of the founding members of 'Song and Friendship' also played in the band of the local militia.[11] Around the mid-century many a local orchestra or brass band gave birth to a (male) choral section. What is striking is the interwovenness of these various expressions of sociability. It is clear that the social background of the male choral society movement is to be found in 'the broad social middle.' Whenever tradesmen are mentioned, they are always independent managers or small businessmen.

'Apollo' was launched in Amsterdam in 1843 as the Deutsche Sangverein and known after 1853 as the *Liedertafel* Apollo. Among its founders were

---

de mogelijkheden voor een geschiedenis van de koorzangbeoefening in Nederland and "De historische studie van koorzang en zangverenigingen in Nederland."

7   See Nuyen et al. (1930).

8   Asselbergs (1966), 240–44.

9   *Algemeene Konst- en letterbode* (11 Jan. 1833), pp. 30–31. See also De Klerk (1965), 235.

10   De Klerk (1965), 241.

11   See Van Eden and Montauban (1930), 46, 153.

J.B.M. Löser and J.J. Nissen, respectively the owner of a furniture or cabinet-making shop and a dealer in pianos.[12] Two professional groups turn up in male choral societies often enough to be considered typical: teachers and typographers. One important indicator of the social class of the *Liedertafels* is that in 1858, inside the movement itself, "the sharp drawing of social distinctions" was blamed for the general malaise in male choral song. The snobbish exclusivity of certain groups was a major obstruction to musical progress. "Don't they understand that nature distributed her gifts over all classes of society, and that talent must be sought where it can be found?"[13] Indeed most of the male choral societies of the first generation had become closed clubs that admitted new members only by vote.

The arrival of the second generation of male choirs, which lasted from about 1865 until 1915 and peaked in the years 1895–1900, is characterized by the collapse of the social exclusivity of the extant *Liedertafels* and by the creation of many new male singing groups among the lower social echelons. Countless choral societies were established for working men, many with names like 'Art for the People,' 'Art After Work,' or the 'Workingman's Fine Art Society.' Here connections can be drawn between industrialization, urbanization, and social differentiation. The 'new middle class' and skilled workers felt an increasing need to take an active part in cultural life. As far as male choral societies are concerned, no direct links can be found with pillarization. There were hardly any choirs whose names or goals indicated a religious or social preference, which cannot be said of the new and equally numerous mixed singing groups. An exception needs to be made for the Catholic church choirs, which are left out of consideration here because of their liturgical function. The reorganization of the venerable 'Confréries van Sint Caecelia' led ultimately to the establishment of secular male choirs that stood formally outside the church.[14]

The Social Situation of the Male Choir

To characterize the male choir as the typical expression of a 'bourgeois' musical culture is problematic.[15] A closer look reveals that the social differences within the world of male choral societies were too broad and often also too subtle

---

12   Soute (1943), 31–32.

13   "Wat kan onze jaarlijksche feesten bloei en duurzaamheid geven?" in *Jaarboek van het Nederlandsch Nationaal Zangersverbond voor het Jaar 1858*, 150–57, 154.

14   Jespers (1988), 114–19 and 230–47.

15   See Dahlhaus (1989), 38.

to be encompassed in catch-all concepts such as 'bourgeois' or 'middle-class.'[16] Forming a more precise image of the social milieux from which male choral societies emerged would require synchronic and diachronic research into the professions of their members, their incomes, life expectancies, marital status, education, etc.[17] For the moment we must be content with a general impression. The most important thing is to remember their importance for social continuity since the eighteenth century,[18] and the appearance in the nineteenth century of such comparable forms of sociability as brass orchestras[19] and chambers of rhetoric.[20]

Of course good fellowship was also important. In Haarlem 'Song and Friendship' took as their first motto: "The aim of our united effort / Is to raise up song with friendship." From the secretary's report we know that, while taking a stroll in 1837, the members of Song and Friendship amused themselves by beating a lame chick with a club and trying to shatter a bottle while blindfolded (the prizes: a leather tobacco pouch and a "tinder-pouch with fire-steel").[21] But singing remained the most important thing. Collective singing gave expression and strength to mutual fellowship, but it could also be used to display a group's ideals or identity to the public by means of the songs selected for public performance on certain socially sanctioned occasions. In this sense the male choral societies stood right in the midst of 'public politics' broadly understood.[22] In the second part of this essay I would like to examine this aspect more closely.

Songfest versus Song Competition: Male Choral Singing and Nationalism

The insistent double marker of both 'Dutch' and 'National' appears designed to call attention to the specifically patriotic character of the Dutch National Song Festivals that were held from 1853 to 1913. These songfests, in which the

---

16 For this problem, see among others Pilbeam (1990), who on her first page describes the concept of the 'middle class' as "a morass, a minefield, even a veritable Pandora's box."

17 See the suggestions of De Jonge and Mijnhardt (1983) for establishing a typology of societies. For a brief survey of the prosopographic approach, see De Jong (1996).

18 See Mijnhardt (1987).

19 See Fassaert (1989).

20 See van den Berg and de Bruijn (1992).

21 Van Eden and Montauban (1930), 153.

22 See De Haan and te Velde (1996).

Liedertafels sang together in public, were indeed heralded as gatherings of national brotherhood, and "Those in whom Dutch blood" was often heard. No one was expected to remember that Hendrik Tollens' national anthem of 1815 had been set to music by the German composer Johann Wilhelm Wilms. The German influence on musical life in the Netherlands in the first half of the nineteenth century was pervasive. According to Eduard Reeser, "one ought not underestimate the degree to which German musical taste has infiltrated our popular consciousness by means of the *Liedertafels*."[23]

As a rule, German historians tend to view the male choral movement from a national-political perspective. The first historical retrospective, published in 1855, highlighted the importance of the movement for the cause of German unification. The 1887 edition of this volume, *Der volksthümliche deutsche Männergesang*, by Otto Elben, is still considered a classic.[24] The note of nationalism has continued to dominate historiography ever since Elben even in the absence of any political content. The struggle for national identity is deemed indispensable in historical accounts of German male choirs, often prefaced by introductions that reveal how deeply the primacy of politics remains anchored in German historiography.[25]

Although these somewhat reductionist tendencies in German historiography raise many questions,[26] let us begin with the question of the Netherlands. It was not just the idea of male choral singing that had been imported in from Germany, but also a large repertoire of German songs.

The world of male choral singing in the Netherlands in the nineteenth century was also affected by nationalism, but nationalism cannot be separated from a broader movement in the top intellectual circles that found expression mostly at the level of culture and was interested most of all in the history of the fatherland. This cultural nationalism has been quite thoroughly studied, with particular attention to the importance of painting and sculpture.[27] Far less attention has been paid to music.[28] The question is: to what extent could the fashion of the *Liedertafels*, imported from Germany along with German songs, be assimilated into Dutch cultural nationalism?

---

23   Reeser (1986), 21.
24   See Elben (1991) and Spitta (1991).
25   See Heemann (1992), and also Düding (1984) and Klenke (1989). For Flanders see Willaert and Dewilde (1987); for Sweden see Jonnson (1983).
26   See my review of Heemann's book in *Volkskundig Bulletin* 22 (1996), 106–8.
27   See Bank (1990), of which van Sas (1992) provides a summary.
28   See Bank (1994).

The Lower Rhine Dutch Song Festivals

The Lower Rhine Dutch Song Festivals held from 1845 to 1852 contributed immensely to the popularity of the *Liedertafels* in the Netherlands. The idea of organizing a festival can be traced back to a reunion of the civic guard in Kleef in 1844, when the local *Liedertafel* decided to maintain contact with 'Eutonia' from Amsterdam, who had been invited to give a performance directed by C.A. Bertelsmann, a German by birth. It was agreed that other German and Dutch *Liedertafels* should also be approached with the idea of organizing an annual song festival.[29] A first call met with positive replies from *Liedertafels* in Elberfeld, Emmerich, Krefeld, Rees, and Wesel in Germany, and from Nijmegen in the Netherlands.

Little is known about the specific reasons for wanting to organize such an international event. Elben's goal was to encourage fellowship among Lower Rhine and Dutch singers, and to popularize and improve male choral song.[30] Kist speaks of "love for the general practice [of singing] among all social classes, and for promoting understanding and brotherhood [through song], also between different nations."[31] For Elben the idea of national brotherhood was self-evident: Flanders and the Netherlands are discussed in his book along with the German parts of Austria and Switzerland under a single heading: *German Land Above All!* Elben was by no means the only German to consider the Dutch as lost members of the same tribe.[32] The Dutch response to this point of view was considerably cooler. To be sure, the Amsterdam orientalist and editor of *De Gids*, P.J. Veth, excited by his visit to the Third Lower Rhine Dutch Festival, was in favor of merging with Germany; but in the world of Dutch male choral societies there was little evidence of support for this position.[33] In the turbulent year 1848, Kist took pleasure in observing that "male singing in our country has always kept its distance from political tendencies, so much so that the efforts of a few Germans to introduce politics into previous festivals were soundly rebuffed and left not the slightest mark on our *Liedertafels*."[34]

The Lower Rhine Dutch Song Festivals, held alternately in Kleef or in Arnhem, were impressive events. The local hostelries found it difficult to house the hundreds of participants, many of whom were obliged to stay in private

---

29   Blommen (1960), 92.
30   Elben (1991), 105.
31   *Caecilia*, 4 (1847), 103.
32   See for example Kloos (1992).
33   See Veth (1847), and also Boogman (1955 and 1978).
34   *Caecilia*, 5 (1848), 149.

homes. The numbers of visitors to the various performances and other events soon reached several thousands. The local middle class profited from this by providing activities such as sack races, greased pole climbings, and firework displays, which gave the entire festival a popular character.[35] This commercial exploitation led to one warning that the Song Festival should try to avoid "looking like a milch cow."[36] Complaints were frequently heard that the festival atmosphere was pushing art too much into the margins. On the other hand, the festivals also made important contributions to the development of public musical life. For example, Musis Sacrum in Arnhem, the largest concert hall in the Netherlands at the time, was built for the Song Festival of 1847.[37]

Participation in the Lower Rhine Dutch Song Festivals was also changing in interesting ways. Six German and two Dutch *Liedertafels* took part in the first festival in 1845. The following year the proportion was eight to four, and at the third festival eleven representatives from each country were present. Thereafter the Dutch share grew quickly, and by the sixth festival in 1851 there were only seven German choirs competing with as many as twenty-two from the Netherlands. The events of 1848 probably played a significant role in these developments. After 1848 the *Liedertafels* of the Lower Rhine began to look more towards the east.[38] At first the Dutch participants complained of this waning enthusiasm, but soon they would draw their own conclusions.

The musical dominance of the Germans had been criticized from the very beginning. The importance of impressive German examples to Dutch choral singing was wholeheartedly acknowledged, but eventually the admiration began to seem somewhat exaggerated. As "one Dutch singer" expressed it: "However little we may be inclined to feel for the political spirit of certain Germans at this moment, we must fight to keep it away from the Song Festivals, and we need never concede that our own roosters crow any less royally than theirs on our very own musical soil."[39] There is no doubt that the Lower Rhine Dutch Song Festivals contributed to the 'Germanization' of Dutch male choral song. Dutch compositions are hard to find either in the general repertoire shared by all the *Liedertafels* or in the programs of the individual choirs. At the first festival in 1845 there was only the "Song of the Fatherland" by J.J.H. Verhulst (along with the "Song of the Fatherland" by F. Kücken). At the third festival in 1847, J.B. van Bree's "Evening Song" was sung, followed by "The Song of the

35   Blommen (1960), 112–14.
36   *Caecilia*, 7 (1850), 155.
37   Kessels (1967), 37–38.
38   Blommen (1960), 98.
39   *Caecilia*, 5 (1848), 184.

High and Low Germans on the Rhine" by C.A. Bertelsmann, and the "Hunter's Chorus" from the opera *The Vow* by W. Smits. Of all the songs performed at this festival, not one out of ten was sung in Dutch.[40]

What is most striking is that these few Dutch songs, with one exception, were performed not by the individual Dutch *Liedertafels*, as one might expect, but in the large general concerts. Apparently the organizing committee that composed the general program felt more responsibility for providing a balanced Dutch representation than did the individual *Liedertafels* themselves. The only Dutch song that could always be heard was "Those in whom Dutch blood," sung together with its German counterpart "What is the German's Fatherland?" at the closing of the festivals. After the festival in Arnhem in 1848, Kist complained that "It has come to the point where one could almost imagine himself in Germany here and not in the Netherlands." Despite his admiration for German singing, he noted that "it rubs me the wrong way and offends my feelings as a Dutchman that we should so desecrate our own independence and—let us admit it with shame—underestimate our own products, among which are some very good things, or at least relegate them too much into the background."[41]

The Dutch National Song Festivals

The smaller numbers of Germans attending after 1848, the cancellation of the festival in 1849 because of an epidemic of cholera, chronic disagreements over whether Kleef or Arnhem should host the next festival, and above all the explosive growth in the number of *Liedertafels* in the Netherlands, all led to the conclusion that the time was ripe for an exclusively Dutch national festival. In 1853 twenty-five Dutch *Liedertafels* formed their own Dutch National Alliance of Vocalists and held their first Dutch National Song Festival in Arnhem.

The stated goal of the Alliance of Vocalists was the "improvement of male choral song, and the promotion of brotherhood among Dutch Singers."[42] It was noted in the by-laws that the National Festival should be held every second year, and that the associated *Liedertafels* should gather to perform choral works by Dutch composers.[43] From the beginning there was a marked discrepancy between the official aims and the actual programs. For example, the

---

40   See Blommen (1960), 275–81.

41   *Caecilia*, 5 (1848), 150.

42   *Jaarboek*, 19.

43   See Buter (1977–78), nr. 9, instalment 1.

following pieces were sung by all the choirs together to celebrate the opening
of the festival in 1853:[44]

1   "Resurrection," (in German) motet by B. Klein
2   Scene and chorus from the opera *Euryanthe* (in German) by C.M. von Weber
3   "Spring Song" (in Dutch) by J.J.H. Verhulst
4   "Springtime Devotion" (in Dutch) by C. Kreutzer
5   "The Song of Hunger" (in Dutch) by J.J. Viotta
6   "A Night at Sea" (solo, choir and orchestra) (in German) by W. Tschirch
7   "To the Lark" (in German) by C.A. Bertelsmann
8   "Hunter's Desire" (in German) by C.G. Reissiger
9   "Sailor's Song" (in German) by H. Marschner

"Those in whom Dutch blood" was sung by way of conclusion. There were no
Dutch compositions at all among the songs performed separately by three of
the attending *Liedertafels*.

At the second Song Festival in 1856 the situation was roughly the same.
Some complained that their societies were quite willing to sing in Dutch, but
that there was almost nothing availble to sing. The journal *Caecelia* responded
by publishing a list of songs in Dutch in three consecutive issues.[45] If we compare this list with the programs of the Song Festivals, it would appear that it
was hardly ever consulted. The third Song Festival of the Alliance of Vocalists
in 1857 also launched a competition calling upon Dutch composers, or other
composers residing in the Netherlands, to compose choral music for two poems
by Jan Pieter Heije.[46] The first poem was aptly titled "The Dutch Language":

> Netherlands! though poor at birth
> Your heart was mild and willing;
> And so are bonded, bold and worthy,
> Strength and mercy in your Tongue, etc.

If a patriotic song were to be made from "The Dutch Language," then it would
have to be of the mild sort for which Heije was famous. Heije was easily the
most popular Dutch poet of his day. His "Spring Song," set to music by Verhulst,
was a special favorite that turned up frequently on the programs:

---

44   *Caecilia*, 10 (1853), 159–61.
45   *Caecilia*, 13 (1856), 111–12, 154, 180. Moreover, these Dutch composers made liberal use of
      German texts in their own compositions!
46   Supplement to *Caecilia*, 14 (1857), nr. 6.

The air is blue, the valley green,
Daisies blooming everywhere
And lilies of the valley;
All is scent and bloom and light
And gleaming glows of sunbeams! etc.

Such simple and natural lyrics filled with love for God's creation and the home-land, mixing reverence with *joie de vivre*, were thoroughly characteristic of male choral song. Nonetheless, the number of songs available in Dutch remained small compared with the wide range of choral works by German compos-ers such as Franz Abt, Conradin Kreutzer, Heinrich Marschner, Julius Otto, or Friedrich Silcher, whom their Dutch counterparts strove to emulate. The programs of the Festivals, and especially the performances of the individual *Liedertafels*, reveal an enduring fondness for songs in German. In 1884 the col-lective part of the program, at the behest of the festival committee, consisted for the first time entirely of works in Dutch, while the various *Liedertafels* con-tinued to sing their own songs as usual in German. At the following festival in 1887, one reporter commented: "The names of familiar Dutch composers like Boers, Brandts Buijs, Coenen, Heijblom, de Lange, Meijroos, Nicolaï, or Worp, graced the walls of the festival building, but made no appearance at all in the program as a whole."[47]

The journal *Caecelia* was not alone in calling for the choral groups to pay more attention to singing in Dutch. This note was voiced with increasing emphasis among the very members of the Alliance of Vocalists. M.A. Caspers, chairperson of the Amstels Men's Choir and after 1867 of the Alliance as well, spoke at length in the society's journal of the urgent need for a national music. Caspers set forth his position in a speech addressed to the Dutch Musical Artists' Union.[48] In his opinion art was viewed too much in terms of divine inspiration, as some otherworldly thing which for this reason alone should have nothing at all to do with nationality. Was not art also a reflection of the personality of the artist, and thus also a reflection of his nation? Nationality mattered therefore even in art. Were there not French, Italian, or German schools in music, and had there not been earlier also a Dutch School?[49]

---

47   *Caecilia*, 45 (1887), 210.

48   *Maandblad van het Nederlandsch nationaal zangersverbond*, 4 (1876/77), 81–85.

49   Caspers was alluding here to polyphonists such as Ockegem, Obrecht, and Des Prez, among others, who, if geographical origin were taken *per se* as the most significant char-acteristic, would constitute a French-Dutch school. On the nineteenth-century myth of the Dutch school, see Vos (1993), 83–86.

The incontrovertible proof of the existence of nationality was of course one's mother tongue. That works written by Dutch composers with Dutch texts expressed a certain national character could not be denied; but when the vocal parts were in a foreign tongue, how could there be any question of national character? Half-hearted compromises lacked any character at all. And according to Caspers the composers were not the only ones to blame: "Many a Dutch composer has sought refuge from the lack of recognition so often encountered here at home by setting German words to music, in order to find buyers and performers for his works in Germany." It must be added that many a Dutch composer sold most of his German lyrics in the Netherlands.

Caspers was no doubt voicing the opinion of the nationally minded portion of the art-loving bourgeoisie and of prominent people in the world of music. The question is rather if the average performer was ever aware of such a pressing need to alter his repertoire. *That* people sang in choirs seems to mattered more than *what* they sang. German songs evidently satisfied their needs; and once the singers grew accustomed to them, familiarity bred the opposite of contempt. Ideological considerations do not appear to have played a significant role in determining the choices of songs. It is also difficult to measure the extent to which the admonitions printed in *Caecelia* and the exhortations of the governing boards to sing in Dutch may have influenced the selection of songs. What cannot be denied is that after about 1870 the traditional German *Liedertafel* repertoire was slowly replaced with songs composed by Dutch or Dutch resident composers. Other factors also played a role in these events.

First of all, the choir directors had a major influence on the choice of songs. Many of them were composers in their own right, and had their own choirs to perform their works, among them for instance Gustav Adolph Heinze, the director of Euterpe Amsterdam, or Richard Hol, who served as director of the Amstels Men's Choir, Caecelia Den Haag, and the Utrecht Male Choral Society. The most important of these composer-directors were often also members of the technical committees of the Song Festivals. In addition, a much larger share of the second generation of male choral singers came from levels of the population that were unfamiliar or only barely familiar with the German language. They chose above all to sing well-known Dutch compositions such as Hol's "Good Morning" and "Peace," Heinze's "Upwards" and "Sunday on the Sea," the "Oarsman's Song" by C.C.A. de Vliegh, and of course Verhulst's perennial "Spring Song."

After about 1870 one other change became apparent. The rise of the second generation of male choirs coincided with the replacement of the simple, strophic song, shaped both musically and textually half of sentiment and half of stolidity, by more thoroughly through-composed pieces with lyrical depths.

While the new male choirs readily accommodated the Dutch songs that were popular at the Song Festivals, the older choirs increasingly took their distance from these songs in favor of more lyrical and challenging pieces, among them oratoria and cantatas such as Beethoven's "Christ on the Mount of Olives" or Wagner's "The Feast of Pentecost," and especially works with national themes like Hol's "Heiligerlee Cantata" and "The Relief of Leiden," or Alex. W.A. Heijblom's "Siege of Alkmaar," or W.F.G. Nicolaï's "Hansken van Gelder."

One could say that just when the national objectives—the singing of Dutch songs by by Dutch composers—seemed finally to be achieved, the social differentiation in the choral world demanded a new outlet and found it in a different musical form and content. No doubt social differentiation also contributed to the drive toward sophistication and avantguardism on the part of the older choirs with respect to the newcomers. The very name 'Liedertafel' gradually fell into disrepute; thenceforth the choirs would be known as 'male choral societies.' Although support for the arts is a major topic in the records of the choral societies, purely aesthetic considerations played only a secondary role in actual practice. The most important goal was active participation in the making of music, as had been the case for the original Liedertafels. Since the artistic ambition of the new male choirs were less clearly defined, the (boards and directors of the) older and more established choirs, united in the Dutch Alliance of Vocalists, suddenly emerged as pioneers and pedagogues.

Chairperson Caspers praised the initiative taken by "one of the groups in our Alliance" (namely his own Amstels Men's Choir) to set up "national singing schools" in Amsterdam. According to Caspers the Dutch had forgotten their own original folk songs and could only sing dreadful street tunes. Improvement of the quality of folk songs was only possible if "the higher and more civilized class" were to set a shining example.[50] At the first congress of the Dutch Alliance of Vocalists in 1887, one of the main items on the agenda was a discussion of how to unify and improve cooperation among the many associations that were seeking to improve the quality of Dutch folk songs.[51]

At the same time, the Song Festivals were becoming less and less exclusive. The twentieth Dutch National Song Festival in 1895 featured performances of A. Krug's *Fingal* for male choir with soprano and baritone solos, along with the Prologue, the Metamorphoses and the Grail scene from Wagner's *Parzifal*, with the boys' parts sung by the ladies of the Mixed Choir section of the Deventer Men's Choir. Henri F.R. Brandts Buys directed his own *The Destiny of Man* for male choir with solos for soprano and baritone. There were

---

50   *Maandblad van het Nederlandsch nationaal zangersverbond*, 2 (1874/75), 41–44.

51   *Tijdschrift van het Nederlandsch zangersverbond*, 3 (1887), 51–53, 84–89.

only two individual choir performances: Aurora (from Arnhem) sang *Chants lyriques de Saül* by F.A. Gevaert, and Apollo (Amsterdam) sang "Thou, Eagle" and "The Poet is a Bird," two songs by their own choir director Philip Loots. J.L. Rijken directed a choral performance with solos for soprano and baritone using selections from his opera *Norma*, followed by Schubert's "The Almighty" as adapted by Franz Liszt for male chorus with tenor solo. Finally there were several solo performances by vocalists Jeanette de Jong, Johannes Messchaert, and Johannes Rogmans.[52]

By the end of the century the Song Festivals appeared to have had their day. An absolute low point was reached in 1900, when only three male choirs attended. In 1913 an effort was made to resuscitate them, but to no avail. This is not to say that the male choral movement was in crisis. On the contrary, during this same period, around the turn of the century, countless male choirs were being established. And there was plenty of singing, if not always of what the aristocracy among the singers wanted to hear. The individual choir performances, those parts of the program in which the musical preferences of the societies were expressed most clearly, had discovered the freedom of the song contest.

Singing Competitions

Along with feelings of brotherhood, the spirit of rivalry had always been present in the world of male choral singing. One song contest even managed to put a stop to all further cooperation between the Lower Rhine and the Netherlands. In 1852 a great many Dutch *Liedertafels* avoided Kleef so they could compete in a song contest in Amsterdam organized by Eutonia, one of the promotors of the international song festival.[53] As early as 1850 the Society for the Furtherance of Music had introduced a competition for *Liedertafels* at their Fifth Public Music Festival.[54] In 1851 the Apollo society organized a competition in Utrecht,[55]

---

52   *Caecilia*, 52 (1895), 169–71.

53   *Tekstboekje en feestregeling van den zangwedstrijd van Nederlandsche liedertafels, uitgeschreven door de Amsterdamsche liedertafel Eutonia, op 3–4 september 1852* (Amsterdam, 1852); *Caecilia*, 9 (1852), 173–74.

54   Maatschappij tot bevordering der toonkunst, *5e Algemene muziekfeest en wedstrijd der liedertafelen te Haarlem, Junij 1850* (Amsterdam, 1850); *Caecilia*, 7 (1850), 121–22.

55   Gemeentemuseum Den Haag, Archief Boers: both concerning the competition held by the Apollo society in Utrecht on 23 Sept. 1851 [Bibl. Haags Gem. mus.: 42 G XIII].

followed in June 1853 by another contest sponsored by Caecelia in The Hague.[56] A contest was also held at the first National Song Festival, if only as an exception. The second part of this festival consisted of a small singing match in which three *Liedertafels* contended for a medal. Eutonia (Amsterdam) sang "In the Woods" by their own director Bertelsmann, along with "Nocturnal Wandering" by Franz Abt. The Utrecht society Aurora sang "Glory to God in the Highest," a motet by M. Hauptmann, together with "Kirmes Rutscher" by H. Marschner. The third contestant, Practice and Relaxation from Den Bosch, performed Bertelsmann's "The Sounds of Bells" and Franz Lachner's "A Hymn to Music."[57] All lyrics were in German.

At first the groups found nothing wrong with the idea of competition. In 1851 Kist had advocated competitions as a way of making the song festivals more attractive to participants.[58] In 1863 a 'rehearsal contest' was introduced to encourage singers to take part in the general section of the program.[59] In 1877 it was even suggested that the Song Festivals might attract more interest if the individual choral performances were also presented in the form of a contest: "Although they lack a jury and a medallion to be won, the individual performances are already quite competitive..."[60] In 1880 the composer, choir director, and *Caecelia* editor W.F.G. Nicolaï added his voice to the discussion: "The question is not whether and to what degree Song Contests serve the cause of art; experience has shown that they are an excellent stimulus to study, and have contributed greatly to the technical development of many a dilettante singer. Without a contest no one wants to practice!"[61]

Some saw the appeal of song contests as direct competition for the Song Festivals,[62] while others complimented the objectivity of the jury members: "they alone remained calm and did not allow their concentration to be disturbed or influenced by the lavishly decorated banners, or the muffled cheers of the audience, or the inspired but often rather unattractive gestures of the directors, or the strangely compelling imitations of barking dogs or echoing horns."[63] Chairman Caspers was strongly opposed to the squandering of national music in favor of "the honor of having company": "Contests or other

---

56 *Caecilia*, 10 (1853), 132–33.
57 Ibid., 160–61.
58 *Caecilia*, 8 (1851), 192.
59 *Caecilia*, 20 (1863), 179.
60 *Maandblad van helt Nederlandsch nationaal zangersverbond*, 5 (1877/78), 27–29.
61 *Caecilia*, 37 (1880), 150.
62 *Caecilia*, 34 (1877), 140.
63 *Caecilia*, 45 (1888), 201.

such violent artistic methods have never found support among a majority of the members of the Alliance of Vocalists; and although some *Liedertafels* have organized them or taken part in them, within the Alliance, such as it has existed for twenty-three years, they have always been condemned."[64] Caspers frequently compared the song contests to modern sporting competitions, which were also flourishing at this time. He rejected the notion that 'singing sports' had anything to do with art: "With sailing or rowing competitions the actual mastery of the art of sailing—with which they are presumed to be connected—is as little served as is the science of warfare or the art of war by holding archery or shooting matches."[65] The same was true *mutatis mutandis* for song competitions.

The Alliance of Vocalists was representative of the Dutch male choral movement to an ever diminishing degree. In 1886 one member of the governing board, G.C. Bunk, voiced strong opposition to director-composer Daniël de Lange's remark that holding a song contest was one way to popularize folk songs. Bunk saw this as an attempt to revive the song contests "which have recently fallen into disrepute." On the other hand he considered it a favorable development "that the song contests were slowly coming to seem a thing of the past."[66] The extent to which the wish was father to the thought here can be expressed numerically. From 1876 to 1885 (at least) twenty-one song contests for male choirs were held, twenty-two from 1886 to 1895, thirty-one from 1896 to 1905, and thirty-eight from 1906 to 1915. In the sixty-five years from 1850 to 1915, at least 130 male singing contests were organized in the Netherlands.[67] To this figure can be added some thirty competitions outside the Netherlands in which Dutch *Liedertafels* took part. Belgium possessed an especially venerable tradition of holding such contests.[68]

There was also legitimate concern about the procedures to be followed in the competitions. The rules for judging were a constant source of disagreement, all the more since jury members were often choir directors or composers in their own right. Participating societies also cheated by 'borrowing' singers from fellow choirs or even by hiring professional singers. Questions were also raised from an artistic perspective about the specially composed 'battle pieces,' into which all sorts of musical obstacles and special effects (such as the 'barking dogs') were interwoven. Yet despite all these concerns and disagreements,

---

64   *Maandblad van het Nederlandsch nationaal zangersverbond*, 2 (1874/75), 81–82.
65   *Maandblad van het Nederlandsch nationaal zangersverbond*, 5 (1877/78), 43.
66   *Tijdschrift van het Nederlandsch zangersverbond*, 11 (1886), nr. 3, p. 34.
67   Compiled from information in *Caecelia* and extant programmes.
68   *Nederlandsch muzikaal tijdschrift*, 5 (1843), 56.

the popularity of the song competitions continued to grow. No doubt much of their popularity was due to the sheer pleasure of taking part in a festive event, and by the excitement of the journey to the festival venue. The element of competition added an extra thrill. In my view these factors counted as much if not more than the honor of any particular society.

Male Choral Societies in Local and Regional Communities

Male choral societies represented first and foremost the local communities in which they had developed, as is clear from the way the home front took part in the festivities. Bringing home the first prize meant that you could count on a reception comparable to what would happen if your local football club won the national championship. The memorial books contain many passages celebrating these triumphs. The winning *Liedertafels* were regaled with celebrations. Singers were welcomed home at their local train stations by conveyances bedecked with flags and garlands, and driven through verdurously decorated streets to the accompaniment of fanfares, brass bands, and other singing groups, to the cheers of sometimes thousands of local residents, in a festive procession to the city hall to be received by the city council.[69] My impression is that many singers were moved to participate in the song competitions by a need to affirm the value of choral societies to their own local communities. And unlike the National Song Festivals where they performed 'under no obligation,' the song contests left them with an independent measure of their accomplishments. The male choral society 'Sappho' from Hoorn, for example, played an important role not only in breaking down social class differences, but also in the development of a new and informal kind of local leadership.[70]

From their musical practice it is clear that the *Liedertafels* were very proud of their autonomy. The biggest complaint at the Song Festivals year after year was of the low attendance at rehearsals and at the performances of the general, 'national' parts of the programme. Many of the participants evidently preferred the local taverns. On the second day, when the individual choirs performed, the motivation to sing was apparently much greater. Against the instructions of their own governing board, participants stuck to their tried and true repertoire in which neither national nor artistic ambitions played a significant role. Either despite or because of its efforts to educate the singing public, by the early years of the twentieth century the Dutch Alliance of Vocalists was

---

69   See for example Gerritsen and Willemsen (1992), 16.
70   Leenders (1992), 79, 201–2.

withering away, while at same time the various local choir groups that emerged from the regional song contests were proliferating. This decentralization of the male choral world could be considered a victory for the democratization of active participation in culture.

In fact the organizational structure of the Dutch National Alliance of Vocalists had always been weak. In its first decade the management consisted *de facto* of the local organizers who were responsible for the following Festival. Not until 1865 was a more permanent Board of Directors established by representatives from several of the most prominent societies, which, as the numbers of male choirs increased rapidly, found itself less and less representative of the choral societies as a whole.[71] In essence the male choral movement was always a local and regional phenomenon. The Confederation of Male Choral Societies 'Frisia' was established in 1849, four years ahead of the National Alliance of Vocalists, and by 1855 a Union of Overijsselsche *Liedertafels* had also come into existence. Regional song festivals were held in Alkmaar in 1855 and again in 1862. In the 1880s annual song contests were organized by an Alliance of Vocalists in the Province of Groningen. In 1896 a choral alliance called 'Singing Uplifts Us' was established in Zeeland, followed in 1902 by the Confederation of Men's Choirs 'Gelre' in Gelderland. At the dawn of the twentieth century the numbers of local and regional singing groups, and also mixed choirs, become too large to keep track of.

My conclusion is that national concerns played a far smaller part in the Dutch male choral movement than German historiography would have us believe, not to mention the doubly insistent message inscribed in the very title of the Dutch National Song Festivals. It is quite possible that the song festivals helped to solidify the idea of a nation, but this happened more likely because they were good places to meet than because of their taste for certain songs. The independence shown by most of the groups in their choice of songs suggests that their first loyalties were regional and local, at levels where cultural life was manifested in practice. Further research into the cultural, social, and political significance of male choral societies in the nineteenth century will need to consider the local networks in which they functioned.

This general sketch of the male choral movement makes it possible to identify a few points for future scholars to keep in mind. In the first place, the continuities in the history of sociability are worth remembering. The *Liedertafel*

---

71 "Notulen der vergadering van feest-gedeputeerden van het Nederlandsch Nationaal Zangersverbond op Zondag den 13. Augustus 1865 te Nijmegen," in: Gemeentearchief Utrecht: Archief van de Koninklijke Utrechtse Mannenzang Vereniging, archiefnr. 135, inventarisnr. 128.

was a new embodiment of a classic type, the society of dilettantes,[72] originating alongside other and older traditional forms of socializing such as gentlemen's clubs, civil guards and militias, or (branches of) the Society for Public Welfare or the Society for the Furtherance of Music, and later all kinds of social and religious fraternities and professional associations. In the second place, male choral societies need to be studied in relation to comparable groups such as brass bands, chambers of rhetoric, etc. Comparison is necessary in order to understand why certain persons or groups chose to gather in one form of association rather than another. The results of such research might provide us with a more accurate understanding of the roles played by various forms of sociability within local communities. Finally, it would be good to compare the development of male choral societies, and *mutatis mutandis* also of other cultural societies, in various locations. This would be necessary in any event for the establishment of a representative national picture.

---

72   Mijnhardt (1990) distinguishes the society of dilettantes from the learned society and the benevolent society.

CHAPTER 8

The Choir Scene in Flemish Belgium in the First Half of the Nineteenth Century

The Vlaemsch-Duitsch Zangverbond

Jan Dewilde

Given the paucity of monographs on the Flemish choir scene in the nineteenth century, no general surveys are available as yet. Therefore this contribution will focus on a brief but significant episode in cultural history, namely the activities of the *Vlaemsch-Duitsch Zangverbond* (1845–47). Although it existed only for barely three years, this supranational choral society played an important role in the development of the choir scene in Flanders. Furthermore, the purpose and the operation of the *Vlaemsch-Duitsch Zangverbond* illustrate different forms of nationalist mobilization in Flanders, Belgium and Germany.

The Choir Scene in the First Half of the 19th Century

The choir as an autonomous music organization, independent of musical performances at courts, churches or operas, is a phenomenon that developed in our area in the first half of the nineteenth century. The earliest evidence of such choirs dates back to the period of Dutch government (1815–30). One of the first choirs documented was allegedly founded in 1817 in Kortrijk (Courtrai) by the composer and music teacher Pieter Vanderghinste (1789–1861), inspired by the contagious enthusiasm of a company of itinerant singers from Vienna.[1] This makes it immediately clear that the choir scene from the German-speaking regions, with their *Singakademien, Gesang-Vereine,* and *Liedertafeln,* was a source of inspiration for the budding Flemish choir scene. However, at the crossroads of Germanic and Romance cultures there was also a considerable influence from the French 'Orphéon' movement showing a manifest pedagogical and social dimension. Both the German and the French choir models would be emulated in Flanders.

Among the early choirs were *De Zangminnaren van Sinte-Cecilia* (Zele, 1823) and *Réunion lyrique* (Brussels, 1825), but most choirs were founded in the latter half of the 1830s. This was largely due to the emancipation of the bourgeois

---

1 Thys (1855), 5; see also Dewilde (2012).

and to changes in the management of time. Work was no longer the exclusive focus of attention, so there was more leisure for passive and active cultural activities, *in casu* choral singing. Autonomous choirs were founded, and extant associations organized choral societies as well: concert and music organizations disposing of their own orchestras started choirs of their own in order to perform the great vocal works. Cultural associations and professional societies also founded their own choral societies. For example, *De Keyser's kunst- en zanggenootschap* (Gent, 1846), a fellowship of literary men and printers, had a choral society of its own. Choirs were *peer groups*, even if the president and the patrons were always prominent citizens. Some choral societies appealed explicitly to workers. In 1849 Charles de Brouckère (1796–1860), the liberal mayor of Brussels, founded an *École de Musique vocale pour les Ouvriers* to sustain the choir *Les Artisans réunis*. This choir gave concerts in order to finance a health insurance and retirement fund. Other workers' choirs bore names such as *L'Écho des Ouvriers* (Brussels, 1850) or *De eenvoudige landlieden* (Hever, 1853). In addition, there were also student choirs, such as the *Société des Choeurs de l'Académie royale d'Anvers* (Antwerp, 1846)—novelist Hendrik Conscience was a member of the board—or the *Société des Choeurs des Étudiants* (Ghent, 1854). Choirs were established even in the army, although they were initially not accessible for the lower ranks. Children's choirs existed only in the framework of schools, although we can assume that children sang together with adults in the Flemish choirs.[2]

Initially, as in the church, choral singing was preponderantly an all-male department, but not exclusively so. Still more research on membership lists and programmes is in order, but the entry of women and the transition to mixed choirs apparently happened gradually, depending on the needs of the repertoire to be performed. Societies ambitious enough to tackle oratorios could not do without women's voices. On 2 December 1837 the *Société d'Harmonie d'Anvers* organized a performance of Joseph Haydn's *Les Quatre Saisons* with "200 male and female voices, and an equal number of instrumentalists."[3] And the *Société d'Orphée* (Antwerp, 1837) first adopted women into their choir for a performance of Gioacchino Rossini's *Stabat Mater* in 1843. It was these women who later, under the guidance of the governor's daughter Constance Teichmann (1824–96), set up the women's choir *Les Dames de la Charité*. Their cooperation

---

2   In a report on choral singing in the provinces written in 1841 at the government's behest, Louis Joseph Daussoigne-Méhul (1790–1875) observed with amazement that many Flemish choirs allowed children to participate.

3   Thys (1855), 111. On the occasion of such a grand musical event, the press referred explicitly to "the example of the large cities of Germany and England" (*Journal d'Anvers*, 4–5 December 1837). Unless otherwise noted, all translations are by the author.

enabled the *Société d'Orphée* to combine forty-three female voices, fifty male voices, and an orchestra with sixty members.[4] Already in its founding year 1841, the choir *Jong en leerzuchtig* from Vilvoorde raised its visibility on the occasion of a choir competition in Aalst with "young girls in their ranks ... [who] sang the upper parts)."[5]

The rapid growth of choirs drew the attention of the public authorities, and in 1841 the Minister of the Interior decided to start keeping numerical data. On this basis we know that Belgium then counted sixty choirs, forty-three of them in Flemish Belgium. The strength of the choirs varied from eight singers (the *Société Haydn* in Ghent) to forty-four (*Les Chanteurs-Campagnards* in Torhout). At the next count, ten years later, 258 choirs were already registered. For the Flemish provinces this breaks down to three in Limburg, sixteen in Antwerp, seventeen in West-Flanders, forty-two in Brabant, and sixty-four in East Flanders. The district of Ghent surpasses them all with thirty-one choirs comprising 1,022 singers.[6]

In addition to the urge to measure and to know, as well as the need for surveillance of the new movement (who sings what?), the special interest of the young Belgian state can also be explained in terms of the awareness that choral singing could produce a positive effect, both morally and pedagogically.[7] Many people shared the conviction that singing (together) improved morals: "Criminals don't have songs," as Johann Gottfried Seume (1763–1810) put it.[8] As the philosopher David Hume (1711–76) argued, aesthetics and ethics were inextricably interconnected, and refinement and taste can be acquired. This idea is also present in *La Musique mise à la portée de tout le monde* (1830), the

---

4   Thys (1855), 11.

5   Ibid., 21.

6   Reliable figures are not available for all periods, but later figures mention 529 choirs just before the turn of the century, and 493 choirs in 1926. According to estimates by the choral association *Koor & Stem*, about 1,250 choirs are active in Flanders today. The discrepancy between these numbers and those of 1926 has to be nuanced to a certain extent; at that time there were more large oratorio choirs, whereas today chamber choirs are prevalent. Even so, the figures prove the great success of the choir as a cultural organization throughout the years.

7   The early interest of the authorities in figures about the budding choir life was not a matter of chance. Ever since the French Revolution, statistics were compiled by civil servants. In 1841 these official statistics were institutionalized in the *Commission centrale de la Statistique*, chaired by the mathematician and statistician Adolphe Quetelet (1796–1874).

8   Seume (1810), 271. The first stanza goes: "Wo man singet, laß dich ruhig nieder, / Ohne Furcht, was man im Lande glaubt, / Wo man singet, wird kein Mensch beraubt; / Bösewichter haben keine Lieder." There were many similar texts in those days.

popular handbook by François-Joseph Fétis (1784–1871), who, as director of the *Conservatoire royal de Bruxelles* and music director of the king, had been commissioned by the authorities to develop a comprehensive plan for the organization of Belgian music life. Education—music education in this case—was very highly regarded. Furthermore, choirs could fulfill an important social and philanthropic role; music societies traditionally organized concerts for fundraising purposes, for the benefit of the poor, the sick, and victims of calamities.[9] And last but not least, the young Belgian state wanted to create a cultural identity of its own in a patriotic move that was both anti-French and anti-Dutch: music was an eminently suitable medium to make Belgium more Belgian.[10] For all these reasons, choirs were supported by the authorities with incentives and free train tickets for trips to competitions and festivals.

Competitions were already popular by the 1840s; almost every city or town organized its own competition or festival.[11] Each festive occasion was used as

---

9   For example: the Brussels choir *Réunion lyrique* (1825–47) managed to raise 4,000 Belgian francs with one single concert in order to provide a bed for an old musician in a Brussels home for the elderly. At a concert in March 1842, in the presence of the king and the queen, 2,000 Belgian francs were collected for the poor, and the following year the victims of a fire in Hamburg received 3,000 Belgian francs from a performance. The last concert of the choir, in March 1847, yielded 4,000 Belgian francs for the Brussels hospices. "Their numerous concerts of choral music were always given for the sake of philanthropy. The costs of these musical feasts were borne by the members and their president, Mr. Lintermans, who always declined a fee, and the proceeds were always given to the suffering classes" (Thys, 19).

10   In his *First Letter on the Present State of Music in Belgium, and on its Future in this Country* (*8 June 1833*), Fétis wrote that he wanted to re-invigorate the rich musical history of his country. He concluded: "Belgium has reconquered a nationality: its government protects both the development of civilization and the restoration of the arts, which have long languished under foreign domination. From now on, it offers the country the educational means that were lacking before; later it will create institutions to sustain artists who will prove their mettle; all conditions are therefore met for Belgium to resume the eminent position in the arts that it held long ago. This is how I understand the situation, and this explains why I have decided to devote the rest of my life to my country" (*Revue musicale*, 15 June 1833).

11   One of the first choir competitions allegedly happened as early as 1834 in Berlare (East-Flanders). According to composer and musicologist Léon de Burbure de Wesembeek (1812–89), himself active in the choir scene in the Dendermonde area, the quality of choral singing was greatly improved by these competitions: "Soon there arose among the competitors a praiseworthy rivalry that made them eager to hear good singers perform and that made them choose works that were harmonically more challenging"; quoted in Thys (1855), 83.

a pretext to organize a choral event, whether competitive (a contest) or not
(a festival). Due to the early development of the Belgian railway system, it was
possible to invite societies from all over the country. This created a community feeling, a considerable audience was reached, and in this way one also
'discovered' one's own country. The authorities themselves organized choral
competitions and festivals with a view to mobilizing the people for national
ceremonies. During the annual September festivities with which the Belgian
nation celebrated its independence and commemorated the victims of the revolution of 1830, choirs received top billing, next to wind ensembles.[12] In 1841,
for example, the *Société Grétry* organized a choir competition supported by the
authorities with 1,000 Belgian francs, and attended by the king and the queen.
It was one of the first great choir contests in Brussels and was therefore considered a landmark occasion.[13] An additional reason was the participation of two
choirs from Aachen, *Concordia* and *Liedertafel*: it was hoped that the high standard of the German choirs would improve the quality of the Belgian choirs.
The *Liedertafel* won the competition by a unanimous decision of the jury.

During the September festivities of 1841, a tremendous effort was made
to bridge the gap between the glorious musical past and the 'renaissance' of
Belgian musical culture. Statues of Orlandus Lassus (1532–94) and André-
Modeste Grétry (1741–1813) were placed on the square in front of the Royal
Palace. Interventions like these clearly demonstrated that making music was
an essential part of being a Belgian, both in the past and in the present. In this
way a national identity was created and cultivated.[14]

The national and international trials of strength during these contests, as
well as the meetings at festivals, no doubt stimulated the quality and expansion of the repertoire. Choirs accustomed to singing harmonized romances
were forced to study choir music for the competitions, and Flemish choirs
were advised to improve their pronunciation of French. Evidently there was
a considerable difference in quality between the choirs from the cities, which
were in a position to hire professional conductors-composers who had spent

---

12   During the official September festivities both early and new music was very prominent.
      Besides large-scale events for brass bands, wind ensembles, and choirs, established com-
      posers as well as promising talents were annually commissioned to write a *Requiem*
      and a *Te Deum*; and from 1843 on, the prize-winning cantatas of the *Prix de Rome* were
      performed.

13   One newspaper reported: "We have seen there the beginning of a new musical era for our
      country, and consequently also a feat of moral progress"; cited in Grégoir (1879), 25.

14   Janssens (2001), 15–16.

their formative years in France or Germany, and choirs from small towns, which were often conducted by well-meaning amateurs.[15]

At any rate, the quality and the size of some choirs in the first decades of the nineteenth century were evidently sufficient to perform the great vocal works of the international repertoire, such as Haydn's oratorios.[16] For example, at the inauguration of the statue of Rubens on the Green Square in Antwerp in 1840 the programme featured, in addition to occasional pieces, Beethoven's *Christus am Ölberge* and fragments from the *Messiah* and *Die Jahreszeiten* (all in French translation).[17] The popular choral repertoire included great vocal works such as *Das Weltgericht* (Friedrich Schneider), *Paulus* (Felix Mendelssohn-Bartholdy), *Stabat Mater* (Rossini), and, from the Flemish repertoire, *Le Sabbat* by Charles-Louis Hanssens "the Younger."[18]

In the early stages choirs drew from German and French choir literature, either in translation or provided with an entirely new text.[19] In this way they

---

15   After the choir contest organized during the September festivities of 1842, Edouard Fétis passed judgement sternly: "Part-singing is generally speaking weak in the societies of the villages. The performers, who have no idea how to project their voice, sing with their mouths barely half open, resulting in a sound that is thin, deaf and almost always nasal. Their pronunciation is almost inconceivably inadequate, often even downright ridiculous, a flaw that would disappear, as we have already observed in a review of the contest in Malines, if the societies sent by Flemish villages would sing in Flemish."

16   Grégoir (1879), 113.

17   The Antwerp *Société d'Orphée* was the nucleus of the great choir then. See Grégoir (1879), 114; and Dewilde (2004).

18   Along with music, painters and painting also had a considerable mobilizing potential. There are many choral works, cantatas, and lyrical dramas in which Rubens, Van Dyck, Teniers, Brouwer or Matsys are praised: "Painting and music were both subject and medium of the cult for and around the Belgian nation. They had to express the greatness of the nation in images or sounds, and concurrently composers and painters from the past were also eulogized in images and sounds. The nineteenth-century developments in the art world were an 'indicator of the level of civilisation of the nation and consequently of its greatness,' but there was also the recourse to the historical art figures and their achievements with a view to proving the nation's greatness" (Ceulemans [2010], 129).

19   These adaptations were not always equally successful. In some cases the new text was out of square with the music. Mendelssohn's drinking song *Liebe und Wein*, which was qualified with the indication "to be sung as if drunk," was transformed into *The Crusader's Song*; Conradin Kreutzer's love song *Abendfeier* was transmogrified into the hunters' song *The Hunt for the Stag*; and Carl Maria von Weber's *Song of the Hussars* became *The Song of the Blacksmiths*.

came in contact with the great repertoire,[20] but the *Liedertafel* repertoire was also a good source. At the same time, a considerable amount of new choir literature was being produced by Belgian composers such as Charles Bosselet, Léon de Burbure de Wesembeek, François De Coninck, Jules Denefve, François-Auguste Gevaert, Charles-Louis Hanssens, Armand Limnander de Nieuwenhove, Joseph-François Snel, and Etienne Soubre. This repertoire vanished together with the male choirs, yet it merits further exploration. Most of these composers conducted choirs themselves, so they knew from the inside how a choir works. Some of their works were written explicitly for competitions; and some of these 'set pieces' are difficult to such a degree that the enabling condition must have been a serious investment of the choirs in the training of their singers. Moreover, some of the choir singers had already enjoyed a good singing education during the period of Dutch government (1815–30), and in the early phase of Belgium, in the 1830s, Fétis and others promoted singing in the schools.[21] Initially this singing education served an explicit pedagogical and moralizing purpose, but at the same time it nurtured the practical aim of producing better choir singers.[22]

This early repertoire, distributed through periodicals such as *Le Choriste, Le Chorophile belge,* and *Journal de chant,* was often steeped in nationalist-didactic discourse. As in other vocal genres such as the lied, the cantata, and the opera, historical events and figures (political icons and artists) were popular subjects. They were instrumentalized for the nineteenth-century hero cult and the concomitant national pride. There were also a great many homages to Belgium, the king and his family. Part of the choral repertoire was clearly aimed at glorifying the past, and designed to provide the young nation with letters of nobility, to legitimate the rich to exist for the nation state, and to construct a national identity and give musical expression to its grandeur. It has already been noted in the study of the history of nineteenth-century nationalism that this often led beyond exact historical facts: the 'invention of tradition'

---

20   A typical festival programme from this period, conducted by Ferdinand at the September festivities of 1842, consisted of works by Méhul, Cherubini, Ries, Haydn, Handel, Beethoven, and Durante. Music critics praised this kind of programme as "all of them first-rate ensemble pieces"; *La Belgique musicale* (28 Sept. 1842), 83.

21   See Dewilde (2000).

22   In 1845 August Valckenaere (1809–63), a sexton-organist, choir conductor and music teacher in Torhout, published a practical handbook in order "to help the youth of our beloved fatherland, who are working so hard to found choir societies almost everywhere, and to offer them a method for the rapid acquisition of a complete knowledge of this praiseworthy science." See Valckenaere (1845).

loomed large.[23] History was re-interpreted as a myth designed to support the nation-building and/or didactic-moralizing discourse. The (historical) figures whose praises the choirs sang—ranging across a wide gamut, from Godfrey of Bouillon to Rubens and King Leopold I—therefore became incarnations of nineteenth-century values and norms. This stereotypical representation of historical heroes and events was supposed to facilitate recognition and identification by the audience, ideally culminating in the collective experience of a common heritage.[24] All this resulted in choral works with titles such as *Le chant du Belge* (Auguste Bouillon), *Vaderlandsch gebed* (Henri Cartol), *Belgisch vredelied* (François Costermans), *Le lion belge* (François De Coninck), *La croisade de Godefroid de Bouillon* (Jules Denefve), *Gloire à Rubens* (Jean Simon Eykens), *César et les Belges* (François-Auguste Gevaert), *De Belgen in 1848* (Edouard Grégoir), *La Belgique* (Charles Miry), *Au roi et au peuple belge* (Joseph-François Snel), or *Chant national à l'occasion de la majorité du duc de Brabant* (Pieter Vanderghinste).[25] Vocal music (and pre-eminently music sung by a group) was a powerful medium to convey an enthusiastic message to an audience that was still partially illiterate.

The young Flemish choral movement involved not only composers and conductors (most often united in one and the same person) but also men of letters, who not only provided texts but also served as board members, organizers and/or propagandists. These writers and *taalminnaars* (language lovers) pleaded for the use of the people's language as a cultural and administrative language within the Flemish subnation. An important 'musical' point of contention was the demand to use a Dutch text for the composition of the cantata for the Prix de Rome (the biennial state prize for composition). The poet Prudens Van Duyse (1804–59) formulated this demand in 1846, which was rejected by the Minister of the Interior.[26] Van Duyse, a vigorous defender of the Flemish cause and until around 1840 a determined Orangist who favored reunification with Holland, was in 1836 one of the founders of the society

---

23 See for example Flacke, ed. (1998).

24 Rigney (1999), 301–3.

25 Such titles constituted of course only a minor part of the choral repertoire produced at that time. Plenty of autonomous art music was also being composed, or choral music sung for the sake of *Gemütlichkeit*, without ideological intentions.

26 Minister de Theux replied that "it requires little thought to realize that only the French language qualifies ... the language that is most widespread and also serves as the vehicle of instruction for music education in our country." Only in 1864 was bilingualism accepted by the Belgian Prix de Rome. See Dewilde (1998).

De Tael is gansch het volk (Language is the Whole People), its name expressing its politically neutral programme.[27]

In 1841 this society issued a call for Dutch texts in the framework of a competition, with a view to promoting the repertoire for choral music in the mother tongue. Here too the system of adaptations was used: new Dutch-language texts were combined with the choral music of German composers such as Heinrich Marschner, Carl Maria von Weber, and Ludwig Spohr, and were published in the volume *Achttien vierstemmige liederen* (Eighteen Four-part Songs). Similar adaptations were also distributed in the periodical volumes *Ryn- en Scheldegalmen* (Sounds of the Rhine and Scheldt) by the brothers Evariste (1808–75) and Robert (1806–93) Van Maldeghem. In 1839 the brothers Van Maldeghem founded the Brussels choir *Gombert's Genootschap*, through which they wanted to distribute Flemish and German music, both profane and sacred. Along with concerts, their publication *Ryn- en Scheldegalmen* contained the Dutchified choral music of German composers (among them Michael Haydn, Conrad Kreutzer, Peter Winter, Carl Gottlieb Reissiger, Ludwig Abeille, and Carl Friedrich Zelter) as well as new choral music by Robert Van Maldeghem. The first instalment, published in 1842, is dedicated to *De Tael is gansch het volk*, "which promotes the dissemination of singing in the mother tongue so powerfully." As a matter of fact, Van Duyse collaborated with this publication, contributing translations and new texts. The Van Maldeghems had a profound interest in 'Flemish' polyphony, which for them prefigured the reinvigoration of Flemish/Belgian music life, coupled with a lively interest in sacred music.[28] A substantial part of their activities consisted of the publication of early choral music, supplemented with new repertoire.[29] As Richard Taruskin remarks, this kind of historical (sacred) choral music, like folk music, was regarded as "artefacts of nationhood, bearers of the national spirit," or, as

---

27   This maxim, tersely encapsulating the conviction that language is the main support of a cultural identity, was coined by Van Duyse himself: the slogan emerges in his anti-French poem *Aen België* (To Belgium, 1835). He recycles the saying for his poem *De Nederduitsche tael* (1840), in which the use of French, "brimming with lustful frivolity," is seen as a moral threat to the Flemish people (and particularly to Flemish girls): a French play makes the young virgin dream of adultery, even before the bridal bed, and a song by Béranger "teaches her how to sing blasphemy." See Kroon and Sturm (1999).

28   The brothers Van Maldeghem published from 1847 in *Cecilia: journal mensuel de musique d'église*, a periodical with old and new religious choral music, on texts in Dutch, with French translations. Their brother Eugene, a historical painter, provided illustrations.

29   Between 1865 and 1893, Robert J. Van Maldeghem published his magnum opus, a series in fifty-eight instalments: *Trésor musical, collection authentique de musique sacrée et profane des anciens maîtres belges*.

he quotes the musicologist Glenn Stanley, "an image of a former, better time" in which the nation's spirituality was as yet "a culture unperverted by secular influences."[30] As a team the brothers also published a textbook for schools and educational institutions, linking music theory and choirs for two, three, and four parts. In several respects they aligned themselves with the work of Hans Georg Nägeli (1773–1836).

With the Van Maldeghems as well as Van Duyse there is an intense interaction of a Belgian patriotic nationalism, a culturally inspired Flemish subnationalism (with special consideration for the mother tongue), a religious feeling, and a didactic-moralistic intention.[31] These feelings found embodiment in their commitment to the Flemish choir scene, which first became concretized in writing and composing, but also in successfully encouraging and publishing choral music on Dutch texts (initially mainly adaptations, and later more and more original music).[32] Like the choirs mentioned above, which originated in a Belgian patriotic context, and for the same reasons, Flemish cultural activists, both writers and composers, produced choral works celebrating historical figures and events from Flemish history. However, this always happened within the Belgian context, certainly in the first half of the nineteenth century. One typical example is the chorale *Belgen, voelt uwe waerde* (Belgians, Know Your Worth) with which Van Duyse and Robert J. Van Maldeghem significantly opened the very first instalment of *Ryn- en Scheldegalmen*. This manifest indictment of language repression ends with:

Long live this holy house of our ancestors!
Let not servility destroy it
Proud feeling glows in our arteries
With the words: I am a Belgian![33]

This attitude was also typical of the *Vlaemsch-Duitsch Zangverbond*, founded in 1845 by Van Duyse and the Van Maldeghem brothers.

---

30   Taruskin (2005), 166.
31   A similar amalgamation is recorded in the *Kunst- en letterblad* 3:1 (1842), 45–47: "Morally speaking, music has a wholesome influence on the civilization of the people; it ennobles the spirit and elevates the soul to its Maker. It also has a patriotic aim, and deserves to be encouraged in this respect;—Flemish song as it sounds from Flemish mouths makes gurgle up in our hearts what the yoke of foreign oppression had repressed so deeply."
32   In the 1840s many composers wrote choral works in Dutch, even though almost nobody did so exclusively.
33   "Leev' dit heilig pand der vaedren! / Dat geen volgzucht haer verdelg' / Fier gevoel gloeit ons door de aedren / By het woord: ik been een Belg!"

The *Vlaemsch-Duitsch Zangverbond* (1845–1847)

The foundation of the *Vlaemsch-Duitsch Zangverbond* fits in with the wave of Germanophilia sustained already in the early 1830s by a good many Flemish cultural activists and lovers of the mother tongue. These Germanophile feelings were enhanced by the special interest in the young Belgian state and in the Flemish language movement mustered by the liberal and national German unification movement. For the champions of a unified German state, language was the most important unifying factor; for them the language border was also the natural border of a future German state. The conviction that 'language is the whole people' thus lived in both the Flemish Movement and in the German unification movement. Groups of Flemings and Germans also shared a romantic feeling of linguistic and ethnic affinities. Dutch and German were called Low and High German, respectively. As the philologist and poet Philip Blommaert (1808–71) wrote: "As far as German is spoken / There extends our fatherland; / From the Alps to the Brocken / From the Oder to the Flemish strand."[34] For historian Joseph Kervyn de Lettenhove (1817–91) and novelist Hendrik Conscience (1812–83) it was clear that Flanders (and by extension even Belgium) had a Germanic identity. One looked for—and 'found'—evidence in vestigial remnants even of antiquity. There was also a shared anti-French mood. In his poem *Fraternization with Germany* (1839) Prudens Van Duyse sings the praises of "the twin offspring of Germanic extraction…unadulterated fruit born from one single people's trunk" and concurrently rejects the inherent immorality of France: "mad Paris…when only the lecherous song could tickle her." During the first years of independence there were constraints in the contacts with those who shared the same language in Holland, so part of the Flemish intelligentsia was eager to lean towards German cultural life.

German interest in Flemish language and culture was concretized in contacts between philologists and collectors of folk songs, e.g. between August Hoffmann von Fallersleben (1798–1874) and Jan Frans Willems (1793–1846).

---

34   Philip Blommaert was among the first to formulate the idea that 'the language is the people.' In his *Aenmerkingen over de verwaerloozing der Nederduitsche tael* (1832) he wrote: "Nothing is so closely connected to the fundamental principles of a nation than the language of the people. It is language that disseminates the same ideas throughout all the ranks of society, that enables us to discern the diversity of peoples, and consequently forms nationality. Therefore a nation's authorities are obliged to promote the language of the people."

These cultural contacts were sustained by economic activities which had been growing in importance ever since the Scheldt was reopened in 1796.[35]

There were also growing connections between the Flemish/Belgian choir scene and that in the Rhineland. In 1841 the *Aachener Liedertafel* was the first German choir to participate in the choir competition organized on the occasion of the September festivities in Brussels.[36] In the following years connections with the Rhineland intensified, particularly through the *Männer-Gesang-Verein* from Cologne. This choir was founded on 27 April 1842 by members of the Cologne *Dom-Chor*, in order "to give pride of place to male singing in its entire greatness and power, and to disseminate German song through public performances for patriotic and municipal, beneficial aims, in keeping with the slogan 'spreading goodness through beauty.' "[37]

The immediate cause for the foundation of the *Vlaemsch-Duitsch Zangverbond* was the participation of the Cologne choir (with forty-eight singers) in the competition that the *Société royale des Mélomanes* (founded in 1838) organized on 7 July 1844 in Ghent. Despite the fact that it had been active for only two years, the *Männer-Gesang-Verein* won the contest, and was held up as an example of perfection for the Flemish choirs.[38] Furthermore, the people of Ghent were impressed not only by the German choir's performance of works by Conradin Kreutzer, Franz Derckum, and Ferdinand Ries, but also by its generosity: in keeping with their motto, they organized a benefit concert for the poor, and they donated their prize money of 200 Belgian francs as well.[39]

---

35   Pelckmans and Van Doorslaer (2000), 11ff.

36   The *Liedertafel* won the contest, surpassing choirs from Bruges, Dendermonde and Aalst; Grégoir (1879), 24.

37   Klefisch (1942), 34.

38   "This contest is memorable, first and foremost because of the participation of the Cologne Männer-Gesang-Verein, which has managed to secure a reputation of superiority all over the world of choral singing, and which shines in the forefront of those German choirs that are recognized as superior to those of all other countries.... in Flanders there had not yet been an opportunity to appreciate this perfection typical of German choirs; it was the Cologne society that initiated the Ghent audience in the harmonious chords of the songs of their country" (Thys [1855], 92).

39   At the benefit concert, choral works by Klein, Marschner, and Weber alternated with string quartets by Mozart and Beethoven executed by the famous Cologne quartet with Franz Hartmann, Franz Derckum, Franz Weber (the choir conductor), and Bernhard Breuer. *Le messager de Gand et des Pays-Bas*, 7 July 1844.

It must have been at this time that Van Duyse conceived his plan for a Flemish-German choral society,[40] a project that he developed with the Van Maldeghem brothers beginning in August 1844. Anticipating the foundation of the society, Van Duyse and the Van Maldeghems tried to persuade as many choirs as possible to sing in 'Vlaemsch.' For this purpose Robert Van Maldeghem travelled all over Flanders, presenting choirs with copies of *Ryn- en Scheldegalmen*. At the same time they appealed also to Francophone Belgians to support the nascent society.[41] The Van Maldeghems were probably interested mainly in musical contacts with Germany, while for Van Duyse the language issue had his first loyalty: in April 1846 he wrote to the Cologne publisher F.C. Eisen: "Belgium is backward in the field of national song, but this genre will develop thanks to the fraternal Rhine, concurrently with our Flemish literature."[42]

With the approval of the *Hoofd-reglement van het Vlaemsch-Duitsch Zangverbond* (Statutes of the Flemish-German Singing Union) in Brussels on 23 December 1845 the society was officially founded. The founding choirs on the Flemish side were the *Gombert's Genootschap* of the Van Maldeghem brothers, the *Société royale des Mélomanes*, the *Société d'Orphée*[43] (Ghent, 1838), *Echoos van den Dender*[44] (Dendermonde, 1841), the *Sint-Gregorius Zangersgilde*[45] (Leuven, 1843) and *La Philomélie* (Leuven, 1845).[46]

---

40   "The participation of the Kölner Männergesang-Verein in the contest of the *Mélomanes* resulted in the idea of the great Belgian-German lyrical confederation. It was the poet Van Duyse who came up with the original project"; *Ephémérides de la Société royale des Mélomanes, fondée à Gand le 1er octobre 1838* (Ghent: De Busscher, 1871), 19.

41   On 27 August 1844 Evariste Van Maldeghem wrote to Prudens Van Duyse: "With great excitement we see how the singing union progresses with giant strides. A considerable number of our Brussels connections, even though they are not fond of Flemish, realize nonetheless that the cause is excellent and of great importance"; Koninklijke Academie voor Nederlandse Taal- en Letterkunde, Ghent: correspondence Prudens Van Duyse.

42   Leo Schwering, "Höhepunkte deutsch-flämischer Beziehungen," in *Der Belfried* 1 (February 1917), 352.

43   This choir was founded in 1838 by students of the Ghent Conservatory. It raised its visibility by performing on the streets and in boats, and in this way contributed to the popularization of choir singing in Ghent. The choir also performed masses by Pieter Verheyen and Sigismond Neukomm, and allegedly disposed of a library holding 1,500 works for male choir, "of which a large share belongs to the German repertoire"; Thys (1855), 37.

44   The choir's first conductor was the composer and musicologist Léon de Burbure de Wesembeek (1812–89).

45   This choir was founded by the chamber of rhetoric De Kersouwe to add lustre to festive occasions with Flemish choral songs.

46   Not all these founding choirs sang exclusively Dutch texts. The choir *Les Mélomanes*, for example, was founded in 1838 in order to "popularize taste and the study of melody and singing," and they sang a lot of French music. The repertoire featured songs by Pierre-

According to Article 1 of the Statutes, the purpose of the Singing Union was: "the practice and dissemination of good music, with choral songs in *Low and High German*. The execution of sacred music, with organ or symphonic orchestra, also belongs to the appropriate range." The main focus was explicitly on choir music, profane as well as sacred, in Dutch, German, and Latin.

The Flemish wing of the Singing Union was led musically by the Van Maldeghem brothers. For the administration there were two presidents: the initiator Van Duyse and the poet and polemicist Jan Nolet de Brauwere van Steeland (1815–88), a Dutchman who lived and worked in Flanders. The poet Johan Michiel Dautzenberg (1808–69) was one of the secretaries. With Van Duyse and Dautzenberg there were two Orangists on the board, while Nolet de Brauwere van Steeland also strove for cultural cooperation with Holland. However, by the appointment as honorary president of Baron E. de T'Serclaes, who had been secretary-general of the Ministry of Foreign Affairs since 1837,[47] the Belgian context of the organization was emphasized. Moreover, according to Article 6 of the Statutes, a singing festival had to be organized annually during the September festivities in Brussels, along with yearly festivals in another Flemish city and in Cologne.

On 20 February 1846 the German wing of the *Deutsch-vlaemischer Sängerbund* was officially founded, under the auspices of the *Männer-Gesang-Verein*. There were explicit references to the participation of the choir in the contests of Ghent (1844) and Brussels (1845), cities with ample sympathy for the German cause. Meanwhile Van Duyse successfully tried to involve Antwerp in the initiative, with *De Scheldezonen* (The Sons of the Scheldt, 1844)[48] and the *Deutsche Gesang-Gesellschaft Teutonia* (1846).[49] The countryside was also represented by the joining of the *Société lyrique* (Zingem, 1843).

Jean de Béranger, sung in alternation by a soloist and a choir, as well as works by Louis Clapisson and Auguste Panseron. Besides that, the choir sang Flemish music in the mother tongue at functions of the drama society *Broedermin en Taelijver*. This situation was the rule with most choirs and, by extension, also with the choral composers, who depending on the occasion composed on Dutch or French texts.

47   http://diplomatie.belgium.be/en/documentation/archives/heritage/diplomatic_archive/ index.jsp (accessed 1 Feb. 2011).

48   The president of this choir was Pieter Frans Van Kerckhoven (1818–57) and the conductor Henri Cartol (1891–96), "one of those composers who pioneered by enriching the national repertoire with choral music on Flemish texts." Cartol was succeeded by François Callaerts (1826–1894), "an artist to whom we owe a series of Flemish choral works as well"; Thys (1855), 12.

49   This *Liedertafel* consisted largely of members of the German colony in Antwerp and sang German repertoire. The choir was conducted by Flemish conductors, first Henri Possoz (1827–97), then François Schermers (1822–74).

Because of the difference in standard between the German and the Flemish choirs a decision was taken to refrain from organizing contests at the common meetings,[50] but to opt instead for a two-day festival modelled after the exceedingly popular *Niederrheinische Musikfeste*. These yearly musical mass meetings were an expression of a rising national pride in the German art of music. The basic model was a two-day festival with a concert on each day, framed by open rehearsals, musical parades, singing exercises, *Garten-Musik*, the presentation of memorial medals, speeches, fireworks, and tourist activities such as boat trips on the Rhine, all generously doused with Rhenish wine.[51]

All these elements were also present at the first meeting of the *Vlaemsch-Duitsch Zangverbond*, organized on 14 and 15 June 1846 in Cologne. From Flanders came 31 choirs, while from the German side 100 choirs participated, totalling 482 Flemish and 1,730 German singers. The accompanying orchestra (winds, supported by twenty-two violoncellos and fourteen double basses) counted ninety musicians. This shows how powerfully attractive the idea of a Flemish-German choral meeting was. By comparison, the *Niederrheinische Musikfest* organized in Aachen in 1846 attracted only 631 musicians (soloists, choir members, and instrumentalists).[52]

The musical advisers for the first Flemish-German choir meeting were Franz Weber, the conductor of the organizing Cologne choir and *königlicher Musikdirektor* in Cologne, and Felix Mendelssohn-Bartholdy (1809–47), then *königlicher Generalmusikdirektor* in Berlin and *Gewandhaus-Kapellmeister* in Leipzig.

The first concert on 14 June in the Gürzenich Hall opened significantly with the *Gebet für das Vaterland* (Prayer for the Fatherland, text by Johan Gabriel Seidl), a double choir work composed especially for the occasion by Franz Weber. This first part also featured the motet *God Have Mercy on Me* by Bernhard Klein (1793–1832), *Calm Sea and Happy Voyage* by Carl Ludwig Fischer (1816–77), *Long Live German Song* by Friedrich Rochlitz (1769–1842),

---

50   Letter from Evariste Van Maldeghem to Prudens Van Duyse, 27 August 1844, Koninklijke Academie voor Nederlandse Taal- en Letterkunde, Ghent: correspondence Prudens Van Duyse.

51   Porter (1980), 216.

52   It must have been an enormous logistical operation to provide accommodation for all the choir members, to organize the rehearsals and the concerts, and to keep the timetable for the abundant programme; but Cologne already had considerable experience in organizing several *Musikfeste* and could count on the support of the municipal authorities and of the high bourgeoisie (Idem., 216–17).

and *Jehova, the King Rejoices in You*, a hymn for double choir by Friedrich Schneider (1786–1853).

The second part opened with the world première of *Festive Song for the Artists*, a cantata composed by Mendelssohn on a text by Friedrich Schiller. The cantata was commissioned for the occasion by the governing board of the *Deutsch-Vlämischen Sängerbund*, who had asked Mendelssohn for a piece with "easy-going melodies" and a duration of three quarters of an hour.[53] He observed the first condition but not the second; the song, for male choir and brass players, takes about seven minutes. He borrowed the text from the final part of Schiller's *The Artists*, which deals with the admonition to strive for perfection through art. Mendelssohn set Schiller's verses mainly homo-rhythmically and kept the part-writing simple, with the music generally serving the declamation of the text. After the *Festive Song*, conducted by Mendelssohn himself, there followed a *Te Deum* by Bernhard Klein, the chorale *O Isis und Osiris* from Mozart's *Die Zauberflöte*, and the hymn *Where Is as Far as Creation Extends* by Heinrich August Neithardt (1793–1861). The first concert was concluded with the *Bacchus Chorale* from Mendelssohn's *Antigone*, no doubt a suitable prelude for the drinking-bout that followed. The whole programme was performed by Flemish and German singers, which means that the Flemish choirs would have received the scores well in advance. It is remarkable that no Flemish work was programmed on the first day.

The second concert, on the following day, was conceived differently: on this day mainly individual German choirs sang. In between, the combined Flemish choirs sang the *Patriotic Hymn* by the Ghent-based composer Martin-Joseph Mengal (1784–1851), and the Flemish choirs together with the *Männer-Gesang-Verein* offered the first performance of *Sounds of the Rhine and Scheldt: the Union's Song of Joy* by Robert Van Maldeghem and Prudens Van Duyse. Finally, all the Flemish and German choirs sang a chorale by Bernhard Klein, the *Rhine-Prussian Warrior Song* by Franz Weber, Mendelssohn's *Farewell of the Hunters*, and Reinhardt's *Des Deutschen Vaterland*. At this second concert, too, the contribution of Flemish choir music was very limited.

The festival was followed by two days of fraternization and tourist excursions. On 16 June the programme included a *Liederfahrt* by boat to Königswinter and the climbing of the Drachenfels. The participants were presented with a song-book especially compiled for this occasion, with adaptations such as the text of *Auf dem Drachenfels* to the melody of *Leb' wohl, o theures Land* (Farewell, O Dear Fatherland). Songs in the dialect of the Rhine region were also included. This was an era of romantic fascination with the Rhine as a mighty monument

---

53   See Koch (2007), 248.

of nature.[54] On 17 June the cathedral and other tourist attractions were visited, and a *Festfahrt* to Brühl concluded the programme.

For this first meeting Dautzenberg wrote the poem *Duitsch en Vlaemsch* in both a German and a Dutch version. Dautzenberg, who had an excellent command of German, emphasized once more the affinities between the two languages: "German and Flemish are next of kin / As close as right and left hand / And German is German, whether High or Low / As resounds from our songs."

The first common choir festival clearly aroused a lot of enthusiasm and national pride, but even so, there remained differences of opinion due to diverging intentions that were often hard to reconcile. On the Flemish side there were controversies between the Flemings from Ghent and Antwerp—based as much on different vantage points as on more personal antagonisms[55]—but problems emerged between the Flemish and the Germans as well. German Pan-Germanic nationalists saw the activities of the *Vlaemsch-Duitsch Zangverbond* mainly as an instrument in their unification movement and in their struggle against France. Many of them differentiated indifferently between Flanders and Belgium, and some of the Flemish resented the lack of empathy for their language struggle. When the *Kölnische Zeitung* deprecated the Flemish and praised only the Belgian constitution and industrial development, a little scandal even erupted. In the run-up to the second Song Festival, to be organized in Brussels on 24 and 25 September 1846, Pieter Ecrevisse (1804–79) wrote a pamphlet to explain and justify the Flemish language demands vis-à-vis the German. He also issued a call to fortify the "Germanic family" against a "greedy and domineering France."[56] At the same time, the *Zangverbond* was increasingly constrained by official Belgian discourse. Against the annexationist threat from France, Belgian authorities emphasized the independence but also the specificity of Belgium, and noted the important role of Flemish language

---

54   On the Flemish side attempts were made to come up with a fluvial counterpart in the Scheldt; see Van Maldeghem's *Sounds of the Rhine and Scheldt* and Van Duyse's verse "The Scheldt thus brings the Rhine her greeting / In songs steeped in Flemish heart"; from *Aen het Keulsch Zanggenootschap* (To the Cologne Singing Society) by Prudens Van Duyse, quoted in Klefisch (1942), 46.

55   On 3 July 1846 Van Duyse sent a letter to Dautzenberg: "Antwerp, whose society Sons of the Scheldt wants to join, should not yet be represented in the board. Conscience acted confused, and is on bad terms with Van Kerckhoven, president of the Sons of the Scheldt." Together with his friend the painter Gustaaf Wappers (1803–74), Hendrik Conscience was the only prominent Antwerpian to have attended the Song Festival in Cologne. He was then appointed an honorary member of the *Männer-Gesang-Verein*.

56   See Ecrevisse (1853), 335–40.

and culture. Thus the second Choir Festival in Brussels was entirely integrated into the official programme of the September festivities, as approved by the Minister of the Interior.[57] The authorities took care to provide free train tickets for the participating choirs. The organization of the choir festival was supported by the Brussels-based literary association *De Vlaemsche verbroedering* which promoted the use of Dutch in Brussels, and in addition cherished societal aims and sought to improve the conditions of workers. From a letter sent by president Jacques-Corneille Van Thielen on 17 September 1846 to a number of prominent writers, it appears that the struggle against the dominance of French as the *de facto* national language was the most important element for these language activists during the choir festival. In his letter the president emphasized that the speeches be held only "in the two sister languages (High and Low German)," that "no songs other than Flemish and High German ones will sound in the Frenchified milieu of Brussels" and that "the deeply sunk Brussels will again become the Low German capital of Belgium."

However, the programme indicates that there was scarcely any Flemish contribution, or any special attention to the Flemish language question. During the two main concerts in the Cirque National and on the square in front of the Royal Palace, the forty-seven Flemish and twenty-nine German choirs[58] mostly sang works that had been performed in Cologne a few months earlier (including works by Franz Weber, Reichardt, Rochlitz, Mendelssohn, and Mozart).[59] These re-runs, meant to reduce rehearsal time, were augmented with only two new Flemish choral works: the hymn *Great is the Lord* by the young Alexander Stadtfeld (1826–53)[60] and the cantata *To the Vlaemsch-Duitsch Zangverbond* by Jules Busschop (1810–96).[61] Busschop's cantata is textually a hymn to Belgium

---

57   *Programma des cérémonies et fêtes qui auront lieu à l'occasion du 16ᵉ anniversaire des Journées de Septembre*, Brussels, 14 September 1846.

58   In this period 106 German choirs were affiliated with the *Sängerbund*.

59   A new feature in comparison with the meeting in Cologne was the programming in Brussels of instrumental works: two works by Jean-Valentin Bender (1801–73), the German-born conductor of the King's Music Chapel, and a Beethoven symphony (in an adaptation for symphonic wind orchestra). The choral performances were conducted by the Van Maldeghem brothers and Franz Weber.

60   Alexander Stadtfeld was of German extraction. A piano prodigy, he was discovered by Leopold I, who gave him a stipend. In 1849 Stadtfeld won the Belgian Prix de Rome.

61   The cantata is a textual rewriting by A. Inghels of an occasional work that Busschop composed in 1846 for the inauguration of the statue of the Bruges mathematician and physicist Simon Stevin (1548–1620). Busschop's Belgian-patriotic cantata *Le Drapeau belge* had won the official composition contest organized by the Belgian authorities in 1834 to add pomp and circumstance to the September festivities.

("O Belgium, splendour of Europe...Hurray, yes Belgium will be reborn!
Hurray! In the lap of ancient Germany!"), while Flanders is mentioned only
once, and in a non-political context ("the Flemish art altar"). Hymns to the
Rhine, to "King and Fatherland" resounded in Brussels much more powerfully than the linguistic ambitions of the Flemish. This second meeting of the
Vlaemsch-Duitsch Zangverbond clearly targeted a discourse that accentuated
the Germanic character of Belgium as a move against the threatening southern
neighbor, a discourse adopted by the young Flemish Movement. This is also
evident from the rhyming speech held by J.-C. Van Thielen during the choir
festival in which he extolled the praises of Germanic fraternization and com-
mended his "dearly beloved sovereign' Leopold I: 'A king of German extraction,
of noble spirit / Whose sons understand High and Low German."[62]

The third and final meeting of the *Vlaemsch-Duitsch Zangverbond* was held
in Ghent on 27 and 28 June 1847 during the fair. Prudens Van Duyse was generously supported by the liberal alderman and MP Hippolyte Rolin (1804–83),
who had studied in Germany. The choir festival in Ghent was co-sponsored by
the municipal, provincial, and national authorities, as well as by the University
of Ghent.

Experience had taught that some Flemish choirs needed lots of time for
rehearsals, so the German works to be programmed for the third time were
published as early as February.[63] There were also new German choral works,
e.g. by Louis Spohr (1784–1859)[64] and Heinrich Marschner (1795–1861).

Commissioned by Van Duyse, the Antwerp poet Theodoor Van Rijswijck[65]
wrote for this gathering *Fraternal Salute*, a text set to music at Van Duyse's
behest by the Antwerp-based composer and choral conductor Jean Eykens
(1812–91), "so as to enable a dignified representation of Flemish Antwerp at

---

62   Van Thielen (1846), 63.

63   Namely: *Rhein-Prussian Warrior Song* (Weber), *O Isis und Osiris* (Mozart, in a translation
      by Dautzenberg), *Hymn to Bacchus* and *Festival Song to Artists* (Mendelssohn), *God Have
      Mercy on Me*, (Klein), *Calm Sea and Happy Journey* (Fischer), and *Jehova, the King Rejoices
      in You* (Schneider).

64   In transit to England, Spohr stopped by chance in Ghent during the choir festival, and the
      organizing choirs from Ghent offered him a serenade. See Spohr (1861), 2: 316–17.

65   Van Rijswijck had recently become a corresponding member of *De Keyser's Kunst- en
      Zanggenootschap* (Ghent, 1846), a guild of writers and printers with a choir of their own.
      The minutes of the inaugural meeting of 29 November 1846 mention that the mem-
      bers should take classes in "Flemish" as well as French, but sing only Flemish songs, for
      "To speak and write Flemish and French well is a civil necessity; but to echo, or want to
      echo French song, is no civil necessity."

the forthcoming great festival in Ghent."[66] Other new Flemish choral works included *Kyrie* and *Victory Hymn* by Emile Beausacq (1815–56), *Ave Regina* by Jules Bovery (1808–68), and Martin-Joseph Mengal's *Rejoice, Rhine!* and *The People of Ghent before the Battle of Beverholt.* However, the most important Flemish work was without doubt the psalm *Super flumina Babylonis* by the young Ghent-based composer François-Auguste Gevaert (1828–1908), a pupil of Mengal then just beginning a remarkable career.

On 26 June, on the eve of the choral festival in Ghent, Van Duyse delivered a remarkable address to the 974 Flemish and 625 German choral singers on the occasion of the first anniversary of the festival in Cologne. In his long speech he quoted at length and with total agreement—in French !—from a letter by a physician from Tournai who claimed that the era of conflicts between the Flemish and the Walloons, two fractions of the same people, belonged to the past. And this opened perspectives: following a reconciliation of Flemings and Walloons, Belgium might be in a position to play a conciliatory and harmonizing role in Europe due to its topography and neutrality. Moreover, Van Duyse recommended reaching out to women with the Singing Union, and argued for the admission of Dutch in official composition contests. The strong religious element that Van Duyse saw in the ties between German and Flemish choirs was also remarkable: in his view it was the "Unnameable" who had given human beings a voice, uniting peoples by choral singing and making steam available as an enabling condition for the choirs to travel by train.[67] This invocation of modernity was also explicitly present in the commemorative medal stamped for the meeting in Ghent, which shows an ancient Germanic bard and the towers of Ghent, but also a smoking factory chimney ("a triumphant column of industry," as Van Duyse put it) and a steam train. Dautzenberg delivered an address too, saying things like: "Whether this salute is German or Flemish I am not in a position to determine myself, but in any case it is genuinely Germanic." During the song festival the Minard Theatre was inaugurated, an important milestone in Flemish cultural history built in reaction to the Théâtre Français, the French opera house in Ghent. In his speech Van Duyse referred to the new theatre: "The Flemish lover of dramatic art will no longer have to blush at the words *Grand Théâtre de la Ville.*"

---

66   Letter from Prudens Van Duyse to Theodoor Van Rijswijck, Ghent, 15 January 1847. Koninklijke Academie voor Nederlandse Taal- en Letterkunde, Ghent: correspondence Prudens Van Duyse.

67   See Van Duyse (1847). The connection between the Belgian railway system and the line Aachen-Cologne was inaugurated in 1843.

On the day after the two-day songfest, tourist trips and all kinds of festivities were on offer. On 30 June the Flemish and German choirs took the train to Ostend, where on the beach they joined together to sing *Des Deutschen Vaterland* by Arndt and Reichardt. The German choirs also collected money for a home for elderly seamen. Out of gratitude, the Flemish promised to donate a stained-glass window to the cathedral in Cologne. After the festival, tentative arrangements were made for a fourth festival in Frankfurt, the venue disclosed in Van Duyse's speech, which ended with: "Three cheers for Belgium! Three cheers for Germania!"

By this time the Singing Union counted more than two hundred German choirs and seventy Flemish choral societies, and two Walloon choirs from Mons and Tournai were also present in Ghent. That the *Vlaemsch-Duitsch Zangverbond* was developing more and more into a Belgian-German choir federation was officially recognized at the meeting of the Flemish board of the Singing Union in Brussels on 26 December 1847. The conclusions of this meeting were laid down in the "*Belgian* principal rules and regulations of the Flemish-German Singing Union," published for the first time not only in Dutch and German but also in French. For the first time it was also mentioned that German and *Belgian* (instead of Flemish) choirs qualified for membership. It is also remarkable that the Van Maldeghem brothers had vanished from the record, and that the new musical director of the singing union was Charles-Louis Hanssens "the Younger" (1802–71).[68] At the same meeting a proposal was accepted to award the title of "Patron of the Singing Union" to Prince Philippe (1837–1905), the third son of King Leopold I and Count of Flanders. Plans were still in the works for a Song Festival in Frankfurt, but the revolutionary year 1848 decided otherwise. This meant the end of the Flemish-German Singing Union.

Despite its brief existence, the *Vlaemsch-Duitsch Zangverbond* provides an important vantage point from which to study the Flemish choral scene in the first half of the nineteenth century, and particularly the role of choral singing in nationalist mobilization. Even so, we have to take into account that, according to estimates, not more than half of the Flemish choirs participated in the Singing Union. Besides, a lot more singing was going on just for the pleasure of making music together. Also, the fact that at Singing Festivals the languages were exclusively Dutch, German, and Latin must not make us forget that in the 1840s only a minimal number of Flemish choirs sang exclusively in their

---

68   Hanssens *jeune*, who in the 1830s cherished Orangist sympathies, was at that moment
      conductor of the *Grande Harmonie* in Brussels and a member of the Académie Royale de
      Belgique.

mother tongue. Only men took part in the three choir festivals, but the choirs sporadically (and increasingly after around 1850) called for female voices when the repertoire demanded them. The choirs liked to venture into the territory of the great oratorios.

Contact with German choirs of superior quality and with works by composers such as Mendelssohn, Marschner, and Schneider was doubtless very stimulating, as were the mutual contacts among Flemish choirs. Most often the choirs consisted of *peers* (e.g., workers from the same branch of industry, university students, students of art schools, former students of a conservatory, members of a German colony, Flemish activists, philantropists, or members of a chamber of rhetoric); but these social and cultural boundaries were crossed at the choir festivals, where everyone met and made music together.

It is striking that after the demise of the *Vlaemsch-Duitsch Zangverbond*, choirs regrouped in other contexts, such as the *Association Royale de Sociétés Lyriques* and the *Union Lyrique Anversoise*, two umbrella organizations founded in Antwerp in 1848. In 1854 Bruges became the seat of the newly established *Belgisch Zangverbond*, grouping choirs from the whole of Flanders "for the organization of annual celebrations devoted to great choral music, after the model of the German lyrical confederations." The German *Musikfeste* remained an important example for part of the Flemish choir scene. They would also remain models for the great choral concerts (often in the open air) and the National Music Festivals that Peter Benoit (1834–1901) was later to organize.

CHAPTER 9

Choral Societies and Nationalist Mobilization in the Basque Country

The Orfeon Donostiarra

Carmen de las Cuevas Hevia

In Spain after 1874 there began a period of Restoration which provided some stability in the state government. At the same time, there was a consolidation of capitalism and its own social groups, while the working class developed in opposition to the capitalist class. Universal male suffrage was introduced in 1890, marking the culmination of an era of fruitful legislative work initiated in 1885, including also the Associations Law, which accommodated the choral societies.

The main social and political events occurred in the industrial regions of the Peninsula, including the beginning of the Basque and Catalan nationalist movements, which involved a large number of choral groups.[1] Some of these choirs were promoted by the power structures as a cultural display of nationalist or regionalist mobilization. Sometimes these choirs took part in national and international choral competitions. Another type of choral society arose from the initiative of groups of workers belonging to various political parties or recreational associations. These choirs were more open and internationalist, and approached relationships with other groups in a social spirit of equality and fraternity.

Despite the different approaches behind the emergence of various choral groups, many of them set forth their non-political and non-religious profiles in their by-laws, which were not amended to maintain good relations with political and ecclesiastical representatives. The choral societies were the heirs of Catholic church choirs which had previously been responsible for providing music for the religious services of the various festivities.

The nationalist movement in the Basque Country involved a combination of elements. On the one hand, the Carlist wars resulted in a loss of economic privileges, followed by an explosion of industrialization and the resulting migrations. The population increased rapidly, generating in the Basque country a middle class which favored the development of a cultural movement to recover their national identity based on language, race, religion, and customs.

---

1 See Labajo (1987).

Specific manifestations of this movement included the Basque Floral Games organized by José Manterola through his magazine *Euskalerria*, with the help of the Regional Council of Gipuzkoa. In 1882 the organization announced as a novelty a musical event to promote the fostering of popular music, offering a special award for the best pot-pourri of Basque tunes. The press remarked that Basque choral competitions should be recognized for their '*Soinu gogoangarriac*' in the same way that the '*Ranz*' of the Swiss, the '*Lieder*' of the Germans and the '*Noëls*' of the French were characteristic expressions of the cultures of these nations.[2]

The port city of San Sebastián was essentially a commercial metropolis where social life was divided between a minority of wealthy individuals and a heterogeneous mass of intermediate layers of non-proletarian condition, with a large number of craftsmen and employed workers who differed from rural laborers.

Cultural and Recreational Societies

The new ruling class was particularly concerned with popular education; they wanted to be able to enjoy the culture previously reserved for the moneyed classes or socially distinguished, and share it with the large masses of workers who swelled the population of areas of industrial and economic development, as was happening elsewhere in Europe at this time. With this aim, they established schools and cultural and recreational societies to promote and provide cultural activities for the disadvantaged. Recreation centres were open during leisure hours to anyone who wished to participate, in accordance with the principles of liberty, equality, and fraternity. The activities of these circles ranged from gatherings and discussions of items in the press to basic activities of instruction and literacy. They also established choral groups or brass bands to liven up meetings, or to perform outdoors at city festivals in squares and boulevards.

The city of San Sebastián pioneered the creation of popular societies for the main purpose of eating and singing.[3] In these popular societies, or along with them, arose countless brass bands and choirs that enlivened and accompanied the most important festivals of the city: the *tamborrada*, the *candelaria*, and the carnival, as well as religious services.

---

2 *El Urumea: Periódico no político* (San Sebastián, 5 June 1879), 1–2.
3 See Aguirre (1983) and Mugica Herzog (1996).

These musical activities always bore the stamp of amateurism, and differed from professional musicians' groups, which occupied different performance spaces in theatres and cafes in the city. The modification of the urban structure in line with the economic development and the increasing population of the city led to the design of open spaces in avenues and boulevards where music kiosks were erected for popular music in the open air.

The main promotor of musical ensembles in San Sebastián was the musician Santesteban (known as *Maisuba*) who brought to this city the ideas of the choral movement of Bocquillon-Wilhem, which resulted in the foundation of the first choral group in the city, the Easonense choir (1866), which was a constant reference for subsequent choral groups like the Choral Society (1886) and the Orfeon Donostiarra (1897), the main subject of this case study.

Along with other institutions, the City Council of San Sebastián worked to promote this type of training in the context of the European choral movement. The City Council provided funds to convene an international choral competition in 1885, awarding the city's own choir, the Choral Society of San Sebastián, a stipend of 2,000 *reales* for training.

The Orfeon Donostiarra

The Orfeon Donostiarra was founded in response to a request from the Consistory of the Basque Floral Games (*Consistorio de Juegos Florales Euskaros*). This Consistory of the city was sympathetic to the recovery of the Basque cultural tradition, particularly its music and language. Accordingly, in its first artistic phase the Orfeon had a specific repertoire of popular Basque tunes as well as popular songs of the choral tradition that were translated into Euskera.

Probably all of these founders of the Orfeon Donostiarra had gained experience in some of the previous choirs developed in the city: the Easonense choir, the Municipal choir, and/or the Choral Society of San Sebastián. Their professions included many different trades, as we can see from the list of the members of the first Board of the Orfeon Donostiarra, established on 21 January 1897: the first Chairman was a printer, the Vice-President a professor of physical education, the Secretary a City Hall employee, the Treasurer a bank employee, the Archivist a finance clerk, and among the board members were a bodybuilder and a plumber.

Unlike its predecessor the Choral Society of San Sebastián, which was chaired by the Marquis of Cubas and had the pianist Leo Silke (the Marquis of Rocaverde) as honorary chairman, the first Board of the Orfeon was not composed of eminent personalities. The Orfeon was chiefly created in order to promote the recovery and fostering of Basque music. Its name was: *Sociedad coral Euskara* (Basque Choral Society) 'Orfeon Donostiarra,' as specified in the first Article of its regulations: "This Society was founded on 17 December 1896, and its primary aims are the promotion and propagation of Basque music by all the means at its disposal..." The Orfeon was different from other previous and contemporary groups, which only reflected in their rules a dedication to vocal music, without specifying the type of repertoire.

Among the Orfeon members two main groups can be distinguished: on the one hand the patrons, who helped to maintain the society financially, and on the other the singing members. The Orfeon was a group of amateur singers, with or without musical training, who attended rehearsals and performances of the Choral Society for the purpose of singing and learning new pieces, in order to perform them in concerts and at public or religious events.

The Choir of San Sebastián went through various stages throughout its hundred-year history, but we will focus here on the choir as a chorus of male voices from its foundation in 1897 until 1909, a period in which it can be related more closely to nationalist mobilization. This period can be further divided into two stages: a first, founding phase (1896–1901) and a second stage involving participation in Orfeon competitions (1902–09).

The Orfeon Donostiarra's first singers met and received institutional support to prepare a repertoire of Basque songs to be performed in the Fiestas Euskaras in Mondragón on 6 and 7 July 1896, organized by the Consistory of Floral Games of Gipuzkoa. Other performances followed, in Mondragón and elsewhere in Gipuzkoa. The remaining activities of this period took place in the city of San Sebastián, in public spaces and in religious services.

After meetings and discussions, the appointment of the Orfeon's first conductor (the professional musician Miguel Oñate) was terminated in 1901, in view of the lack of understanding between himself and the choir.[4] In 1902 the Board proposed as the new director of the Orfeon the conductor Secundino Esnaola, who had previously worked with the Choral Society of San Sebastián. The new director would modify and extend the lines and artistic ways of the Choir. The first seven years were spent preparing the choirs to participate in choral competitions both nationally and internationally. These contests were in fashion at the time, and were not only a musical test but also a competition between the towns and cities represented by the choirs that participated in them.

---

4   See De las Cuevas Hevia (1996).

In 1904 the Orfeon Donostiarra took part in the Concours d'Orphéons in Royan, France. Here the group's profile would change. It was no longer a matter of singing a repertoire of popular songs to liven up parties and out-ings; here they had to prepare for competition with other choirs, to sight-read works composed especially for these events, and to master choral music with characteristics and dimensions very different from those of the folk repertoire. Some of the compositions written for the French *orphéonistes* (Adolphe Adam, Laurent de Rillé, and Dard Janin) can still be heard nowadays in San Sebastián at special events of the Gastronomic Societies *Gaztelupe* and *Gaztelubide*, as examples of the legacy of the Orphéonic movement.

The City Council of San Sebastián again approved financial support for the Orfeon to go to these international competitions. The Orfeon issued appeals through the press calling on singers to join their ranks, which would soon be composed of more than a hundred voices.[5]

Performance Spaces

The Orfeon had a wide and varied number of performance spaces in which it presented music programs, without a regular venue as occurred in other parts of Europe. Popular festivals were typical settings for the early Orfeon Donostiarra. Generally these were outdoor performances at a kiosk or pub-lic square, and for a broad audience, with free access. The programs were popular, and could be accompanied by an instrumental ensemble, a band or a brass band.

They also performed music for religious services such as those to celebrate the patron of musicians, Santa Cecilia, in November, or the celebration of San Sebastián in January, or the celebrations of the Virgin on 14 and 15 August.

Competitions and festivals confronted the choirs not only with different physical spaces but with a different kind of musical space, since they were singing in competition or combination with other choirs. Public events con-sisted of performances in places where there was an official opening or event. The repertoire did not reach the category of a concert; only some illustrations accompanied the songs and were selected in accordance with the type of event.

---

5   Ibid.

CHAPTER 10

Choral Societies and Nationalist Mobilization in Catalonia, 1850–1930

Dominique Vidaud

How could an activity as apparently harmless as choral singing become in Catalonia a very strong vector of identity that contributed significantly to the emergence of a national culture starting from 1891, the date of the foundation of the Orfeó Català? How, at the end of the nineteenth century, did a regional culture that cultivated the Catalan personality without questioning its allegiance to the Spanish community change into an exclusively national culture? Why was Catalan society enthralled by a repertoire that widely referred to the past and idealized Catalonia, with no real links to its everyday life? Who were the actors in what came to be called the 'choral movement,' and what motivated them? On what support for resistance was Catalan choral singing able to rely in such a movement, while in the rest of Spain, except for the Basque Country and Galicia, such activity attracted far less attention?

Three Rival Federations of Choirs

The first choral society in Catalonia, La Fraternidad, was created in 1850 by Josep Anselm Clavé. In 1857 its name was changed to Euterpe and it was quickly emulated. An association called the Asociación Euterpense was created to organize festivals in Barcelona and broadcast Clavé's work by means of a periodical, *El Eco de Euterpe*, which become a weekly in 1863 under the name of *El Metrónomo*. By 1864, at the fourth festival of Euterpe, there were some 2,000 choir-singers and eighty-four societies in Catalonia.

The death of Clavé in 1874 marked the beginning of a period of decline for the Association, which carried on the repertoire created by its founder until it split in 1886 with the creation of the Asociación de los Coros de Clavé. A reunification occurred in 1901, followed by a new split in 1915. The Clavérian movement still exists today, carried on by the Federación de los Coros de Clavé.

In 1891, a new type of choir was created in Barcelona by Lluís Millet i Bagès and Amadeu Vives: the Orfeó Català. Although it invoked the legacy of Clavé, its innovative repertoire was open to traditional songs and to new works by young musicians such as Francesc Alió, Antoni Nicolau, or Lluís Millet himself, based on poems written by their contemporaries. Unlike the Choirs of Clavé, the Orfeó Català was mixed, and on this model eighty-eight Orpheon groups developed and federated in 1917 under the name of Germanor dels Orfeons de Catalunya.

The Clavérian choirs had performed extracts from *Tannhäuser* since 1862, but the Orfeó Català was the first choral group to undertake an ambitious repertoire by interpreting for the first time in Spain such vocally complex works as J.S. Bach's *Mass in B minor* or the *Magnificat*, the *Requiem* of Hector Berlioz, the *Ninth Symphony* and *Missa Solemnis* of Beethoven, Handel's *Messiah*, and *Les Béatitudes* by César Franck. Some Orpheons were even more ambitious, such as the Orfeó Gracienc, which performed difficult works by Liszt, Brahms, Kodaly, and Stravinsky.

In 1895 a third choral society, Catalunya Nova, was founded by Enric Morera, who four years later, in 1899, created the Federació dels Cors Catalans, which remained very active until the early 1920s and often took part in the cycle of Festes Modernistes organized by the painter Santiago Rusiñol at Sitges, a small sea-side resort close to Barcelona. Its repertoire was based on the works of Clavé and numerous traditional songs harmonized by Morera, but also included songs which Morera composed for poems by his friends E. Guanyabens, I. Iglesias, and A. Guimerà.

The Spread of Choral Societies in the Catalan Area

Creating a reliable database of choral societies is difficult because sources are not always reliable and the results are often contradictory. In the case of the Choirs of Clavé, the newspaper of the main Association, *L'Aurora*, makes it possible to compile a list of affiliated choirs at the end of every year when subscriptions were renewed. But there were numerous splits in the Clavérian movement after the death of its founder in 1874: in 1886, the old Asociación Euterpense was challenged by the creation of the Asociación de los Coros de Clavé. A reunification in 1901 gave birth to the Asociación Euterpense de los Coros de Clavé, but in 1915 a new split appeared that would finally be resolved only in 1936. The total number of Clavérian choirs is therefore difficult to determine precisely except for the period 1901–1915, when it varied from 158 to 171, reflecting the flux of registrations and lapses. The year 1924—the fiftieth anniversary of Clavé's death—appears to mark the high point of the Clavérian movement, with a peak of 171 listed choirs.

The situation is clearer in the case of the Orpheons because there were no splits within the association; the Germanor dels Orfeons de Catalunya was created in 1918 to group together the fifty-two choirs created since 1891 on the model founded by Millet. Several people strongly connected to the Orfeó Català served in the permanent council of the Association from 1918 till 1931, that is, from the first to the last assembly of the Association. As Pere Artis i Benach reminds us, the numbers of Orpheons represented at the three assemblies of 1918, 1920, and 1931 varied,[1] which suggests that if some groups appeared after 1920, others could have disappeared before 1931 (the dictatorship of Primo de Rivera from 1924 to 1931 had an impact on certain societies connected to Catalanism, even on the right wing).

There were apparently fifty-two Orpheons in 1918, seventy-five in 1920, and sixty-three in 1931. However, to give a complete image of the real spread of the Orpheonic movement, it seems preferable to count choirs at their peak (in 1920) by adding those present in 1918 and 1931, whose absence from the assembly in Vic was presumably only momentary and not a sign that they had ceased to exist. This method produces a total figure of eighty-seven choirs, or a little more than half the number of the Choirs of Clavé, which is surprising since the Clavérian sphere of influence was often considered, by its contemporaries as well as by historians of the choral movement, as decadent compared to the supposedly much more dynamic Orphéonism.

Massive population increases privileged the eastern regions of Catalonia, especially the urban areas. A map of Orpheons and Choirs of Clavé indicating the number of choral societies by district in 1924 shows that out of forty districts, only seven had no choral society: these were in the regions most remote from Barcelona, and the most rural ones. The region of Barcelona and its surroundings, the Barcelonès, was dominant with fifty-three permanent choirs, while the western Vallès (with Terrassa and Sabadell, two major industrial areas) followed with twenty-six. The less industrialized districts close to this nucleus followed, with between ten and twenty choirs each: the oriental Vallès, the Maresme, the Baix Llobregat, the Alt Penedès, and the Bagès. Then, with between five and ten choirs, came districts that were more distant but included important cities such as Tarragona and Gérone (with 23,000 and 15,000 inhabitants respectively in 1900), and industrialized regions such as the Anoia (Igualada) and the Osona (Vic). Certain areas (the Berguedà and the Ripollès, the Garrigues, the Urgell, and la Selva) look like exceptions to this pattern: less heavily industrialized and with no important cities, they nonetheless gave rise to a considerable number of choirs.

Everywhere else choirs were less numerous and were concentrated in small urban areas (with 2,000 to 5,000 inhabitants) or large villages (of between

---

1 Artis i Benach (1980), 75–79.

500 and 2,000 inhabitants). There was one big surprise: the inclusion of a large rural city in the choral landscape: Lleida (with 21,500 inhabitants in 1900).

Of the total of 231 cities or villages with choirs, thirty-eight (or 16%) had two coexisting networks, representing both the Choirs of Clavé and brass bands, sometimes with several groups. This was the case in Barcelona naturally, but also in the western Vallès, the valley of Llobregat, and the cities of the Maresme; a group to the North which connected Berga, Ripoll, Olot and Figueras; and a group to the West which connected Tarragona with Lleida. In these privileged places for choral singing, it seems that coexistence was a source of rivalry and mutual challenge, but joint concerts were not rare, especially after 1917. Thus two choral societies could be found even in villages of from 1,300 to 2,500 inhabitants.

This proliferation can be explained by several factors: economic, political, and in terms of human resources. The economic link with industrialization is evident, the Choirs of Clavé having served initially as 'surrogate communities' for the uprooted workers of Barcelona. The phenomenon then spread to other industrial areas, including the rural workshops, because the message of Clavé was encouraged by paternalistic employers. The Orpheons, on the other hand, recruited later among the rapidly growing middle classes (unprecedented in the rest of Spain) who identified all the more easily with the choral movement as they were themselves in search of identity.

Although the choral societies embodied rival political projects, they shared a common character because their singing could serve as an expression of resistance. Republican federalism, conservative Catalanism, and progressive Catalanism all found in these choirs important vectors for their projection into the national area, even if, in their internal statutes, the societies asserted their non-political character. As Emilio S. Pastor expressed it:

> Thanks to the musical education of the Catalan people, we could see the development of a political ideology through singing which would never have been possible in another region of Spain. Thanks to the replacement of the club by the concert hall, what had been a doctrine of cultured persons spread to the masses.[2]

The choral societies were often founded by natives of small towns or villages who lived or trained in Barcelona before returning to their native regions. The importance of these teachers and choirmasters for the development of choral singing partially explains the role of Barcelona as a major center of impulse.

---

2   Pastor (1899), 18.

The Choirs of Clavé in Industrial Catalonia

According to Jaume Carbonell i Guberna, choral societies first appeared in Catalonia outside Barcelona in cities where the process of industrialization was strongest: in Gràcia, Sants, Hostafrancs, and Sant Martí in the suburbs of Barcelona; farther out, in the industrial areas of the Vallès such as Sabadell, Terrassa, and Granollers; farther still, in the productive centres of central Catalonia like Igualada, Manresa or the valley of Llobregat; and finally very far, in Berga, Vilafranca del Penedès, Girona, or Tarragona.[3] There were almost no choral societies in most of the rural districts of the western half.

Clavérian societies prospered especially in the industrialized regions and recruited essentially among the workers of the heavy textile industry or in the more modest workshops of the rural villages. In 1940 the membership list of the Clavérian company Euterpe shows mostly men of modest occupations (some of whom had been members since 1899!): painters, tanners, laborers, shoemakers, carpenters, tapestry-makers, watchmakers, lathe operators, electricians, business employees, fishermen, mechanics, chauffeurs, railroad employees, and electrical engineers. There were very few women, but from the end of the century women do appear in certain choirs of Clavé; they were often unemployed, but included a hairdresser, a student, a seamstress, and a milliner.

The Clavérians were not only choral societies but also clubs offering leisure, where collective singing was an essential but not a unique activity: there were also sections for dancing, games, and sometimes mutual help. An article in the bulletin *L'Aurora* provides the following analysis:

> Why did the choral societies spread and take root so much in Catalonia while they barely existed in the other regions of Spain? ...
>
> It is in the economic situation of our people that we need to look for the causes of the exuberant life shown in the choral societies. The laborious, sober and thrifty Catalan worker saw in the choral societies an adequate means to satisfy his appetite for leisure without giving up his virtues: it cost him only a réal a week to be a member of the society. With this réal, he paid the maestro who conducted the choir, paid the rent of the premises where they met, acquired the vocal scores, etc.
>
> As he had two or three weekly rehearsals plus a meeting, he visited the premises of the society at least three or four evenings a week. In addition, for thirteen pesetas a year, he could attend concerts, outings, and theatre performances accompanied by his wife and children. Furthermore, if the

---

3 Carbonell i Guberna (1994), 71.

choir-singer paid an extra subscription fee to cover the expenses of these artistic outings, it wouldn't exceed two réals a week, or twenty-six pesetas a year; but during these outings, the choir-singer would pay nothing else because the revenue from concerts and donations was sufficient!

Thus, the choral societies constituted an adequate means for the labourer to be able to make the most of an affordable entertainment and a cultural enrichment.[4]

The society was thus intended above all to create social links, and the gathering place, at least in the early days, was often the back-room of a café in the village or the urban district, as was the case for the Unió Santcugatenca when it was founded in 1900. Not until 1913 did this group have its own premises, the property of the members, a vast ground-floor room with a café-bar and billiard table, followed in 1924 by a permanent headquarters built by fund-raising, including a concert hall with 1,000 seats, a billiard room, a café, a dance floor, a library, and a conference room. Along with its choral activity, the society could boast of a dance section in 1906, with a cinema section added in 1918, a drama section in 1923, an 'artistic impulse for youth' group in 1924, a society of mutual help in 1924, a music section in 1928, and a chess section in 1929. It thus played a major part in the civic and cultural life of Sant Cugat, according to Climent Ribera i Villanueva and Joan Auladell in their study of this small choral society, La Unió Santcugatenca.

The Associacion Euterpense dels Cors de Clavé was very proud to count among its members choral societies located in other provinces of Spain. When one critic denounced the lack of patriotic feeling in the Choirs of Clavé, he was answered as follows by Eusebi Benages: "It is false to claim that our Association is Catalan, given that, by welcoming societies of various provinces, it is on the contrary highly Spanish!"[5] Clavé Choirs existed also in Saragossa, Madrid, Palma and Valencia.

The Orpheons and Catalanist Nationalism

The Orphéonic movement grew rapidly, probably because membership in a choral society of this type was in itself a sign of strong political commitment: from 1898, Orphéonism became one of the main vectors of Catalanism. With

---

4   Anonymous, "The choral societies from the point of view of the economy of the worker," *L'Aurora*, 1 March 1896. This and all other translations are by the author.
5   Benages (1899), 6.

the crisis of the Spanish state aggravated by the defeat in Cuba, the last psycho-logical barriers that had kept many Catalans from participating in the move-ment were lifted.

Some 145 Orpheons were created between 1891 and 1934: thirty-four appeared between 1891 and 1908, fifty-four from 1909 to 1917 (the peak period), and another fifty-seven between 1918 and 1934. It was thus a mass phenomenon that numbered approximately 10,000 singers by 1931. This geographic expan-sion started in Barcelona, then spread to the main towns of the surrounding districts: Manresa, Sabadell, Vilafranca del Penedès, Reus, Olot and Terrassa, and naturally Lleida, Girona and Tarragona. After 1900, choirs were formed in villages like El Vendrell, Besalú, La Garriga, Cardedeu, Masllorenç, Falset, Sitges, Palafrugell, etc. Very often, natives of these cities and villages founded new Orpheons while living in Barcelona.

The differences between the growth of the Orpheons and that of the Choirs of Clavé are not obvious: the Orpheons were more widely scattered in the Catalan area, but less prevalent in the most industrialized regions and more common in the rural districts of the North and West.

In 1980 Pere Artis i Benach compiled a set of index cards listing singers who had joined the Orfeó Català between 1898 and 1915.[6] Out of sixty-one entries, there were thirty shopkeepers, four cabinetmakers, four businessmen, three shoe-shop managers, two tailors, two sculptors, two printers, one teacher, two laborers, three carpenters, one picture framer, one tile-layer, one watchmaker, one gilder, one confectioner, and two salesmen. The difference from the Choirs of Clavé is huge, especially given that the first singers of the Orfeó had presum-ably received a bourgeois education if they could sight-read a score. The social composition of the Orpheons was thus dominated by the middle classes.

The Germanor of the Orpheons of Catalonia

In 1917 the Orphéonic movement was restructured with the foundation of a Federation encompassing all the orpheons: La 'Germanor' (Fraternity) of the Orpheons of Catalonia. The aim was to hold group events through regional gatherings and encourage the spread of Catalan choir music. On 23 and 24 June 1918, during the Germanor Assembly held in Manresa, the main direc-tors of the Orpheons, Lluís Millet, Francesc Pujol, and Joan Llongueras, gave speeches encouraging the artistic, economic, and social life of choir insti-tutions. The second assembly took place in Vic in 1920 with the support of

---

6   Artis i Benach (1980), 63.

seventy-six choir institutions; and the third and last assembly took place in 1931 in Manresa with a total of fifty organizations present. A year before, in 1930, a solemn ceremony of the Germanor was held in the Barcelona Olympic Stadium to celebrate the end of the dictatorship of Primo de Rivera despite political tensions between republican power and the representatives of the Germanor. Between meetings, the life of the Germanor consisted of regional gatherings, the "Festes de Germanor" that were held in Manresa (1918 and 1931), Vic (1921), Figueres (1922), and Reus (1923).

Different Venues for Choral Societies

Concerts were organized in theaters, cultural centers, and, in the biggest cities, at the Opera. Lluís Millet recalled one concert at the grand Theater of Liceu, the Barcelona Opera, on 30 March 1901:

> When we came to the Liceu, we had some fears.... Everything there was new: theater and public ... composed of elements totally unaware of the Orfeó which, when there was no comedy on the stage, were usually yawning with boredom.... We gave them humble songs of the Land which must have shocked the lovers of opera melodies ...[7]

The competitions apparently shared space with other types of music, orchestral or vocal, except when the halls were fitted out by the societies themselves. The case of the Orfeó Català is exemplary, with the construction, by popular subscription, of the Palace of Catalan Music from 1907 onwards.

It is difficult to estimate the share of these concerts in the musical offerings of that time. What is certain is that choral singing found its place, musically speaking, somewhere between popular music (zarzuelas, flamenco shows, music hall) and classical music (operas or symphonic music). The rivalry between popular music of Castilian or Andalusian origin and Catalan popular songs appears to have favored the former in the two last decades of the nineteenth century: according to Joan-Lluís Marfany, two-thirds of the advertisements in the Barcelona press dealt with the '*genero chico*,' a mixture of Castellan zarzuelas, popular songs, and arias borrowed from Italian opera.[8]

Churches offered another kind of specialized venue, mainly for concerts of sacred music, which was fervently promoted by the Orpheonic movement

---

7   Millet i Bagès (1917), 19.
8   Marfany (1992), 313.

and also by the Catalanist and conservative leaders. For holidays (Caramelles, Carnestoltes, Festes Majors), the main square of the village or the district would be requisitioned. In Barcelona, the Place of Catalonia was often used for commemorations and anniversaries (such as the tribute to Lluís Millet in 1917 on the occasion of the twenty-fifth anniversary of the Orfeó Català).

During their tours, the choral societies observed an immutable ritual which involved, as soon as they arrived, giving a first informal concert in front of the City Hall located on the main square. Countless pictures show the Orfeó Català in the midst of a huge crowd which fills the whole public space, a particularly impressive image of a fusion between the population and the singers.

There were also more surprising venues, including bullfight arenas and stadiums (such as the stadium of Montjuich where 5,000 chorus-singers met in 1930, conducted by Lluís Millet). In 1897 the Tarragona arenas hosted a contest of choral societies where the Choirs of Clavé and the society Catalunya Nova (led by Enric Morera) competed in their interpretations of compositions by Clavé that Morera wanted to modernize and Catalanize.

Finally there are *lieux de mémoire* that became places of pilgrimage for the politically committed choral societies, such as the statue of Clavé on the Rambla de Catalunya (for example, in 1924, for the fiftieth anniversary of his death), or the statue of Rafael Casanova (a martyr to the resistance of Barcelona against the troops of Philip v) built in 1888, which became a central place for nationalist gatherings. Despite recurring incidents until the beginning of the twentieth century, the Catalanists sang "Els Segadors" in front of the statue to commemorate the *Diada*, which finally became a national holiday in 1980.

The Palace of Catalan Music, Symbol of the Orpheonic Project

According to Ignasí de Solà-Morales,

> Culturally, the Barcelona of the end of the century was a Wagnerian city, a society seeking to save itself from industrialism and the loss of its national roots through Art. . . . The work of L. Domènech i Muntaner corresponds to the project of architecture as a comprehensive work of art.[9]

The Palau de la Música Catalana built in 1908 is one of the most symbolic modernistic buildings of Barcelona. Ordered by the Orfeó Català and financed by fund-raising, it became the prestigious headquarters of Catalan choral high

---

9   Solà-Morales (1992), 39.

society. Thanks to the use of very advanced techniques for the time (a metal structure and transparent façades which allow for removal of the walls of the classic theater à l'italienne and an unprecedented play of light), an ample and harmonious space was created without discontinuity between the stage and the auditorium. The ceramic and stained glass on all the inner walls reflects the immense glass chandelier that takes up all the central part of the ceiling of the auditorium. The Palace of Catalan Music was thus transformed, thanks to natural light or the electricity fairy, into a colorful area of twinkling reflections. As Solà-Morales observed: "We are looking at a building designed for collective use of the greatest architectonic subtlety, but also one of the most symbolic of social choralism which the architecture of the end of the century produced, as a sign full of hope at the dawn of new times."[10]

The Musical Project of the Orfeó Català

The Catalan identity of the Palace is signalled by many symbols: the emblem of the Orfeó (an escutcheon with four blood-red vertical bars on a field of gold), the mountains of Montserrat, birds, and the Cross of Sant Jordi. These ornamental items also signify the amalgamation of Wagnerian, Romantic and Clavérian cults: busts of Beethoven and Wagner are joined by a statue of Clavé outside; a horde of walkyries seem to fall from the ceiling onto the stage; Greek muses decorate an entire wall; and ornamental subjects from the repertoire of Clavé and a general medieval atmosphere evoke the Catalan Renaissance.

As Ernest Gellner notes, "Nationalism is, essentially, the general imposition of a high culture on society, where previously low cultures had taken up the lives of the majority...of the population."[11] For the Catalanist project of the Orfeó Català, the will to unite high and low culture is evident, along with the legacy of Clavé and the effort to create a national music.

Itinerant Societies: Excursions, Festivals, and Competitions

The Catalan choral societies often travelled within Catalonia. In the context of charitable exchanges, the Orpheons and Choirs of Clavé organized frequent excursions, which sometimes triggered ironic comments about their immoderate taste for contests and honors, or their inclination to take inexpensive

---

10   Ibid., 146.
11   Gellner (1983), 57.

trips to the detriment of purely musical goals. These complaints were directed mostly at the Choirs of Clavé, but the whole choral movement was involved. The federations also organized excursions that mixed the members of various choirs. The creation of the Germanor dels Orfeons de Catalunya was the result of a huge choral gathering in Barcelona in 1917, followed by several others, in Manresa, Terrassa, and Vic, until 1931.

Finally, there were more remote expeditions, into Spain and beyond its borders. The Orfeó Català was the most itinerant group, given its exceptional status as ambassador of Catalan music during the domination of the Lliga Regionalista on the political scene in Catalonia from 1905 to 1917. Prestigious trips to London and Paris in 1914, and then to Latin America, were financed mainly by the Mancommunitat de Catalunya, directed by a friend of Lluís Millet, Francesc Cambó.

A detailed examination of the trips of each society reveals diverse strategies to conquer, or at least to occupy the national territory. All of them benefitted from the rapid expansion of the railway network in Catalonia between 1870 and 1920, and from the social networks created by the choral associations to multiply the town-to-town exchanges. Yet each choral society had different goals during these trips.

The Choirs of Clavé organized exchanges that often forged links of friendship between choral groups: for instance, Jordi Morant pointed out that between 1891 and 1912, the choir L'Ancora from Tarragona travelled to Espluga de Francoli (a small town located in the district of Conca de Barbera) four times, almost as often as they visited Barcelona. They also organized major tours open to all the societies of the Association: trips to France in 1899, 1914, and 1922 allowed hundred of choir members from all Catalonia to visit Béziers, Narbonne, Nîmes, Marseille, Nice, Lyon, and Paris. They participated in competitions, and also traveled widely within Spain: Asturias, Cantabria, Andalucía, Castilla, and of course Madrid were visited regularly by the Choirs of Clavé, which probably reflected their attachment to a united Spain, even if some leaders like Eusebi Bages preferred the Republican option to the monarchy restored in 1874.

The Orpheons were often more willing to travel up and down the national land, even to very remote towns, as shown by the story of the Orfeó Català expedition to Camprodon (transcribed below). The Orfeó Gracienc was also a good example of the Barcelona choirs with a high musical level which, under the guidance of their director Joan Balcells, multiplied their Catalan excursions: forty-nine trips between 1905 and 1931, an average of two trips a year. The wish to impact the whole Catalan community strongly influenced the Orfeó Català with its sixty-one trips, along with ten 'foreign' trips between 1891 and 1931: to France (Nice in 1879, where the Orfeó received an award, then Marseille,

Montpellier, and finally Paris in 1914), the United Kingdom, Italy (Rome in 1925, during Primo de Rivera's rule), and Spain (Madrid, Valencia, Sevilla and Córdoba). These trips took on proportions that can hardly be imagined nowadays, with huge gatherings and concerts that looked like patriotic celebrations, ending with the audience and the choirs together singing "Els Segadors" and "El Cant de la Senyera."

In contrast, the choral society Catalunya Nova appeared a sorry sight: despite the charismatic personality and the musical skills of its director Enric Morera, it could never compete with its rivals, who were better organized and had more powerful political support. Morera's anchoring in liberal Catalanism gave him interesting aesthetic perspectives, including Modernism, with the complicity of the painter Santiago Rusiñol, who often invited Catalunya Nova to Modernist gatherings in Sitges in the last years of the nineteenth century. The fourteen trips the choir took between 1895 and 1908 to working-class towns close to Barcelona, and above all the failure of a trip to Paris because of the lack of political support, must have disappointed the fiery director, who after 1901 dedicated himself almost exclusively to musical composition.

The Orfeó Català: A Typical Trip

The trip by the Orfeó Català to Camprodón in 1899 was described by Lluís Millet:

> The arrival in Camprodón was typical and a new thing for us. A crowd of people welcomed us with cries of joy; Children with red hats jumping up and down greeted us with twigs of green branches. Richly dressed heralds on horseback escorted the welcoming committee organizing the holiday, accompanied by tourists from Barcelona.
>
> We went amidst a great flood of people up to the square, in front of the city hall, where we sang "El Cant de la Senyera"; the mayor welcomed us from his balcony. Then we continued in procession to go and greet the priest. By then it was pitch dark. There, at the door of the church, four or five priests awaited us. The excitement suddenly stopped; lanterns illuminated the old walls of the church, giving a solemn color to this moment. The priest broke the silence by welcoming us with simple and sincere words; we then sang two traditional songs.
>
> Then we went to greet Doctor Robert, then mayor of Barcelona, who was in Camprodón to forget the worries such responsibilities were causing him. He greeted us with a patriotic speech; down from his manor house, it was pleasant to hear him talk about Ripoll, about some Pyrenean

parts of the country where the Catalan sap stays pure as the snow of the very high mountains; only then can we feel Catalan, that's why our songs sounded free and powerful, saying: oh Pyrenees, we are still your sons!

Then, we start singing "Els Segadors" in this pure air which Jofres and Tallaferros, the fathers of the free, strong, and honored Catalonia, our unique homeland, had inhaled.

That same evening, we gave a concert at the Casino. The premises were not big, but they were fully packed. We sang traditional songs, Clavé, and even "Aucellada" by C. Jannequin. The great opera singer Mrs. Wehrle sang, with her usual good taste, songs by García Robles and me. She was much applauded.

But the most beautiful memory of our stay in this Pyrenean valley was the following evening in Vernetar. From there, we dominated all the city surrounded by close summits and the river Ter. An orchestra played a sardana. Night fell. We sang "Flors de Maig"; the voices sound odd in the solemn peace of open nature. The soft melody and the simple harmony of Clavé were in harmony with the shades of the sunset; our spirits rose up, and a feeling of peace enraptured us.

Surprised by the effect produced, we sang "The Emigrant": "Sweet Catalonia, homeland of my heart!" There she was, our mother so sweet! Stroking our forehead with the pure air of the mountains, thoughtful and letting us share her dreams. We had them, those high Pyrenees just over our heads, raised, huge. Oh, strong sap of nature! Oh, sap of the Homeland! Oh, poetry of the soul!

At night, there were sardanas in tribute to Orfeó, and we all danced. We held hands with the people of the country and they guided us; mountain and city hats were together in this big circular dance, because we are all the sons of the same mother.

The following morning, Holy Mary's Day, at the service we sang the "Mass of Pope Marcello" by Palestrina. In the afternoon, there was a gathering in Can Moy and the celebration was even more popular than the day before, and less poetic... but what a lively celebration! And how good it was to be among these mountaineers who danced and danced without ever getting tired! Friends, that's living! Near the river we sang "Flors de Maig" and, I think, also "El Cant de la Senyera"; all around us, the farmers escorted us enthusiastically.

In the evening, we gave the last concert. The success was enormous. After the concert, it must have been one o'clock in the morning, we ate a little, and at three o'clock we left the Casino to go catch the horse-drawn carriages that would take us back to Sant Joan, where the earliest train for Barcelona was waiting for us. Then, spontaneously, we did a very original dance: all in a circle, as a finale to our beautiful stay in Camprodón, we went through the streets of the city singing "Els Segadors" and repeating endlessly the Catalan anthem. People came out on their balconies in white nightdress (there are always some who sleep!). On the main square, in spite of the late hour, there were still cries of enthusiasm. We kissed the organizers of this trip who had been so kind to us, taking with us into our carriages the happy memories that life can give us.[12]

A Choral Repertoire to Build the Nation

The songs most frequently performed by various choirs between 1891 and 1931 can be surveyed from the concert programmes of the Orfeó Català (several hundred of them), the magazines of various town bands (the *Revista de l'Orfeó Gracienc*, for example), the concert notices of various associations of the Coros de Clavé in the newspaper *L'Aurora* during this entire period, and the concert programmes of the choir Catalunya Nova recorded in the magazine of the same name between 1896 and 1919. In total, more than 200 vocal pieces are registered in the repertoires for all the choirs.

Songs were composed for male or mixed choirs after 1890: at a conference held in 1917 on Popular Catalan Songs, Lluís Millet distinguished several genres: pastoral songs, love songs, marching songs, lullabies, Christmas and religious songs, work songs, prose songs, and legends. There are dozens in the repertories of different choirs, but only some thirty songs appear frequently in the concert programmes.

These songs possess a fundamental ambiguity, as they were re-written by folklorists of the Renaixança who, as was the case throughout Europe in the mid-nineteenth century, were concerned about safeguarding 'popular traditions' as the industrial revolution, particularly pronounced in Catalonia after 1830, was supplanting traditional rural culture. Their works, in particular the collection of rural popular songs, facilitated a return to the origins of the 'Catalan soul' with its legends and pure language (unlike urban Catalan, which was 'contaminated by Castilian').

Pau Piferrer i Fàbregas was the first to collect traditional songs at the end of the 1830s, followed by Marià Aguiló, who published the first *Cançoner* of Majorcan songs but became known chiefly for his *El romançer popular de la terra catalana* (1893), and by Francesc Pelau Briz, who in 1866 produced the first series of *Cançons de la terra*, with the fifth and last series published ten

---

12   Millet i Bagès (1917), 14–17.

years later. In 1882 Manuel Milà i Fontanals compiled the most complete collection entitled *Romancerillo catalán: Canciones tradicionales*, gathering 523 songs and their variants.

As Joan-Lluís Marfany reminds us in *La cultura del catalanisme*, a new generation of folklorists emerged, due to the growth of the touring choirs in the years between 1880 and 1890, which proposed to "promote a positive knowledge of the country and its many aspects, and establish a love for the image of Catalonia created by the Renaixança."[13] In 1891 the Centre Excursionista de Catalunya was formed, whose principal objective, as outlined in an article in its first press release, was "to take part in a peaceful Catalan crusade with folklore and the natural, historical and geographical sciences ... to improve this land that we love so much."[14] The Orfeó Català extended this folkloristic work, and several musicians, guided by Francesc Pujol, continued the collection which was completed in 1926 with the publication of *L'Obra del Cançoner Popular de Catalunya*.

As the composer and great ethnomusicologist Felip Pedrell noted, the ethno-musicians who gathered, assessed, and classified these traditional songs often lacked any real musical competence, and proceeded to sort the songs into those they considered authentic and those that were not; the notion of 'authenticity' was confused not only by national considerations and those of ethnic purity, but also by the strictly aesthetic interest of the music.[15] It was even possible that a certain moralism caused some songs to be favored over others: in fact, the objective of the Revival was not simply to recreate the world as it was but as it should have been. With the notable exception of Cels Gomis, linked to the progressive republican movement, the Catalonian folklorists were all representatives and active agents of a conservative and Catholic ideology which called for the social and moral regeneration of Catalonia through 'faith, history, art and tradition' in accordance with the renaixantist formula.

As they saw it, the mission of the folklorists was to discover the original purity of corrupted cultural products and to reconstitute objects perverted by popular usage. It is therefore important not to confuse the terms 'popular' and 'traditional' precisely because the folklorists imposed a re-interpreted culture often by marginalizing rival expressions of Catalan culture, in particular those of popular culture.

J.A. Clavé produced a corpus of about thirty songs for male voice, forming a group apart in popular choral music. These include long poems composed

---

13   Marfany (1992), 312.
14   Ibid., 300.
15   Pedrell (1906), 11.

between 1850 and 1873 which focus on everyday work, pastoral images, patriotic hymns, or songs that pay homage to typical Catalonian traditions. These choral pieces were for the most part to be sung *a cappella*, but some of them, composed from later European dance rhythms (polkas, valses, mazurkas), were performed with an orchestra. Clavé thus managed to revive a popular lyrical tradition in forms such as refrains, bagatelles, serenades, and in particular the old French *pastourelles* which emerged in the Middle Ages, by exceptionally combining tradition and innovation, thus enabling him to create an updated historical memory. As J. Llongueras, a musician and teacher of the Orfeó Català, acknowledged in his tribute to the Maestro in 1924 on the hundredth anniversary of his birth in 1924: "Clavé has written a simple music but one that is Catalonian in sentiment, character, ideas and form; he had the indisputable ingenuity to initiate and reveal in a succinct and definitive manner the existence of a Catalonian musical nationality that will reach maturity later."[16]

The heart of the repertoire consisted of about 125 lyrical pieces composed for poems by well-known authors such as the priest Jacint Verdaguer (twenty-one poems), Joan Maragall, Emili Guanyabens, Angel Guimerà (a dozen poems each), and by young musicians who were highly influenced by the melodious lines of traditional songs, such as Eric Morera (twenty-seven songs alone!), or composers related to the orpheonic scene, among them Lluís Millet, Anton Nicolau, Francesc Pujol, Felip Pedrell, Joan Balcells (with between five and ten compositions each). For these composers, the desire to create a truly Catalan music meant satisfying stringent requirements: namely following the traditional song model while also developing new artistic modes of art music. According to Enric Morera, the result was not always conclusive:

> Having grown up in Argentina with the popular songs of this country, but also nurtured in Brussels on modern music with no real concern for Catalan nationalism, I must admit I did not give much thought to the popular songs composed by the young musicians here when I returned to Barcelona.
>
> When I realized how beautiful and rich our songs were in melody and rhythm, I became interested not in the song itself but in the approximate harmonization which had been carried out. When one of these young musicians wanted to give it a Catalan touch, he simplified to the extreme and produced a copy deprived of everything: melody and harmony![17]

---

16   Llongueras (1924), 72.
17   Morera (1936), 39.

Despite this highly critical viewpoint, the network that was very active in this domain contributed by giving new works a nationalist sensitivity, legitimacy, and recognition in Catalan society by celebrating the national heritage and defending works composed for this purpose by contemporary musicians.

These 'contemporary' songs fall into distinct categories. Most are a form of nationalized *Lied* (art song) and are purely descriptive. But some pieces are more specifically Catalan: *Caramelles* composed for the occasion of popular fêtes were highly prized by the Choeurs of Clavé, while *Sardanes*, composed from the rhythm and melody of a traditional dance from the region of Empordà, were popularized by Enric Morera or J. Sancho Marraco.

The *sardana*, known by the name of *contrapas* in the sixteenth century, was rediscovered by folklorists in the mid-nineteenth century; a musician from Figueras called Pep Ventura gave it its modern form. The dancers hold hands in a circle and dance to the music of an instrumental ensemble called a *cobla*. Joan Maragall thus praised it in his poetic work *Visions and Chants* written in 1898:

> The most beautiful dance is the sardane
> Of all the dances that are done and undone
> It is the jewel, magnificent and mobile
> Swaying slowly to the rhythm[18]

A large number of hymns were created by the Orpheons to give themselves an identity ("El Cant de la Senyera" for the Català band, "Voltant la Senyera" for the Gracienc band, "Cant al Penó" for the Choirs of Clavé), to honour the memory of a great man ("Himne a Wagner," from a text by A. Pena), along with numerous hymns dedicated to Clavé, or written more generally to celebrate a patriotic cult. Morera specialized in these hymns, writing as many as eighteen of them between 1898 and 1936.

In 1931, J.M. de Gibert wrote his "Chant du peuple" harmonized by A. Vives for a melody by Clavé. Its first verse is very characteristic:

> Glory, Catalonians, let's sing!
> Sing with the soul,
> One cry and one voice,
> And the fatherland will triumph![19]

---

18   Maragall (1961), 632.

19   Unpublished score, archives of the Foundation Orfeó Català, Palau de la Música, Barcelona.

Numerous settings of lyrical poems by Jacint Verdaguer or Joan Maragall also allude explicitly to Christian ideals. Religion was an important element of the Catalan repertoire, with the desire to restore ancient liturgical chants, the discovery of Gregorian chants, and the religious music of Palestrina encouraged in 1902 by the *Motu proprio* issued by Pope Pius X, who recognized a quality in Gregorian chant that could act as a model for sacred music. Religious polyphony was represented by Bach chorales and the anthems of Vitoria and Palestrina. In addition, contemporary religious chants were frequently composed for the poems of Jacint Verdaguer, a priest whose work was crowned by two epic poems, *L'Atlantidà*, and *Canigó*, which were conceived as a mystical re-reading of the collective history of the Catalan people. The *Cants franciscans* by J. Llongueras and the *Cants religiosos per al poble* by V.M. de Gibert also belong to this religious tendency in Orpheonic music.

The repertoire of course also included 'foreign' works, among them a dozen songs for male voice composed by great musicians such as Schumann, Grieg, Richard Strauss, or Berlioz, along with other songs by less illustrious composers, such as "El Himne Boer" by C. Van Rees, or "Els Emigrants d'Irlanda" by F. Gevaert. There were a few madrigals and other songs of the Renaissance (barely a dozen pieces), but these few signified a desire by some bands to return to the origins of secular polyphony: Dowland, Lassus, Jannequin and Brudieu are the composers most often cited.

The symphonic works and chorales of Beethoven, Franck, Stravinsky, Berlioz and Richard Strauss also featured in the programmes of some groups, but only occasionally. Finally, special mention should be made of the Wagnerian repertoire, much appreciated by the Catalan bourgeoisie at the end of the century. The Orfeó Català often interpreted extracts from his operas, notably during concerts organized in Madrid in 1912 by the Wagnerian Association of Madrid for the Symphonic Orchestra competition, and also during a large Wagner festival organized at the Palau de la Música Catalana in 1913 to commemorate the centenary of the great German composer. Performed for the occasion were the "Chœur des fileuses," an extract from the *Fligende Holländer*, an extract from Act II of *Lohengrin*, and excerpts from Act III of *Parsifal*, with 250 singers and 130 musicians—not to forget the "Hymn to Wagner" composed by G. Zanné and J. Pena and sung to the tune of the march from *Tannhäuser*.[20]

---

20   Unpublished score, archives of the Choirs of Clavé's Federation, Barcelona.

An Idealized Portrait of the National Territory

Certain common features can be identified in the entire Catalan repertoire with regard to a sung description of the homeland. The most frequent words occurring in the repertoire (out of a total of 9,000 words that occur more than once) are the words 'love,' 'song,' 'earth' (associated with 'our'), and 'heart': combinations of these five words occur more than 140 times and inevitably recall the Orpheonic project (Millet often defined choral singing as a patriotic labor of love!). However, the words 'love' and 'heart' may also refer to more prosaic situations, particularly in the pastoral songs of Clavé, and may also reveal the influence of a religious vocabulary. Nevertheless, the coincidence is striking and unquestionably indicates the dominance of Orpheonism in the repertoire of the ensembles.

A second category of common words includes 'typically Catalan' elements of the natural landscape: 'sky,' 'sea,' 'sun,' and 'flowers' are each mentioned more than ninety times, reflecting the poets' fervor in describing Catalan nature and its seductions. The word 'mountain' features less prominently, with fewer than fifty occurrences, although the Pyrenees, Monserrat, and Monseny are often perceived as symbols of the country's core values.

A third category, with over fifty occurrences, contains the words 'fatherland' and 'people' as well as 'son'; while the words 'brothers' and 'companions' appear somewhat less frequently in the repertoire (forty-five and thirty-five occurrences), although they are widely used in the nationalist lexicon in Catalonia to denote the 'good Catalan.'

Finally, in a fourth category (with over thirty occurrences), the words 'dance,' 'freedom,' 'cry,' and 'youth' may also reflect a celebration of the life force that claims to define the new country as vigorous and free. The relative frequency of words with strong religious connotations, such as 'God' (ninety-six times), 'saint' and 'mother' (seventy-five and seventy-six times), 'Jesus' and 'Lord' (forty-five and thirty-three times) reveal the importance of religion in the Catalan repertoire. According to Didier Francfort: "Even when not explicitly part of a nationalist project, choral music maintains a certain religious message. The analysis of nationalism replacing religion as a phenomenon in contemporary societies is influenced in the music of choirs by this meeting point between a national and religious sentiment."[21]

---

21   Francfort (2004), 165.

The Myths of the 'Catalan Renaissance'

According to Stéphane Michonneau, Victor Balaguer, the main 'myth-maker' of the Catalan Renaissance in the 1850 and 1860s, exerted a profound influence on all national literature.[22] Passed on by the folklorists and the Modernist poets of the twentieth century, this influence is clearly visible in the Catalan repertoire: it passes through the content of traditional songs that evoke courtly love or various episodes of medieval or modern history in "El Comte Arnau," "Els Segadors," "La Dama d'Arago," or "Bach de Roda"; but it is also found in contemporary songs that perpetuate the cult of King Jaume I and an idealized rural Catalonia.

In "L'Empordà," for example, the poet Joan Maragall evokes a northern region of Catalonia: "Just next to the Pyrenees, surrounded by hills and right by the sea, opens a smiling plain, the Empordà!"[23] As "La Santa Espina," a poem by A. Guimerà harmonized in 1907 by Morera, declares with enthusiasm: "We are and will be the Catalan people, whether or not we want it, because there is no prouder land under the sun!"[24] In "L'Emigrant," Jaume Verdaguer uses a softer and more nostalgic tone to describe the grief of departure:

> Sweet Catalonia,
> The homeland in my heart,
> When we are distant from you,
> We die of nostalgia . . .[25]

Reconstitution of the Medieval 'Great Catalonia'

In the choral suite *Catalunya!*, harmonized by Morera in 1932, Vives i Miret celebrates the constituent elements of the national territory: *Canigou*, "harsh citadel of the Conflent, eternal guardian of our beautiful homeland"; *Montserrat*, "inextinguishable flame of the holy Grail, which belongs much more to the glorious future than the past"; *the rivers* "that are a great artery of a people who love freedom"; *the olive trees*, "signs of peace"; and *the lakes, the valleys, the fountains . . .* Even if history has left some of these elements on the wrong side of the border, the song proclaims their indisputable Catalan identity and reintegrates them vividly into the national memory. This is true for the

---

22   Michonneau (2007), 32–34.
23   Unpublished score, Foundation Orfeó Català.
24   Ibid.
25   Ibid.

Canigou, celebrated in the traditional song "Muntanyes Regalades": "Dripping mountains are those of the Canigou, that flourish all summer long," and it remains true for North Catalonia and for the Roussillon in general.

Thanks to the magic of language and song, Catalonia recovers its medieval frontiers.

In "Nostre Hymne," for example, written by A. Guimerà and harmonized by Morera in 1917, the Catalan countries are similarly evoked: "Catalonia and Valencia, Majorca and Roussillon, branches of an incomparable tree. They remain part of one single homeland since its creation; unique is our language, and unique is our courage."[26]

An evident change occurred in the repertoire of the nationalists in 1914: the Great War appeared to give wings to the partisans of Catalan autonomy, both on the side of the conservative Regionalist League led by E. Prat de la Riba and on that of the Catalan Republican Party founded in 1917 by F. Macià. Up until the dictatorship of Primo de Rivera, there is a noticeable increase in the number of anthems: "L'Ombre du roi," "Marche roussillonnaise," "Notre chanson," "Hymne de notre parler," "Empordà et Roussillon," "La Sardane de la patrie," "Hymne à la Catalogne". These musical pieces all advocate fighting as a method to restore freedom and re-establish borders in better accordance with the glorious past.

A Homeland of Changing Geometry According to Different Repertoires

Clavé's choir had a rather limited repertoire of only fifty-seven songs in total, most of them composed by Clavé, and thirty-five of them sung only by Clavé's choirs. People did not always sing in Catalan, and Clavé's songs were not exclusively in Catalan: he wrote songs in Castilian as well, and even hymns that left no doubt about his Spanish patriotism. As the lyrics of "Gloria à Espanya!" declaim:

> Glory to Spain, the heroic matron
> Who humiliated the foreign arrogance
> Invincible in Sagunto, Numancia,
> Covadonga, Girona and El Bruc!
> Glory to you, Glory to you, beloved Homeland![27]

---

26   Ibid.

27   Ibid.

Clavé's Republican and Federalist political beliefs (under the influence of the Proudhonian F. Pi i Margall) and above all his closeness to the working class made him one of the representatives of the popular and progressive movement of the Renaixança, which did not challenge a provincial vision of Catalonia. Other provinces are also mentioned in his songs, such as "Las Galas del Cinca" or "Las veladas de Aragón," where he celebrates the Jota, Zaragoza and Aragón. His pacifism led him to assert in his compositions that art is a supreme value that should make us forget all particularities. His adaptation of "La Marseillaise" into Catalan in 1871 is a tribute to the role played by Catalonia after the 1868 revolution in establishing a federal republic in Spain (created in 1873, but it didn't last long) and the defence of freedom. When he writes "Sons of Catalan soil, rather die than be slaves," we must interpret this more as an encouragement to fight against the monarchy than a reference to any struggle against Spain.

Another example of universalism in the repertoire of Clavé's Choirs is the bellicose "Marche Roussillonnaise" composed by C. Grandó in 1916 to encourage the Catalan volunteers' involvement alongside France, which begins:

> Move forward, brave Catalans!
> It's the Homeland which calls you
> Everyone shall take his rifle
> And show of whose father he is the son!
> In the deafening storm,
> Did you hear it?
> Move forward, brave Catalans![28]

The Association of Clavé's Choir tried to preserve the liberal, provincialist, and pacifist orientation of the Claverian repertoire by praising its founder for example in the "Homenatje a Clavé" written by C. Roure in 1906, the "Cant al Poeta" written by E. Guanyabens and harmonized by Morera in 1909, the "¡Gloria a Clavé!" written by A. Mestres and harmonized by J. Sancho Marraco in 1916, and "Salut als Cantors!" written by the president of Clavé's Choir, Eusebi Benages, at the beginning of the twentieth century, based on a melody by A. Thomas:

> Hail to the Singers! Hail to the Singers!
> Hail to all those who cultivate this fine art
> Hail, Hail to the honourable choral societies![29]

---

28   Unpublished score, archives of the Choirs of Clavé's Federation.
29   Ibid.

Nevertheless, if they respect the spirit and the content of Clavé's work, these uninspired compositions appear completely outdated on a musical and cultural level. Some musicians even blamed Clavé's Choirs for wrongly interpreting the master's pieces! As Jaume Pahíssa wrote: "After Clavé's death, those who replaced him as choir director did not have talent enough to continue his work, and even less to give it a new direction...the splendour of the Association diminished and its musical prestige was shattered".[30]

Clavé's Choirs were criticized most heavily for his desire to keep them on the fringes of the nationalist momentum that overwhelmed Catalonia in the late nineteenth century. The intransigent position of Benages in this regard, expressed in several articles called "A la Nació Catalana" in *L'Aurora* in August and September 1899, was evidently not shared within the association, since he was forced by Clavé-inspired Catalonists to resign his presidency in 1901. The split between radical Republicans (Lerrouxists) and solidarity Republicans, which appeared with the birth of Solidaritat Catalana in 1906, split the Clavé's Choirs as well.

The Catalunya Nova choral society was founded in 1895 specifically to fill the musical void into which Clavé's Choirs would have sunk. Its founder, Enric Morera, was intimately linked to them; he had also been their musical director a few years earlier. Morera endeavoured to extend the work of Clavé by renewing the repertoire. As he wrote in 1896, "We firmly believe that the stream of popular Catalan songs and choral works from other countries will help the development of choral music from the Catalan land, so finely established by the immortal Clavé, and let it simultaneously contribute to the musical education of our people, and the production of national works of great artistic value."[31] It is therefore not surprising to find a high proportion of traditional compositions and songs in his repertoire: of the forty-two choral pieces performed by Catalunya Nova and the Federation of Catalan Choirs, he composed twenty-one and harmonized twelve, the others mostly being songs by Clavé (six), or foreign songs, by Grieg, Gevaert, or Van Rees, all related to the theme of the suffering homeland or the hope of liberation.

What is most striking in the compositions of Morera is the number of patriotic hymns he composed between 1898 and 1930 from texts by contemporary poets such as Iglesias and Guanyabens. The remarkable continuity in his patriotic effort places his work in the most radical stream of Catalan Republicanism, which was propounded by the Catalan Center of V. Almirall until 1887, then by Solidaritat Catalana from 1906, and finally by the Catalan Republican Party after 1917. This political engagement did not prevent Morera

---

30   Pahíssa (1900), 2.
31   Morera (1896), 3.

from being actively involved in an intense effort to spread the avant-garde music of his time: he introduced, for example, the music of César Franck and Vincent d'Indy to Catalonia.

He even managed to involve his workers' choir in the Modernist parties that his wealthy friend, the painter Rusiñol, organized in Sitges at the end of the century, the same Rusiñol who wrote in the publication of Morera's Choir, *Catalunya Nova*:

> Our folk songs are humble and simple, but beautiful in their modesty. They are about rugged landscapes with Greek lines...they cry while laughing and laugh while crying...We would not want foreign airs to spoil them or make them die, songs that were born bad and artificial, songs carried not by the air of the mountain, nor transmitted by our memory, turning the green and beautiful vine into disreputable taverns...Let us sing in Catalan, we who were born in Catalonia! Sing, and keep in mind that the integrity of Greece and the French Revolution were made with one song alone.[32]

Rivalry with the Orpheonic Movement

The entire choral work of Morera aims to create *the* national song through a merging of traditional melodies with poems by his contemporaries. In this attempt he encountered fierce competition from the musicians of the Orpheonic movement, who had the advantage of controlling the musical institutions and had an efficient and much wider associative network.

He responded to this relative marginalization in a very critical autobiography, *Moments viscuts*, published in 1936:

> Francesc Alió ... composed a collection of melodies for voice and piano, some of whom at first give an impression of Catalanity, but they eventually sound like Mendelssohn. From Lluís Míllet, I heard an orchestra piece that was so insignificant I didn't dare tell him that I didn't like it. Another one, Amadeu Vives, who could have done something interesting if he had studied, seized the opportunity to leave Barcelona for Madrid, where he limited himself to the easy zarzuela music, among musicians who, in that case, were born musicians. Yet another, Enric Granados, the musician-poet as they used to call him, who also had some talent, gave in

---

32   Rusiñol (1897), 3.

to the influence of Pedrell and held on to Spanish music with the intention of exploiting it.[33]

Such violent criticism reveals the divisions that existed between liberal and republican Catalanism, well represented by the figure of A. Guimerà, who appeared more and more nationalist from 1905 onwards, and the conservative Regionalist League, which exerted a dominant political and cultural influence (since the foundation of the Unió Catalanista in 1887) by recuperating the figure of Verdaguer.

The Orpheons had a much wider repertoire which included 110 songs exclusive to them and twenty-seven songs that were shared with other choral societies. Since they recruited in less popular environments, the Orpheons could count on a higher level of musical competence than that of the other choral societies. Enric Morera stated that "all the members of [his] choir were workers, and not one of them knew how to sight-read a score, so [he] had to teach them through listening to a wide repertoire of Anselm Clavé's pieces and [his own] . . ."[34] The Orpheons improved by training their singers in musical theory, which allowed them to tackle much more demanding pieces.

The Orpheons' repertoire was a subtle mixture of contemporary and traditional songs, religious pieces, madrigals, and often various genres that coexisted within a single concert. For a concert at the Théâtre des Nations in Marseille on 21 November 1901, the first part included two sixteenth-century madrigals, four contemporary songs by Millet, Noguera and Nicolau, one popular song, and one song by Clavé. The second part included four Renaissance pieces, one piece by César Franck, another by Bordes, and finally the inevitable *Els Segadors* in the version harmonized by Millet. It became normal for the programs of Orfeó Català to mix various works, secular and sacred, as if to show the 'ecumenical' spirit of a choral ensemble able to integrate everything as long as the songs meant to elevate the soul. At a grand concert at the Palais du Trocadéro in Paris on 16 June 1914, Orfeó performed "El Cant de la Senyera," a hymn created for them by Millet, five traditional songs, two sardanes, a motet by Bach, and the "Hymne" of sixteen voices for two choirs by Richard Strauss.

This type of programming reflects one of the objectives of the promoters of the chorus movement: reintegration of the folk song into the Arts, and the development of the nationalized Catalan lyrist. As Felix Pedrell expressed it in his speech during the first Festival of Catalan Music in 1904, "the restoration of religious song and folk song allows the modern artist to find the principles

---

33   Morera (1936), 39.
34   Ibid., 45.

upon which a nationalist lyric can be based";[35] this echoed the project of the Schola Cantorum created in Paris by Charles Bordes and Vincent d'Indy in 1894, which encouraged the spreading of an elitist spirituality as a basis for national education.

A similar motive inspired the ideological concerns of the Vic group, who were very influential in the Lliga Regionalista. As Bishop Torras i Bagès wrote: "only the Church is able to awaken the deep currents that lie under the political surface and make sense of Catalan identity."[36] The choir appears in this context as a tool for reclaiming the cultural space largely occupied by popular music of 'foreign' origin: Andalusian ('flamenquists'), Madridian (the 'zarzuelas') or Italian (the 'lusty opera melodies' denounced by Millet in 1901, at the first concert of Orfeó at Liceu).

Observing the trajectory of the Orfeo Català, it seems that Catalanism at the end of nineteenth century followed the same course that Eric Hobsbawm described for the Irish and Polish cases:

> Indeed, the very fact that the new mass political movements, nationalist, socialist, confessional or whatever, were often in competition for the same masses, suggests that their potential constituency was prepared to entertain all their various appeals. The alliance of nationalism and religion is obvious enough, especially in Ireland and Poland.[37]

If the Orfeó essentially shared the Catalan conservative and Catholic values, it also demonstrated a remarkable ability to transcend social boundaries. In 1903, Millet addressed the Board of Directors of the Choral Society in the following terms:

> Oh friends, we too can do something about the social issue, by dispensing decent art by those who are noble and Catalan among poor people who are in greater need of bread for their spirit than for their body . . . and if we can't do everything by ourselves, we will facilitate the creation of societies such as our own, giving us the upper hand to be even stronger. This is not a dream! Look how in Barcelona various artistic circles are established that share the same ideals with us.[38]

---

35   Pedrell (1904), 161.

36   Torras i Bagès (1935), 1: 164.

37   Hobsbawm (1992), 124. These two nations and the essential role of their Catholic clergy in building a national identity at the end of the nineteenth century are cited by Torras i Bages (1: 160) as an example for the regeneration of Catalan society.

38   Millet i Bagès, 30.

The spreading of choral movements in the most remote villages in Catalonia and in the popular districts of Barcelona seems to confirm his sincerity. In 1925 the Orfeo headquarters (the Palace of Catalan Music) was closed by the Primo de Rivera government, while the leaders of the Lliga Regionalista and its political allies were thriving under the new regime. During the dictatorship, the Orpheons would keep alive the emotional values that underlay the permanence of the national community.

The Nationalization of Popular Memory

The Orpheons' repertoire represented a clever synthesis of all the components of choral song. Morera's criticisms notwithstanding, the Orpheons did not hesitate to perform his songs and even took part in the tribute to him at the Fine Arts Palace on 15 October 1911, along with Catalunya Nova and the Association of Clavé's Choir; such fraternization shows that the relationships between the different choral societies were not always inimical. Another aspect of this common ground can found in the distribution of the repertoire: the fact that Clavé's songs, traditional songs, and Morera's songs were sung by all the choirs reveals a common patrimony. The Orpheons shared twelve songs with Catalunya Nova and seven with Clavé's Choir, while the latter shared seven songs with Catalunya Nova; the three choirs shared eight songs altogether. Of the thirty-four songs of this shared repertoire, seven were composed by Morera, seven were traditional songs, and thirteen were composed by Clavé. Along with rivalry and competition, there was a common element whose pivot was the Orpheonic movement, which was more open and able to assimilate diverse musical influences. The integration of Clavé's and Verdaguer's works might also have served as a way for Catalan nationalists to nationalize popular memory and thus bind Catalan society ('the Homeland in unison') in a shared acceptance of the national land.

Nevertheless, this myth of national unity is hard to square with the facts. In 1931, at the end of the third assembly of the Germanor dels Orfeons de Catalunya, the leaders of the Orfeó Català seemed completely disheartened: even if the end of the dictatorship allowed Catalonia to proclaim its autonomy, they were worried by the anticlerical Constitution of the Second Republic. Beyond the political problems, they felt detached from their era. As Millet expressed it: "The time for self-sacrificial ideals, respect and veneration for everything that rises and purifies the popular soul, the time for the recovery of a forgotten spirituality, for the most pure and incorruptible Catalanity, has passed."[39]

---

39   Millet i Loras (1930), 345–47.

This distress found an echo in the musical content of the concerts given by the Orpheons at that time, as suggested by Joan Balcells, in the editorial of his Orfeó Gracienc's Review: "The folklorism that inspired the Orpheonic repertoire is already outdated . . . in fact, patriotism evolves as art evolves, as music renews itself . . . the Orpheonic repertoire must be renewed because it has been silent for too long."[40]

If national musicians must count on an associative and institutional framework that gives meaning to their music, they are also constantly forced to institute a new national music, adapting their creations to new political and cultural contexts. This lesson had been well learnt by the Orfeó Català when it criticized the stasis of Clavé's Choir at the end of the previous century, but the lesson was not implemented. It was no accident that in 1931 the Association of Catalan composers was created, gathering a new generation of very active musicians in choral song, which gave a new impetus to those choral societies with the courage to perform their pieces, such as the choral Sant Jordi, the Orfeó de Sants, or the Orfeó Gracienc.

The Invention of a National Anthem

The history of the national anthem is very revealing of the political and cultural context of the time. "Els Segadors" was originally a traditional Catalan song whose text was obtained by Jacint Verdaguer around 1863 and was published by Milà i Fontanals in 1882. In its original version, the song recalls a Catalonian peasant revolt in June 1640 against abuses committed by the royal troops of Philip IV of Castile, who were ordered into the province by the Count of Olivares, viceroy of Catalonia. This popular riot known as the "Corpus of blood" brought fire and devastation to Barcelona. The original poem ended with the following verses:

> The bishop blessed them, with his right and left hand,
> Where's your leader, where is your banner?
> They will find the good Jesus, covered with a black veil
> That's our leader, that's our banner
> With Catalan weaponry! they have declared war on you![41]

The poem attracted little attention until in 1892 the first musical version of the poem was published by F. Alió in his collection of Catalan folk songs; but the

---

40   *Revista del Orfeó Gracienc* n°149 (Nov. 1932).
41   Massot i Muntaner et al. (1983), 12.

musicologist introduced a few small changes into the text.[42] The original text was generally respected, but Alió replaced the original melody with another popular song whose tone seemed to him better suited to the vibrant and patriotic content of the text. Alió's replacement of the traditional melody apparently did not shock his friends from the Orfeó Català, who added the song to their repertoire from 1892 in an arrangement by Lluís Vives, and in 1899 in a version harmonized by Lluís Millet himself.[43] Even Morera, who had already harmonized it in 1897 for Catalunya Nova, cited it in a patriotic choral poem, *Catalonia*, written by Guanyabens in 1899.

When Spain was defeated in the Cuban war, this protest on behalf of Catalan nationalism was very badly received in Madrid, which banned the song, thus of course ensuring its success in Catalanist circles. On 27 September 1897, Maragall noted that the song "Els Segadors" was "arranged recently by our modern composers for choirs, and has recently become the essential patriotic anthem in all the Catalanist celebrations and demonstrations, performed with solemnity, acclaimed and sometimes warmly sung by the public, and considered with suspicion by all those who consider it a symbol of hostility towards the Spanish state."[44]

One final event brought about a change in the text of the anthem: on 10 June 1899, the newspaper *La Nació Catalana* proposed a contest to change the lyrics of "Els Segadors" in order to create a text "that would give a clearer idea of Catalonia's thirst to recover its lost identity, whose brave strophes would encourage the sons of this land to try to free [Catalonia] from the oppression it currently suffers, with modern poetry and traditional popular song tenderly entwined to create the national anthem of Catalonia."[45]

This initiative provoked a sharp reaction from folklorist circles, supported by the moral authority of Jacint Verdaguer and Bishop Torras i Bages, who were fond of the previous versions of the anthem. The scandal exposed Alió's dishonesty, but did not prevent the text from changing. The old lyrics were rewritten by Guanyabens, and now start with the famous "Catalunya triomfant!":

> Triumphant, Catalonia,
> Will once again be rich and fertile!
> We must not be the prey
> Of those proud and arrogant invaders! Let us swing the sickle!
> Let us swing the sickle, defenders of our land! Let us swing the sickle!

---

42   Ibid., 13.
43   Ibid., 23.
44   Maragall (1961), 586.
45   *La Nació Catalana*, 10 June 1899, 36.

The final word is given to Maragall, who wrote in *El Diario de Barcelona* of 27 September 1899: "A national song, a patriotic anthem, is not a definition of aspirations, nor a political platform; it is the soul of a people who dream with their past, present and future, revealing their spirit through the centuries."[46] This is tantamout to saying that the content of the national anthem refers to an altogether invented memory in which an idealized past mingles with the dreams of the present. Nevertheless, it is worth noting that Clavé's Choir eventually accepted the song from 1930 onwards,[47] and that after a period of prohibition under Franco lasting nearly forty years, it rose from its ashes with the return of democracy in Spain.

In conclusion, the Catalan choral movement seems a particularly interesting case in the European context. First of all, competition and rivalry created a sort of civic 'awakening' that stimulated the sense of national belonging through collective practice: to create the homeland through singing is to dream aloud of unity, harmony, beauty, and a glorious past, even if this is done differently on different sides. In this sense, choral singing is essentially civic. Secondly, the willingness to participate in a work of national redemptive construction was coupled with a desire to reconnect with a supposed Golden Age: Catalans would thus be able to disregard the 'Castilian' interim as a reaction to the inglorious present time for Spain. Finally, a cumulative process can be observed in Catalan choral movements which, from Clavé to Millet to Enric Morera, managed to introduce Catalonia to the "Chorus of Nations" with a strong and durable personality (it has survived two dictatorships!) at the same time that it helped to bring modernity and new ways of singing to Catalonian music.

---

46   Cited in Marfany (1998), 89.
47   Carbonell i Guberna (1998), 184.

CHAPTER 11

"By Means of Singing to the Heart, by Means of Heart to the Homeland"

Choral Societies and the Nationalist Mobilization of Czechs in the Nineteenth Century

Karel Šima, Tomáš Kavka, and Hana Zimmerhaklová

Czech historiography has paid considerable attention to the role of national-ist societies—including choral societies—in the context of Czech nationalist mobilization in the nineteenth century. However, existing research has focused on three levels of analysis that have introduced two barriers to recognition of the activities of choral societies as the principal factor in the process of nation-building. Firstly, a number of studies have examined the origins and composi-tion of particular societies and their functions in local contexts.[1] These valuable works present a rich collection of facts, but they have not examined this phe-nomenon in the context of nationalism. Secondly, disciplinary research based in musicology has made important discoveries concerning repertoires in the context of the history of musical genres.[2] However, this approach ignores the socio-economic and cultural context in a broader sense. A third approach rec-ognizes the role of choral societies in the process of nation-building as a part of the widening of the social background of the process.[3] Typically this inter-pretation places choral activities only in the third phase of nation-building, as a mass movement at the time when most members of society were already involved in the nationalist project.

These lines of research have raised barriers to a better understanding of the phenomenon in two ways: they either disregard the broader context of the success of choral societies, or they treat their success as a side-effect of a larger socio-economic process and neglect the symbolic and performative importance of their actual activities. An integrated and comparative analysis should consider not only evidence of the size, composition, funding, and social background of the societies, but bring these aspects together to explain their

---

1 See for example Kopalová (2005) and Řeřichová (2005).
2 The most comprehensive book on the history of Czech musical culture is the monograph by
   Kotek (1994).
3 See for example Ledvinka and Pešek (2000).

mutual dynamics in relation to the process of national identification and the performative generation of national identity.

In this paper we argue that the social and economic background and the performative and musical context of the Czech choral movement were shaped by its role in the framework of national mobilization. In the 1860s this role involved bottom-up funding strategies, participation of the intelligentsia, an explicitly patriotic repertoire, and occupation of public space. In later decades this central role declined gradually, which for choral societies meant a diversification of their social status and financial background, transformation of the repertoire towards more thematic variety, and a retreat from nation-wide performative situations to more closed and traditional musical and cultural contexts.

Choral Societies: Initial Conditions and Expansion

Choral societies emerged in the Czech lands as voluntary associations in civil society after the revolutionary year of 1848. This initial situation was defined in law by the first wave of constitutionality in the Habsburg monarchy. Societies could be established thanks to the provisional associational law of 1849, followed in 1852 by the imperial patent for associations and statutes.[4] There were two traditional types of choral activities in Czech lands: church choirs and military choirs in the Austrian army. The newly established choral societies could build on this foundation. The first registered civil choral association was called *Svatopluk*, founded in the town of Žďár nad Sázavou in 1849; and in that same year the German *Akademischer Männergesangverein* was established in Prague. The numbers of such societies increased slowly during the era of so-called Bach absolutism (1850–59), with a majority of societies established in smaller towns (for example, in Chrudim or Jaroměř in 1856). The choral movement expanded significantly after the October Diploma adopted in 1860 by Emperor Franz Joseph, who promised to initiate constitutional reform. Many new associations were registered at this time, which had possibly existed earlier unofficially. Most likely they originated in the unorganized singing of men within the activities of popular educational organizations (in Czech Beseda) or in readers' clubs, probably because of the complicated process of obtaining permission from the Austrian authorities until the end of the 1850s. Starting in 1860—following the abandonment of the absolutist regime—these voluntary

---

4 Rataj and Ratajová (1998), 11–12.

associations flourished into a strong network of organizations that brought vital impulses and energy to the Czech nationalist movement, especially in the shaping of symbolic public space.

The most important Czech choral society, *Hlahol* from Prague, was established in January 1861. Its first appearance in public was a concert at the funeral of Václav Hanka, the famous national poet and writer well known for his 'discovery' of the 'Manuscripts' of Dvůr Králové and of Zelená Hora, considered as medieval relics of ancient Czech culture.[5] This choir was led by the most reputable Czech choirmaster, Jan Ludevít Lukes, who was also a respected vocalist and originally a brewer by profession. *Hlahol* was registered by the Austrian authorities four months later as the first nationalist society with nationwide ambitions.[6] Like all of the nationalist associations at this time (e.g., Sokol for physical training, Umělecká beseda for art), *Hlahol* was registered as an exclusively male society.

The choral societies gained significant visibility also in the regional context. They played a vital role in introducing Czech nationalist ideas to a wider public. They were among the first organizations to occupy the 'public sphere' in an urban space, especially by arranging national festivities and concerts. *Hlahol* intended not only to develop a socially relevant space for spreading nationalist beliefs, but also symbolically to proclaim them with their name ('Hlahol' means ringing of bells in Czech) and their motto: *Zpěvem k srdci, srdcem k vlasti* (By means of singing to the heart, by means of heart to the homeland). In association with Czech literary, fine arts, and other clubs and societies, *Hlahol* helped to form a basis for the development of genres of high culture within Czech nationalist society. Regional choral societies also followed this pattern in their use of Czech and Slavic symbolism. Some names of the societies were derived from the names of Slavic mythological heroes, such as *Slavoj* (in the town of Chrudim), *Jaromír* (Jaroměř), *Slavjan* (Hradec Králové), *Záboj* (Rokycany), or *Svatobor* (Sušice). Only a few of the names were derived from their geographical location, as for instance *Moravan* in Kroměříž, *Střela* in Plasy (after the name of the local brook), or *Prácheň* in Horažďovice. Furthermore several 'regional' *Hlahols* were established as well (in Nymburk, Písek, Plzeň and Tábor). The overall symbolic framework of their activities was, however, the discourse of national unification, as was also evident from their mottos: the Czech choral society *Brněnská beseda* based in the city of

---

5   These manuscripts were composed by Hanka and handwritten by his colleague Linda at the beginning of the nineteenth century.

6   Rataj and Ratajová (1998), 25.

Brno (with a majority German population) adopted the slogan *Zpěv jednotí,
jednota sílí!* (Singing unifies, unity strengthens!); while the other choral society in the same city, *Řemeslnická beseda Svatopluk* (Craftmen's Organization
of Svatopluk), had as its motto *Buďmež svorni, vlasti věrni!* (Let us be united,
devoted to our country!).[7]

Social and Financial Background and Networking Activities

The initiators of Czech choral societies were often leaders of nationalist culture who were in touch with amateur or professional musicians or pedagogues.
Music teachers from the regional high schools, either general or specialized,
often took positions as choirmasters. For example, the first choirmaster of
Hlahol, Jan Ludevít Lukes, together with several music-loving men (including
the teacher František Pivoda and the lawyer and amateur musician Ludevít
Procházka) organized the first meetings of *Hlahol* and also supported it financially. The first chairman of *Hlahol* was Rudolf von Thurn and Taxis, a noble
Czech landowner known as a "democratic prince," who was an ardent orga-
nizer and supporter of Czech nationalist activities at the beginning of the
1860s.[8] Later he supported the Czech liberal political party that was formed in
1874 after the National Party split into conservatives and liberals.[9]

Although the regional networks of the nationalist activists were not as dense
as in Prague, the social background of the initiators of choral activities was
similar: they were typically from the local intelligentsia, mainly teachers, journalists, or lawyers. For example, the society *Záboj* from the town of Rokycany
separated its activities from the male choir of the local popular educational
organization (*Měšťanská beseda*) initiated by a teacher at the local boys' school,
František Václav Karlík.[10] However, there were usually not enough generous
donors to fund the choirs' expenditures. One exception was the choral society
Moravan in the Moravian city of Kroměříž, which was subsidized by the local
Czech patriot, lawyer, journalist, and member of the Moravian assembly Jan
Kozánek. But many other societies were not so fortunate.

The position of choirmaster was regularly held by well-reputed men who
had won respect in specifically urban communities. The choirmasters of
Prague and of Plzeň's *Hlahol*, the two most prestigious societies of this kind,

---

7   Bajgarová (2005), 55.
8   He co-founded both the central physical training union *Sokol* and the art society *Umělecká
        beseda*.
9   Malíř (2000), 42–62.
10   See *Památník k 75letému trvání pěveckého spolku Záboj v Rokycanech* (Rokycany, 1936).

were replaced relatively often. The most famous choirmaster of the Prague *Hlahol* was composer Bedřich Smetana (from 1862–65), who was succeeded by the popular composer Karel Bendl in the 1870s. The *Hlahol* of Plzeň had as its director, choirmaster, and composer Hynek Palla, who was also the leader of the Sokol society in Plzeň and one of the most active nationalists in the region.[11] High-school teachers carried out the role of choirmasters in the choral societies of smaller towns like Rokycany or Tábor (with populations of about 5,000). Accordingly, students also formed a significant part of the choral movement, especially in its initial phase. They often took part in the societies' performances, even though they were not usually permanent members of the choirs. The representatives of the most significant Czech choral societies (*Hlahol* in Prague and Plzeň) aimed to establish their own singing schools.

Czech choral societies were largely financed by membership fees. There were usually several categories of membership, of which in general the most important were active, contributory, and honorary. Active members often sang in the choir and also performed administrative duties in the society, and they usually paid a lower membership fee. Contributory members could have official functions in the society and paid a higher fee. They established a fund to support the main activities of the societies, and their numbers were crucial for the scope of choral activities. The role of contributory members could be defined as one of 'collective patronage,' as they served as minor sponsors. The honorary members were wealthy citizens such as local mayors, or national celebrities or reputable artists. Unlike the other membership groups, students were not required to pay a membership fee.

The range of membership fees also differed according to the size, social status, and regional location of a given choral society. Generally, the highest fees were paid in bourgeois associations in large cities, while working-class ensembles levied lower fees. For example, the first specialized craftsman's choral society, *Typografická beseda* (the Association of Printers), was established in Prague in 1862; by 1864 it had forty members, and the fee was one gulden per month, so that its monthly revenue from fees was forty gulden. This sum was not enough to meet the society's operating costs; it also needed income from performances at various social events where entrance fees were collected. Paid concerts could represent a significant contribution to the assets of a society, and for the singing printers of Prague, these additional revenues were much more important than membership fees. The printers' choir performed on many social occasions, including festivities outside Prague. One of them—a

---

11   Frolík (1993), 39–48.

concert in support of a Czech Technical School in Vienna—brought a profit of 260 gulden that was divided equally between the society and the school.[12]

The size of choirs was determined chiefly by the size of its home town and the level of activity of nationalist circles in the town. The Prague *Hlahol* began to perform in 1861 with 120 men in the choir. By 1879 the male choir had 200 members, and a new ladies' choir with 143 members was established. The *Hlahol* from Plzeň had 100 men by the mid-1860s. On the other hand, membership in the *Střela* society from the small town of Plasy (population about 3,000) ranged from fifty-one to seventy-one members between the years 1870–1914.[13]

Of the various Czech choral societies established during the second half of the nineteenth century, the Prague *Hlahol* played the initial and the most nationwide role. A number of societies with regional ambitions helped to foster the nationalist movement in local contexts and contributed to the dissemination of the nationalist fervor. Choral societies organized along professional lines were formed in larger cities as well, like the printers of Prague and a similar organization founded in 1868 in Brno called *Řemeslnická beseda Svatopluk* (the Craftsmen's Organization of Svatopluk). These professional societies began to emerge earlier than women's choral societies, which usually originated from within the men's choral groups. The originally male choirs were regularly complemented with female sections from the 1870s. The male choir of the Prague *Hlahol* was enlarged with ladies' voices in 1873, and a separate ladies' choir was constituted six years later. The first effort to create a mixed choir came from the art society *Umělecká beseda*.[14] The leaders of its music section made a first attempt in the years 1867–70, which failed due to disagreements among the musicians. However, the first women's choirs were formed within the women's educational associations. The female choir of *Ženská vzdělávací jednota Vesna* (the Female Educational Union Vesna) in Brno is well documented since 1870.[15]

In general, Czech nationalist society was interconnected through a wide cultural (and not only choral) organizational network. Choral societies supported each other in the name of national solidarity. Smaller societies enrolled as members of the central associations from Prague. The largest Czech cultural associations like *Hlahol* or *Umělecká beseda* had many of the local and regional choral societies among their members. In return, the central associations supplied their regional members with songbooks, sheet music, literature, pictures, etc. In some cases they supported the regional societies also financially,

---

12   Jindra (1934), 4–10.

13   Nejedlý (1911), 82–83.

14   Šilhan (1913), 23.

15   Bajgarová (2005), 33.

organizationally, or symbolically. For example, during the ceremony to consecrate the flag of the Chrudim society *Slavoj* in 1863, the Prague *Hlahol* was
represented by several members with their own societal flags, and more than
fifteen other regional choirs were also present. This entire network was formed
in opposition to the German choral societies.[16] In fact, the parallel Czech and
German organizations often mirrored each other.[17] For instance, the German
Deutscher Gesangverein Flöte constituted in 1861 was a reaction to the establishment of the Prague *Hlahol*; while the German choral society in Brno, the
Brünner Männergesangverein, was founded about one year earlier (in 1861)
than the local Czech society *Brněnská beseda*.

In the 1860s the network also assumed the official status of an association—the Union of Czech-Slavic Choral Societies (*Jednota zpěváckých spolků
českoslovanských*)—initiated by the leading Czech choir *Hlahol* from Prague.[18]
After three years of negotiations, the Union received state approval at a meeting held in Prague in 1869; among its aims were mutual support for choral
activities, expanding the singing of Czech and Slavic choral music, and publishing songbooks and sheet music. Thirty-nine societies were present at
the constitutive meeting: thirty-six from Bohemia, only one from Moravia
(*Brněnská Beseda*), one from Silesia (from the smaller city of Klimkovice), and
two deputies from similar societies in Vienna (*Slovanský spolek* and *Lumír*).[19]
The activities of this newly established network were discontinued after
its third meeting in the year 1873. Among the reasons given was the passivity
of the choral members; but the decrease of interest could best be explained
by the deterioration of the economic, political, and social conditions for their
existence. The collapse of the Vienna stock exchange in 1873, the splitting of
Czech national political representation, and the controversy about Bedřich
Smetana and the 'nature' of the Czech musical tradition[20] were all factors that
made the situation worse for choral societies. The 1870s were characteristically
described as an 'era of crisis' for the Prague *Hlahol*.[21] Leading personalities in
the societies made efforts to revive the movement during the 1870s by opening
the repertoire to a wider audience. This strategy was designed to attract the
lower social classes to fill the gap left by the departure of the intelligentsia and

---

16   Nejedlý (1911), 78.
17   For comparison with tensions concerning national memorials, see Hojda and Pokorný
     (1995).
18   Nejedlý (1911), 82–83.
19   Ibid., 83.
20   Hostinský (1904), 5–53.
21   Srb and Tadra (1886), 84–85.

fragmented political representation, but it was supported only by a minor part of the choral leaders, and in the end it served only to provoke more controversy among the societies.

During the late 1880s the economic depression was fading out in Czech lands and the political leadership was overtaken by the liberal faction of the Young Czechs (*Mladočeši*). Moreover, the variety of national societies had grown in the meantime, so that choral societies became only one among many active components of the national movement, on the same level as, for instance, associations of firemen or theater clubs. In fact choral societies had not lost their significance (especially during the national festivals in urban environments), but they were not perceived as a constituent part of national mobilization. Paradoxically, with the decline of the potential for performative mobilization, the number of societies continued to grow, and they became ever more specialized according to the social backgrounds of the members and their audiences. By the beginning of the twentieth century the structure of choral societies more or less reflected the social structure of Czech national society.

During the 1890s the Union of Czech-Slavic choral societies was re-established with better organization than the old one. Its new central committee held regular meetings, and a professional administration published an official bulletin (*Věstník Ústřední Jednoty zpěváckých spolků českoslovanských*). After continual expansion, a district structure was established comprising twenty districts in Bohemia and six in Moravia. By the turn of the century—during the peak of its activities—the association counted 324 choral societies, of which 116 were male choirs, 20 female, and 188 mixed.[22]

Representatives of the renewed Union tried not only to build a stable organization, but also to integrate as far as possible all of the (ethnically) Czech choirs of the time.[23] While they continued to stress the symbolic importance of collective singing for national mobilization, they had no overt political ambitions, which facilitated the integration of a diversified body of societies and enabled them to concentrate their activities on musical performance and repertoire. According to the Union's own figures (from 1903) published in its bulletin, craftsmen and members of the lower intelligentsia were the most numerous social groups represented in the societies (see Table 11.1). In the early years of the movement the lower intelligentsia had outnumbered teachers, students, and other groups, and they were still slightly overrepresented in the association in comparison with the whole of Czech society.

---

22   *Věstník pěvecký Ústřední Jednoty . . .*, Vol. 8, Nos. 3–4 (20 March 1903), 124–25.
23   Ibid., 10: 1 (5 January 1905), 1–2.

TABLE 11.1   *Social Structure of the Union of Czech Choral Societies in 1903*

Profession	Percentage	Individuals
Craftsmen	21,5	882
Lower intelligentsia	20,1	826
Teachers	14,8	604
Workers	13,5	552
Traders	12,2	501
Students	5,7	234
Doctors	4,9	199
Professors	3,1	128
Farmers, Peasants	2,1	86
Priests	1,6	62
Builders	0,5	20
Total	100	4,094

Source: Tureček (1903), 124–25.

Despite controversies during the preparatory phase of its first national music festival in 1904 (when a newly elected committee resigned), the Union survived the First World War, and after the proclamation of the Czechoslovak republic in 1918 it became the only officially recognized corporation of singing societies acknowledged by the patronage of President Tomáš Garrigue Masaryk.

The Repertoire: Tradition, Topicality, and High Culture

The principal historical sources of most of the choral societies' repertoire are two widely popular songbooks published in many editions in the second half of the nineteenth century: the *Societal Czech Songbook* of *Hlahol* (first edition 1861) and the very first *Societal Czech Songbook* composed by Josef Bohuslav Pichl (first edition 1851). These collections—together comprising more than 350 songs—shaped the regular repertoire of every Czech choral society. Thematically they included most of the categories described below.

In general, the musical form of the repertoire depended on singing skills, finances, and personal abilities. The basic musical form was a simple adaptation of songs for male quartet. This *liedertafel* style was commonly used on various civil and also church ceremonial occasions. Richer societies that were able to raise the repertoire level arranged more exacting programmes, including fragments from operas or classical music.

The repertoire could be divided into seven categories, each representing certain genres with different social functions.

Folk Songs

By definition, folk song is a spontaneous singing genre which focuses on everyday life in an agricultural or urban environment. Folk song was rehabilitated during the second half of the nineteenth century when it became a part of nationalist efforts to build up Czech national identity on the basis of folkloric traditions. The most important drive in this sense was a Czech ethnographic exhibition (1895) which greatly encouraged the recognition of Czech folklore. Czech folk songs served as important tools for building national consciousness, and many choral societies included them as an indispensable part of their program. However, not only Czech folklore was perceived as a necessary element of the choral societies' performances, but a common Slavic folk musical heritage was also re-interpreted and re-performed in a contemporary context. This genre was later gradually replaced by the so-called broadsheets, which became more popular in urban society at the beginning of the twentieth century.[24]

Cantastoria

This tradition comprises songs with provocative but also moralistic themes produced by professional authors since the seventeenth century. Cantastoria had an epic character, recounting political, military, or criminal news, and news about natural disasters. It became very popular and competed in popularity with folk song. The basic motifs of these songs began to change due to social changes in the eighteenth century. The themes became more linked to civilian life and love, but also involved political and public topics (e.g. wage labor, railway construction, etc.). Especially during the revolutionary year of 1848, many songs of this kind reflected current events and were very popular. K.H. Borovský, a leading activist of the revolution, applied this genre on the ironic open letter to the famous Frankfurter parliament. His song "Shuselka Writes to Us" became widely popular, reflecting the refusal to integrate Czech society and culture into the pangermanistic movement.[25]

In the second half of the nineteenth century the popularity of cantastoria declined mainly because of new media technologies. However, these songs were still in the repertoire of many choral societies. They remained popular

---

24   Kotek (1994), 13.
25   Ibid., 38.

because of their familiar structure amenable to comments on up-to-date public topics with parody and hyperbole. At the same time, they could be used for national mobilization due to their moral appeal.[26]

Patriotic Songs

This form represented a core genre of nationalist propaganda. These songs were meant to inspire unity and fervor based on their strongly emotional appeal. However, its evolution in the Czech national movement was relatively slow because of a lack of appropriate lyrics in the Czech language in the first third of the nineteenth century. This led to a differentiation of this genre into variety of modes.[27]

In addition to explicitly patriotic themes directly celebrating the homeland and other symbols associated with Czech culture, this category also included love songs and humorous and satirical songs. Such a broad range of topics would certainly require a much more detailed analysis, but in the latter half of the nineteenth century they can generally be separated into two categories.

The first type is the song with an exclusively patriotic theme. The form can be characterized as sentimental and tendentious. A good example is the later Czech national anthem "Kde domov můj" (Where is My Home), written by J.K. Tyl in the 1830s.[28] Its content expresses a personal relationship to the homeland, highlighting the beauty of home and the pathos of homecoming. (The song was initially presented in a theatre performance where it was sung by a blind hobo). It starts with words: "Where is my home / where is my home / Water roars across the meadows / Pinewoods rustle among the cliffs." Its role in the choral movement and collective singing culture can be illustrated by its changing position in the national songbook compiled by Pichl. In editions from the 1850s the first song in the book presented as the 'national anthem' was the Austrian anthem (*Volkshymne*) "Gott erhalte"; but after 1863 the song "Where Is My Home" took its place without explanation or comment.

Many songs of this kind are simple chants about emotional attachment to the Czech nation, language, and culture. Examples include "My beautiful Bohemia, my soul is straitened by desire," and especially the pan-Slavic anthem "Hey Slavs" with the lines "Hey Slavs / our Slavic language still lives / as long as our loyal hearts / beat for her." The principal function of these songs was a direct appeal to the patriotic feeling and unity of the Czech nation or the entire Slavic ethnic group.

---

26   Ibid., 39.
27   Václavek and Smetana (1940), 10–55.
28   Kotek (1994), 58.

The second form of patriotic song can be defined as the patriotic love song in which the lovers personify various patriotic virtues. For example, a girl is loved by boy due to her exemplary patriotism. Many of these songs were included in a collection published monthly from 1835–39 under the title *A Wreath of Patriotic Songs Tied Up for Patriotic and Self-sacrificing Girls*.[29] In Czech nationalist culture, the sub-genre of the patriotic love song was evidently the most popular form for expressing patriotic feelings. The semantic context of love enabled a transfer of the symbolic object of love from woman/ man to homeland/nation (in Czech *vlast*, feminine and *národ*, masculine).

Stories of National History

This genre could be described as artificial, sentimental, and patriotic. Its themes reflected national history (unlike the above genres), and focused on the events and personalities that played a crucial role in the formation of a national mythology. Karel Tůma, a Young Czech journalist, wrote many texts of this type. One example is the very famous song "On the Banks of the Rhine," which celebrates the memory of the Czech reformer Jan Hus, who was burned to death in Constance in 1415. Tůma re-used the melody of a heroic song sung by the Warsaw insurgents of 1830. The lyrics are characteristically sentimental and patriotic, expressing heroic sacrifice, the resiliency of the nation, and the image of the enemy of the nation:

> On the banks of the Rhine the stakes burn up
> And we ask, Who is in the flames?
> It is Master Jan, our famous Czech . . .
> However, live still, Czech nation, for revenge . . .
> Anger rises in the holy arm, plunges hot flashes into the dark of delusions,
> Bent to the hard crown of Rome . . .[30]

Political Songs

Some pieces in the choral society repertoire had a clear political content responding to contemporary political situations, persons, or cases. These songs gained importance in the 1870s, in the time of escalating fights against the centralization policy of the Vienna government and also due to a split among the Czech political representatives. The song "Rebels" (1868) denounced the Austrian-Hungarian government for its unrealized promises of autonomy for Czech lands, while at the same time criticizing domestic national policy for

---

29   Ibid., 58.
30   Pacák (1873), 1.

being ineffective and defensive. This motif was later elaborated in the song "The Man Without Tears," referring to Karel Havlíček Borovský, the famous Czech political prisoner and 'martyr' who was one of the most active political journalists of the Revolution of 1848, and after his death became a symbol of active and uncompromising liberal politics, and thus an ideal for Czech liberal-democratic choral societies.[31] This song celebrated him as an imprisoned patriot lamenting the plight of the Czech national movement. The lyrics refer to the figure of a man who survived prison but whose heart turned to stone after he was released as he realized that his nation had fallen into slavery. In the early 1870s this symbol clearly reflected the failure of Czech nationalist aspirations and the split between conservative and liberal Czech political parties (Old Czechs vs. Young Czechs). It should be noted that most of the choral societies of this period were on the side of the Young Czechs and often took part in their political campaigns.[32]

"Sokol" Songs

The Sokol (Falcon) association represented the most radical nationalist organization of the young Czech bourgeoisie, linking physical training with moral and intellectual training for the nation, generally based on the German Jahnian tradition of the Turnverein. The varied activities of the Sokols (as they called themselves) included hikes, public exercises, and marching during national festivals, and also choral singing, which gave rise to the genre of the Sokol song. The massive popularity of such songs expanded during the 1880s when the Sokol movement spread quickly. Sokol songs were strongly militant, unifying, and rousing, most of them being marching-songs. The symbolism of these songs was straightforward and bellicose, using simple slogans. For example, a traditional patriotic song beginning "I am Slavic and I will be Slavic" was paraphrased in the Sokol piece "I am a Falcon and I will be a Falcon." A good many of these songs were based on lyrics from the 1848 revolution, as in the case of Karel Havlíček Borovský's poems/epigrams criticizing Austrian conservativism and calling for freedom, nation, and brotherhood.[33]

Elements of High Culture: Opera and Literature

A significant part of the repertoire of choral societies was made up of contemporary choral music based in neo-romanticism, with special emphasis on the

---

31   In 1851 Borovský was deported by the Austrian police to South Tyrol, where he spent five years in confinement; upon his return he fell ill and died shortly thereafter.

32   Pabian (2009), 221–28.

33   Kotek (1994), 110–11.

Wagnerian tradition. Among contemporary composers, Bedřich Smetana was a leading figure, the choirmaster of the *Hlahol* society and the composer of a number of choral pieces performed by Czech choral societies. A great many arias from his operas became regular parts of the choral repertoire. The most famous example—his opera *The Bartered Bride*, with its final chorus "Why Should We Not Be Merry?"—is the best illustration of an orientation towards a 'national' folklore with the neo-romantic taste for folk motifs and popular culture.[34] Smetana's operas also contributed to the dissemination of nationalistic mythology by using stories from Czech history and mythology: *Dalibor, Brandenburgers in Bohemia*, and *The Devil's Wall* all have medieval settings, while *Libuše* is a ceremonial opera with a pre-Christian mythological plot based on the story of the first female ruling princess of the Czechs.

The rapid acceptance of high culture into the popular choral societies movement (in the 1860s and 70s) brought a significant shift to the dissemination of neo-romantic musical culture in Czech lands and considerably influenced subsequent Czech popular culture.

Workers' Songs

In its early days the musical culture of the working class was associated mainly with traditional folklore. Its original motifs were centered on a social critique directed against the aristocracy, foremen, rich peasants, etc. The factory proletariat, a still growing and changing component of urban society in the second half of the nineteenth century, needed a new type of song. The traditional form was brought from rural areas and transformed by workers under the influence of particular (urban) conditions. The key element of this form was the lyrics, while the melody mattered relatively little. Because the goal of this collective singing was to encourage and unify the labour movement, texts had to be alarming and militant, with simple melodies accessible to untrained singers.

Many of these songs were anonymous; choirmasters mostly edited the original melody and added new lyrics. Later in the 1870s, with the growing organization of the labour movement, journalists and writers from working-class milieux began to write original songs, which were published in the workers' daily press and later also in songbooks. However, most of the workers' songs were banned by Austrian censorship offices, so the first songbook (*Songs of Workers*) was published in New York. The First 'Prague' songbook of workers was printed in 1894. In addition to original Czech material, translations of German and Austrian workers' songs were popular.

---

34   Ibid., 109.

A typical example is a very popular song entitled "Men of work, wake up!":
*'Men of work, wake up! | Know your power: If you want, every wheel stands still. /
Overthrow the yoke of slavery. We need freedom!'*[35] The text appeals distinctly to
a specific social group that is not nationalistic, and promotes the international
solidarity of the workers' movement. This international theme was an important characteristic of the workers' songs.

Even though the level of workers' collective singing was not as high as in the
case of bourgeois choral societies, and its contribution to nationalist mobilization was limited, choral singing became a significant part of the workers'
movement. From the 1890s to the First World War, the number of workers' choral societies grew to several hundred.[36]

To sum up, mixing the repertoires of choral societies from different musical
traditions (both popular and high culture) proved a very effective tool for
mobilizing national sentiment. In the 1860s patriotic songs became the most
important part of the choral societies' repertoire, emphasizing the emotional
relationship to the homeland and its virtues. These patriotic songs reveal the
influence of folk songs, whose original form could be used by composers as
a template for the creation of patriotic songs (and a form of cantastoria was
also suitable for the same purpose). At this time, songs derived from opera
and the classical repertoire also became more popular, and were performed
not only by choral societies but also in middle-class salons. They served the
cause of national mobilization as reminders of the high value of Czech musical culture, whose quality bears comparison with well-established European
national cultures.

An important shift in repertoire occurred in the 1870s when the leaders of
the national movement split into two political parties (Old Czechs and Young
Czechs). As mentioned above, this division was caused by differing attitudes
towards the centralist policy of the Vienna government. Czech political representatives who favoured active intervention founded the Young Czechs party,
and the use of political song as an active mobilizing instrument gave them an
advantage. Sokol songs also became popular and soon crossed the borders of
their original sport associations. The appeal of such songs was underlined by
their stimulating character, reflected also in the symbolism of the Sokol movement: the Czech nation was metaphorically seen as a falcon endowed with
strength, vision, and the freedom of flight. These characteristics became part
of the political rhetoric of the Young Czechs during the 1870s.

---

35   Ibid., 124.
36   Ibid., 126.

After the 1870s the activities of workers' choral societies increased slowly. The workers' songs were based on folk tradition, but adapted for a growing urban proletariat. They helped to integrate the workers' movement in a limited way as part of the Czech national mobilization, but more significantly under the strong influence of the international social democratic movement. In this sense the workers' songs exceeded the national framework; but their melodic elements were often based on famous Czech folk songs and patriotic songs which were very popular in this period. As far as fully organized workers' singing is concerned, their choral societies were not as active and numerous as (petit-) bourgeois ones until the 1890s, when workers' political activities increased and their organizational structures developed quickly in all their fields of interest.

Performances[37] and National Identification

In the Czech case the context of choral performances played a crucial role in building national identity. The most important period of these activities started in the late 1850s, reached its peak in the late 1860s, and subsequently declined; but this period witnessed the massive entering of nationalist efforts into public space. The dynamics of this evolution starts with the rapid growth of activities of the choral societies when their contribution to the organized public action was central, followed by a period of slow decline ending in the merging of collective singing into a more widespread activity with clear political goals.

In the late 1850s Servác Heller, a Czech journalist and author of many nationalist brochures, recorded in his memoirs his own experience of the performative power of choral singing. He described a gathering held in a ballroom in spring 1859 in memory of Karel Hynek Mácha, the famous Romantic poet who died in 1836. Heller noted that this was the only venue and form (*beseda* = ball) allowed by the Austrian police at this time. The celebration culminated when participants gathered into a circle around the poet's bust and read (silently!) an occasional poem dedicated to Mácha. The only communicative part of the program came afterwards, with the singing of 'national songs' that were always enthusiastically applauded.[38] This example shows that in the time of state restrictions of the public sphere, nationalists used rather closed spaces with fewer participants. On the other hand, collective singing (at least at closed social events) was not repressed, unlike public speeches and declamations.

---

37   For a detailed disscusion of the concept of the performative and performance (in Austin, Derrida, and others) see Šima (2006), 81–85.

38   Heller (1916–23), vol. 1, 148.

The opening of public space to collective singing is also illustrated in the memoirs of the Czech poet and lawyer Ladislav Quis.[39] One day he met a group of fellow students who were carrying the flag of the revolutionary society *Concordia (Svornost)* from 1848, singing patriotic songs[40] and heading out from the city centre of Prague. Quis joined them 'spontaneously,' singing songs all the way to a popular park not far from the city walls. There they continued to sing, dance, and declaim, which he describes as a proper national enjoyment. Such collective singing still had a rather unofficial character, but it had already entered into public space, even if it was outside the symbolically closed space of the busiest and most prestigious streets of the city centre.

In the 1860s the situation changed rapidly. The *Hlahol* society was established in early 1861 and quickly gained respect in the Czech nationalist community. After a year of existence they were able to organize a large meeting of choral societies which took the form of a national festival. In May 1862, on the traditional St. John's Day when thousands of countrymen made a pilgrimage to Prague, more than five hundred members of several choral societies came to Prague for a joint performance and a festive program.[41] The rehearsal of all the groups took place on an island in the Vltava river, i.e. in the open air. According to witnesses, the rehearsal of such a large number of singers was a complicated task. Furthermore, the quality of the choirs was very diverse, because "choristers of younger choral societies were not yet trained enough."[42] Nevertheless, the main concert in the largest theatre hall in Prague reportedly went well. A performance of the present-day national anthem "Kde domov můj" (Where Is My Home?) provoked the audience to stand up and listen "piously to these luscious sounds,"[43] so the song had to be sung once again. Since this was a concert performance, the audience expressed its common experience 'in the name of the nation' with applause and standing ovations. This act brought performers and audience together in a moment of identification which gave them a common understanding of the symbolism of the nation.

During the 1860s national festivals spread widely across Bohemia and Moravia, and choral societies were a regular part of their program.[44] Whether it was festive tappings on foundation-stones or ceremonial unveilings of national memorials, choirs accompanied the central festive act with performances

---

39   Quis (1902), vol. 1, 129–30.

40   Among the songs mentioned are the revolutionary "Šuselka nám píše" (Shuselka Writes to Us), "Slovan jsem" (I Am Slavic), and other songs with historical motifs.

41   Rank and Vichterle, eds. (1862), 89–96.

42   Ibid., 91.

43   Ibid., 94.

44   See Pokorný and Rak (1997).

of patriotic songs.[45] The most important national festival in the nineteenth century—laying the foundation stone of the National theatre in 1868—had also its peak in the collective singing of the *Hlahol* society. The placing of the stone was performed collectively, symbolizing the different entities comprising the nation (politics, music, theatre, sports, workers, students, women, etc.), and collective singing united the audience in a single choral body that brought these differences into one 'unified nation.'

After 1873 the number of large national performances decreased rapidly. Although choral societies played a special role in various local or municipal, political or historical festivals, they were slowly becoming only one among many types of participating organizations. As the number of diverse nationalist societies grew, choral societies were losing their central organizational role for the national movement. In the 1870s they were still performing on various public occasions with a national program, but they were not the organizers of such events.

After a period of relative decline in national performative culture in the 1880s, a new upheaval came with a widely popular national exhibition in 1891 designed to bring together evidence that the Czech nation had reached a high level of social, cultural, and economic development.[46] Czech choral societies were back on stage again, not during the main ceremonies, but by organizing accompanying concerts with both a popular and a classical repertoire. Over the following years this type of performance began to prevail, and choirs with specific professional or social backgrounds performed in concerts or on festive occasions for like-minded groups. For example, the 1892 anniversary of the birth of Jan Amos Komenský, who was celebrated as 'the teacher of nations,' found musical expression in a concert given by the choral society of Bohemian and Moravian teachers.[47]

Conclusions

Czech choral societies played a significant role in the nationalist mobilization of Czechs in the nineteenth century, having their principal impact in the 1860s, starting with nation-wide choral festivals and contributing to the entry of the Czech nationalist movement into public space. During the 1870s the choral movement suffered from controversies within nationalist politics. Political

---

45   For a detailed disscusion of this period, see Šima (2006).
46   Pešek, ed. (1995), 5–21.
47   Pokorný (2000), 207–12.

songs were exploited by the Young Czechs against the conservative Old Czechs, and performance culture declined accordingly. By the end of the 1870s workers' choral societies began to spread slowly, followed by other societies based on professional links. The core of nationalist activities moved into the political and economic spheres, and choral societies became only a minor part of the whole nationalist mobilization. On the other hand, the choral movement itself diversified socially and culturally, which brought integrative tendencies to the movement that culminated in the re-establishment of the nation-wide Union of all Czech choral societies. Despite initial struggles about the organization and form of this national union, this association continued to play a significant role in the Czechoslovak Republic after the First World War. While the performance culture diversified during this period, choral societies generally lost their role in nationalist mobilization, retreating to more closed performances.

These dynamics corresponded to the social background of the Czech choral societies. The first organizations were usually in the hands of the intelligentsia (teachers, writers, journalists), and in the 1860s funding was based on member fees differentiated according to the members' wealth and prestige in the nationalist community. In the 1870s and 80s the number of societies organized by professions grew, along with working-class societies. These societies tried to gain more funds from performances and benefits. By the end of the nineteenth century the social structure of members of societies corresponded more or less with the social structure of Czech national society, while the funding strategies also reflected the social status of particular societies.

Finally, Czech-German tensions also contributed significantly to the nature and dynamics of Czech national mobilization in the nineteenth century. The Czech choral movement evolved in parallel with German choral societies in Czech lands. The interconnectedness of both sides was deep, given their shared initial inspiration, parallel roots in neo-romantic musical culture, and interest in nationalist mobilization. These mutual interests accelerated the dynamics of both movements, but also contributed to tensions between Czech and German nationalist societies in Czech lands that ended by the turn of the twentieth century in national communities that were almost completely separated.

CHAPTER 12

Collapsing Stages and Standing Ovations
Hungarian Choral Societies and Sociability in the Nineteenth Century

Krisztina Lajosi

Almost every Hungarian town and hamlet has its own choral society, and some can boast even two; this is perhaps not a bad thing, since what comes up from the throat does less damage than what goes down. One or two fiery songs can intoxicate the mind more than three bottles of wine. However, to be honest, I prefer listening to a village girl singing her sorrow on the meadow, or a sulky village lad singing his woe in soft or robust tunes, to watching a ridiculous group of elderly men with white mustaches and deformed faces wailing in unison with the flapping arms of a conductor.... Singing suits them about as much as ballet suits a cow.... Small-town caterwauling societies[1] are notorious for many a *casus bibendi*.... At least people are not bored, so they won't start revolutions.[2]

This satirical appraisal of choral societies was written by Kálmán Mikszáth (1847–1910), a famous nineteenth-century novelist who made fun of the attitudes and rituals associated with the singing culture that defined the social life of Hungary in the late nineteenth century. After criticizing the quality of their voices, Mikszáth mocked the pride and eagerness of choirs to win prizes at singing competitions. He ridiculed the prize-winning ceremony at the national song festival held in Debrecen in 1882, where the jury had to give some sort of certificate to almost every participant in order to avoid a scandalous fight among the choral societies who all claimed to have delivered the best performance. When they returned home with their prizes, each choral society was celebrated with great pomp and circumstance by passionate crowds who took pride in the extraordinary achievements of their melodious townsmen.

Choral societies were a matter of prestige that involved whole communities, and sometimes divided them. They provided for many happy occasions advancing social cohesion, but often they became the breeding grounds for political conflicts and class struggles. According to the writer Ferenc Móra

---

1 In the original text the word *dalárda* (choral society) is replaced with *dalárma*, combining *dal* (song) with *lárma* (noise).

2 Mikszáth (2005), 588. Unless otherwise noted, all translations are by the author.

(1879–1934), who published a history of the choral society in Szeged, political oppression forged unity, while liberty created dissent among the people. After the Ausgleich of 1867,[3] some 'good Hungarians' formed a green-tag party and wanted to elect a mayor who supported the Austro-Hungarian compromise, while the 'even better Hungarians,' cherishing the memory of the failed anti-Habsburg revolution of 1848, formed a white-tag party and campaigned for a mayor who did not disavow this revolutionary heritage. In order to resolve this excruciating difference, an anonymous cartoonist proposed to have both candidates sit on a hot stove, and the one who remained seated the longest should become the new mayor of Szeged. However simple and effective this solution might have seemed, the elections were not decided by the hot-stove method. Instead, the city of Szeged itself became a hot hell for a while. The Greens and the Whites did not greet each other, did not shop in the same stores, and did not frequent the same pubs. "The Whites were cursing the Germans in the Zrínyi Restaurant on the church square, while the Greens were glorifying the homeland in the Grapevine pub. Of course, where patriots are so divided even over drinking matters, singing will also reflect dissonance."[4] The director of the first choral society in Szeged, Ede Hánki, was a white-tagged 'true' Hungarian, whose relentlessly temperamental and outspoken nature became the source of much irritation among the Greens, who eventually paid him back for all the discomfort by establishing their own 'élite' choral society. The differences between the old and the new 'élite' society were magnified by the two local newspapers, who were looking for dramatic stories. Finally the 'élite' choral society fell apart and Hánki, with all the active members of his choral society, founded a new choir which he called the 'civic' choral society, as against the 'élite' one that had been disbanded. This 'civic' society was active, and there was hardly any charity in the town which the society did not support.[5]

---

3   The Ausgleich or Compromise of 1867 was the result of many exploratory talks and negotiations between the Austrian and the Hungarian governments after the failed Hungarian revolution and war of independence in 1849. The compromise led to the formation of the Austro-Hungarian Monarchy. In the dualist system Hungary and Austria each had complete independence in domestic affairs, but surrendered their sovereignty in matters relating to foreign and military policy. The emperor had more power than a traditional constitutional monarch, since he could interfere in the decisions of the executive and had absolute authority over his dominions. Public opinion in both countries was divided about the success of the Compromise, and many were convinced that the other party had the better deal.

4   Móra (1922), 10.

5   Ibid., 11–13.

The proliferating choral societies, whether loved or hated, provided musical and social entertainment for Hungarians in the second half of the nineteenth century. As Carl Dahlhaus says of the German *Liedertafeln* and *Gesangvereine*, these choral societies "formed an increasingly dense web of musical societies mingling companionship and music in equal measure."[6] Most of the choirs were formed between the 1860s and 1880s. Fifty choirs participated at the festival in Pest in 1865.[7] Many of these choral societies became members of an overarching national association, the *Országos Magyar Daláregyesület* (Hungarian National Association of Choral Societies), founded in Arad in 1867.

The first amateur male choral society was formed in Pest in 1840 under the leadership of Mihály Havi (1810–64), a singer at the National Theatre. They were the first choir to perform Ferenc Kölcsey's (1790–1838) *Hymn* set to music by Ferenc Erkel (1810–93), which later became the national anthem of Hungary.[8] By the 1840s, choral works were becoming ever more popular in operas. The chorus plays a prominent role in the works of József Ruzitska (ca. 1775–1824), who composed the first Hungarian opera, *Béla Futása* (Béla's Flight) in 1822. Choruses also figure importantly in the operatic works of Károly Thern (1817–86), Béni Egressy (1814–51), Kornél Ábrányi (1822–1903), and Ferenc Erkel, who would later be known as the Hungarian national opera composer.

Hungarian theatres followed the general European trend in staging crowd scenes, creating gigantic historical tableaus, and enhancing the spectacle with 'national' costumes and decorations. Like famous opera arias, the operatic chorales took on a life of their own as part of the repertoire of choirs that sang at festive occasions. Next to these opera choruses, composers set to music popular poems by famous Hungarian poets. The "Bordal" (Wine Song) by Mihály Vörösmarty (1800–55) was a particular favorite, and after Erkel included it in his opera *Bánk bán* (1861) it became a standard piece in the programmes of choral societies all over the country, along with Vörösmarty's other poem, the "Szózat" (Appeal). The poems of the Hungarian national poet Sándor Petőfi (1823–49) were also set to music by Béni Egressy, one of the most prolific choral composers before Erkel. He set to music Petőfi's "Nemzeti Dal" (National Song), which became one of the most popular poems during the anti-Habsburg revolution of 1848. Patriotic songs were ubiquitous in the revolution and the war of independence. Some tunes, like the "Rákóczy induló" (Rákóczy March) and well-known opera choruses like the "Meghalt a cselszövő" (The Schemer Died) from Erkel's opera *Hunyadi László* (1844), gained wide circulation already

6 Dahlhaus (1989), 47.
7 Kacz (1889), 16.
8 Mihálka (1986), 19.

before the revolution; they were disseminated outside the theatre by professional and amateur choirs all over the country.[9] The *Marseillaise* was translated into Hungarian and set to music in 1848 by Mihály Mosonyi (1815–70), a renowned composer of that time.[10] Songs that mocked the Austrians and glorified the Hungarian leaders, especially Lajos Kossuth (1802–94), were sung by soldiers and supporters of the revolution all over the country. The memory of the revolution in folk music has recently been studied by the ethnomusicologist Lujza Tari, who collected these songs in a digital anthology that is now also available online.[11] According to Tari, the "Kossuth nóta" (Kossuth Song) has many variants and was probably sung by thousands of peasants and commoners during 1848; it became one of the best-known relics of the revolution.

After the failed war of independence, communal singing became scarce in Hungary. The so-called Bach regime of the 1850s, named after the infamous Minister of Interior Alexander Bach (1813–93), is remembered as one of the darkest ages in Hungarian politics, ruled with a heavy hand by Haynau's dreaded secret police who retaliated against every suspect political assembly.[12] These circumstances were not conducive to musical and social gatherings. However, the gloomy air had cleared by the 1860s and societal organizations began to flourish among the Hungarians: literary groups, choral societies, reading societies, bourgeois and civic clubs (*polgári kör* and *társas kör*) were founded all over the country. These grass-root civil initiatives of the bourgeoisie were all the more important since under the Bach regime the only way to participate in public life was by showing loyalty to the Austrian political system. "Because of the Germanization of the public administration, the nobility and the bourgeoisie were excluded from the running of the country. Anyone who, nevertheless, assumed office for existence reasons could expect to become a social outcast."[13] It is therefore no surprise that the writer Ferenc Móra, in his short history of the choral society of Szeged, claimed that the choral festival of 1866 organized by the city of Szeged was not only an entertainment for the local population but a celebration of the whole country.

---

9   Ibid.

10   See Lujza Tari's website *Revolution, War of Independence in 1848/49 and its Remembering in the Traditional Music.*

11   See Tari, *A szabadságharc zenei emlékei.*

12   Julius Jacob von Haynau (1786–1853), also called "the Habsburg Tiger" or the "Hyena of Brescia," was an Austrian lieutenant who became famous for his ruthless and aggressive military leadership. In Italy and Hungary he was remembered for his brutality and merciless oppression of the anti-Habsburg revolutionary insurrectionists.

13   Toth, ed. (2005), 404.

The devil put the Bach regime in his sack, but did not take it away completely yet. The double-headed eagle turned both its necks towards his fatherland, but its claws were still holding tight to the Hungarian wool. It was still a patriotic duty to show resistance by wearing the Hungarian national costume and a Kossuth-beard and to sing Hungarian songs. National resistance was bursting in every song and every rhythm, and we had to make singing a national cause not only because we liked it, but also because it infuriated the oppressive power. The national song was not only a delight for the heart, but also a political weapon.[14]

This "political weapon" proliferated in the 1860s and it was also encouraged by the leading composers of that time: Kornél Ábrányi, Ferenc Erkel, and Mihály Mosonyi. The first Hungarian musical journal, *Zenészeti Lapok* (Musical Papers),[15] published articles regularly about the choral festivals and about newly formed choral societies. From 1868 the *Zenészeti Lapok* became the official journal of the Hungarian National Choral Society. Kornél Ábrányi, who was appointed editor-in-chief by the Society, "made the support of the Hungarian choral movement his new goal."[16]

Given the proliferation of choral societies in Hungary and their prominence in the press and public sphere in the latter half of the nineteenth century, it is remarkable that they have not received more scholarly attention. As far as I am aware, there are no comprehensive studies of Hungarian choral societies, except for one unpublished doctoral dissertation that focuses on children's and women choirs.[17] Both cultural and music historians either ignore them completely or mention them only in a few dismissive paragraphs.[18] This disparaging attitude towards choral societies could perhaps be explained by the quality of the music they were propagating, the folksy character of their repertoire, and the lack of musical education of most of their members. Music histories traditionally chronicle the production of art music and overlook low-brow music-making. However, choral societies in Hungary formed a bridge between high art and low-brow entertainment: they made certain high-brow pieces accessible to the general public, and popularized musical education

---

14   Móra (1922), 9.
15   *Zenészeti Lapok* (1860–76), published in Budapest.
16   Szerző (1986), 5.
17   Fazekas (2007).
18   One of the best-known histories of Hungarian music, László Dobszay's *Magyar Zenetörténet* (1998), devotes less than one page (p. 324) to a description of the nineteenth-century Hungarian choral movement.

and musical culture by involving as many people as possible in their ritualized gatherings and festivals. Choral societies may not have improved the quality of musical production, but they certainly played an important role in spreading musical culture. When the *Zenészeti Lapok* became the official newsletter and journal of the National Association of Hungarian Choral Societies, subscriptions to the journal soared, and more people supported the publications of the musical press than ever before.[19]

Choral societies organized societal life, shaped and cultivated national consciousness, and increased the demand for original Hungarian choral compositions. The social and political functions of these societies were closely intertwined with their artistic, entertaining, and educative aspects. Though most of them had from ten to twenty-five active members, the number of the supporting members could exceed 600, which was a significant basis for sustaining a regular musical culture in Hungarian towns.

The first records of Hungarian choral music in a modern sense date from the eighteenth century. Choral singing developed in the Protestant colleges— especially in Debrecen, Sárospatak, Kolozsvár, and Miskolc—and the choirs participated not only at school festivities but also at town celebrations. These choirs sang mainly church music and occasionally German songs, usually in Hungarian translation. The poets of the so-called Western School, László Amadé (1703–64) and Ferenc Verseghy (1757–1822), had both received Catholic educations and sought to elevate Hungarian musical culture by imitating and translating German songs. Because the population of Hungarian cities was largely German, and the Hungarian bourgeoisie also spoke German, the domestication of German models was not difficult. Following the examples of the college choirs and the advice of eighteenth-century poets, the first amateur choirs were formed, and they sang German songs in German. The popularity of the German-style *Liedertafeln* was a first phase in the history of choral singing in Hungary, but at the same time it hindered the development of Hungarian choral works.[20]

The growing reputation of *verbunkos* music[21] in the so-called Reform Era (1825–48) also had an impact on the development of vocal music. Verbunkos originated as recruiting music for the Austrian army, but by the nineteenth

---

19   Szerző (1986), 5.
20   Mihálka (1986), 15.
21   The word *verbunkos* is derived from the German *Werbungsmusik* (recruiting music). Since
      the late eighteenth century it came to be seen as the typical Hungarian national music. It
      was first used mainly in instrumental pieces, but later also became popular in vocal music
      and operas.

century it came to be associated with the anti-German *kuruc*[22] identity, mainly because of its role in the anti-Habsburg Rákóczi war of independence (1703–11). Because of its complicated ornamentations, the verbunkos style was not ideal for vocal music, as it did not follow the natural rhythm of the Hungarian language. However, composers like Ferenc Erkel, Béni Egressy, and Károly Thern shaped the verbunkos to fit Hungarian diction, and most of the choral pieces they composed were written in verbunkos style. In the Reform era the cultivation of Hungarian music and the popularity of verbunkos went hand in hand. Musicologists assume that most of the songs during the revolution of 1848 were sung in verbunkos style recalling the memories of the earlier anti-Habsburg Rákóczi insurrection. Verbunkos thus came to be seen as the music of the Hungarian resistance throughout the first half of the nineteenth century.[23] Nevertheless, the choral societies formed in Hungary in the 1840s sang exclusively in German and had only German works in their repertoires.[24] These pioneers were towns in West Hungary with a substantial German population: Győr, Pécs, Pozsony, Sopron, Veszprém, etc.

As mentioned earlier, the first male choir was formed as a private initiative of Mihály Havi in 1840. The *Pestofner Liedertafel*, active for two years, was founded by Antal Dolezsnák in 1844. In the same year the choral society in Pozsony, the *Pressburger Männergesang-Verein*, was established by János Sroffregen and provided musical entertainment until the revolution of 1848. This society also sang mainly in German, but occasionally they performed Hungarian folk songs and the famous "Meghalt a cselszövő" (The Schemer Died) chorus from Erkel's *Hunyadi László*. In 1846 a male choir was founded in Pécs under the leadership of József Ede Wimmer (1820–59). The founder and director of the choral society in Győr was Antal Richter (1802–56), an accomplished musician, kapellmeister, and teacher in the Esterházy family.[25] These choral societies founded in the 1840s did not have a long life, and their activity was put to a halt by the political events of 1848–49.

The crushed war of independence of 1849 was followed by difficult years of reprisal characterized by strict censorship and prohibitions on assembly, which was not favorable for the cultivation of communal singing. Kölcsey's "Himnusz"

---

22   The word *kuruc* refers to the armed anti-Habsburg rebels—mainly of Hungarian and Slavic origin—who fought over a period of almost 100 years against Habsburg rule. The most famous anti-Habsburg uprising was led by Francis II Rákóczi (1676–1735) and led to a war of independence (1703–11).

23   Mihálka, 16.

24   See Kaskötő-Buka (2014).

25   Fazekas (2007), 7.

(Hymn), a popular favorite, was banned, along with other Hungarian music, Hungarian theatre performances, balls, and every form and manner of societal activity that might have presented an occasion for the expression of patriotic feelings.

A Catholic kapellmeister in Pest, Nándor Thill, formed the first post-revolutionary choral society in 1852 under the name *Pest-Budai Dalárda* (*Pest-Ofner Gesangverein*). He and his society operated under the close scrutiny of Haynau's secret police. Only when the state officials noticed that they could not provide music of quality for the king's visit to Pest did they lift the strict restrictions regarding musical gatherings.[26] According to the first article in their statutes, which were published in 1857 in both Hungarian and German, the goal of the society was the cultivation of church music. This specification could also be seen as a strategy to avoid censorship, since there could be no objection to singing Catholic church music. However, the second article of their statute, which elaborates on the 'activities' of the society, mentions monthly singing evenings and excursions along with other educational and charitable pursuits. The article about membership distinguishes between two categories of members: active and honorary ones. The active ones were required to have "some experience with singing so that they won't hinder the singing of the choir."[27] Thill's concert for the king was a success, and with his payment of twenty guilders he commissioned original choral compositions. This was the first competition organized for Hungarian choral works, and many composers responded with enthusiasm. Among the winners were Károly Thern, Károly Huber (1828–85), and Ferenc Doppler (1821–83).

Control was so strict in the 1850s that the programme of every public concert had first to be approved by the censor. In his memoirs Kornél Ábrányi recalled the way his concert in Nagyvárad in 1851 was policed and almost forbidden by the authorities. He traveled from Szolnok to Nagyvárad without a passport, pretending to be a doctor's apprentice. When he arrived after eight days of exhausting travel, he was received with great hospitality by the governor and his music-loving family. The governor approved the programme which contained the following pieces: 1. "Emlékkönyv (magyar ábránd)" (Book of Memories: A Hungarian Dream), 2. "A hegyek között" (In the Mountains) by Ferenc Liszt, 3. "Polonaise" by Chopin, and 4. "Ne sírj hazám (magyar hallgató nóta)" (Don't Cry, My Homeland: Hungarian Song). The first and the fourth pieces were Ábrányi's own compositions. After the poster was printed and the concert was sold out, the police, who had not received notice that the governor approved

---

26   Ibid., 9.
27   *A Pest-Budai Dalárda alapszabályai* (1857), 4.

of the pieces, took action against Ábrányi, who was arrested and questioned at the office of the military commander because of the 'rebellious nature' of his repertoire. Ábrányi explained that the second and the third pieces are well known, and the first and the fourth have nothing insurrectionary about them, quite to the contrary, as their titles suggest, they are wistful in tone; but the general became very angry and reproached Ábrányi for misleading the governor about his concert, since all the titles contained some rebellious allusions to the past. In the interpretation of the general, the "Book of Memories" was inviting the public to bemoan the deaths of the Hungarian heroes of the revolution of 1848; "Among the Mountains" referred to the apotheosis of Görgei[28] above the Carpathian Mountains; the Polonaise celebrates Polish patriotism; and the last piece "Don't Cry, My Country" is a direct "Anspielung," a straightforward reference to the return of Lajos Kossuth from emigration. Ábrányi and his concert were saved only thanks to the intervention of the governor.

The news about the scandal regarding the programme spread quickly in the city, so Ábrányi had no need to worry about publicity for his musical evening. The concert room was packed with a very enthusiastic audience, and also a large number of police to keep an eye on the potentially revolutionary crowd. Some people did express their patriotic sentiments during the final piece, which resulted in a number of arrests. The chief of police, unwilling to admit defeat, showed up the next day at the house of the doctor where Ábrányi was lodging and asked to see his passport. Since he did not have a valid passport, the police tried to convince the governor that Ábrányi had political motives and that his artistic activities were just an excuse to create unrest. In the end, Ábrányi was asked to cancel his second concert and leave the city at once.[29]

In the 1860s, when the political and social climate was becoming less tense and restrictive, choral societies spread rapidly all over the country. The choral society in Szentes was founded in 1861, and that same year Hungarian choral societies were established in Pécs and Arad, followed by Jászberény in 1862, Kecskemét and Szekszárd in 1863, and the following year in Baja, Balassagyarmat, Buda, Debrecen, and Szarvas. By 1864 there were approximately one hundred choral societies.[30] The choral society in Lugos was founded in 1852, the same year as Thill's *Pest-Budai Dalárda*. Its director, Konrád Pál Wusching (1827–1900) was an organ teacher, violinist, and esteemed composer whose choral works were published by several musical journals in Hungary (*Apolló, Zenelap*,

---

28   Artúr Görgey (1818–1916), a Hungarian military leader who was serving in the Austrian army but supported the Hungarian rebels in the 1848 revolution.

29   Ábrányi (1891).

30   Fazekas (2007), 13.

Dalárzsebkönyv). He was awarded a silver medal by the Pope for his church music, and in 1883 the king distinguished him with a golden cross. For forty-six years he edited the yearbook of the choral society in Lugos, *Lugosi Dal- és Zeneegylet Évkönyve*, setting thus a good example of record-keeping for other choral societies to follow.[31] The *Zenészeti Lapok* also wrote appreciatively about the choral society in Lugos: "There are not many choral societies in this country that contribute as much to the cultivation of Hungarian culture as the choral society in Lugos."[32] This society had twenty-eight singers, 166 supporting members, and nineteen honorary members.[33] The society maintained a music school for twenty-six students and had 512 music scores in their library, a mixture of German and Hungarian choral pieces.[34] The same article contains the names of other towns with active choral societies. According to the records from the yearbook edited by Konrád Wusching, the director of the choral society in Lugos, there were choral societies in Arad, Baja, Buda, Csongrád, Debrecen, Eger, Eperjes, Eszék, Fehértemplom, Győr, Hatzfeld, Kőszegh, Kalocsa, Kassa, Karcag, Kisbér, Komárom, Nagykőrös, Lugos, Mohács, Miskolc, Nagykanizsa, Nyíregyháza, Pécs, Pest, Pancsova, Pozsony, Rimaszombat, Szalonta, Szatmár, Szombathely, Orsova, Magyaróvár, Tapolca, Zenta, and Zombor. The journalist of the *Zenészeti Lapok* complained that only a few of these choral societies had contacted their journal, and probably there were more societies around the country, but since they did not officially report their existence, the journal had no information about them.

The choral society in Pécs was arguably the best known and most successful choir in the country. It was founded in 1861 by Károly Wachauer (1829–90), a Catholic kapellmeister. Pécs organized the first national choral festival in 1864, to which only Hungarian choirs were invited. Eighteen choral societies with altogether about 200 members competed for the prize.[35] At this event the flag of their choral society was consecrated, and participants expressed their wish to establish a national overarching association for choral societies; but conditions were not yet optimal yet for the implementation of this initiative, which

---

31   Ábrányi (1892).
32   *Zenészeti Lapok*, (14 Jan. 1864), 123.
33   To get a sense of the scale and the circumstances it is perhaps worth mentioning that in 1880 Lugos (today part of Romania and probably best known as the birthplace of the famous actor Béla Lugosi [1882–1956]) had 11,287 inhabitants of whom 43% were Romanian, 41% German, and 12% Hungarian. In 1910 the total population was 19,818, of whom 35% were Hungarian, 32% Romanian, and 31% German.
34   Ibid.
35   Haksch (1902), 36.

was finally realized in 1867 at the choral festival organized by Arad. It is remarkable that the speech of the main guest, György Majláth (1818–83), who in 1866 had become the Hungarian chancellor, was highly political; he advocated the coronation of Austrian Emperor Franz Joseph I as King of Hungary as a gesture of pacification towards the Hungarian nation. His dream turned into reality in 1867, after the Ausgleich, when Emperor Franz Joseph I was indeed crowned the Hungarian king. But already in 1864 Majláth's words were received with applause and cheers, though as the author points out, "these were very bold words"[36] at that time.

In Pécs the first mention of a choral society dates from 1819, but this was a German group, which is not surprising given that the population of Pécs was largely German. However, in the Reform Era of the 1830s and 40s, as the cultivation of Hungarian culture gained more and more supporters throughout the country, the choral society of Pécs sang more songs in Hungarian: their repertoire ranged from folk songs to opera choruses translated into Hungarian. The first singers of this society were the members of the Catholic church choir reinforced with a number of amateurs. They took the name *Pécsi Dalárda* in 1847, and this is the forefather of the choral society of Pécs founded in 1861. The freshly organized choral society relied on the old statutes of its predecessor from 1847. The first article of the statutes asserts that music occupies a prominent position in the culture of the modern age, and that "the more civilized a nation is and the more highly developed its bourgeois culture, the more attention it pays to the elevation of the arts" and especially to singing, as the human voice is the most beautiful musical instrument.[37]

Thanks to the contributions of their members and well-to-do sponsors, the choral society of Pécs could buy a piano and could even invest in the stocks of the local railway company. By the end of the first year, their collection of scores amounted to 896 Hungarian and German choral songs and some music for piano and orchestra.[38] In the beginning they sang German songs in Hungarian translations, which were not always of the highest quality, but the aesthetic aspect was overlooked for the sake of the "cultivation of our dear Hungarian mother tongue... which in those times was enough to kindle the hearts of the people."[39]

The choral society in Pécs invited students with some knowledge of music from the local college to join their members, hoping that when they became

---

36   Ibid.
37   Ibid., 3.
38   Ibid., 9.
39   Ibid., 12.

teachers in provincial towns they would spread the love of singing and form similar choral societies. Unfortunately the students were less enthusiastic about this plan, and since they did not attend rehearsals, the board of the choral society decided to relieve them from joining the choir. The director also complained of the lax attitude of the regular members who did not show up for weekly meetings and did not learn the pieces. Those members who did not practice and were not able to be present at the rehearsals were fined a small sum for every missed session.[40] Thanks to their stricter discipline and higher level of musical training, the choir from Pécs could participate in every national singing competition, which they won three times over the course of forty years: in Debrecen (1868), Kolozsvár (1874), and Debrecen again (1882).

After conquering the hearts of the Hungarians with their singing, the choral society in Pécs decided to travel abroad and tour in Germany to let the world "pay homage to Hungarian song."[41] However, the world was not very interested in listening to Hungarian songs. According to Haksch, in Austria and especially in Germany they were received with "cold indifference" and "suspicious rejection."[42] In Graz the police asked them to provide a valid permit certifying that they had the right to sing in the territory of Styria. Before they were allowed to advertise themselves and print posters, the director of the choral society had to guarantee that they were not a 'Sängertrupp' of wandering minstrels and would not entertain the public with immoral songs. The choral society of Ischl rejected them, saying that "they do not wish to meet the Hungarian choral society, who should refrain from contacting them in the future." In Salzburg they were told that they "should not accept any honorarium." In Nürnberg they were bluntly informed that they were "not desirable visitors because they are Hungarians," while in Switzerland they were expected to sing dressed up in "national costumes." In Gmunden a lady asked her companion, "Who are these stately people (*stattlichen Leute*)?" and when the man at her side replied that they were Hungarians (*Aha, ich weiß schon, das sind Ungarn!*), the lady remarked with amazement, "*So, die sehen ja aus wie Menschen!*" (So, they actually look like humans!).[43]

Despite these unfriendly remarks and the unwelcoming attitudes, the choral society decided to pursue their goals and to sing at the choral festival in Zürich, Switzerland. They were determined to show the German public that their image of the Hungarians was false, and to convince them of the artistic quality

---

40   Ibid., 14.

41   Ibid., 117.

42   Ibid.

43   Ibid., 118–19.

of their singing. Though the authorities in German cities were not always hospitable, some German choral societies did extend a welcoming hand and sent warm notes to the choral society of Pécs when they read about their upcoming visit in the local newspaper. For example, the *Männergesangverein Nürnberg* sent a kind letter inviting them to Nürnberg and expressing their delight in getting to know the Hungarian singers. On the other hand, the city officials were rude in their response and did not want to admit them to any concert venue. The reason they gave was that they doubted whether the German public would be interested in a Hungarian choral society, since the city of Nürnberg had several excellent choral societies who provided enough musical entertainment for their audiences. The director of one of the local choral societies sent an apologetic letter to Pécs about their unfriendly treatment and reassured the Hungarians about the warm-hearted invitation of the German singers: "even though the public opinion created by journalists is against you simply because you are Hungarians, please do come to Nürnberg." They suggested that given the hostile circumstances, it would perhaps be a better idea to give a joint performance together with the German choral society, and the programme of the two societies would fill the concert hall.[44] After so many humiliating messages the singers of Pécs decided not to go to Nürnberg, and instead to tour only in those cities that eventually were more welcoming. They sang in Aussee, Ischl, Salzburg, Zürich, and Luzern. Despite the hostile reception, after hearing their concerts, the German public changed their mind about the Hungarians, and the singers received standing ovations accompanied with excellent reviews in the newspapers. The journalist of the *Tagepost* (Daily News) from Graz was pleasantly surprised to find "Das Deutsche Lied" on the programme of the Hungarians, and asserted that the choral society from Pécs was not chauvinistic if they chose to sing this song: "das sind keine Chauvinisten, die singen das 'Deutsche Lied' von Kalliwoda."[45] The next day the same newspaper published a rave review of the performance, praising the Hungarian conductor, Károly Wachauer, and the singers who could interpret German songs with such passion. "When the Hungarians started singing 'Das Deutsche Lied' the audience stood up in standing ovation, and the ardor with which they applauded the choir beggars description."[46] In Aussee they were also warmly received, and the reports in the newspapers after the concert were passionately positive. According to the author, "no choir received stronger applause in Aussee than the choral society of Pécs." The director of the local choral society offered to

---

44   Ibid., 126.
45   Ibid., 131.
46   Ibid., 132.

keep them company on their way to Ischl. After this kind reception it was quite disappointing to receive a curt telegraph from Ischl informing them that "the queen was honored by the choral society's offer of a serenade, but she did not wish to receive them." Nevertheless they held a successful concert in Ischl and offered all the proceeds for the support of the local library. The audience in Ischl was moved to tears by this gesture.

In Salzburg they received if not a royal, at least a princely reception. Prince Rohan greeted them personally and invited them to his own residence, which was unheard of even for local choral societies.[47] Following the sensational news about the hospitality of the prince, the public in Salzburg was curious to see the Hungarian choral society. After a very successful concert there was a joint dinner with the local *Liedertafel*; they sang together through the night, and the members of the two societies became good friends. Even the journalist of the *Salzburger Volksblatt* who at first did not welcome the Hungarian singers admitted in his article *"Die Sängergäste aus Ungarn"* that the choral society from Pécs sang with impressive mastery (*Männerchor von solcher Meisterschaft*). The twenty-three singers were praised for their musical education, the quality of their voices, and the rich repertoire they presented. Their performance of five Hungarian and four German songs was outstanding; with their German pieces they conquered the hearts of the Salzburgian public. Finally the author concluded that "if all Hungarians were like the singers from Pécs, Austria could not wish for better neighbors than the Hungarians."[48] In Zürich they were also praised to the skies for their concert and for their generosity in donating all the money they earned to a local charity helping the victims of an avalanche. The director of the local choral society acknowledged that *"Die Ungarn sind bekannt von ihrem Edelmuth!"* (The Hungarians are famous for their magnanimity!). The tour ended in Luzern, where the Swiss public treated the singers from Pécs to standing ovations, especially when they offered the income of their concert partly to a charity helping the poor of Luzern and partly to another charity for poor school children. In the local newspaper they were praised again for the strength of their voices and for their cultivated musical skills. "No amateur choir ever sang so well in Luzern as the choral society from Pécs."[49] They returned from their triumphant German tour to face a chaotic situation at home, where the national association for Hungarian choral societies almost fell apart as a result of internal fights, biased juries, and dissatisfied choir directors.

---

47   Ibid., 138.
48   Ibid., 142.
49   Ibid., 148.

In response to the encouragement and the passionate appeals of Kornél Ábrányi in the *Zenészeti Lapok*, more and more Hungarian choral societies started to join the national association that was formed in 1867 at the choral festival in Arad. However, from its birth, this joint umbrella organization was characterized by conflict and disagreement among its members. The most common complaints were that at the national singing competitions the decisions of the jury were subjective and biased, and that member choirs were not paying their dues, with the result that the national association had to cope with deficits almost on a regular basis. In his history of the Hungarian choral societies Kornél Ábrányi paints a detailed picture of the unruly festival organizations and the rows among the choirs that accompanied almost every national competition. Even the simplest decisions about the location of the next choral competition, or the compulsory song for all the choirs, could lead to polemics. Under these circumstances Ábrányi, who became the president of the national association, found it difficult to keep the peace and prevent the association from falling apart.

As already mentioned, the first national choral festival was held in Pécs in 1864, and was memorable not only for the ceremonious consecration of the flag and the subsequent pompous banquet, but also because the stage proved too flimsy and collapsed under the weight of the choirs who were preparing for a joint performance.[50] The next national festival took place in Pest in 1865, where Liszt premiered his oratorio *The Legend of St. Elizabeth*. Liszt's presence immediately enhanced the zest for participation, and forty-three choirs enrolled for the festival. Five hundred singers performed his oratorio, about which Ábrányi published a detailed review in the *Zenészeti Lapok*.[51] The choral competition took place two days later in the Városliget, a central park in Pest, and according to Ábrányi the singers were all wearing various ornate Hungarian national costumes; Pest never hosted a more colorful crowd. The march of the choirs on the streets of Pest was welcomed by cheering local crowds who then joined them at the festival venue in the Városliget. The stage did not collapse this time, but perhaps to avoid the collapses of the two previous years, the stage was built too low for the audience to see the singers, and because of the open air venue the acoustics were also not the best. Nevertheless, the public was satisfied and the director of the festival, Ferenc Erkel, was lavishly praised.

The next choral festival was held in Arad in 1867, but because of the parallel festivities in Pest around the coronation of Franz Joseph I following the Ausgleich, this festival was almost cancelled. Eventually forty-three choirs

---

50   Ibid., 32.
51   *Zenészeti Lapok*, 17 Aug. 1865 (online version: ZL 1864/65: 361).

participated and the festival was well received, but not as glamorously as the one in Pest two years earlier. In Arad it was decided that the choirs would unite in a national association and would hold choral competitions every second year. In 1868 Debrecen organized the next choral festival, which followed a familiar routine: the choirs arrived by train (usually 1,000–1,200 singers); they were welcomed by the members of the local choral society at the train station; they marched through the city with their banners flying, and were admired and celebrated by the local population. The next day they participated at a church ceremony, rehearsed their songs, and had a joint banquet, and the national committees held their meetings. The third day was devoted to the competition, and at the end of the day the jury announced the results. The last stage of this ritual was the expression of discontent with the decision of the jury and the usual fights of the choir directors who all felt wronged by the final judgment. In the beginning the winners were given a silver cup that was usually awarded by the local women supporters. Later the choirs received only a diploma. In the following years the national choral competitions and festivals were held in Pest (1870), Nagyvárad (1872), Kolozsvár (1874), Szeged (1876), Kolozsvár (1880), Debrecen (1882), Miskolc (1884), Pécs (1886), Szeged (1889), Budapest (1892), Fiume (1894), and Budapest (1896).

Some choral festivals were also disturbed by ethnical conflicts, since the national association admitted only Hungarian choirs and the choral festivals regarded themselves as the guardians of Hungarian songs, which meant that the choirs of the ethnic minorities living on the territory of Hungary were excluded from the choral festivals since they would not—and in many cases could not—sing in Hungarian. The strongly nationalistic atmosphere of the choral festivals and competitions led to serious frictions and conflicts with the choirs of the minorities. The *Zenészeti Lapok* tried to encourage the choirs of the ethnic minorities to take part in the festivals, but "none of the Romanian or Saxon choirs wanted to accept the invitation."[52]

Although contacts with the choirs of the ethnic minorities were far from optimal, there were a few exceptions. When the choral society of Pécs visited Eszék (Osijek, now Croatia) in 1863, the locals greeted the singers and their companions with banners written in three languages: Croatian, German, and Hungarian. The river port was decorated with Hungarian and Croatian flags, the welcoming speeches were also given in three languages, and the choirs of the different ethnicities were very friendly towards each other.[53] Another example

---

52   Ábrányi (1892), 178.
53   Reberics (1886), 15.

of a positive attitude towards minorities was the festival held in Brassó in 1888 where the Hungarian organizers also invited Romanian and German choirs.[54]

The more numerous the choral societies became, the more influence they demanded in the musical press, *Zenészeti Lapok*. After they agreed with Kornél Ábrányi that the *Zenészeti Lapok* would be the official journal of the choral societies, they treated the journal as theirs and insisted that Ábrányi should publish more news about choral events. However, Ábrányi did not want to alter his editorial policies drastically and fill the journal only with news about the choral societies, so he repurchased the proprietary rights in 1873 and reclaimed the journal from the dominating policies of the choral movement. After this year, the choral coverage was relegated to a subsidiary position.[55]

The popularity of the choral societies were often linked to other social gatherings and caused many *casus bibendi*, as Kálmán Mikszáth noted in his satirical essay quoted at the beginning of this essay. One such drinking bout led to a good deal: the choral society of Komárom was offered a venue for ten years by a local squire for a token price. The members of the society were very pleased with the offer and wanted to thank the generous man in person for his kind proposal. They visited him and gave him a serenade, after which they were all invited for a drink, after which the generous host revoked his first offer and gave the choral society the use of the venue for twelve years free of charge.[56] Often the choral evenings were followed by ballroom dancing, or sometimes by bowling and other societal entertainments which were seen by some purist critics as a sign of degeneracy.

Almost all the conductors complained of the lack of discipline among the regular members who did not attend the weekly rehearsals.[57] Choral societies had to cope with clashes among their regular and supporting members over the right to vote and decide on important matters regarding the rules of the society. The societies competed among themselves to invite famous composers as honorary members. Erkel and Ábrányi were the honorary members of more than one choral society.

Social conflicts among the members also presented the conductors with a challenge. For example, the life of the Hungarian choral society from Brassó (1863) was marked by interdenominational tensions and problems related to the different social backgrounds of the members. Though the choir split along the social lines, after a few years they reunited again, since their willingness

---

54   Józsa (1886), 74.
55   Szerző (1986), 5.
56   Kacz (1889), 25–26.
57   Zoltsák (1889), 13.

to have a local Hungarian choral society and their love of singing together helped them through the problems; in the end they managed to stay together despite the conflicts.[58] "The choral movement," Philip Bohlman argues, "was the embodiment of the nation-state as an amalgam of different classes and types of people. This is not to say that many nineteenth-century choruses were openly democratic."[59] The Hungarian choral societies were exclusively male. The first women's choir was formed in 1870 in Vác, but it was not until the first decades of the twentieth century that women became actively involved in a national network of choirs.[60] Socially mixed choirs also led to many polemics. The priests speaking at the flag consecration festivity in Baróth also warned the choral society against letting social tensions stand between their members.[61] Towards the end of the nineteenth century choral societies were mushrooming, and almost every village had its own choir, but the critics complained more frequently about the lack of musical education of the singers and the remarkably poor quality of their performances at the national festivals, where many choirs arrived totally unprepared and did not even learn the compulsory piece. "There are 1,200 people on the stage of whom only 200 can sing."[62]

Though by definition the raison d'être of the choral societies was singing, many regarded music as a secondary goal compared to the cultivation of Hungarian culture. This is clear from the mottos of the choral societies or from their statutes: the most often used words were 'dear fatherland' and singing for 'the glorification of the Hungarian nation.' Newspaper articles, reports and histories of the choral societies and festivals are all more concerned with the societal aspects of these events than with the singing proper. The ritual of the flag consecration was one of the main elements of the festivals: the flag was taken to the church and consecrated in the framework of a religious ceremony. Each flag had a 'mother.' This role was played by a highly regarded lady in the local community who had also given a large financial contribution for the manufacturing of the flag. At the ceremony, the flag mother, accompanied by 'flower girls,' crowned the flag with a laurel.[63] The coronation of the flag was followed by the hammering of so-called nails into the staff of the flag by the local sponsors of the choral society. These 'nails' were in fact tiny metal shields with the names of the sponsors, and each person or society who had a nail also

---

58   Józsa (1886), 12.
59   Bohlman (2004), 50.
60   Fazekas (2007), 51.
61   Török (1894), 15.
62   *Zeneközlöny* (1905), 277.
63   Török (1894), 12.

recited a slogan in praise of the choral society and of Hungarian culture. After a choral society emerged victorious from a competition and arrived back home, they were celebrated like heroes by the people of their city, who organized fireworks, street marches, and balls in their honor. The crowds that gathered to glorify the singers could be compared to present-day football supporters who celebrate when their club wins a match.

By the end of the nineteenth century choral societies were ubiquitous in Hungary and provided access to social participation and musical entertainment for a large section of society. While celebrating the local, they raised awareness of the national. They were intermedial cultural elements uniting literary, musical, and political discourses in performative acts. They did not change the structure of the public sphere, but through their performative acts they accentuated group solidarity and became vehicles for the solidification of national identity. As Christopher Small argues, music should not be seen as an aesthetic category, as a thing, but rather an activity, which he calls "musicking." He warns us against the "trap of reification" when it comes to appreciating and studying music: "Music is not a thing at all but an activity, something that people do."[64] Examining the history of choral societies in their local, national, and international networks can contribute to the renegotiation of the musical canon and to a better understanding of the cultural and social function of music. Choral societies can be regarded as catalysts which transformed their listeners into a socially engaged public and the public into political crowds. Studying rituals of performance and their ensuing "riotously interactive relations"[65] could lead to a creative reinterpretations of social and national movements.

---

64   Small (1998), 2.
65   Gramit (2002), 127.

CHAPTER 13

Choral Societies and National Mobilization in the Serbian (Inter)national Network

Tatjana Marković

Choral societies in nineteenth-century Europe served as socio-cultural, political, and artistic centers, and in the case of Serbia, their activities were of key significance in the network constructed between the diaspora and the homeland. Serbian choral societies are indispensable for understanding Serbian national mobilization in the nineteenth century. This paper examines the activities of the numerous societies and their network, which extended from the United States to the Ottoman Empire. The nationalist idea was embodied in the vernacular language and presented first of all through folk and also patriotic songs, cherished by national as well as foreign (mainly Czech) composers.

Serbian national identity was established outside the state territory due to activity in the diaspora and emigration from the Austrian (and later Austro-Hungarian) Empire, forming a kind of double identity as a result of the different historical, political, social, and cultural backgrounds of the Habsburg Monarchy and the Ottoman Empire. The border between the two empires divided the Serbian people, so that their culture developed in two very different contexts. The shifting military border between the two empires passed through Serbia (the Banatian military frontier) and Croatia (the Slavonian military frontier). Invaded by the Ottoman Empire in 1521, Belgrade was later occupied three times by Austria (in 1688, 1717, and 1789), and each time recaptured by the Ottomans. In Vojvodina, the province of the Monarchy, music institutions such as the Musikvereine, municipal orchestras, national theatres, music schools, and conservatories provided a musical life based on European models. On the other hand, life in the Ottoman provinces was marked in the first place by the struggle for liberation, and only during the rare intervals of

* This research was conducted within the postdoctoral project *Opera and the idea of self-representation in Southeast Europe* supported by the Austrian FWF (Fonds zur Förderung der wissenschaftlichen Forschung; Elise-Richter project V143-G18) at the Institute of Musicology, University of Graz (2010–2012) and at the Department of Musicology, Institute for Art History and Musicology, Austrian Academy of Sciences (since 2012).

peace, or after achieving independence in 1878, could a similar cultural life be established or revived.

The two kinds of national identities have been defined theoretically in various ways. One of these assumes differences between so-called Western and Eastern embodiments of national identity based on different ways of understanding national memory. It is emphasized that national identity in the Western sense implies "a 'political nation' . . . referring exclusively to the population living within an area defined by borders," while in the East a common language and culture play the main role.[1] Although this distinction is applicable in some cases, a strict division of Europe into East and West is not fully accurate since, for instance, German national identity is historically closer to the 'Eastern' identity due to its lack of unified territory. It seems that newer colonial and postcolonial theories of national identity might be more appropriate, with the concept of hybrid identity, assuming diversity in one unique geographical space along with the lack of such a unique space within the influential diaspora.[2] Narratives of identity are expressed through various media, one of which is certainly the opera, reflecting contemporary national self-representation, often based in the nineteenth century on a mythologizing of national history.

Serbian national mobilization will thus be considered in the context of intense cross-border transactions between the diaspora and the homeland.[3] Two perspectives on the process of building national cultural identity through diaspora can be distinguished: on one hand, the communication between the diaspora and the homeland directed from outside cultural centres to the national territorial centre, and on the other, the circulations and interactions within the diaspora itself, the Serbian network based outside the home country proper.[4]

Singing Bridges between Diaspora and Homeland

Serbs were disseminated over a large part of Europe, where they spoke a variety of languages but were unable to communicate with people speaking

---

1   See Bischof and Pelinka, eds. (1997), 26. The authors clearly follow the theory of two kinds of national identity developed by Anthony Smith (1993).
2   See Bhabha (1994).
3   See Faist (2010), 15.
4   See Siu (2012), 147.

the vernacular language in Serbia proper;[5] so language reform (starting with Dositej Obradović [1742–1811], Sava Mrkalj [1783–1835] and the pre-romanticists and culminating with Vuk Stefanović Karadžić [1787–1864] in Vienna) was especially important in the context of Serbian culture.[6] It was in fact intellectuals, mainly from Vienna and southern Hungary, who made the biggest contribution to Serbian national culture by establishing the national (vernacular) language,[7] which constituted a national identity in spite of an often explicit lack of support in their own country. Establishing a national culture in the diaspora was characteristic not only of the Serbian community but also for other Slavic peoples living in the Habsburg Monarchy. "Many cultures live in diasporas; many cities, even in early modern and nineteenth-century Europe, are receptacles for the influx of many different cultures."[8]

As in other areas, the first professional Serbian musician was educated in Vienna: Kornelije Stanković (1831–65), from the Serbian community in Buda, was a private student of Simon Sechter, a professor at the University of Vienna. Following the program of Vuk Karadžić, his collaborators, and the circle of Slavic students around him in Vienna, as well as the recommendation of the Serbian Patriarch Josif Rajačić and Professor Sechter, in Sremski Karlovci Stanković systematically transcribed the Serbian Orthodox chant (1855–57), which had been transmitted orally for centuries, and later also Serbian folk melodies (1861–63). Thanks to the support of Prince Mihailo Obrenović (1823–68), he published his collections in Vienna and promoted the Serbian Orthodox chant, which

---

5   Serbian citizens lived in "new two-storey buildings, were travelling in coaches, led discussions... in Latin, spoke the Russian redaction of Church Slavonic language, and on their way to Vienna, Pest, Leipzig and Krakow communicated in German"; Popović (1985), 8. This and all subsequent translations from Serbian are by the author.

6   Karadžić started with a systematic notation of Serbian epic poems, lyric folk songs, and other literary forms. After he published his first collections of Serbian folk poems in Vienna in 1814, reviews by Jakob Grimm (1785–1863) and Jernej Kopitar (1780–1844) in the *Wiener Allgemeine Literaturzeitung* and the *Litterarisches Conversationsblatt* encouraged him to further activity and, on their recommendations, six additional folk melodies were included for the first time in his second collection of folk poems (1815). Serbian folk poetry and other literary forms aroused great interest from Goethe, Mickiewicz, and the Grimm Brothers, as well as composers such as Brahms, Dvořák, Čajkovskij, Huber, Rubinstein, Reger, and Janáček. See Marković (2006).

7   Karadžić's *Srpski rječnik* (1818), a Serbian-German-Latin dictionary containing 26,270 words, presented an adapted version of Serbian grammar for his model of literary language based on the Neo-Shtokavian dialect of epics, and also a new writing system. This had extensive consequences not only for constituting Serbian Romantic literature, but also for the foundation of music terminology in the Serbian language.

8   Leerssen (2006), 176.

was arranged for choir for the first time, at two concerts given at the Wiener Musikverein (in 1855 and 1861).

Choral Music as a Dominant Genre in Nineteenth-Century Serbian Music

Collecting the Serbian musical heritage, including folk songs and melodies, and their four-part arrangements for voice and piano, or a male choral ensemble, were the first steps in constituting a Serbian national culture. The primary means in this process was choral singing.

There were a variety of reasons why this was so. Some were political. For example, cultural societies (whether choral, literary, or gymnastic) and church services were the only forms that allowed Serbs to gather in public spaces. Through patriotic poetry it was possible to express ideas about liberation that were otherwise prohibited. Choral societies also provided an important means to establish bourgeois culture inside Serbia, since they were the most accessible form of cultural and musical life for numerous amateurs in Serbian society, and membership did not require a professional musical education. The choral singing of songs in the vernacular facilitated networking among Serbs from different parts of Europe. The associations of the choral societies also contributed to education more generally: musical performances were often combined with lectures on topics about geography, medicine, or national poetry. In addition, some associations (such as the *Ujedinjena omladina srpska* [United Serbian Youth] or the *Savez srpskih pevačkih društava* [Association of Serbian Choral Societies]) published their own journals with news of European musical life and productions. The choral societies provided places where Serbian citizens could exchange journals from Vienna, Paris, Pest, and other cities about contemporary architecture, fashion, and art, as well as political and financial news.

The first Serbian choral societies were established in the 1820s and 1830s, mainly within the Habsburg Monarchy. It was no coincidence that they should be established in multi-ethnic environments such as Pančevo (situated on the military border between the Austrian and Ottoman Empires), Novi Sad, or Kotor. It is understandable that the choral societies were founded first in the territory of Vojvodina, first of all in the free royal cities: Novi Sad (the 'Serbian Athens'), Sombor, Velika Kikinda, and others. They formed a very wide institutional network by increasing their numbers and occupying a gradually wider and wider territory. The list of places where choral societies appeared is certainly not definitive, yet it confirms the widespread dissemination of this cultural, socio-political, and artistic network. Consequently, choral and reading societies were very significant in the process of national networking, especially in multi-ethnic environments such as the towns in the Habsburg Monarchy, particularly in the Banat, where they coexisted with Hungarian, German, and also Romanian choirs.[9] Serbian choral societies were established not only in the cities, but in numerous towns and villages as well, including both citizens' and farmers' vocal ensembles.[10]

The dominance of male choirs until the 1880s was in accordance with European (German) practice, but also with a patriarchal society like the Serbian. There were several exceptions, like the independent female choirs of specific institutions such as women's institutes. Choirs for children and young people were set up in primary schools and gymnasia.

Choral societies were often established in orthodox churches, since an administrative procedure, establishing definite and published regulations, with a statement of aims and planned activities, was necessary before the official public work of a choral society could begin. Without this procedure, a choral society would not be allowed to work officially. Nevertheless, many choral societies were active without official permission, although illegal gatherings and performances could cause certain police restrictions. The choral societies had their own recognizable national signs, such as a flag or an anthem.

Choral Societies and the United Serbian Youth

The national-political mission of the choral societies was embodied in all their activities as well as their iconography: their aim was to promote liberation, independence, and above all—unity. It seems that those who were most far-sighted and successful in surmounting the division of the Serbian people and in achieving their union were the members of the liberal Serbian youth. Together with Vladimir Jovanović, the leader of the Liberal party, they established "one of the biggest organizations in recent Serbian and Yugoslav history,"[11] the *Ujedinjena omladina srpska*, precisely in Vojvodina, in Novi Sad. Their annual assemblies were held in the multi-ethnic Vojvodina cities (Novi Sad, Kikinda, Vršac), so that the Constitution of the United Serbian Youth was published in both the Serbian and Hungarian languages. This organization included at the beginning of its work sixteen institutions best suited for a very wide process of networking: literary and choral societies, later in collaboration with the

---

9   See Ilić (1978) and Marković (2006).
10   See Pejović (1991), 21–22.
11   Milisavac, ed. (1968), 13.

sokol (gymnastic) societies. All the activities of the United Serbian Youth were aimed at the education of the Serbian people in order to make the struggle for national unity widely accepted and to preserve it in the multi-ethnic communities in Vojvodina or, more widely speaking, in the Habsburg Monarchy.

Political circumstances, such as the lack of national unification reflected in cultural and musical life, resulted in a focus on a political and cultural strategy similar to that of German students several decades earlier:

In the War of Liberation of 1813, the German nation rose to preserve its pride and ancient traditions, to halt the advance of Napoleon, and to avenge its earlier defeats at Jena and Auerstadt in 1806. From 1806 to 1813 the idea of Germany had begun to take shape. Johann Fichte found the answer to German problems in national education, using Pestalozzi's ideas of a culture of the intellect, practicality, and patriotism. The famous *Turnvater* Jahn organized students at German universities into a patriotic national force through his work in gymnastics. The fiery poet Ernst Arndt placed the greatest value of a nation in its common language and common origins. From 1806 on, the social and national growth of the German nation was simultaneous with the growth of the male chorus.[12]

In other words, as might also be said about the Serbian male choral societies: "the German male chorus became both the symbol of a united Germany through the bond of German song, and an agent of social and political change."[13] Members and collaborators of the United Serbian Youth expressed not only the same aim, but also an awareness of this similarity. Thus, on 9–10 June 1869, a ceremony was held to consecrate the flag of the *Vršačko srpsko crkveno pevačko društvo* (Serbian Church Choral Society of Vršac), with the attendance of Serbian choral societies from Belgrade, Novi Sad, Pančevo, Timisoara, and Vršac. This was their programme:

I. The First Day
1. At 8:00 a.m. the procession with the flag will go from the music school through the market and the royal street to the cathedral, where the flag will be consecrated after the liturgy.

   Afterwards: a) The president's speech; b) Driving the nails; c) The speech of the godmother while giving of the flag to the president; d) The speech of the flag-bearer while receiving the flag from the president; e) "Ne dajmo se" (Let's Not Give Up) sung by all the choral societies.

---

12   Brinkman (1970), 17.

13   Ibid., 16. The author is clearly wrong to claim that "the growth and development of German male singing in the early nineteenth century represents a unique historical phenomenon."

2. At 2:00 p.m. there will be a banquet.

3. At 8:00 p.m. "Beseda" (Speech).

II. The Second Day

1. At 7:00 a.m. there will be an assembly of the singers to discuss the following topics: a) ways in which fellowships for music students could be established; and b) the needs of Serbian music and ways to fulfill them.

2. At 8:30 p.m.: "San na javi" (A Dream in Reality) by J. Subotić and *Lek od punica*, a theater play in the honor of the celebrators.

Everyone who would like to attend the festivity can, with the identification paper of our choral society, travel for half-price by ship or train in both directions.

In Vršac. The Committee.[14]

Next to the festive concert part of the manifestation, there was also an official meeting attended by the elected president of the assembly, the politician Vladimir Jovanović, the vice-president and conductor of the Vršac society, Vojtěch Hlaváč, the author Aleksandar Sandić, and others. Comparing Serbian choral societies with those of Prussia, Milan Jovanović from Belgrade said that choral societies

> were coming closer and closer to fulfilling their mission, since they were starting to accept genuine Serbian ideas. The same was occurring in Germany: shorter songs were being united into one long song that became a song of freedom. We need a freedom song too, and in order to achieve this, it is necessary to call the people to support the already existing choral societies as well as to establish new ones.[15]

Within the Diaspora: National Choral Societies in a Multi-Ethnic Context

Serbian choral societies played a more complex role in the multi-national (multi-ethnic, multi-lingual) context of Vojvodina or other parts of the then Austro-Hungarian Empire. Every individual ethnic group defined its own national, political, and cultural space by means of language, education, and the

---

14   Programme leaflet *Osvećenje zastave vršačkog Srpskog crkvenog pevačkog društva* (Vršac, 1869).

15   *Pančevac, nedeljni list za prosvetne i materijalne interese*, 22 June 1869.

establishment of certain institutions and media. Serbs resisted Magyarization and Germanization through their journals, theatre plays, and choir songs.

The Serbian community had the longest tradition of choral singing in Banat. Among Pančevo choral societies, for instance, undoubtedly the most significant and active one was the still extant *Pančevačko srpsko crkveno pevačko društvo* (Serbian Church Choral Society in Pančevo), and there were two more Serbian choral societies: *Venac* (Wreath, est. 1886) and *Zanatlijsko pevačko društvo* (Craftsmen's Choral Society), as well as three German choral societies: the *Deutscher Männergesangverein* (1863), *Deutscher Gewerbegesangverein* (1886), and the *Evangelischer Kirchengesangverein* (1883). The conductors of the Serbian societies were Czech, German, and Serbian musicians who wrote compositions to verses of Serbian poetry. However, when it came to membership, equal tolerance did not exist. German and Hungarian choral societies collaborated much more, compared with Serbian ones, which is understandable regarding their common religion. Serbian amateur musicians participated only in the work of Serbian societies. One article of the *Srpsko zanatsko pevačko društvo* (Serbian Craftsmen Choral Society) regulations stated that craftsmen could join the society "regardless of their religion or nationality"; but the Serbian journal *Glas* published a sharp critique saying that "it would then no longer be a Serbian choral society," and expressed doubt whether "decent craftsmen" would care to join such a society at all.[16]

The Viennese music periodical *Fromme's musikalische Welt*, which reported on musical life in Vienna since 1876, also included a list of music institutions in the Monarchy. Among others, it is a source of data (such as the name of the conductor and the number of members) for Serbian choral societies from Vojvodina.

The Association of Serbian Choral Societies

Choral societies formed a unique network through various types of cooperation, contributing to a cultural area of Serbs unified in spite of geographical and political boundaries. The network was institutionalized by the establishment of the *Savez spskih pevačkih društava* in Sombor from 1911–14.[17]

The Association of Serbian Choral Societies (ASCS), including thirteen choral ensembles, was founded in December 1910 (by the Julian calendar used in

---

16   *Glas*, 11/23 April 1887.

17   The idea had been mooted several times since 1865–66, but was not realized until 1911. See Marković (1995).

Serbia at that time) or in January 1911 by the Gregorian calendar. A president was elected, along with members of a governing board, and a steering committee was formed consisting of the presidents of the various choral societies (from Sombor, Stari Bečej, Novi Sad, Veliki Bečkerek, and later Zrenjanin and Velika Kikinda). The aims of this institution were stated as follows:

1)   to bring together in one association all the Serbian Orthodox church and secular choral societies and all other non-political societies which cherish, among other purposes, the Serbian Orthodox Church chant;
2)   to support Serbian traditional and classical vocal and instrumental music;
3)   to help all the members of the Association to be equally ... active in order to achieve these aims.[18]

The Rules of the ASCS reflect Enlightenment ideas and the ideology of romanticism embodied in the interaction of the discourse of folklore and the discourse of patriotism:

1)   to form choral societies in the choral singing parishes;
2)   to identify the places and areas where no church or secular choral societies yet exist, and promote their establishment there as well;
3)   to encourage discipline, work, and progress for individual choral societies;
4)   to purchase and issue church/spiritual and secular compositions for Serbian choral societies;
5)   to collect traditional church and secular vocal music and to publish them in professional editions;
6)   to establish a central federal archive to include all earlier and more recent compositions by Serbian musicians;
7)   to publish a music journal designed to announce all decisions and intentions of the Association and to serve as the official organ of the Association and its members;
8)   to convene meetings of the parish choral societies and of the Association;
9)   to give educational lectures on the occasion of the parishes' or the Association's meetings ...
10)   to hold regular annual competitions of the parish choral societies, along with song festivals of the Association;
11)   to organize educational courses for choir conductors;

---

18   *Pravila Saveza srpskih pevačkih društava* (Sombor: M. Bikar i drugovi, 1911), Articles 2 and 3.

12) to provide for regular visits to the chairs of the parish choral societies and ASCS board members for supervision and direct instruction to ensure that all members of the Association achieve the same working methods...;

13) to present awards for choral compositions and their publication;

14) to explore the possibility of founding a music school for the professional education of musically talented children;

15) to support talented young Serbian men and women to attend foreign music academies and conservatories;

16) to recognize deserving Serbian and foreign musicians and other activists for spreading Serbian songs.[19]

Membership in the Association of Serbian Choral Societies required filling in an application form and paying dues. These forms are kept in the Historical Archive of Sombor, and they are a precious source of data about choral societies. Here, for example, is the application form submitted by the *Srpska akademska pjevačka tamburaška družina 'Balkan'* (the Serbian Academic Choral and Tambura society *Balkan*) from Zagreb:

- Date of foundation: October 16/29, 1904
- The first committee: President: Milan Ćurčić; Vice-President: Đuro Helbet; Secretary: Uroš Trbojević; Treasurer: Mirko Kosijer; Committee Members: Andrija Frušić, Dušan Đermanović; Review Committee [not named]
- Date of confirmation: January 20, 1905
- Brief history of the Society's activity up to the present. The main moments: In its seven years of continuous existence, *Balkan* has visited almost all Serbian areas. In its first year the society was in Banja Luka for the consecration of the flag of the Serbian Choral Society *Jedinstvo* (Unity)...During their second year they visited some places in Banat and Srijem. In its third year the 'B.' traveled all through Bosnia, Herzegovina, Montenegro, and Dalmatia....This year it was...in Trieste, that conscious, rich trading Serbian colony, and during the holidays, it traveled all around Serbia, all the way to Vranje and Pirot. Along with this, during the seven working years of its existance, the 'B.' has organized more than 100 concerts.
- Number of members: 43; number of males: 43, number of females: 0
- Property and assets: the membership fee; the membership fee for new members is one crown. By the way, the Society has no ready cash...

---

19   Ibid., Article 2.

- Where does the singing school take place? In private houses, or if not, where? And how many times per week?: In the building of the Serbian parish church, together with the supportive literary society. At least three times per week.
- Members of the current administration: President Nikola Ćurčić, cand. phil.; Vice-President Jovan Ranković, cand. iur.; Treasurer: Milan Stajić, phnd. phil.; Councillors: Mihajlo Matić, cand. phil., Dimitrije Petrović and Đuro Čutuković, phnd. phil.
- The library, scores and all music works in full, otherwise numbers: (see the list of compositions).
- In Zagreb, May 20, 1911[20]

The practice of working without a license can be proved, for instance, by the fact that *Srpska crkvena pevačka zadruga iz Zemuna* (the Serbian Church Choral Society in Zemun), was established "ca. 1855, no exact data about that," and its activity was officially confirmed only on 15 September 1866.[21]

Among the societies interested in becoming members of the Association was also the *Srpsko pevačko društvo 'Gusle'* (Serbian Choral Society "Gusle") from New York. The letter they sent to Sombor is worth quoting:

New York, 18 March 1914
To the respected Association, the Serbian choral society 'Gusle'

We have decided to become a member of the respected Association, but since we are not familiar with the membership conditions from America (the United States), we would like to ask you to send us your rules, and we will act according to them as soon as we receive them.

We are also asking you to send us several newest scores for singing and for the music (Tambura ensemble). We shall send you the money as soon as we receive the bill. . . .

Looking forward to the respected news from you very soon, we are sending you Serbian greetings and with respect,

Serbian Choral Society "Gusle"
Vid Vuić, secretary[22]

---

20   Istorijski arhiv Sombora, Fond 42.
21   Ibid.
22   Translated from Serbian by the author.

Ideas of Yugoslavism and the establishment of a common state of South Slavs resulted in proposals to establish a unique music organization for the region: "It is understandable that the new as well as renewed institutions cannot be organized on a narrow tribal basis: all of them should be permeated by the idea of national Serbian-Croatian-Slovenian unity."[23] This led in 1924 to the establishment of the *Južnoslovenski pevački savez* (Association of South Slavic choral societies).

The Association of Serbian Choral Societies gathered societies from cities, towns, and villages in Austro-Hungary and Serbia as well as the United States. Due to the institutional structure of the Association, and the documentation of the individual choral societies that had to be provided, precious data about their work has been preserved.

The Association of Serbian Choral Societies encouraged not only choral performance practice, but also music production. They organized competitions for the best choral compositions, and also published a collection of the choral works:

> we have published the first volume of scores for choral societies. We are convinced that this volume, with its scope and content, has brought something new into Serbian music literature... The professional Slavic music journals, such as the Czech *Hudba, Novi akordi*, and *Pjevački vjesnik*, have expressed high praise for this edition.[24]

The official journal of the Association of Serbian Choral Societies, *Gusle* (1911–14) reported on the work and performances not only of Serbian choral societies, but also information about musical life, especially among choral societies abroad which they took as their model. Serbian cultural and musical writings of the nineteenth century found aspects of contemporary musical life in German countries and the Habsburg Monarchy not only familiar, but also worthy of emulation. Evidence for this includes, for example, articles like the following "News from musical life," published in the journal *Gusle*:

> The Nuremberg all-German vocal meeting. As many as 1700 German vocal groups, with 1100 flags, have applied so far. Among them are vocal groups from Hungary, Russia, Turkey and America. Special premises are built for this occasion. The concert hall will be 132 meters long and

---

23   Konjović (1920), 140.

24   *Izveštaj Upravnog...* (1914), 7–8.

9000 [sic] meters wide... This is how it is done where there is organization and a strong national consciousness. The vocal groups are a force that the highest circles take into account; and they became that way thanks solely to their work and tight organization.[25]

It is obvious that in the Austro-German context outlined above, music criticism had now become a focal point for ideological reflections on the nature of music.

The First Serbian Choral Festivity

The activity of the Association of Serbian Choral Societies could be illustrated by the largest event they organized: the *Prva srpska pevačka slava*, which was held over three days in June 1914, shortly before the institution ceased to function. They received support from the free royal city of Sombor, and also from the command of the Fourth Artillery Corps in Budapest.[26] The jury consisting of three members (one composer, Miloje Milojević, and two musicians, Dušan Kotur and Cvetko Manojlović), had the task of choosing the three best choral societies from among the seventeen that took part in the competition; the winners were *Srpsko građansko pevačko društvo* (the Serbian Civil Choral Society) and the *Akademsko pevačko društvo 'Balkan'* (the Academic Choral Society *Balkan*), both from Zagreb, in Croatia. As was pointed out,

> in its scope, and the reception by choral societies, this festivity was in accordance with the plan and intent of the Association's presidency, which was able to offer with this celebration a nice pleasure not only to choral societies and Serbian singers, but also a stronger élan and enthusiasm to our people from this side. Our national optimism, now awake and developed in all layers of the folk more than ever, is expressed this time too, and strongly.[27]

---

25   The author of the report probably meant to say that the concert hall was 90 meters wide. "Nirnberški svenemački pevački savez," *Gusle* no. 5 (1912), 79.

26   Istorijski arhiv Sombora, Fond 42: 42.78, 42.79.

27   Konjović, 140–41. By "our people from this side" Konjović had in mind Serbs who lived outside the homeland or, more precisely, in Croatia.

The Model of Viennese Performance Practice

West and Central European (and above all Germanic) Romanticism pervaded Serbian art directly and indirectly: directly in the same contexts (of Austria and Hungary), and indirectly via the first Serbian professional musicians educated in centres such as Vienna, Pest, Prague, or Leipzig, who brought their experiences back to the Serbian cultural environment of their homeland. This process of migration witnessed a particular mixture of elements of European Romantic music with local tradition.

These influences are obvious in the repertoire and certain aspects of the performance practice of Serbian choral societies. The early history of Serbian choral singing was marked by a dearth of compositions in the Serbian language, so that works by composers of the eighteenth and early nineteenth centuries were adapted for national purposes. For instance, the famous slow movement from Beethoven's "Appassionata" (opus 57, no. 23) was arranged for male choir under the name "Molitva pod zvezdama" (A Prayer under the Stars).

The repertoire of the Serbian choral societies, especially in Serbia proper, included first of all patriotic songs. They were more frequent and much more popular than lyrical, sentimental compositions based on love poems or descriptions of landscapes. Patriotic poetry set as choral music ranged from second-rate amateur songs to poems of the highest quality written by the main representatives of the Serbian Romantic poets (Jovan Jovanović Zmaj or Đura Jakšić). Since the patriotic message was the most important aspect of choral music, the compositions were mainly of homophonic texture, homorhythmic, providing for a clear pronounciation of the verses. They owed their popularity also to certain topics which played a major role in the construction of Serbian national identity: the Battle of Kosovo (1389) and its heroes, the medieval Serbian Empire of the Nemanjić dynasty (the 'golden age' of Serbia, especially the reign of Stefan Uroš IV Dušan Nemanjić, known as Dušan the Great, the Serbian medieval king 1331–45 and the first Serbian tzar 1346–55), and heroes from the more recent First Serbian Uprising (1804–13).

Vienna was not only a centre of Serbian culture, but also a model for the repertoire policy of the choral societies; the Viennese musical canon was redefined in accordance with the new (Serbian) context. While salon music was developed among Serbs from the Habsburg Monarchy, in Serbia itself the main form of musical life was concerts by choral societies with mixed programs. In both cases, arrangements of folk melodies were a recognizable sign of the newly established national culture.

The programmes of numerous choral societies within the *Gesellschaft der Musikfreunde* (such as the *Wiener Männergesangverein*, the *Wiener*

Singakademie, and the *Wiener akademischer Gesangverein*) show that the dominant ideological concepts in the nineteenth century were nationalism and historicism. On the one hand, there were subscription concerts entitled *Historische Konzerte* or *Geistliche Konzerte*, and on the other hand, *Volkskonzerte*. While the former were set up as educative histories of music in sound and held in concert-halls, the latter, in accordance with their function, very often included popular songs and arrangements of folk melodies and were held in public spaces. Along with songs for choir, both groups of concerts included compositions for vocal quartets, chamber ensembles, and also *Lieder*. This was the model for the programs of Serbian choral societies.

The most significant example of the concept of historicism in the repertoire is certainly Stevan Stojanović Mokranjac's (1856–1914) historic concert planned on the occasion of the twenty-fifth anniversary of the *Beogradsko pevačko društvo* (Belgrade Choral Society, founded in 1853), entitled "A History of Serbian Song in Song." This concert presented the history of Serbian music in chronological order, from the sung declamation of epics accompanied by the *gusle* to Romantic compositions.

The program opened with a epic recitation with *gusle* accompaniment, followed by choral renditions of "the oldest Serbian songs in notation": two sixteenth-century songs by Petar Hektorović from his epic poem *Ribanje*, followed by three folk songs transcribed by F. Mirecki in 1815 (all arranged for mixed choir by Mokranjac). Then followed a number of songs by Nikola Đurković and Atanasije Nikolić, two Serbian composers known for writing songs in the 'foreign' idiom, arranged for male choir.

The second part of the concert opened with works by Kornelije Stanković and his followers, Aksentije Maksimović and Mita Topalović, arranged for male or mixed choir. Then came works by "Slavic" (Czech and Slovenian) composers who worked on Serbian songs (Václav Horejšek, Quido Havlasa, and Davorin Jenko), arranged for male choir.[28] The last part of the concert was devoted to "new Serbian music," represented by Josif Marinković and Stevan Mokranjac with two works each for both male and mixed choirs.

This concert was clearly influenced by the historic concerts staged in Vienna by Leopold Alexander Zellner between 1859 and 1869 at the *Gesellschaft der Musikfreunde* or *Musikverein*. Such historic and spiritual concerts were specific for the two Serbian choral societies in Vršac and Pančevo. The society in Vršac performed a concert in 1913 which included an overview of Russian religious music from the seventeenth to the nineteenth centuries modeled upon

---

28   One of Davorin Jenko's songs was entitled "Dvori davorovi" (Davor's Manor-house).

spiritual concerts by choral societies from Vienna (such as the The *Geistliches Konzert* by the *Wiener Caecilien Verein*).

One further aspect of the choral societies' practice—namely excursions, guest performances, or journeys to visit other Serbian vocal ensembles both in and outside the country—was also very characteristic of Serbian choral societies. And in this case too, in organizing short trips, they followed the Viennese model.

The most mobile society was undoubtedly the Belgrade Choral Society with its numerous international guest performances under its conductor Stevan Stojanović Mokranjac, who was regarded as the most significant Serbian composer. In the six years between 1893 and 1899 this group ventured ever farther from Belgrade: first to Dubrovnik and Skopje; then to Thessaloniki and Budapest; then to Sofia, Plovdiv, and Constantinople; then to Moscow, St. Petersburg, Kiev and Nizhny Novgorod; and finally to Berlin, Dresden, and Leipzig. The Belgrade Society's performances received excellent reviews.

Therefore, Viennese or, more broadly speaking, Germanic bourgeois culture played a key role in providing both ideological and technological models for the Serbian musical discourse of Romanticism, ranging from social order and establishing a way of life for the newly-founded middle class to the development of a national character in cultural and musical manifestations.

Choral societies played a very significant role in national mobilization, forming the most powerful network among Serbs dispersed all over the world. In the second half of the nineteenth century about four million Serbs were living outside Serbia in Montenegro, Slavonia, Hungary, Croatia, Dalmatia, Herzegovina, Bosnia, Albania, and Macedonia, while only one million lived in Serbia proper. Consequently, a unique Serbian cultural space was formed via the transcultural dynamics between the diaspora and the homeland along with interactions within the diaspora. An entire network formed by choral societies was based on the culturally and politically motivated activities of amateur musicians (both performers and to some extent composers) who were at the same time farmers, pharmacists or doctors, or authors and poets from a wide geographic area far beyond the borders of the Serbian state.

CHAPTER 14

Choral Societies and National Mobilization in Nineteenth-Century Bulgaria

Ivanka Vlaeva

Compared with the histories of many national movements in nineteenth-century Europe, in Bulgaria the industrial revolution was delayed and modern culture arrived late. Lagging behind most other Europeans, the Bulgarian population had to compensate for its lack of modern cultural development. Thus, one important characteristic of Bulgarian culture is its evolution at accelerated rates.

Before liberation in 1878, for almost five centuries the Bulgarian lands were under Ottoman rule, without their own governmental and religious institutions. Foreign rule, a feudal economy, a weak middle class, and the absence of national cultural institutions were serious obstacles to the development of a new culture on the western European model. The most important aims for the Bulgarians (led by educators, intellectuals, and revolutionists) were to struggle politically against Ottoman governance, economically for new industrial processes in the Ottoman Empire, and culturally for a national identity. The leaders of the revolutionary movement called for a struggle not against the Turkish people, but against Ottoman rulers and foreign clerks.[1]

These historical processes resemble those elsewhere in Europe, especially in the central and southeastern regions. Nineteenth-century Bulgarian culture therefore needs to be considered along with that of the Balkans more generally because of the cultural similarities, interactions, and fluctuations in this region.[2] The establishment of a new economy and the fight for modern education were among the main priorities in Bulgarian communities.

The eighteenth and nineteenth centuries are the so-called Revival period in Bulgarian cultural development, strongly influenced by the ideas of the Enlightenment. As the conservative culture with its predominantly religious

---

1   According to a popular revolutionary platform advocated by the Bulgarian national hero Vassil Levski, Turks, Armenians, and other ethnic and religious communities were to enjoy equal rights in the Bulgarian state.

2   Many politicians and scholars now prefer the term "Southeastern Europe" to "the Balkans" because of its pejorative connotations; Todorova (2009), 28.

consciousness shifted slowly from a theocentric to a humanistic perspective, secularization and rationalism provided opportunities for modernization. Traditional values coexisted with more modern attitudes, and the native coexisted with the foreign to create a basis for contemporary musical culture in Bulgaria.

The Bulgarian Revival encouraged democracy and tolerance, and a multicultural Empire with a decentralized cultural life was a good medium for Bulgarians to assimilate different traditions. Initially the monasteries and their small schools were centers of enlightenment and especially music, but from the 1820s and 1830s most new developments in culture, education, and music took place in the towns.

Urban circumstances and urban life opened new horizons and perspectives for establishing a modern culture in which modern education could be realized and secular art and culture could flourish. The Bulgarian Revival was a process of Europeanization and Westernization in which a Bulgarian national identity and national culture were constructed through the assimilation of foreign traditions (mostly from the West) and through a process of self-development. Urban cosmopolitan musical traditions and imported novelties formed the core of the new Bulgarian musical culture. Popular songs and mass musical culture were important vehicles for the Bulgarian Revival, as against the higher genres that were important in other regions in Europe.

Choral Singing from the 1830s to the 1870s

The Bulgarian musical tradition in the early nineteenth century was predominantly monophonic. Its main elements were, on the one hand, instrumental performances and the folk tradition (with some regional exceptions for two-part singing), and on the other, church monody chanting with the ison (drone). The development of a Bulgarian language was the basis for the national revival. All the holy texts for the year-round ritual cycle were translated into modern Bulgarian by monks from Rila, one of the oldest and most important Bulgarian monasteries. New fiction and poetry were also published in the Bulgarian vernacular.

The period from the 1830s to the 1850s also witnessed the growth of Bulgarian schools. Music was included in the syllabus, and in the following decades choral singing played an increasingly important role. The Greek influence on education was replaced thanks to the development of Bulgarian institutions and specialists. In a few decades some 1,500 primary schools and dozens of secondary schools were established in the Bulgarian lands, set up on advanced European models such as the Bell-Lancaster method. Along with traveling to schools in Tzarigrad (as Istanbul was known by Bulgarians, literally "the town of tsars"), thousands of Bulgarians enrolled in high schools and universities abroad, in Austria, France, Germany, Romania, Russia, and Serbia. Some returned to their homelands, and soon a highly educated cultural élite was formed.

The earliest extant writings about choral singing in Bulgarian communities date from the 1830s. Neofit Rilski founded a church choir at the school of Gabrovo (1835) and in Koprivshtitza.[3] At about the same time, Catholic missionaries in the town of Plovdiv founded a church and established a choir in 1839 on the initiative of a Czech, Joan Ptachek. In the 1840s, in the town of Kotel, Sava Dobroplodni organized two students' choirs, one to sing at each side of the church.[4] The Bulgarian choral movement was thus rooted in two different church traditions: the monody of the Eastern Orthodox church and the polyphony of Catholicism and later Protestantism. The choral movement was also stimulated by the need for musical and cultural activity, social life, and modernity. These first choral ensembles show the connection between the church and the school, and between church singing and school singing. The same groups of singers would sing in both institutions. Early in the nineteenth century the Bulgarian schoolteacher and the priest were often the same person. To some extent this fact reveals the more secular character of Bulgarian church life at that time.[5] At first the repertoire was mixed, and the first initiators of choral singing were teachers and priests (or monks).

Among the most important centers for musical education and choral development were the thriving towns of Plovdiv, Shumen, Samokov, and Varna. In some towns the population was in the spheres of influence of *superpowers* like France and Great Britain, which had their own interests in the region. Various religious missions also worked there. Russia had a strong effect on Bulgarian culture after the 1830s, and its intellectual impact overlay the previous Greek influence. The Pan-Slavic idea of closer relations with other Slavic lands began after the Russo-Turkish War in 1828–29 and continued especially after the next two wars. This idea was later developed with different manifestations in music and other arts, as well as in the field of choral singing.

In the Ottoman Empire, Bulgarian schools and choral ensembles had been set up without subsidies from either a state tax or the official Orthodox Church under Greek rule. All expenses for school construction and other costs were

---

3   Balareva (1992), 19.
4   Hlebarov (2003), 65.
5   Hadzhiiski (1974), 486–94.

paid with donations from Bulgarian patriots or church communities whose budgets were dependent on voluntary contributions. In many places the Bulgarian local community paid for all school expenses.

School singing was a part of the secularization of Bulgarian society, but it co-existed with church patterns in the school practice. Choral songs were sung in schoolrooms (at the end of the school year, for example), but performances were also held in churches or outdoors as part of traditional community festivals (for Christmas, St. Lazar's Day, or the welcoming of important guests). The idea of a concert as a special event on a special stage was unknown to most Bulgarians at that time. Choral singing was only one element of the celebrations. The Bulgarian population was not yet ready for this form of entertainment, and circumstances in the Ottoman Empire did not support such social forms of aesthetic and leisure activities. Among other reasons were the lack of expertise and sometimes a lack of understanding from Bulgarian society, which saw multi-voiced singing as a symbol of the foreign (Western) church. This is evidence that the Bulgarians assimilated selectively from western traditions, and chose to accept principles of secular culture from the West as a way to move forward. Choral singing symbolized modern musical culture for the most educated Bulgarians, but it was accepted with difficulty because of the local tradition which had a different type of melody, mode system, and texture.

Initially, choral singing did not necessarily mean multi-part singing; sometimes monophonic group singing was called 'choral'. If Bulgarian choirs are compared with that of Catholic schools in Plovdiv in the 1840s or the later Protestant school, it appears that multi-voiced singing was among the priorities of the foreign teachers from whom the Bulgarian students learned religious songs. Among the foreigners with a great impact on the spread of choral singing were Joan Ptachek, Dominicus Francisk Martileti (known as "Beliyat Domin," the White Dominican), and James Clark. Martileti founded a choir and also an orchestra, and brought an organ to the Catholic Church in Plovdiv.[6] Clark, an American Protestant missionary, was invited to the local Bulgarian high school to teach European music.[7] Thus, one of the most successful ways to disseminate multi-voiced musical culture in the Bulgarian lands was through the activity of religious missions. The multicultural context in Plovdiv created a good atmosphere for the success of the national movement; it was here that the Day of Saints Cyril and Methodius was first celebrated (in 1857) as a sign of Bulgarian language and culture, i.e., Bulgarian identity. In this way a tradition was founded which spread to other places as well, and exists to this day.

---

6   Genchev (1981), 488.
7   Ibid., 398–99.

Songs were written in honor of these ninth-century Byzantine brothers who devised the Glagolithic alphabet, the ancestor of Cyrillic. Among the leaders of the movement was Naiden Gerov, who was also a music educator.

In the town of Shumen, Hungarian and Polish emigrants and French and Italian musicians from Turkish military orchestras performed not only a Turkish repertoire (sharkiya, hava, march), but also European instrumental music. The Hungarian Mihály Sáfrány founded the first orchestra in the Bulgarian lands in 1851. There was evidently a connection in Shumen between choral singing and orchestral practice; Dobri Voinikov, one of Sáfrány's students, was the next conductor of the orchestra. He founded a many-voiced school choir in 1856 whose repertoire included songs in two, three, and four voices.[8] For the choral repertoire Voinikov wrote his own songs.

In this way choral singing in Bulgarian schools developed with more elaborate songs and a little more understanding in the society, which was often precarious because of the predominantly traditional attitudes. The 1850s were a key period with an important impact on the development of Bulgarian arts, connected largely with the increasing struggle for church and national independence.

The choral activity of Yanko Musstakov, which began in the 1860s in the town of Svishtov, was typical of musical culture at this time. As in other towns along the Danube, there were various European influences in the context of trade, not only from the neighboring countries Romania and Serbia, but also from other countries further upstream. Like his predecessors and contemporaries, Musstakov worked at a school where he founded a four-voiced choir (1868). He was the first person in that period to dedicate himself chiefly to the idea of music and choral singing instead of literature or theater. His choral repertoire consisted at first of parts for two voices, but was later enlarged to include sopranos, altos, tenors, and basses. The performers were male students and young men. Initially the choir was meant to serve the church liturgy, but singers in Svishtov soon took part in other festivities, such as the Day of Saints Cyril and Methodius, and also sang to welcome the Russian soldiers who liberated the town in 1877. The exact nature of their repertoire is not known; except for songs composed by Musstakov himself, choral scores were ordered from Russia through Bucharest. Perhaps it was Musstakov who initiated a request for church music that was sent to the Russian Consulate in Rousse on behalf of the Library in the Svishtov Cultural center.[9] Following Dobri Voinikov, who had introduced music as a school subject in Shoumen in the 1850s, Musstakov

---

8 Balareva (1992), 33.
9 Ibid., 41.

developed a similar tradition in Svishtov. Graduates of his school were proud that they could read notes at a time when many of their contemporaries had no idea of notation.[10] Among these students was Georgi Baidanov, who later conducted the cathedral choir and ensemble in the town of Plovdiv, where some of the first Bulgarian professional composers started as singers.

Bulgarian music is characterized by the co-existence of two traditions of notation. The first is the neumatic system derived from Byzantine and old Bulgarian church practice, especially in the form simplified in the nineteenth century by Chrysanthos and Chourmouzios. This was the main notation in the Bulgarian lands until the 1850s, with a few exceptions, as in the Catholic missions. The first Bulgarian songs were written in neumes to be sung by one or two voices. One example of this practice in church and also at school was mentioned for the town of Lom,[11] where the teacher, writer, and theater activist Krastyu Pishurka sang the melody solo while boys accompanied him with a drone, the basic tone of the scale sung not to a text but simply to the vowel 'A'.

Western notation was generally in use from the 1850s, and both Dobri Voinikov and Yanko Musstakov taught this notation. It is documented that Krastyu Pishurka, among others, knew both musical notations.[12] Voinikov and Musstakov had studied Western music in the Bulgarian lands as well as abroad: Voinikov had private lessons from a teacher of Czech origin in the town of Zemun, while Musstakov, thanks to his talent, was sent by the citizens of Svishtov to study music in Bucharest. Like many Bulgarians educated abroad, they assimilated the modern musical system and tried to introduce it into Bulgarian education. Foreigners—musicians, missionaries, and the officers of foreign companies—also had an impact on the dissemination of Western notation and music. New musical forms and genres became fashionable in urban circles, and European songs and dances such as the polka became popular.

The long co-existence of the Orthodox or folkloric and the European secular traditions determined another peculiarity of Bulgarian choral developments. Church music used modal structures and intonations similar to folk songs, while urban music reflected more the system of major and minor and the principles of homophonic vertical structures. In Bulgarian choral music these two inherited trends later became known as *pesni v obsht ton* (songs in urban mode) and *pesni v naroden ton* (songs in popular mode).

Along with schools, the cultural centers called *chitalishte* (from the verb *cheta*, to read) were also important for Bulgarian music and choral

---

10   Brashovanov (1932), 3–4.
11   Balareva (1992), 30.
12   Ibid., 31.

development. The *chitalishte* were formed to accommodate the increasing cultural interests of the Bulgarians, to expand their knowledge of music and the arts and to serve the national revival. The first centers of this type were founded in the towns of Svishtov, Lom, and Shoumen in the 1850s, and then in many other places.

The new Bulgarian music and singing were often closely connected with cultural activities involving Bulgarian literature and especially theater. Theater performances and choral singing were products of the revolutionary upswing and the national revival. At mass events and collective manifestations, text and sound could strongly affect emotions and convey a sense of identity. These activities originated in the 'speaking choir' in schools, a kind of musical declamation.[13] The musicians of that time were often teachers, writers, poets, choirmasters, the authors of songs, and sometimes conductors or dramatists. Many of the leaders of the national movement were well-educated intellectuals whose central interests were literature and theater, while music was ancillary to their complex work in the fields of education and the arts. The complexity of their cultural roles expresses the spirit of the Enlightenment, but it also is a result of the quantity and quality of the specialists of that time; there were not enough professionals, so before the 1880s most musicians were amateurs.

Popular songs reflected the topical issues of the time—education, revolution, and the patriotic ideas of the Enlightenment—in titles such as "A Plea for Studies," "Hymn to Saints Cyril and Methodius," "Fatherland," or "Try Again."[14] These were songs for *a cappella* choirs with three or four voices. The ideas of the Enlightenment and revolution were two sides of the same coin in the Bulgarian Revival, and choral singing served both interests. Another institution with an impact on choral singing was the Music Society (*muzikalno druzhestvo*), another model of European musical culture in the Bulgarian lands. The first society of this kind was established in the town of Varna in 1861 by a Polish emigrant, Vladislav Bohinski, an employee who worked to build Baron Hirsch's railway. Bohinski conducted an orchestra that was part of the Music Society, with performers of various national origins. The West European repertoire of the orchestra set the tone for the new music in Varna, and by the end of the nineteenth century the Music Societies became spaces for choral activity in Bulgaria.

In 1870 Todor Hadzhistanchev founded the Bulgarian Church Singing Society (*Bulgarsko cherkovnopevchesko druzhestvo*) in Rousse. In the Bulgarian context a 'music society' (*muzikalmo druzhestvo*) and a 'singing society'

---

13   Ibid., 26.

14   Petrov (1959), 166–68, 172–73. Unless otherwise noted, all translations are by the author.

(*pevchesko druzhestvo*) were basically the same thing, namely a choral society. Hadzhistanchev knew that such societies existed in other countries in almost every town, and he believed the institution would serve educational and religious purposes. He hoped that choral singing would chase 'Greek mumbling' (*gratzkoto tananikanie*) out of the Bulgarian church rituals. The core of his institution in Rousse was the choir as a permanent basic structure. The Music Society also organized instrumental performances (mostly string quartets), a musical circle, and lecture courses on solfeggio and the history of music. Society members also staged theatrical performances, and because they were choir singers, Hadzhistanchev chose plays that included singing. The Music Society also held revolutionary meetings under the specious pretext of music and theater rehearsals. The first Music Society in Svishtov was founded by Yanko Musstakov in 1871 as an extension of the school choir he had created in 1868.

Choral singing was performed in many contexts, but the choirs themselves consisted either of boys or of boys and men. There are no records of female choral singing (or mixed choirs) until the 1880s. Perhaps at school the girls could sing together with the boys. Hadzhistanchev was a teacher in one of the seven Bulgarian schools that also had female classes (out of a total of about sixteen schools: one Jewish, two Armenian, one Catholic, and three Turkish, among others). In Rousse, performances were held both in the auditorium of the School for Young Girls and in the hall of the then-famous Hotel Islyahhane. Rehearsals were held either at schools or in other buildings, such as the monastery buildings in Lyaskovetz. When Ottoman Sultan Abdülmecid had visited a Bulgarian school in Rousse in 1841 and a teacher and his students sang Turkish songs, they were rewarded with the sultan's blessing and also permission for a new school building.[15]

In the 1870s choirs were also founded in Bulgarian communities in neighboring countries, for example in Bolgrad (then in Russia, now Ukraine) and in Gyurgevo (Giurgiu, now Romania). Nikolai Iv. Nikolaev, who worked in Sofia after the Liberation, was the conductor of the first choir, and Dobri Voinikov the leader of the second. In Russia, Romania, and Serbia, Bulgarians not only received a higher and more modern education but also engaged in various social and cultural activities such as publishing, staging theater performances, and organizing cultural and scientific circles such as the Bulgarian Learned Society (founded in Braila, Romania, in 1869), now the Bulgarian Academy of Sciences.

---

15   See "Obrazovanieto v Ruse . . ."

Bulgarian choral singing from the 1830s to the 1870s was part of urban life and an important element of the new secular culture that served the needs and interests of the bourgeoisie and intellectuals. Choral developments helped Bulgarian society to shift from the traditional to the modern, and from the religious to the secular. In the Ottoman Empire these processes of modernization were generally known as 'à la Franga' ('in the French style', also written as *alafranga* and *alafranka*) versus the traditional 'à la Turka' (*alaturka*). For the Bulgarians, models for modernity in choral art were sought in many directions but mainly from foreigners in the native lands and in neighboring countries like Austria and Russia. Accordingly, the choir of Yanko Musstakov in Svishtov followed 'Romanian' and 'Russian' models, while the choir in Rousse was more 'Serbian'.

Choral singing was at this time a movement of amateurs; it began with simple musical forms and functions that were elaborated over the years. The songs had a maximum of four voices and a simple structure for non-professionals (often students), some of whom understood notation while others learned the music by rote. The choirs were polyfunctional, performing at various places (both religious and secular) and events (schools, fairs, theaters, for charity, or to support political groups). The activities of Hadzhistanchev's choir in Rousse is a good illustration of this polyfunctionality. Choristers sang in church and at funerals and celebrations. In 1872 they greeted the first Bulgarian exarch Antim I with the song "Sing Gladly, O Ye Bulgarian People," (*O, ti, bulgarskii narode, radostno vech zapei*). In this way choral groups helped to unite the Bulgarian communities in the towns.

Choral singing was involved in all national movements for social education, modernity, and Bulgarian identity and statehood. These aims shaped the characteristics of the choral songs. For example, traditional Bulgarian folk patterns were not used for school or patriotic songs. Folk traditions were preserved in villages but were not suitable for the needs of the new era. The idea of the national in music was realized largely by way of foreign intonations.[16] Partly these were echoes of the revolutionary nineteenth century.[17] Urban melodies of various ethnic origin were in use all over the Balkans and received various transformations.[18] Often the composers were anonymous, since the text and its message were considered more important, and the music was meant to serve actual social and political aims. The Bulgarians claimed they were getting away from Turkish and Greek musical patterns, which they disparaged

---

16   Belivanova (2002), 44.
17   Hlebarov (2003), 76.
18   Kaufman (1968), 25–27; Katzarova (1973), 115–33.

as 'goat singing' (*kozloglasovanie*). But there were also cases where Turkish songs were transformed into Bulgarian patriotic songs and continue to exist in social memory as Bulgarian.[19] Turkish and Greek models were unwelcome, but melodies of Serbian, Russian, Ukrainian, Czech or Polish origin were accepted. These were then transformed melodically, arranged with Bulgarian texts, and harmonized, i.e. 'Bulgarianized'. This kind of intonation met the needs of the new Bulgarian music, and its Slavic affiliation was possibly another reason for its assimilation. The choral repertoire consisted of songs by (sometimes anonymous) Bulgarian composers, music from Central Europe and Russia, and music from immigrants and missionaries. The Bulgarian choral repertoire of this time includes compositions by Dobri Voinikov, Yanko Musstakov, and Todor Hadzhistanchev.

In general, the choral repertoire at first consisted of school or religious songs, *a cappella* works for not more than four voices that were easy to sing. The establishment of the first cultural centers and music societies then made it possible to organize social events (to help poor students, for example, or for community aims) and political gatherings around music. The repertoire thus reflects musical needs and occasions. For religious purposes Yanko Musstakov composed the "Two-voiced Liturgical Songs" (*Dvuglasni liturgichni pesni*) in 1868 and the four-voiced "Funeral of Jesus Christ" (*Opeloto na Isusa Hrista*) in 1870.[20] These works, along with fifteen other secular songs by Musstakov, are among the earliest Bulgarian works whose authorship is known.

Secular choral works tended to express pathos or glory. Only a few were humorous, like the four-voiced composition "Grandfather Red Like a Crab" (*Cherven dyado kato rak*) by Dobri Voinikov, which remained popular in concert programs in Shoumen throughout the twentieth century. The main genres in choral singing were the hymn, the march, and the romance.[21] The first category covers works in honor of saints, political figures, homage to the motherland, and celebration of knowledge. Such songs were written by Voinikov ("The Song of Saints Cyril and Methodius") and by Musstakov, among them "Welcome, Tsar" (*Tzaryu, dobre doshel*) from 1877, in honor of the Russian Emperor Alexander II, with lyrics by Ivan Vazov. Among the marches were the two-voiced song "Glory to the Merit" (*Da proslavim pametta*) with lyrics

---

19   Among these songs is "The Wind Blows, the Balkan Moans" (*Vyatar echi, Balkan stene*), which Nikolai Kaufman (1968) mentions in his collection of Bulgarian urban songs, pp. 46–47.

20   This work was translated into the new Bulgarian language by Krastyu Pishurka.

21   Petrov (1959), 247; Hlebarov (2003), 76.

and probably also music by Voinikov. Other songs included "After Thousands of Years" (*Sled tisyashta godini*) by Naiden Gerov and "Solemn Assembly" (*Tarzhestveno sabranie*) from 1877 by Musstakov. The romances included popular songs like "You Are Beautiful, My Forest" (*Hubava si moya goro*) with Lyuben Karavelov's lyrics, but the composer is unknown. Teachers' assemblies (first organized in the town of Stara Zagora in 1868) helped to transmit the song repertoire, as did personal contacts, the relocation of teachers, and the training of students.

Choral Singing after 1878

After the Liberation from Ottoman rule, Bulgaria began to develop its culture under new conditions. The Revival and consolidation of the Bulgarian nation led to the building of a system of state structures, and also to the idea of unification with Bulgarians in Eastern Rumelia and Macedonia who remained under Ottoman rule after the Berlin Treaty. These events not only influenced other revolutionary movements and even wars in the region, bringing vast political and social changes, but also had an impact on the arts. Europeanization was a strategy of the state, and the government supported this process. The Turkish past was deemed retrograde by the intelligentsia and the bourgeoisie whose education and economic status were linked with western (European) types of culture and music. Much of the old organization of culture and its civil institutions persisted into the 1890s, but state funding for culture was entirely new. Not only did initiatives of the civil communities continue as before, but the authorities were anxious to build a state infrastructure and train specialists to meet the needs of modern culture and progress.

The year 1878 marks a historical divide in Bulgaria, but this border is not absolutely fixed because music and other cultural processes continued their previous development into the 1890s. The next period extends from the 1890s to the second decade of the twentieth century (including the war years of 1912–1918). Modern music and the idea of individual creativity evolved later in Bulgaria than in many other European countries.

At the state level, education occupied a central place in the new order of things. Musstakov had promoted singing as a necessary element of school curricula as early as 1878, and by 1879 music was a major subject in Bulgarian schools. Choral singing was included in school practice and was considered a higher form of music than the folk music performed in educated social circles. However many issues had to be resolved, among them the need for well-educated professionals, syllabi, workbooks and songbooks.

The Bulgarian musical heritage at that time included layers of folk, urban, and church music which interacted with each other. Especially love songs and humorous songs were borrowed and became part of a wider culture of entertainment. Instead of the Turkish and Greek songs that had long been popular in the towns, more and more songs of Czech, Polish, Croatian, Russian, and German origin were disseminated, and some of them became 'naturalized' as Bulgarian songs. The famous Bulgarian composer and educator Dobri Hristov noted that even fragments from Giuseppe Verdi's *La Traviata* and Gaetano Donizetti's *Lucia di Lammermoor* were rearranged musically with Bulgarian texts and accepted as Bulgarian songs.[22] Such examples of assimilation and popularization were later criticized by professional musicians like Hristov.

Throughout the 1880s folk song material was imported for use by composers. Borrowing folk melodies was at that time a novelty in Bulgarian music. Czech musicians in particular had an important influence on modern Bulgarian musical culture. Czech kapellmeisters invited by the state authorities to organize military bands and teach music in the schools were among the first to create works based on Bulgarian folk songs. Their instrumental and vocal compositions met the Bulgarian public's need for a larger repertoire. Folk-song arrangements were the first stage in this long-lasting process; later, composers would incorporate folk elements into their own works.

This new attitude towards the folk heritage reflected the aims of the new historical moment. If the national idea in Bulgarian music before the Liberation had been realized through foreign (non-Bulgarian) melodies very popular in urban circumstances or imported from abroad, by the 1890s the position of musicians with regard to folk music had changed. The Czech Karel Mahan was among the first to look for national origins in Bulgarian folk music, and to collect folk music not only as lyrics but also as melodies.[23] These tendencies were developed by other non-native musicians as well as Bulgarians. The first editions of Bulgarian folklore (like the Miladinovi brothers' collection from 1861)[24] consisted only of texts, but after the Liberation folk music and melodies were also published in notation. The beginning of musical score printing in Bulgaria provided more and more possibilities.

The choral movement developing in this context played an important role in Bulgarian music by integrating the main areas of musical activity to become one of the pillars of modern Bulgarian music, perhaps the first to achieve widespread popularity. Choral songs created a democratic base and generated

---

22   Balareva (1992), 64.

23   Mahan (1894), 221–35.

24   *Bulgarian Folk Songs (Bulgarski narodni pesni)*, published in Zagreb.

an increasing number of choirs. The song was the central genre for Bulgarian music over the following decades.

Choral singing was an integral part and a very popular expression of the newly built system of Bulgarian musical culture. Other elements included pedagogic schools, wind orchestras, military bands[25] (*duhova muzika*), music journals, music theater, and book and note publishing; but most important of all was the creation of the first professional musicians and composers. The shift to a new music system partly governed and supported by the state changed the sound atmosphere mainly in the towns, but also to some extent in the villages. In rural areas folk music was still vital, and the calendar of ritual customs continued to be of great importance. Modern Westernized music was not the only layer in urban surroundings. The multiethnic traditions typical of the Balkans made for a multifaceted musical image in the biggest towns in Bulgaria, such as Rousse, Varna, Kazanlak, Sofia, and Plovdiv (after the Union of Eastern Rumelia with the Bulgarian Principality in 1885). As major political and economic centers, towns continued to be where cultural reforms were most visible, along with the mixing of diverse tendencies. Various social and religious groups lived together, and their daily and festive activities were good conditions for the coexistence of various old and new layers of music.

By the end of the nineteenth century the main institutions where choral singing was concentrated were the schools, cultural centers (*chitalishta*), the church, the army, and especially the singing societies (*pevcheski druzhestva*) which reflected various forms of urban life, including athletic groups, charities, and women's organizations.

Russian military and later civilian choirs played a crucial role in the choral singing establishment in Bulgaria. Their activities were perhaps the most powerful impulse to accept a new type of choral singing not only in secular institutions but also in the church. Russian singers accomplished what Catholic and Protestant missionaries could not achieve in the field of multi-part singing. Many of the Russian troops in the last Russo-Turkish war had church choirs which sang for the Sunday liturgy, for holidays, and after military victories. The Bulgarians were impressed by these male choirs full of passion and energy. In the emotional memory of the Bulgarians, the Russian people had helped them to win their freedom and create their own state after centuries of struggle against the Ottoman Empire. The Russians are also Slavic and Orthodox, and these features were important for the ordinary people and their acceptance of Russian singing.

---

25   By the end of the nineteenth century, military bands also performed concerts in civilian contexts and were used as symphony orchestras with strings added to the main ensemble.

The choir led by Yanko Musstakov greeted the Russian army when it crossed the Danube into Svishtov in 1877.[26] Choral songs were written especially for the event. The Russians also created a choir in Svishtov and invited Bulgarian boys to sing with them in church liturgies. After Russian troops had left the town, the Bulgarian singers continued this activity and became widely popular. The choir was invited to Veliko Tarnovo in 1878, where the singers performed in special events: the Constituent Assembly for the Bulgarian Parliament and The Easter Liturgy.[27] This choir concert was one of the first separate musical events of this kind mentioned by contemporaries. A studio photograph of sixteen of the choir's members (dressed in European costumes with bow-ties) commemorates only a part of the whole ensemble. In 1879 a choir of Russian officials was organized in another large town, Varna. Russian musicians founded choral ensembles, among them Aleksei Shulgovski and Konstantin Tarasevich. Shulgovski was the first professional musician in Razgrad, where from 1884–1895 he organized a church choir of about thirty boys and men between the ages of twelve and twenty-six. Their repertoire was both religious and secular. Like other musicians of this period, Shulgovski was a teacher; he also formed an amateur orchestra and collected folk songs.

After 1878, Sofia, the new national capital with no traditions in new music, began to develop culturally. Nikolai Iv. Nikolaev was invited from Bolgrad to lead the cathedral choir in the new capital. As usual, the first choral ensembles there were entirely male. Nikolaev also established a choir in the Military School, a choir in the First Male High School, and another in the Slavyanska Beseda Society.

Many music societies were established in 1885 to develop a love of music, to promote folk music, and to disseminate the works of Bulgarian and Slavic composers. This process of mass civil activity continued until the 1920s, reflecting a greater social and musical organization. While school and church choirs depended on the state and the initiatives of leaders, music societies were an initiative of the citizens. The choirs of the music societies had primarily a social function, but also served musical, educational and aesthetic needs. This process culminated in the establishment of the Bulgarian Music Union in 1903, whose members were all music teachers, though a year later kapellmeisters and musical societies could also receive affiliate memberships.

---

26   Balareva (1992), 58–59.

27   All costs for the visit of the choir were paid by Prince Alexander Dondukov-Korsakov (1820–93), the head of the Russian administration in Bulgaria after the last Russo-Turkish war; he also helped to draft the first Bulgarian constitution.

The music societies organized lectures about music, various music courses including the study of instrumental performance, traditional festivals, charity events, etc. Their statutes and aims were printed, as were the programs of their events. There were three categories of membership: regular, affiliated, and honorary. The main aim of the societies was to promote social communication through music. In thirty-five years about sixty music societies were founded, mainly Bulgarian, in almost every large town, but Greek societies (in Varna and Plovdiv) and Jewish societies (in Rousse and Sofia) also existed. The music societies were usually named after musical instruments (often local ones like the gusla, kaval, gaida, or lyre) or other musical symbols such as Orpheus, etc. The choirs were amateur, but the choirmasters were kapellmeisters and teachers— the only professions (together with members of the military orchestras) for state musicians in Bulgaria at the turn of the twentieth century.

The composer Angel Bukoreshtliev recalled that the Singing Society in Plovdiv was organized on the model of Western European societies. Thanks to donations, the members bought a grand piano and ordered the society's flag from Bonn, the birthplace of Beethoven. The slogan on the flag was "Song Unites, Cheers, and Consoles" (Pesenta sdruzhava, razveselyava i uteshava).[28]

At the turn of the twentieth century different types of choirs were formed: secular choirs (male, mixed, and childrens' choirs, and also students' and workers' choirs), church choirs, and military choirs (by the order of the Ministry of Defense in the 1890s). Most of the choirs were amateur ensembles. The church choirs in Plovdiv, Sofia, Pleven, Varna, Rousse, and Stara Zagora received state subsidies at a time when the foundations of semi-professional singing were being laid. These were the best-trained choirs, with a diverse repertoire, and they performed at various events, not only in church. The singers in the choral movement were students, teachers, officials, and later workers. Gradually specialized ensembles emerged, according to age or profession, such as the Teachers' Choirs in Varna (1896) and Tutrakan (1897). Social distinctions led step by step to the organization of the workers' movement, whose political and cultural activities included workers' choirs. One of these was in Kazanlak in the last decade of the nineteenth century. In their memoirs local residents recalled the young staff singing "in one, two, and even in three voices."[29] Another Singing Society, 'Gusla' (1899) in Plovdiv, was founded by printers.

At first, the singers in the choirs were boys and men (recordings mentioned predominantly young men). Socially they were representative of the intelligentsia and middle-class bourgeoisie. Mixed ensembles were found later.

---

28   Bukoreshtliev (1936), 48–51.
29   Balareva (1992), 87.

Historiography mentions such choirs in the towns of Harmanli (1893–1894), Tutrakan (1897), and Kazanlak (1899–1902), where the choir included both male and female teachers along with students.[30] A choir with female teachers was also organized by Angel Bukoreshtliev in Plovdiv (1894–95). Unfortunately, local communities and clerks were initially opposed to female singing in the church, but this resistance was gradually overcome. The Russians by the end of the 1870s had also contributed to the emancipation of women in the churches. Tours of foreign choirs in Bulgaria in the 1880s and later show the presence of mixed choirs. Among the most popular and acclaimed was the choir of Dmitrii Agrenev-Slavyanski, which consisted of various male, female, and children's voices. The audience "tasted the sweetness of the cultural music" and "went into ecstasies" about their performances.[31] Guest concerts of this choir were reported in the periodical press, along with tours by other foreign groups like the Belgrade Singing Society in 1895,[32] the Greek troupe 'Tespis,' and the American Musical Troupe.[33] Music critics reviewed these events with praise or criticism, but most periodicals were not specialized in music, with a few exceptions.[34]

Separate choral concerts were rare in Bulgaria at this time, and usually involved touring choirs from abroad. Although it was not common, some Bulgarian choirs also went on tour. The four-voiced students' choir of Alexei Shulgovski (with some thirty singers) walked the sixty-four kilometers from Razgrad to Rousse to perform at the invitation of the citizens there. They gave more than one concert, and were soon invited to other places in the region. The Plovdiv Singing Society also travelled to Bourgas in 1898, where its thirty-five members entertained the local Bulgarian and Greek audience with two concerts. The program included patriotic songs and marches by Bulgarian composers. Bulgarian choirs also began touring abroad at the turn of the twentieth century.

Most choral concert activity concerned events in which choral singing was only part of the program, together with poetry recitations and other vocal and instrumental offerings. Such events, called *vecherinki* ('evening gatherings'), became a popular and democratic art form in the last decades of nineteenth-

---

30   Ibid., 88–89; Kazasov (s.d.), 25–28.
31   Balareva (1992), 78.
32   Ibid., 82.
33   Vlaeva (2006), 74.
34   The first music magazine in Bulgaria was *Gusla* (1891), which published only one issue. The next were the magazine *Kaval* in 1894 and *Muzikalen vestnik*, which appeared irregularly from 1904 to 1928.

century cultural life. Choral music was transmitted by telephone during the First Bulgarian International Trade Exhibition in Plovdiv (1892). In this manner an audience in Slavyanska Beseda Hall in Sofia could listen through amplified speakers to a concert from Plovdiv that was specially organized for the International Fair. Later, Bulgarian radio made international broadcasts of concerts possible.

The choral repertoire was enlarged during this period and gradually came to include a large number of works by both Bulgarian and foreign composers. European music was assimilated in various directions: there were songs by Slavic composers, and German repertoire and opera choral parts.[35] At this time, most Bulgarians received their musical training in Slavic cities (in Belgrade, Zagreb, Prague, Odessa, Moscow, or Kiev) and brought home the traditions they had learned. Press reports and concert programs often listed the names of composers like Brahms, Schubert, Wagner, Verdi, Donizetti, Gounod, Smetana, Glinka, Tchaikovsky, and Rubinstein. Among the many Slavic composers in the programs were the Croatian Ivan Zajc and the Serbian Stevan Mokranjac, both listed along with other foreign composers whose works are now largely forgotten. Elementary school songs in repertoires and programs appeared together with high-class European compositions, confirming Hristov's remark that everything at that time was new to Bulgarian musical culture. Nineteenth-century music dominated the repertoires of the choirs.

Changes in the choral repertoire reflected newly composed works by Bulgarian composers, but also by kapellmeisters and teachers who were not trained as composers. The increased number of choirs created favorable conditions for new compositions, where new elements included folk origins and the discovery of a traditionally Bulgarian form of rhythm and meter, the so-called asymmetric (uneven or irregular) rhythms.[36] These characteristics were important for the emergence of a Bulgarian national style.

School songs were a major part of the choral works and perhaps had the longest life of all. For example, the hymn dedicated to Saints Cyril and Methodius, "Go, Reborn People" (*Varvi, narode vazrodeni*) by Panayot Pipkov (1901), is sung even now at schools, celebrations, marching protests, strikes, or simply for entertainment. Impoverishment and the wars in the Balkans provided material for new types of songs, including choral works for workers and soldiers such as the "Workers' March" (*Rabotnicheski marsh*) by Emanuil Manolov (1899) and "We Shall Vanquish" (*Nie shte pobedim*) by Alexander Morfov (1900).

---

35   Balareva (1992), 64; Vlaeva (2006), 83–86.

36   The theory of these asymmetrical rhythms in Bulgarian folk music was explained by Dobri Hristov in 1913.

During the Serbian-Bulgarian War in 1885, Tzvetan Radoslavov composed "Dear Motherland" (*Mila, Rodino*), which became very popular and is now the Bulgarian National Anthem.

The choral *kitka* (bouquet or pot-pourri) became important for both a cappella and instrumental works.[37] The pot-pourri was a popular way to entertain listeners, and its compositional structure challenged composers to develop larger, more complex forms and thus helped to broaden the stylistic range of the first professional composers in Bulgaria. The structure of these compositions is built on different bright melodies presented as songs, and on contrasts between the various parts depending on tonality, rhythm and meter, tempo, texture, and register. Among the best-known composers of works of this kind are Emanuil Manolov, Dobri Hristov, and Angel Bukoreshtliev. Songs like Hristov's "Lilyana, Lovely Girl" (*Lilyana moma hubava*) of 1897, "These Girls from Zheravna" (*Pusti momi zheravnenki*) of 1898, and Manolov's "What a Girl I Saw, Mother" (*Kakva moma vidyah, mamo*) of 1899, are familiar classics of the Bulgarian choral repertoire to this day. These a cappella compositions, along with instrumental works for military bands, made it possible for other genres to flourish at the turn of the twentieth century, such as the cantata for choir and orchestra.

The first Bulgarian compositions in the field of church music date from the 1890s. Atanas Badev wrote his "Liturgy of St. John Chrysostom" (*Zlatoustova Liturgiya*, 1898) and Georgi Baidanov composed the "Liturgy of St. Basil" (*Vasilieva Liturgiya*). Later Dobri Hristov added his "Liturgy of St. John Chrysostom" which was added to the church service because the music coexists with the ritual (and thus cannot be performed as an autonomous work). The unreformed Orthodox Church and its closed practice did not allow novelties. Composers found church music unsuited for their modern efforts and the idea of a national style. At the same time, an interest developed in Old Bulgarian church music, the so-called Bolgarskii rospev with its intonations and diatonic scale, which influenced the music of later composers.

Conclusions

For Bulgaria the nineteenth century was a time of transition: from a feudal to a bourgeois economy, from a religious to a secular culture, from traditional to modern, from the struggle for statehood to restoration of the state, and from a revolutionary movement to political conflicts both inside and outside the

---

37   Petrov (1959), 274–81.

country. The final result was the construction of a national culture with its own system and infrastructure. Music and choral singing played an active part in this cultural development.

The models and measures were generally European, but Europe was represented mainly by the neighboring countries: the Slavic lands, Austria (later Austria-Hungary), and Russia. Russian choirs had a very strong impact on church music and altered the manner of singing, leading to a mixed repertoire and female singers in the 1890s; but secular music was also subjected to many influences. Before the 1870s and even 1880s, the national idea was realized by non-Bulgarian musical material from multi-ethnic urban cultures provided with Bulgarian lyrics on topics important for national identity. 'Bulgarianized' songs and innovative works in major and minor modes became the basis for a new type of singing. Choral singing in church, at school, and in other cultural centers helped to catalyze the process of national revival. The national idea went together with the idea of national education, and school choirs formed the core of choral singing. Educated young people accepted the new music more easily than older people. At first, European works were imported rapidly and randomly. The point was to cast off the Turkish past and Greek chanting, but this was realized through a mixing of multi-faceted, multi-ethnic urban traditions with music from other countries. The last decade of the nineteenth century witnessed a shift in understanding the relation of national music to Bulgarian folk music (melody, rhythm and meter, and especially asymmetric patterns). Some analogies with Romantic style arose in the use of local color and national identity, but in Bulgarian music they were mixed with many other influences (the Enlightenment, social problems, modernization). The process of forming a national Bulgarian music began in the 1830s and in choral singing it continued until the 1920s.

Bulgarian song and choral singing were well suited for the realization of the main ideas of the time: the Enlightenment, education, national independence, and modernization. The democratic nature of choral singing, along with its large social accessibility, reflected the democracy of the Bulgarian national revival and the consolidation of the Bulgarian nation. The popular song is often considered a low form of music in Europe, but such songs became the most popular genre in nineteenth-century Bulgarian music, and choral singing proved able to unite different social groups for a long period. After the Liberation in 1878, the state authorities promoted choral singing by adding music to the school curriculum. In the 1890s music societies became places for cultural and social gatherings more than for politics, with certain exceptions.[38]

---

38   For example, organizations of Bulgarian Macedonians (Bulgarians of Macedonia region).

The first professional composers appeared at this time, and took the national idea in music to the next stage by exploring new forms like the choral pot-pourri. By the turn of the century new wars, increasing numbers of Bulgarian soldiers, and the establishment of military bands and choirs stimulated the development of another new genre: choral patriotic soldiers' songs. Bulgarian music in the nineteenth century generally followed contemporary musical tendencies in Europe in harmony with the major ideas of modernization. In this sense, the development of the Bulgarian national movement and of choral singing was a process of Europeanization.

Bibliography

Ábrányi, Kornél. "Egy zsandáros hangverseny, 1850-ik évi emlékeimből" (A concert with police). In *Vasárnapi Újság*, issue 42 (1891). Accessed 30 March 2015 at http://egyvaradiblogjanagyvaradrol.blogspot.nl/2014/10/abranyi-kornel-egy-zsandaros-hangverseny.html.

———. *Az országos magyar daláregyesület negyedszázados története.* Budapest: Országos Magyar Daláregyesület Kiadványa, 1892.

Aguirre, Franco, R. *Las sociedades populares.* San Sebastián: Caja de Ahorros Provincial de Gipuzkoa, 1983.

Alten, Michèle. "Les Formes de sociabilité musicale dans les écoles primaires de la République." In *Les Sociabilités musicales, Cahiers de* GRHIS, 6 (1997), Presses de l'Université de Rouen, n° 227, 49–60.

———. "L'Ecole républicaine et la musique, 1880–1939." In Tournès, ed., 232–46.

Anderson, Benedict. *Imagined Communities: Reflections on the Origin and Spread of Nationalism.* London and New York: Verso, 1983.

Anderssen, Otto. *Den norske studentersangforening 1845–1895: festskrift udgivet i anledning af foreningens 50aars jubilæum.* Kristiania: Grimsgaard og Malling, 1895.

Anonymous. "Glasgow International Exhibition." *Glasgow Herald* (9 Nov. 1888), 9.

———. "Handel Festival." *The Era* 2440 (27 June 1885), p. 9, cols. 1–3.

———. "Handel's 'Messiah' as performed under the direction of Mr. John Hullah." *The Era* 1124 (Sunday 8 April 1860), p. 12, col. 1.

———. "Music, a Means of Popular Amusement and Education." *Musical Times* 3 (1849), 240, 245.

———. "The Tonic Sol-Fa College." *The Daily News* 15956 (18 May 1897), p. 8, col. 5.

Artis i Benach, Pere. *El cant coral a Catalunya (1871–1979).* Barcelona: Barcino, 1980.

Arvesen, Olaus. *Vaagaa-presten: folkeopdrageren, provst Hans Peter Schnitler Krag og hans samtid: et livsbillede fra 30–40 aarene.* Kristiania: Cappelen, 1916.

Asper, Ulrich. *Hans Georg Nägeli: Réflexions sur le chœur populaire, l'éducation artistique et la musique de l'église,* trans. Jean Giraud. Baden-Baden: V. Koerner, 1994.

Asselbergs, Alphons J.M. *Dr. Jan Pieter Heije of De Kunst en het Leven.* Utrecht: Oosthoek, 1966.

Bajgarová, Jitka. *Hudební spolky v Brně a jejich role při utváření "hudebního obrazu" města 1860–1918.* Brno: Centrum pro studium demokracie a kultury, 2005.

Balareva, Agapiya. *Horovoto delo v Bulgaria ot sredata na 19 vek do 1944 godina.* Sofia: Izdatelstvo na Bulgarskata akademiya na naukite, 1992.

Bang, Herman. *Rundt i Norge: skildringer og billeder.* Kristiania: Aschehoug, 1892.

Bank, Jan. *Het roemrijk vaderland: Cultureel nationalisme in Nederland in de negentiende eeuw.* Oratie Rijksuniversiteit Leiden. 's-Gravenhage, 1990.

————. "Muziek: een vergeten hoofdstuk in de Nederlandse cultuurgeschiedenis." In P. van Reijen, ed., *Muziek en muziekwetenschap in de Nederlandse cultuur: Beschouwingen bij het 125-jarig bestaan van de Koninklijke Vereniging voor Nederlandse Muziekgeschiedenis.* Utrecht: KVNM, 1994. 21–29.

Baptie, David. *Musical Scotland Past and Present: Being a Dictionary of Scottish Musicians From About 1400 Till the Present Time.* Paisley: Parlane, 1894.

Bashford, Christina, and Leanne Langley, eds. *Music and British Culture 1785–1914: Essays in Honour of Cyril Ehrlich.* Oxford: Oxford University Press, 2000.

Behrens, Johan Diederich. *Sanglære for Skoler. Første Trin.* Kristiania: Joh. D. Behrens, [1868].

[————, ed.] *Udvalgt Samling af norske, svenske og danske flerstemmige Mandssange: udgiven ved en Del Studenter* [= Behrens's quartet]. Kristiania: Winther, 1845 and 1846.

————. *Udvalgt Samling af tyske firstemmige Mandssange.* Kristiania: Winther, 1846.

Belivanova, Kipriana. "Istoricheskite urotzi na bulgarskoto Vazrazhdane." In Ganka Konstantinova, ed., *Izsledvaniya, kritika, publitzistika.* Sofia: Artkoop, 2002, 35–51.

Beller, Manfred and Joep Leerssen, eds. *Imagology: The cultural construction and literary representation of national characters. A critical survey.* Studia imagologica 13. Amsterdam: Rodopi, 2007.

Benages, Eusebi. "A la Nació catalana." *L'Aurora*, 15 Aug. 1899, p. 6.

Bennett, Joseph. *Forty Years of Music.* London: Methuen, 1908.

Berg, W. van den, and A. de Bruijn. "Negentiende-eeuwse rederijkerskamers, een inventarisatie." *De negentiende eeuw* 16 (1992), 163–84.

Bhabha, Homi. *The Location of Culture.* London, New York: Routledge, 1994.

Billig, Michael. *Banal Nationalism.* London: Sage, 1995.

Bischof, Günter, and Anton Pelinka, eds. *Austrian Historical Memory & National Identity.* New Brunswick: Transaction Publishers, 1997.

Blommen, Heinz. *Anfänge und Entwicklung des Männerchorwesens am Niederrhein.* Doctoral thesis, Universität Köln. Köln: Arno-Verlag, 1960.

Boeva, Luc. *Rien de plus international: Towards a comparative and transnational historiography of national movements.* Antwerp: ADVN, 2010.

Bohlman, Philip. *The Music of European Nationalism.* Santa Barbara, CA: ABC-CLIO World Music Series, 2004.

Boogman, J.C. *Nederland en de Duitse Bond 1815–1851.* 2 vols. Groningen: Wolters, 1955.

————. *Rondom 1848: De politieke ontwikkeling van Nederland 1840–1858.* Bussum: Unieboek, 1978.

Bouchor, Maurice. *Chants populaires pour les écoles*, troisième série. Paris: Hachette, 1909.

Brashovanov, Stoyan. "Za podviga na edin zabraven". In *Rodna pesen* 5: 1 (1932), 3–4.

Brinkman, James M. "The German Male Chorus of the Early Nineteenth Century." *Journal of Research in Music Education* 18 (Spring 1970), 16–24.

Brophy, James M. *Popular Culture and the Public Sphere in the Rhineland, 1800–1850*. Cambridge: Cambridge University Press, 2007.

Brüggemann, Karsten, and Andres Kasekamp. "'Singing oneself into a nation?' Estonian song festivals as rituals of political mobilisation." *Nations and Nationalism* 20: 2 (2014), 259–76.

Bruyneel, Elisabeth et al., eds. *Veel volk verwacht: Populaire muziekcultuur in Vlaams-Brabant sinds 1800*. Leuven: Peeters, 2012.

Bukoreshtliev, Angel. "Spomeni". *Plovdivsko pevchesko druzhestvo*. Plovdiv: Hr. G. Danov, 1936. 48–51.

Bull, Jacob Breda. *Knut Veum: et Folkelivsbillede*. Kristiania: Gyldendal, 1910.

Burrows, Donald. *Handel: Messiah*. Cambridge Music Handbook. Cambridge: Cambridge University Press, 1991.

Burton, Nigel. "Oratorios and Cantatas." In *The Romantic Age*, edited by Nicholas Temperley. Athlone History of Music in Britain, vol. 5. London: Athlone Press, 1981.

Buter, J. "Het Koninklijk Nederlands zangersverbond 1853–1978." Eight instalments in *Nederlands Zangersblad* 30, nrs. 8–31 (1977–78).

Butt, John. "Choral Music." In Samson, ed., 213–36.

Carbonell i Guberna, Jaume. "Los Coros de Clavé, un ejemplo de música en sociedad." *Bulletin d'Histoire Contemporaine de l'Espagne* 20 (CNRS, Dec. 1994), 68–78.

———. "Els Cors de Clavé i Els Segadors entre 1892 i 1936: in contribució a l'estudi de la consciencia d'Himne nacional a Catalunya." *Miscellania Oriol Martorell*. Barcelona: Universitat de Barcelona, 1998. 171–89.

Ceulemans, Adelheid. *Verklankt verleden: Vlaamse muziektheaterwerken uit de negentiende eeuw (1830–1914): tekst en representatie*. Coulissen 1. Antwerpen: University Press Antwerp, 2010.

Chanet, Jean-François. *L'Ecole républicaine et les petites patries*. Paris: Aubier, 1996.

Coeuroy, André. *La musique et le peuple de France*. Paris: Stock, 1941.

Corten, René. "Wat zongen de Belgen in 1830? Een onderzoek naar de liederen bij de Belgische afscheiding in 1830 en 1831." Master's thesis, Universiteit van Amsterdam. Amsterdam: Nederlandse taal & cultuur, 2009.

Cox, Gordon and Robin Stevens, eds. *The Origins and Foundations of Music Education*. London: Continuum International Publishing Group, 2010.

Croll, Andy. "From bar stool to choir stall: music and morality in late Victorian Merthyr." *Llafur: The Journal of Welsh Labour History* 6: 1 (1992), 17–27.

———. *Civilising the Urban: popular culture and public space in Merthyr c.1870–1914*. Cardiff: University of Wales Press, 2000.

Curwen, John. *An Account of the Tonic Sol-fa Method of Teaching to Sing: a Modification of Miss Glover's Norwich Sol-fa Method, or Tetrachordal System*. London, 1855.

————. *Singing for Schools: a Grammar of Vocal Music, Founded on the Tonic Sol-fa Method and a Full Introduction to the Art of Singing from the Old Notation*. 7th ed. London: T. Ward, ca. 1857.

Dahlhaus, Carl. *Die Musik des 19. Jahrhunderts*, vol. 6 of *Neues Handbuch der Musikwissenschaft*. Wiesbaden: Athenaion, 1980.

————. *Nineteenth-Century Music*. Translated by J. Bradford Robinson. Berkeley and Los Angeles: University of California Press, 1989.

Davies, John. *A History of Wales* (1990). Rev. ed. Harmondsworth: Penguin, 2007.

De Haan, I. and H. te Velde. "Vormen van politiek: Veranderingen van de openbaarheid in Nederland, 1848–1900." *Bijdragen en mededelingen betreffende de geschiedenis der Nederlanden* 111 (1996), 167–200.

De Jong, J. "Prosopografie, een mogelijkheid: Eliteonderzoek tussen politieke en sociaal-culturele geschiedenis." *Bijdragen en mededelingen betreffende de geschiedenis der Nederlanden* 111 (1996), 201–15.

De Jonge, A. and Wijnand Mijnhardt. "Het genootschapsonderzoek in Nederland." *De negentiende eeuw* 7 (1983), 253–59.

De Klerk, Jos. *Haarlems muziekleven in de loop der tijden*. Haarlem: Tjeenk Willink, 1965.

De las Cuevas Hevia, Carmen. "Fundación y primera etapa artística del Orfeón Donostiarra (1896–1901): Rastreo hemerográfico, bibliográfico y documental, Trabajo de investigación" (unpub.). Cursos de doctorado bienio 1994–96: "Sociedad y Educación en Euskal Herria." Dpto. Tª e Hª de la Educación, UPV-EHU, 1996.

Dewilde, Jan. "Muziek en Vlaamse Beweging." In *Nieuwe Encyclopedie van de Vlaamse Beweging*, vol. 2. Tielt: Lannoo, 1998. 2114–34.

————. "De kleine zanger . . . Historische schets van het aanvankelijk solfège- en zangonderwijs in Vlaanderen tijdens de negentiende eeuw." In *Prometheus zoekt Aquarius: reflecties over creatief muziekonderwijs*. Peer: Alamire, 2000. 23–37.

————. "Muziek ter ere van Pieter Paul Rubens: de Rubensfeesten van 1840: wat zong Rubens?" *Forum* 12: 1 (2004), 19–28.

————. "Het rijke Vlaamse koorleven: recente tendensen." *Stemband* 10: 13 (2012), 11–12.

Dobszay, László. *Magyar Zenetörténet*. Budapest: Planétás, 1998.

Dolar, Mladen. *A Voice and Nothing More*. Cambridge, MA: MIT Press, 2006.

Dompnier, Nathalie. *Vichy à travers chants*. Paris: Nathan, 1996.

Düding, Dieter. *Organisierter gesellschaftlicher Nationalismus in Deutschland (1808–1847): Bedeutung und Funktion der Turner- und Sängervereine für die deutsche Nationalbewegung*. München: Oldenbourg, 1984.

————, ed. *Öffentliche Festkultur: Politische Feste in Deutschland von der Aufklärung bis zum Ersten Weltkrieg*. Reinbek bei Hamburg: Rowohlt, 1988.

Dunk, H.W. von der. *Der deutsche Vormärz und Belgien, 1830–1848*. Wiesbaden: Steiner, 1996.

Duyse, Prudens Van. *Bij het eerste verjaringsfeest van het Vlaemsch-Duitsch Zangverbond door deze voorzitter voor Vlaenderen: aenspraek ter bijeenkomst der Duitsche en Belgische Zangers, op het eerste verjaringsfeest van 't Verbond, in de zael van het Casino te Gent, den 26 Juny 1847.* Ghent: Annoot-Braeckman, 1847.

Ecrevisse, Pieter. "Het Vlaemsch-Duitsch Zangverbond en de Kölnische Zeitung." In *Vlaemsche bloemkorf: keus van stukken uit de beste schrijvers.* Brussels: Greuze, 1853. 335–40.

Eden, K. van, and C. Montauban. *Gedenkboek uitgegeven ter gelegenheid van het honderdjarig bestaan der Koninklijke liedertafel 'Zang en Vriendschap' te Haarlem.* Haarlem, 1930.

Edwards, Owen M. *Tro i'r De.* Wrexham: Hughes & Son, 1907.

Elben, Otto. *Der volksthümliche deutsche Männergesang: Geschichte und Stellung im Leben der Nation.* 1887. 2nd ed. Reprint, Wolfenbüttel: Möseler, 1991.

Ehrlich, Cyril. *The Music Profession in Britain Since the Eighteenth Century: A Social History.* Oxford: The Clarendon Press, 1985.

———. *The Piano: A History.* Oxford: The Clarendon Press, 1990.

Ephémérides de la Société royale des Mélomanes, fondée à Gand le 1er octobre 1838. Ghent: De Busscher, 1871.

Erll, Astrid. *Memory in Culture.* Translated by Sara B. Young. Basingstoke: Palgrave Macmillan, 2011.

Evans, Eric J. *The Forging of the Modern State: Early Industrial Britain 1783–1870,* 2nd ed. Essex: Pearson Education Limited, 1999.

Faist, Thomas. "Diaspora and transnationalism: What kind of dance partners?" In Rainer Bauböck and Thomas Faist, eds., *Diaspora and transnationalism: Concepts, theories and methods.* Amsterdam: Amsterdam University Press, 2010.

Farmer, Henry George. *A History of Music in Scotland.* London: Hinrichsen, 1947.

Fassaert, R. " 'Aangename uitspanningen en het genot der burgerlijke relatièn': Op zoek naar de vroegste sporen van de blaasmuziekvereniging in Nederland." *Volkskundig Bulletin* 15 (1989), 148–76.

Fauser, Annegret. *Musical encounters at the 1889 Paris World's Fair.* Eastman Studies in Music. Rochester: University of Rochester Press, 2005.

Fazekas, Ágnes. "Magyar zeneszerzők világi kórusművei a 20. század nagy zenei változásai előtt." Ph.D. diss., Budapest: Liszt Ferenc Zeneművészeti Egyetem, 2007. Accessed 29 March 2015 at http://docs.lfze.hu/netfolder/public/PublicNet/Doktori%20dolgozatok/fazekas_agnes/disszertacio.pdf.

Fétis, François-Joseph. "Première lettre sur l'état actuel de la musique dans la Belgique, et sur son avenir dans ce pays (8 June 1833)." *Revue musicale* (Paris), 15 June 1833.

Flacke, Monika, ed. *Mythen der Nationen: Ein europäisches Panorama.* München: Koehler & Amelang, 1998.

Florack, Ruth. "Nationalcharakter als ästhetisches Argument." In Jens Häseler, Albert Meier, and Olaf Koch, eds., *Gallophobie im 18. Jahrhundert*. Berlin: Berliner Wissenschaftsverlag, 2005, n. p.

———, ed. *Tiefsinnige Deutsche, Frivole Franzosen: Nationale Stereotype in deutscher und französischer Literatur*. Stuttgart: J.B. Metzler Verlag, 2000.

Folkehöjskolens sangbog: Foreningen for höjskoler og landbrugsskoler. Odense: Foreningen for höjskoler og landbrugsskoler, 1942.

Foucault, Michel. "Qu'est-ce qu'un auteur?" In *Dits et écrits*, vol. 1. Paris: Minuit, 1996, 789–821.

Francfort, Didier. *Le Chant des Nations: Musiques et Cultures en Europe, 1870–1914*. Paris: Hachette, 2004.

Frech, Kurt; 1996. "Felix Dahn: Die Verbreitung völkischen Gedankenguts durch den historischen Roman." In U. Puschner, W. Schmitz and J. Ulbricht, eds., *Handbuch zur "Völkischen Bewegung," 1871–1918*. München: Saur, 1996, 685–98.

Freeden, Michael. "Is Nationalism a Distinct Ideology?" *Political Studies* 46 (1998), 748–65.

Frolík, Jiří. "*Hynek Palla a jeho význam pro hudební rozvoj Plzně*." *Hudební kultura* 12 (1993), 39–48.

Fulcher, Jane. "The Orphéon Societies: 'Music for the Workers' in Second-Empire France." *International Review of the Aesthetics and Sociology of Music* 10: 1 (1979), 47–56.

Geisler, Ursula, and Karin Johansson, "Introduction: Histories and Practices of Choral Singing in Context." In Geisler and Johansson, eds. *Choral Singing: Histories and Practices*. Cambridge: Cambridge Scholars Publishing, 2014. 1–24.

Gellner, Ernest. *Nations and Nationalism*. Ithaca: Cornell University Press, 1983.

Genchev, Nikolai. *Vazrozhdenskiyat Plovdiv*. Plovdiv: Hristo G. Danov, 1981.

Gerald of Wales: The Journey through Wales and the Description of Wales. Edited and translated by Lewis Thorpe. Harmondsworth: Penguin, 1978.

Gerritsen, Harry, and Jan Willemsen. *125 Jaar Koninklijke Zangvereniging Breda's Mannenkoor: Kroniek van een koor 1865–1990*. Tilburg: Gianotten, 1992.

Geyer, Myriam. *La Vie musicale à Strasbourg sous l'Empire allemand (1871–1918)*. Mémoires et documents de l'Ecole des Chartes n° 57. Paris: Ecole des Chartes / Société savante d'Alsace, 1999.

Ginkel, John. "Identity Construction in Latvia's 'Singing Revolution': Why inter-ethnic conflict failed to occur." *Nationalities Papers* 30 (2002), 403–33.

Girardet, Raoul. *Le nationalisme français, anthologie 1871–1914*. Paris: Seuil, 1983.

Graham, John. *A Century of Welsh Music*. London: Kegan Paul, 1923.

Gramit, David. *Cultivating Music*. Berkeley: University of California Press, 2002.

Grégoir, Edouard. *L'Art musical en Belgique sous les règnes de Léopold I & Léopold II, rois des Belges, 1830–1880*. Bruxelles: Schott frères, 1879.

Grijzenhout, Franz. *Feesten voor het vaderland: Patriotse en Bataafse feesten 1790–1806.* Ph.D. diss. Vrije Universiteit Amsterdam. Zwolle: Waanders, 1989.

Gumplowicz, Philippe. *Les Travaux d'Orphée: 150 ans de vie musicale amateur en France. Harmonies, chorales, fanfares.* Paris: Aubier, 1987.

Hadzhiiski, Ivan. *Bit i dushevnost na bulgarskiya narod.* 2 vols. Sofia: Bulgarski pisatel, 1974.

Haksch, Lajos. *A negyvenéves pécsi dalárda története: 1862–1902.* Pécs: Taizs Ny., 1902.

Hanssen, Christopher. *Kristiania haandverker sangforenings historie gjennem sytti aar.* [Kristiania: Kristiania haandverker sangforening], 1919.

Harvie, Christopher. *Scotland and Nationalism: Scottish Society and Politics 1707 to the Present*, 3rd ed. London: Routledge, 1998.

Heemann, Annegret. *Männergesangvereine im 19. und frühen 20. Jahrhundert: Ein Beitrag zur städtischen Musikgeschichte Münsters.* Frankfurt am Main: Peter Lang, 1992.

Hegtun, Halfdan. *Rundt fabrikken.* Oslo: Aschehoug, 1984.

Heller, Servác. *Z minulé doby našeho života národního, kulturního a politického. Vzpomínky a zápisky. 5 vols.* Praha, 1916–23.

Herbert, Trevor. "Popular Nationalism: Griffith Rhys Jones (Caradog) and the Welsh Choral Tradition." In Christina Bashford and Leanne Langley, eds., *Music and British Culture 1785–1914: Essays in Honour of Cyril Ehrlich.* Oxford: Oxford University Press, 2000. 255–74.

Herresthal, Harald. *Med spark i gulvet og quinter i bassen: musikalske og politiske bilder fra nasjonalromantikkens gjennombrudd i Norge.* Oslo: Universitetsforlaget, 1993.

———. *Fra privat til offentlig engasjement: musikkpolitikken 1814–1858 (Norsk kulturpolitikk 1814–2014).* Oslo: Unipub, 2004.

Heydenrijck, C.J.A. *Het oude Nijmegen aan de liedertafels van het vijfde nationaal zangersfeest.* Nijmegen: H.C.A. Thieme, 1861.

Hlebarov, Ivan. *Novata bulgarska muzikalna kultura.* Vol. 1 (1878–1944). Sofia: State Music Academy 'Pancho Vladigerov'/ Haini, 2003.

Hobsbawm, Eric J. *Nations and Nationalism since 1780. Programme, Myth, Reality.* 2nd ed. Cambridge: Cambridge University Press, 1992.

——— and Terence Ranger, eds. *The Invention of Tradition.* Cambridge: Cambridge University Press, 1983.

Hoegaerts, Josephine. *Masculinity and Nationhood, 1830–1910: Constructions of Identity and Citizenship in Belgium.* Basingstoke: Palgrave Macmillan, 2014.

———. "Little citizens and petites patries: Learning patriotism through choral singing in Antwerp in the nineteenth century." In Ursula Geisler and Karin Johansson, eds., *Choral Singing: Histories and Practices.* Cambridge: Cambridge Scholar Publishing, 2014. 14–32.

Hojda, Zdeněk, and Jiří Pokorný. "Denkmalkonflikte zwischen Tschechen und Deutschböhmen." In Hanns Haas, ed., *Bürgerliche Selbstdarstellung. Städtebau,*

Architektur, Denkmäler Bürgertum in der Habsburgermonarchie, vol. 4. Wien–Köln– Weimar: Böhlau, 1995. 241–51.

Hopkins, K.S., ed. *Rhondda Past and Future*. Ferndale: Rhondda Borough Council, 1975.

Hopstock, Carsten. *Bogstad: et storgods gjennom 300 år*. Oslo: Boksenteret/Bogstad stiftelse, 1997.

Horatius Flaccus, Quintus. *Satires; epistles; and ars poetica*. With an English translation by H. Rushton Fairclough. The Loeb Classical Library no. 194. Cambridge, MA: Harvard University Press, 1929.

Hostinský, Otakar. *Bedřich Smetana a jeho boj o moderní českou hudbu*. Praha, 1904.

Hristov, Dobri. "Ritmichnite osnovi na narodnata ni muzika." *Sbornik za narodni umotvoreniya i narodopis* 27 (1913), 1–48.

Hroch, Miroslav. *Social Preconditions of National Revival in Europe: A Comparative Analysis of the Social Composition of Patriotic Groups Among the Smaller European Nations*. New York: Columbia University Press, 2000.

———. *Das Europa der Nationen: die moderne Nationsbildung im europäischen Vergleich*. Göttingen: Vandenhoeck & Ruprecht, 2005.

Huldt-Nyström, Hampus, ed. *Sangerliv: et verk om korsang*. 2 vols. Oslo: Børrehaug, 1958–59.

Ibsen, Henrik. *The Pretenders*. In *The Oxford Ibsen*, edited by James Walter McFarlane. London: Oxford University Press, 1963. Vol. 2, 217–341.

Ilić, Sava. *Srpski horovi u Banatu*. Bucharest: Kriterion, 1978.

Izveštaj Upravnog odbora Saveza srpskih pevačkih društava o radu g. 1911–1914. Sombor: P. Bajić, 1914.

Jaarboek van het Nederlandsch Nationaal Zangersverbond voor het Jaar 1858. Utrecht: H.A. Banning, 1858.

Janssens, Jeroen. *De Belgische natie viert*. Leuven: Universitaire Pers, 2001.

Jespers, F. *"Het loflyk werk der Engelen": De katholieke kerkmuziek in Noord-Brabant van het einde der zeventiende tot het einde der negentiende eeuw*. Ph.D. diss. Katholieke Universiteit Brabant. Tilburg, 1988.

Jindra, Hynek. *Dějiny Zpěváckého spolku pražských typografů 1862–1932*. Praha, 1934.

Johnson, David. *Music and Society in Lowland Scotland in the Eighteenth Century*, 2nd ed. Edinburgh: Mercat Press, 2003.

Johnson, James. *The Scots Musical Museum*. Edinburgh: Johnson, 1790.

Jones, Anthony. *Welsh Chapels*. Stroud: Sutton Publishing, 1996.

Jones, K. Davies. "Coleridge Taylor and Wales." *Welsh Music* (Autumn 1999), 3–14.

Jonnson, A. "Uppfostran till patriotism: En idéhistorisk exposé over manskörsangens århundrade ur ett upsaliensisk perspektiv." *Svensk Tidskrift for Musikforskning* 65 (1983), 15–68.

Jonsson, Leif. *Ljusets riddarvakt: 1800-talets studentsång utövad som offentlig samhällskonst*. Studia musicologica Upsaliensia, n. s., 11. Uppsala: University of Uppsala, 1990.

Józsa, Mihály. *A brassói magyar dalárda 25 évi fennállásának története.* Pécs: Koller Lipót kiad., 1886.

Kacz, Lajos. *Huszonöt én a komáromi dalárda történetéből.* Komárom: Ziegler Károly, 1889.

Kaskötő-Buka, Marietta. "Dasselbe Jahrhundert—verschiedene Epochen. Die Entwicklung der Chorliteratur im 19. Jahrhundert in Ungarn im Spiegel der Rukoveti von Stevan Mokranjac." *Musicologija* (Serbian Academy of Sciences and Arts) no. 17 (2014), 243–60.

Katzarova, Raina. "Balkanski varianti na dve turski pesni." *Izvestiya na Instituta za Muzikoznanie* 16 (1973), 115–33.

Kaufman, Nikolai. *Bulgarski gradski pesni.* Sofia: Izdatelstvo na Bulgarskata akademiya na naukite, 1968.

Kazasov, Dimo. "Osnovite zaslugi na 'Gusla.'" In *Mazhki hor 'Gusla' 50 godini.* Sofia, s.d. 25–28.

Keen, Basil. *The Bach Choir: The First Hundred Years.* Aldershot: Ashgate Publishing, 2008.

Kessels, Jan A.W. *Mensen en muziek in Arnhem.* Arnhem: Stichting Nato Taptoe, 1967.

Kist, Florentius Cornelis. "Mannenzang en mannen-zangvereenigingen; eene korte schets van derzelver oorsprong en voortgang op onzen tijd." *Caecilia* 3 (1846), 145–47, 153–55.

———. "Toestand der toonkunst in Nederland gedurende de eerste helft der 19e eeuw." *Caecilia* 9 (1852), 211–13.

Klefisch, Josef. *Hundert Jahre deutscher Männergesang, dargestellt am Werden und Wirken des Kölner Männer-Gesang-Vereins, 1842–1942.* Köln: DuMont Schauberg, 1942.

Klenke, Dietmar. "Bürgerlicher Männergesang und Politik in Deutschland." *Geschichte in Wissenschaft und Unterricht,* 40 (1989), 458–85, 534–61.

———. *Der singende "deutsche Mann": Gesangvereine und deutsches Nationalbewusstsein von Napoleon bis Hitler.* Münster: Waxmann, 1998.

Kloos, Ulrike. *Niederlandbild und deutsche Germanistik 1800–1933: Ein Beitrag zur komparatistischen Imagologie.* Amsterdam: Rodopi, 1992.

Koch, Armin. "Felix Mendelssohn Bartholdys *Festgesang an die Künstler,* op. 68." In *Schiller und die Musik,* edited by Helen Geyer et al. Köln: Böhlau-Verlag, 2007.

Kohn, Hans. "Romanticism and the Rise of German Nationalism." *Review of Politics* 12 (1950), 443–70.

Konjović, Petar. "Muzika u Srba." In *Ličnosti.* Zagreb: Ćelap i Popovac, 1920.

Kopalová, Dana. 'Zpěvácký spolek Střela v Plasech." In *Spolkový život v Čechách v 19. a na počátku 20. století: Sborník k životnímu jubileu Jany Englové.* Ústí nad Labem: Univerzita J.E. Purkyně, 2005. 73–106.

Kotek, Josef. *Dějiny české populární hudby a zpěvu.* Praha: Academia, 1994.

Krebs, Christopher B. *A Most Dangerous Book: Tacitus's "Germania" from the Roman Empire to the Third Reich.* Cambridge, MA: Harvard University Press, 2011.

Kroon, Sjaak, and Jan Sturm. " 'De taal is gansch het volk': een zoektocht naar de oorsprong en het gebruik van een sententia." *Spiegel* 17/18: 1–2 (1999), 25–66.

Kuhn, Hans. *Defining a nation in song: Danish patriotic songs in songbooks of the period 1832–1870.* Copenhagen: Reitzel, 1990.

Labajo, J. "Aproximación al fenómeno orfeonístico en España (Valladolid 1890–1923)." Unpub. Dip. Prov. de Valladolid, 1987.

Landon, H.C. Robbins. "Music." In *The Cambridge Cultural History VI: The Romantic Age in Britain.* Cambridge: Cambridge University Press, 1992.

Langewiesche, Dieter. *Nation, Nationalismus und Nationalstaat in Deutschland und Europa.* München: Beck, 2000.

Ledvinka, Václav, and Jiří Pešek. *Od středověkých bratrstev k moderním spolkům.* Praha: Scriptorium, 2000.

Leenders, J. *Benauwde verdraagzaamheid, hachelijk fatsoen: Families, standen en kerken te Hoorn in het midden van de negentiende eeuw.* Ph.D. diss. Universiteit van Amsterdam. Den Haag: Stichting Hollandse historische reeks, 1992.

Leerssen, Joep. *National Thought in Europe: A Cultural History.* Amsterdam: Amsterdam University Press, 2006.

———. *De bronnen van het vaderland: Taal, literatuur en de afbakening van Nederland 1806–1890.* Nijmegen: Vantilt, 2011a.

———. "Viral Nationalism: Romantic Intellectuals on the Move in Nineteenth-Century Europe." *Nations and Nationalism* 17:2 (2011b), 257–71.

———. *When was Romantic Nationalism? The onset, the long tail, the banal.* Antwerp: NISE, 2014.

———. "The nation and the city: urban festivals and cultural mobilisation." *Nations and Nationalism* 21: 1 (2015), 2–20.

Lewis, E.D. *The Rhondda Valleys.* London: Phoenix House, 1959.

Llongueras, J. "Tribute to Josep Anselm Clavé." *Revista Musical Catalana* n° 252 (Dec. 1924), 72.

Locke, Ralph P. *Music, Musicians and the Saint-Simonians,* Chicago and London: University of Chicago Press, 1986.

Loit, A. ed. *National movements in the Baltic countries during the nineteenth century.* Uppsala: Almqvist & Wiksell, 1985.

Lönnecker, Harald. " 'Unzufriedenheit mit den bestehenden Regierungen unter dem Volke zu verbreiten': Politische Lieder der Burschenschaften aus der Zeit zwischen 1820 und 1850." *Jahrbuch des Deutschen Volksliedarchivs* 48 (2003), 85–131. [theme issue *Lied und populäre Kultur,* edited by M. Matter and N. Grosch].

Lysdahl, Anne Jorunn Kydland. "Light up every home: The Social and Cultural Meaning of Song in Norway in the 1800s." *I.A.H. Bulletin. Publikation der Internationalen Arbeitsgemeinschaft für Hymnologie* (Graz), no. 30 (2004), 9–27.

————. "Sang i politikkens og nasjonsbyggingens tjeneste." In *100 år var det alt?* Edited by Øystein Rian, Harriet Rudd, and Håvard Tangen. Oslo: Nei til EU, 2005, 60–67.

MacAloon, John J. "Introduction: cultural performances, culture theory." In MacAloon, ed., *Rite, drama, festival, spectacle: Rehearsals toward a theory of cultural performance*. Philadelphia: Institute for the Study of Human Issues, 1984.

MacCunn, Hamish. "A Scottish College of Music." *Dunedin Magazine* 1 (1913), 153–58.

MacKay, D. Leinster. "John Hullah, John Curwen and Sarah Glover: A Classic case of 'Whiggery' in the History of Musical Education?" *British Journal of Educational Studies* 29: 2 (2 June 1981), 164–67.

Mackerness, E.D. *A Social History of English Music*. London: Routledge and Kegan Paul, 1966.

Mahan, Karel. "Nashite napevi." *Sbornik za narodni umotvoreniya, nauka i knizhnina* 10 (1894), 221–35.

Mainzer, Joseph. *Singing for the Million*. London: The Author, 1841.

Maldeghem, Robert J. Van. *Trésor musical, collection authentique de musique sacrée et profane des anciens maîtres belges*. Fifty-eight instalments. Bruxelles: C. Muquardt, 1865–93.

Malíř, Jiří. "Mladočeská strana v Čechách a promladočeské strany na Moravě." In Pavel Marek, ed., *Přehled politického stranictví na území českých zemí a Československa*. Olomouc: Katedra politologie a evropských studií Filozoficke fakulty Univerzity Palackého v Olomouci, 2000. 42–62.

Maragall, Joan. *Obres completes*. Barcelona: Arial, 1961.

Marfany, Joan-Lluís. *La cultura del catalanisme*. Barcelona: Empuries, 1992.

————. "Al damunt de nostres cants: nacionalisme, modernisme i cant coral a Barcelona del final del segle." *Recerques* 19 (Curial, 1998), 85–113.

Marković, Tatjana. "Istorijski arhiv Sombora—muzički fond." *Novi zvuk* 4 (1995), 91–108.

————. "The specific nature of the activities of choral societies in a multi-ethnic context: A case study of Serbian choral societies in Banat (Pančevo and Veliki Bečkerek) in the 19th century." *New Sound* 28 (2006), 115–130.

————. "From cultural memory to multiplying national identities." In Marković and Vesna Mikić, eds., *Musical culture & memory*. Belgrade: Fakultet muzičke umetnosti, 2008. 34–41.

Marr, Robert A. *Music for the People: A Retrospect of the Glasgow International Exhibition, 1888 with an Account of the Rise of Choral Societies in Scotland*. Edinburgh: J. Menzies, 1889.

Massot i Muntaner, Josep, Salvador Pueyo, and Oriol Martorell. *Els Segadors, hímne nacional de Catalunya*. Barcelona: Generalitat de Catalunya, 1983.

McCormick, Lisa. "Music as Social Performance." In Ronald Eyerman and Lisa McCormick eds., *Myth, Meaning, and Performance: Toward a New Cultural Sociology of the Arts.* Boulder: Paradigm, 2006. 121–44.

Merwe, Peter van der. *Origins of the Popular Style: The Antecedents of Twentieth-Century Popular Music.* Oxford: Oxford University Press, 1992.

Michonneau, Stéphane. *Barcelone: Mémoire et Identité, 1830–1930.* Rennes: Presses Universitaires de Rennes, 2007.

Mihálka, György. *Karvezetés IV., Kórustörténet és a kórusélettel kapcsolatos elvi és gyakorlati tudnivalók.* Budapest: Tankönyvkiadó, 1986.

Mijnhardt, Wijnand W. *Tot heil van 't menschdom: Culturele genootschappen in Nederland, 1750–1815.* Amsterdam: Rodopi, 1987.

———. "Sociabiliteit en cultuurparticipatie in de achttiende en vroege negentiende eeuw." In M.G. Westen, ed., *Met den tooverstaf der ware kunst: Cultuurspreiding en cultuuroverdracht in historisch perspectief.* Leiden: Martinus Nijhoff, 1990, 37–69.

Mikszáth, Kálmán. "Piktorok és dalárok." In Kristóf Pétery, ed., *Cikkek és karcolatok.* Szentendre: Mercator Studió, 2005. 586–90. Accessed 26 March 2015 at http://www .akonyv.hu/klasszikus/mikszath/mikszath_kalman_cikkek_es_karcolatok_2.pdf.

Milisavac, Živan, ed. *Ujedinjena omladina srpska.* Novi Sad, Beograd: Matica srpska, Istorijski institut 1968.

Millet i Bagès, Lluís. *Pel Nostre Ideal.* Barcelona: J. Horta, 1917.

Millet i Loras, Lluís. "L'Obra dels Orfeons de Catalunya." *Revista Musical Catalana* n° 320 (Aug. 1930), 345–47.

———. "El llegat historic de l'Orfeo Catala (1891–1936)." *Recerca musicológica* 14–15 (2004–05), 139–53.

Milojković-Djurić, Jelena. "The role of choral societies in the nineteenth century among the South Slavs." In A. Loit, ed., *National movements in the Baltic countries during the nineteenth century.* Uppsala: Almqvist & Wiksell, 1985. 475–82.

Minor, Ryan. *Choral Fantasies: Music, Festivity, and Nationhood in Nineteenth-century Germany.* Cambridge: Cambridge University Press, 2012.

Moohan, Elaine. "The Sacred Music Institution in Glasgow, 1796–1805." In Gordon Munro et al., eds., *Notis Musycall: Essays on Music and Scottish Culture in Honour of Kenneth Elliott. Historical Studies of Scottish Music.* Glasgow: Musica Scotica Trust, 2005.

Móra, Ferenc. *Az ötvenéves szegedi polgári dalárda.* Szeged: Mars Könyvnyomdai Műintézet, 1922.

Morera, Enric. "Al Public." in *Catalunya Nova* (March 1896), p. 3.

———. *Moments viscuts.* Barcelona: Ed. Graficas, 1936.

Morton, Graeme. *Unionist Nationalism: Governing Urban Scotland 1830–1860.* East Linton: Tuckwell Press, 1999.

Mugica Herzog, F. *Breve crónica de un siglo de vida donostiarra. La sociedad Unión Artesana en su centenario (1870–1970).* San Sebastián: Kutxa Fundazioa–Fundación Kutxa, re-ed. 1996.

Mussat, Marie-Claire. "Les Enjeux politiques du kiosque à musique au début de la troisième République." In Tournès, ed., 193–206.

Nagel, Joane. "Masculinity and nationalism: gender and sexuality in the making of nations." *Ethnic and Racial Studies,* 21: 2 (1998), 242–69.

Nagore, Maria. *La revolución coral: Estudio sobre la Sociedad Coral de Bilbao y el movimiento coral Europeo (1800–1936).* Madrid: Instituto Complutense de Ciencias Musicales, 2001.

Narváez Ferri, M. "L'Orfeó Català, cant coral i catalanisme (1891–1951)." Ph.D. diss., Universitat de Barcelona, 2005.

Nejedlý Z., "Dějiny pražského Hlaholu." In Rudolf Lichtner, ed., *Památník zpěváckého spolku Hlaholu v Praze, vydaný na oslavu 50tileté činnosti. 1861–1911.* Praha, 1911, 54–97.

Nettel, Reginald. *Music in the Five Towns 1840–1914.* Oxford: Oxford University Press, 1944.

Netzer, Katinka. *Wissenschaft aus nationaler Sehnsucht: Verhandlungen der Germanisten 1846 und 1847.* Heidelberg: Winter, 2006.

Newmarch, Rosa. *Henry J. Wood.* Living Masters of Music, vol. 1. London: John Lane, 1904.

Nickelsen, Trine. "Bærere av akademisk kunnskap—og samfunnet." *Apollon* 2. Oslo: Universitetet, 2011, 14–16.

Novikova, Irina. "Constructing national identity in Latvia: gender and representation during the period of the national awakening." In Ida Blom, Karen Hagemann, and Catherine Hall, eds., *Gendered Nations: Nationalisms and Gender Order in the Long Nineteenth Century.* Oxford: Berg, 2000. 311–34.

Nuyen, N.J.W.M., et al. *Koninklijke zangvereeniging 'Cecilia': Gedenkboek eeuwfeest 1930.* 's-Gravenhage, 1930.

"Obrazovanieto v Ruse prez Vazrazhdaneto." In *Regionalen istoricheski muzei—Ruse.* Accessed 7 January 2011 at http://www.museumruse.com/ruseznanie/education .html.

Ozouf, Mona. *La fête révolutionnaire, 1789–1799.* Paris: Gallimard, 1976.

Pabian, P. "Czech Protestants and national identity: commemorating Jan Hus in 1869." In Zdeněk David, ed., *The Bohemian Reformation and Religious Practice,* vol. 7. Praha: Filosofia, 2009. 221–28.

Pacák, Bedřich. "Husova slavnost v kriminále." *Svoboda: politický časopis.* 7 (1873), 1.

Pahíssa, Jaume. "La Federació de coros catalans." *Catalunya Nova* (March 1900), p. 2.

Palmer, Fiona M. *Vincent Novello (1781–1861): Music for the Masses.* Aldershot: Ashgate Publishing, 2006.

Památník k 75letému trvání pěveckého spolku Záboj v Rokycanech. Rokycany, 1936.

Pastor, Emilio S. "Los Segadors." *Heraldo de Madrid* (11 Nov. 1899), 18.

Pedrell, Felix. *Por Nuestra Musica*. Barcelona: Ed. Heinrich, 1891.

———. In *Revista Musical Catalana* (1904), 161.

———. *La Cansó Popular Catalana, la Lírica Nacionalisada y l'obra de l'Orfeó Català*. Barcelona: La Neotipia, 1906.

Pejović, Roksanda. *Srpsko muzičko izvođaštvo romantičarskog doba*. Beograd: Univerzitet umetnosti, 1991.

Pelckmans, Geert, and Jan Van Doorslaer. *De Duitse kolonie in Antwerpen, 1796–1914*. Kapellen: Pelckmans, 2000.

Pešek, J., ed. *Pražské slavnosti a velké výstavy. Sborník příspěvků z konferencí Archivu hlavního města Prahy 1989 a 1991*. Praha: Archiv hlavního města Praha, 1995.

A Pest-Budai Dalárda alapszabályai—Statuten des Pest-Ofner Gesangvereines. Pest: Müller Emil Könyvnyomdája, 1857.

Petrov, Stoyan. *Ochertzi po istoriya na bulgarskata muzikalna kultura*. Sofia: Nauka i izkustvo, 1959.

Pilbeam, Pamela M. *The Middle Classes in Europe 1789–1914: France, Germany, Italy and Russia*. London: Palgrave Macmillan, 1990.

Platou, Ludvig Stoud, ed. *Indberetninger om National-Festen den 11te December 1811, i Anledning af Hans Majestæts Kong Frederik den Sjettes Befaling om et Universitet i Norge: udgivne af Det Kongl. Selskab for Norges Vel*. Christiania: Lehman, 1812.

Pokorný, Jiří. "Oslavy J.A. Komenského v roce 1892." *Studia comeniana et historica* 30 (2000), 207–12.

———, and Jiří Rak. "Öffentliche Festtage bei den Tschechen." In Emil Brix, ed., *Der Kampf um das Gedächtnis: Öffentliche Gedenktage in Mitteleuropa*. Wien–Köln–Weimar: Böhlau Verlag, 1997. 171–87.

Popović, Miodrag. *Istorija srpske književnosti 2: Romantizam*. Belgrade: Zavod za izdavanje udžbenika i nastavna sredstva, 1985.

Porter, Cecilia Hopkins. "The New Public and the Reordering of the Musical Establishment: The Lower Rhine Music Festivals, 1818–67." *19th-Century Music* 3: 3 (1980), 211–24.

———. *The Rhine as Musical Metaphor: Cultural Identity in German Romantic Music*. Boston: Northeastern University Press, 1996.

Prebble, John. *The Darien Disaster*. London: Secker & Warburg, 1968.

Pritchard, Brian W. "Some Festival Programmes of the Eighteenth and Nineteenth Centuries: 3. Liverpool and Manchester." *RMA Research Chronicle*, vol. 7, 1969.

Quis, Ladislav. *Kniha vzpomínek. 2 vols*. Praha: Nakladetelské družstvo máje, 1902.

Rainbow, Bernarr. *The Land Without Music: Musical Education in England 1800–1860 and Its Continental Antecedents*. London: Novello, 1967.

———. "Hullah, John." In *Grove Music Online. Oxford Music Online*. Accessed 15 March 2011 at http://www.oxfordmusiconline.com/subscriber/article/grove/music/13535.

Rank, J., and F. Vichterle, eds. *Sokol. Národní kalendář českoslovanský na obyčejný rok 1863*. Praha, 1862.

Rataj, Tomáš, and Jana Ratajová. "Úvodní studie." In Marek Lašťovka, Barbora Lašťovková, Tomáš Rataj, Jana Ratajová, and Josef Třikač, eds., *Pražské spolky: soupis pražských spolků na základě úředních evidencí z let 1895–1990*. Praha: Scriptorium, 1998. 2–35.

Rauline, Jean-Yves. "Les Sociétés musicales sous le second Empire et la troisième République: entre sociabilité et propagande politique." In Ludovic Tournès, ed., *De l'acculturation du politique au multiculturalisme*. Paris: Honoré Champion, 1999. 173–91.

Raun, Toivo U. *Estonia and the Estonians*. 2nd ed. Stanford: Hoover Institution Press, 1991.

Reberics, Imre. *A pécsi dalárda 25 évi fennállásának története*. Pécs: Koller Lipót kiad., 1886.

Reeser, Eduard. *Een eeuw Nederlandse muziek*. 2nd. ed. Amsterdam: Querido, 1986.

Řeřichová, Jiřina. "Činnost prvního teplického mužského pěveckého spolku jako iniciátora Německého pěveckého svazu v Čechách." In *Spolkový život v Čechách v 19. a na počátku 20. století: Sborník k životnímu jubileu Jany Englové*. Ústí nad Labem: Univerzita J.E. Purkyně, 2005. 49–72.

Ribera i Villanueva, Climent and Joan Auladell. *Societat coral La Unió Santcugatenca: cent anys d'història, 1900–2000*. Barcelona: Generalitat de Catalunya, 2001.

Richter, Joachim Burkhard. *Hans Ferdinand Maßmann: Altdeutscher Patriotismus im 19. Jahrhundert*. Berlin: De Gruyter, 1992.

Rigney, Ann. "Epiloog." In Robert Hoezee, Jo Tollebeek, and Tom Verschaffel, eds., *Mise-en-scène: Keizer Karel en de verbeelding van de negentiende eeuw*. Ghent: Museum voor Schone Kunsten/Mercatorfonds, 1999.

———. "Embodied communities: Commemorating Robert Burns, 1859." *Representations* 115 (2011), 71–101.

———. *The Afterlives of Walter Scott: Memory on the Move*. Oxford: Oxford University Press, 2012.

Roverud, Lars. *Et Blik paa Musikens Tilstand i Norge: med Forslag til dens almindelige Udbredelse i Landet, ved et Instituts Anlæg i Christiania*. Christiania: Lars Roverud / Chr. Grøndahl, 1815.

———. *Tale af L. Roverud. Holden i Christiania den 9de November 1827*. [1827?].

Rusiñol, Santiago. "Cançons del Poble." *Catalunya Nova* (July 1897), 3.

Russell, Dave. "Music in Huddersfield 1820–1914." In E.A. Hilary Haigh, ed., *Huddersfield: a most handsome town*. Kirklees: Kirklees Metropolitan Council, 1992.

———. *Popular Music in England 1840–1914: A Social History*. 2nd ed. Manchester: Manchester University Press, 1997.

Samson, Jim. "Nations and nationalism." In Samson, ed., *The Cambridge History of Nineteenth-Century Music*. Cambridge: Cambridge University Press, 2002. 568–600.

Sas, N.C.F. van. "Nationaliteit in de schaduw van de Gouden Eeuw: Nationale cultuur en vaderlands verleden 1780–1914." In Frans Grijzenhout and Henk van Veen, eds., *De Gouden Eeuw in perspectief: Het beeld van de Nederlandse zeventiende-eeuwse schilderkunst in later tijd*. Nijmegen/Heerlen: SUN/OU, 1992. 83–106.

Sayers, W.C. Berwick. *Samuel Coleridge Taylor: Musician. His Life and Letters*. London: Cassell, 1915.

Schiørring, Nils. *Musikkens historie i Danmark*, vol. 2, edited by Ole Kongsted and P.H. Traustedt. [København]: Politiken, 1978.

Schneider, Ute. *Politische Festkultur im 19. Jahrhundert: Die Rheinprovinz von der französischen Zeit bis zum Ende des Ersten Weltkrieges (1806–1918)*. Essen: Klartext, 1995.

Schulz, Johan Abraham Peter. *Gedanken über den Einfluss der Musik auf die Bildung eines Volks, und über deren Einführung in den Schulen der Königl. Dänischen Staaten: Zum Besten einer armen Wittwe*. Kopenhagen: Christian Gottlob Prost, 1790.

Seip, Jens Arup. *Utsikt over Norges historie*. 2 vols., 1974–1981. Vol. 2: *1850–1884*. 2nd ed. Oslo: Gyldendal, 1981.

Seume, Johann Gottfried. *Gedichte*. 3rd ed. Vienna and Prague, 1810.

Šilhan, Antonín. "Hudební odbor v prvním půlstoletí Umělecké besedy. Doba první. Sbírání sil a prostředků (1863–1885)." In *Padesát let Umělecké besedy 1863–1913*. Praha, 1913.

Šima, Karel. "Národní slavnosti šedesátých let 19. století jako performativní akty konstruování národní identity." *Český časopis historický* 104: 1 (2006), 81–110.

Siu, Lok. "Serial Migration." In Sukanya Banerjee, Aims McGuinness, and Steven Charles McKay, eds., *New Routes for Diaspora Studies*. Bloomington: Indiana University Press, 2012.

Small, Christopher. *Musicking. The Meanings of Performing and Listening*. Middletown: Wesleyan University Press, 1998.

Smith, Anthony D. *National Identity*. Reno: University of Nevada Press, 1993.

———. *The Antiquity of Nations*. Cambridge: Polity Press, 2004.

Smith, James G. and Percy M. Young. "Chorus (i)." In *Grove Music Online. Oxford Music Online*. Accessed 15 March 2011 at http://www.oxfordmusiconline.com/subscriber/article/grove/music/05684.

Smither, Howard E. "*Messiah* and Progress in Victorian England." *Early Music*, 13: 3 (1985), 339–48.

Solà-Morales, Ignasí de. *Arquitectura modernista: fin de siglo en Barcelona*. Barcelona: Ed. Gustavo Gili, 1992.

Soute, Joh. B. *Apollo's negende decennium, 1853–3 juni–1943: verhaal van gebeurtenissen uit het negentig-jarig bestaan in tijdsorde weergegeven*. Amsterdam: Mannenzangvereeniging Apollo, 1943.

Spitta, Philipp. *Der deutsche Männergesang*. In Friedhelm Brusniak and Franz Krautwurst, eds., *Musikgeschichtliche Aufsätze*, 1894. Rpt. Wolfenbüttel: Möseler, 1991.

Spohr, Louis. *Louis Spohr's Selbstbiographie*. Kassel: Wigand, 1861.

Srb, Josef, and Ferdinand Tadra. *Památník pražského Hlaholu. Na oslavu 25leté činnosti spolku*. Praha, 1886.

Strindberg, August. "Jäsningstiden: en själs utvecklingshistoria" (1867–72). *Tjänstekvinnans son. Samlade skrifter*, vol. 18. Stockholm: Bonnier, 1913.

Stynen, Andreas. "'Muziek moet evolueren': Wisselende accenten in het vocale repertoire." In Bruyneel et al., eds., *Veel volk verwacht: Populaire muziekcultuur in Vlaams-Brabant sinds 1800*. Leuven: Peeters, 2012. 200–15.

Szerző, Katalin. "The Most Important Hungarian Music Periodical of the 19th Century: *Zenészeti Lapok* (Musical Papers) (1860–1876)." In *Periodica Musica* (Vancouver) 4 (1986), 1–5.

Tall, Johannes. "Estonian song festivals and nationalism in music toward the end of the nineteenth century." In A. Loit, ed., *National movements in the Baltic countries during the nineteenth century*. Uppsala: Almqvist & Wiksell, 1985. 449–54.

Tari, Lujza. *Revolution, War of Independence in 1848/49 and its Remembering in the Traditional Music*. Accessed 28 March 2015 at http://48asdalok.btk.mta.hu/tanulmanyok/revolution-war-of-independence-in-1848-49-and-its-remembering-in-the-traditional-music.

——. *A szabadságharc zenei emlékei*. Accessed 28 March 2014 at http://48asdalok. btk.mta.hu/zeneiadatok.

Taruskin, Richard. *The Nineteenth Century. The Oxford History of Western Music*, vol. 3. Oxford: Oxford University Press, 2005.

Taylor-Jay, Claire. "'I am blessed with fruit': masculinity, androgyny and creativity in early twentieth-century German music." In Ian Biddle and Kirsten Gibson, eds., *Masculinity and Western Musical Practice*. Farnham: Ashgate, 2009. 183–86.

Thaulow, Harald Conrad. "Christianias Sangforeninger." *Morgenbladet* (Kristiania) nr. 216 (4 August 1846).

Thielen, Jacques-Corneille Van. "Het Vlaemsch-Duitsch Zangverbond." *De Broederhand: Tydschrift voor Hoogduitsche, Nederduitsche en Noordsche letterkunde* (Brussel, 1846).

Thiesse, Anne-Marie. *La création des identités nationales: Europe XVIIe–XXe siècle*. Paris: Seuil, 1999.

Thys, Auguste. *Historique des sociétés chorales de Belgique*. Ghent: De Busscher Frères, 1855.

Todorova, Maria. *Imagining the Balkans*. Rev. ed. New York: Oxford University Press, 2009.

Török, Ferencz. *A baróthi dalárda történelme és zászlószentelési ünnepélye*. Brassó: Alexi Könyvnyomda, 1894.

Torras i Bagès, Josep. *La Tradició Catalana*. In *Obres completes*, vol. 1. Barcelona: Biblioteca Balmes, 1935.

Toth, István György, ed. *A Concise History of Hungary*. Budapest: Corvina/Osiris, 2005.

Tournès, Ludovic, ed. *De l'Acculturation du politique au multiculturalisme*. Paris: Honoré Champion, 1999.

Tureček, J. In *Pěvectvo české dle stavů, Věstník Ústřední jednoty zpěváckých spolků českoslovanských* 8: 3–4 (20 May 1903), 124–25.

Václavek, Bedřich and Robert Smetana. *Český národní zpěvník*. Praha: Melantrich, 1940.

Věstník Ústřední Jednoty zpěváckých spolků českoslovanských, Praha, 1896–1904.

Vadelorge, Loïc. "L'Orphéon rouennais, entre protection et promotion sociale." In *Les Sociabilités musicales. Cahiers de GRHIS*. 6 (1997). Rouen: Presses de l'Université de Rouen. 61–86.

———. "Un Vecteur d'intégration républicaine: l'orphéon. L'exemple de Rouen sous la troisième République." In Ludovic Tournès, ed., *De l'acculturation du politique au multiculturalisme*. Paris: Honoré Champion, 1999. 81–110.

Valckenaere, August. *Muziekael handboek of leerwijze der grondregels van het muziek*. Brugge: Vandecasteele-Werbrouck, 1845.

Vanchena, Lorie A. *Political Poetry in Periodicals and the Shaping of German National Consciousness in the Nineteenth Century*. Frankfurt: Peter Lang, 2000.

Verhandlungen der Germanisten zu Frankfurt am Main am 24., 25. und 26. September. Frankfurt: Sauerländer, 1847.

Veth, P.J. "Het derde Nederrijnsch-Nederlandsch zangersfeest te Arnhem." *De Gids* 11: 2 (1847), 397–409.

Vlaeva, Ivanka. "Muzikata v periodichniya pechat na Plovdiv prez 80-te i 90-te godini na 19 vek." In Kipriana Belivanova, ed., *Musical and Scientific Almanac* 4 (2006), 71–88.

Vos, Jozef. *De spiegel der volksziel: Volksliedbegrip en cultuurpolitiek engagement in het bijzonder in het socialistische en katholieke jeugdidealisme tijdens het interbellum*. Ph.D. diss. Katholieke Universiteit Nijmegen. Nijmegen, 1993.

———. *Rapport betreffende de mogelijkheden voor een geschiedenis van de koorzang-beoefening in Nederland*. Universiteit Utrecht: Onderzoekinstituut voorgeschiedenis en cultuur, 31 Jan. 1995.

———. "De historische studie van koorzang en zangverenigingen in Nederland." *Muziek & Wetenschap* 4 (1994), 209–26.

Wahl, Hans Rudolf. *Die Religion des deutschen Nationalismus. Eine mentalitäts-geschichtliche Studie zur Literatur des Kaiserreichs: Felix Dahn, Ernst von Wildenbruch, Walter Flex*. Heidelberg: Winter, 2002.

Wallem, Fredrik B., ed. *Det norske studentersamfund gjennem hundrede aar: 1813–2. oktober–1913.* 2 vols. Det norske studentersamfund. Kristiania: Aschehoug, 1913.

Webb, Keith. *The Growth of Nationalism in Scotland.* Harmondsworth: Penguin, 1978.

Weber, Eugen. *Peasants into Frenchmen: The Modernization of Rural France 1870–1914.* Stanford: Stanford University Press, 1976.

Weber, William. *The Rise of Musical Classics in XVIIIth Century England: A Study in Canon, Ritual and Ideology.* Oxford: Clarendon Press, 1992.

──────. *The Great Transformation of Musical Taste: Concert Programming from Haydn to Brahms.* New York: Cambridge University Press, 2008.

Widmaier, Tobias. "Ich hab mich ergeben." In *Populäre und traditionelle Lieder. Historisch-kritisches Liederlexikon,* 2011. Accessed 6 May 2013 at www.liederlexikon. de/lieder/ich_habe_mich_ergeben/.

Wigard, Franz, ed. *Stenographischer Bericht über die Verhandlungen der Deutschen Constituirenden Nationalversammlung zu Frankfurt am Main.* Frankfurt: Sauerländer, 1848–50.

Willaert, Hendrik, and Jan Dewilde. *"Het lied in ziel en mond": 150 Jaar muziekleven en de Vlaamse Beweging.* Tielt: Lannoo, 1987.

Williams, Gareth. *Valleys of Song: Music and Society in Wales 1840–1914.* Rev. ed. Cardiff: University of Wales Press, 2003.

Williams, M.I. "Did Handel ever visit Cardiganshire?" *Ceredigion* (1959), 337–44.

Williams, Roger, and David Jones. *The Cruel Inheritance: Life and death in the coalfields of Glamorgan.* Pontypool: Village Publishing, 1990.

Zin[c]k, H[ardenack] O[tto] C[onrad]. *Frimodige Yttringer over Musikens gavnligste Anvendelse i Staten ved offentlig og grundig Underviisning og Dyrkelse.* Kjøbenhavn: Th. E. Rangel, [1810].

Zoltsák, János. *Az ungvári dalárda története. 1864–1889.* Ungvár: Kelet Nyomda, 1889.

Index